Sharing Our Biblical Story

Children & the Eucharist

D1373643

Sharing Our Biblical Story

A Guide to Using Liturgical Readings as the Core of Church and Family Education

Joseph P. Russell

MOREHOUSE-BARLOW
Wilton, Connecticut

Emily

I have enjoyed my time in west Tennessee

in peace

[signature]

9/28/

Morehouse-Barlow Co., Inc.
78 Danbury Road
Wilton, CT 06897

Library of Congress Cataloging-in-Publication Data

Russell, Joseph P.
  Sharing our Biblical story: a guide to using liturgical readings
as the core of church and family education/Joseph Russell.
      p. cm.

  Reprint. Originally published: Minneapolis: Winston Press,
  ©1979. Bibliography: p. 325.

  ISBN 0-8192-1425-6

  1. Bible stories. 2. Bible—Study. 3. Church year. 4. Bible—
Liturgical use. 5. Storytelling—Religious aspects—Christianity.
6. Christian education. I. Title.

BS546.R87 1988   88-8399
268'.6—dc19   CIP

Unless otherwise credited, all Bible quotations are from the
Revised Standard Version Common Bible, copyrighted © 1973
by the Division of Christian Education of the National Council
of Churches of Christ in the U.S.A. Used by permission.

Printed in the United States of America
by
BSC LITHO
Harrisburg, PA

Table of Contents

Chapter 3:   Sharing Our Story in the Liturgy: The Liturgy as Dramatization—87

Chapter 4:   How to Design a Parish Religious Education Program Based on the Church's Liturgy; Three Model Programs—97

Chapter 5:   A Commentary on the Eucharistic Lectionary, Year A—139

Chapter 6:   A Commentary on the Eucharistic Lectionary, Year B—197

To Jane, my wife—
  whose love is a living experience of the Gospel;
to Parker and Carolyn, our son and daughter—
  whose joyful discovery of life is a constant sign
  to me of the sacredness of creation.
I see the image of God and the vision of eternity
  in the deep moments of our sharing.

"God is love,
  and he who abides in love
  abides in God,
  and God abides in him"   (1 John 4:16b).

Introduction

This is an idea book for religious educators and parents—a book to stimulate thinking and creativity. This book is a guide to centering Christian education, both at church and at home, around the Bible and liturgy. More precisely, it shows how to base Christian education on the Bible stories that come to us in the context of worship. The intimate connection between the Bible story and liturgy is succinctly stated by John Westerhoff III.*

> . . . in the community's liturgy, story and action merge; in worship we remember and we act in symbolic ways which bring our sacred traditions and our lives together, providing us with both meaning and motivation for our daily existence.

Perhaps the best illustration of the Bible story coming alive in the liturgy is our reaction to hearing the Christmas story. Hardly anyone in the entire Christian Church is unfamiliar with the second chapter of the Gospel of Luke. Many of us get somewhat misty-eyed upon hearing the familiar words "And in that region there were shepherds out in the field, keeping watch over their flock by night. . . ." When we hear this reading as part of the Christmas liturgy, the story somehow becomes part of *our* story, and it helps

us to proclaim Christ's birth into our own lives as we feel his presence in the loving community that is celebrating the mystery of Christmas.

Christmas is so meaningful because we *participate* in the action and feeling of the story expressed in the liturgy. During Advent the pastor, parents, musicians, and religious education team have lively dialogue as they plan the Christmas celebration. When Christmas arrives, out come the angel costumes, the creche, the figures of Mary, Joseph, and the baby Jesus. We light candles and sing carols. Little children come to the midnight Mass, and though they may fall asleep during the sermon, they sense the power of the story and of the total moment. As a result, all who participate in the celebration share a feeling of fulfillment. They have lived the story. For many, the Christmas liturgy is the most meaningful worship experience of the whole year precisely because they have lived out the story.

But why can't we experience the same kind of "learning" on the sixth Sunday after Easter, on the Feast of Saints Peter and Paul, or even on the third Sunday in August when many church schools are closed for the summer?

If we would use a model of parish education designed around the richly varied Bible-centered celebrations of the parish church, everyone would share in those experiences week after week. Parents would not need to ask their

*John Westerhoff, *Will Our Children Have Faith?*, p. 60.

children, "What did you do in Sunday school today?" They would *know* because they themselves would have been a part of the child's experience. In a vibrant worship service, even the youngest children can sense the drama of the faith story. They will naturally miss much of the intellectual content, but over the weeks, months, and years the story of their people dramatized in the liturgy will become theirs, and they will become empowered by it.

If the liturgy of the parish is to be the focal point for education, then the church-school program needs to be tied directly to what is happening in the liturgy. This means that the liturgical Bible readings, the seasons and festivals of the church year, and the sacraments and other rites of the Church that mark the growing points in each person's life must become the curriculum of the church school. In a program so oriented, adults and adolescents will be exposed to an in-depth study of biblical passages that will help them see their lives and their world through the eyes of God as he is revealed in the biblical story. Children will know the Bible because they will have participated together in the faith story as it is experienced and passed on within the faith community. They will know the Creed, the Lord's Prayer, the Ten Commandments, and other fundamentals of Christianity, but they will have learned them by experiencing them in liturgical celebrations over the years. They will know the Bible stories intimately because they will have heard them over and over as awe-filled readings in the liturgy and in celebrations of the Judeo-Christian festivals of the church year both in their homes and in their parish learning community. And the children will have been exposed to Christian ethics and moral formation because the story and the covenant in which they have been actively engaged have much to say about values, about the right use of the world's precious resources, and about respect for every living creature in God's creation.

Centering our religious education around the Bible story as it is dramatized in the Church's worship is actually the traditional approach to Christian religious education. In this approach, the community of the faithful lives out and hands on the story of salvation in the life its members lead together as the people of God. That story of salvation shapes the view of the world that all of us, as members of God's people, see and respond to. As we realize that we are truly a part of that faith story, we find a strength and an identity that in turn shapes our values and actions. If we come to have a loving concern for our neighbor, it is not because we have been taught in a classroom to do so. It is rather because we have found our identity, our convictions, and our strength in being part of a faith community whose very way of life is to show loving concern for others.

With this traditional model of Christian education in mind, the concern of parents and religious educators is not to "teach" the faith but to help child and adult alike feel themselves to be part of the faith story that shapes our understanding of God's creative action in our lives and in the world about us. In a program based on this model, we come to know Christ in the life and love we celebrate together. We become part of the Christ story; we are caught up in the drama—the acted-out story—of his presence among us. Even our most painful moments can be transformed when we realize that we are part of this eternal drama that Christ lived out and continues to reenact in our midst. Our ancient liturgy proclaims in joyful times and sad times, in birth and death and resurrection times that Christ is with us. We share his story, and he shares ours.

So the Bible story lies at the root of our faith and of our response to God. Living out that story and sharing it so that we feel its power shaping our lives in the present moment is our primary responsibility and joy as members and leaders of the Christian community.

In the model for religious education that I share in this book, the church school meets either before or after the liturgy and is tied directly to the liturgical experience. If the gospel reading appointed for the day is the parable of the prodigal son, that parable will be the focus of the church school program. By the way, I would like to abandon the term *church school*. Since we are not concerned with "teaching" the faith but with sharing the faith story, I suggest the title *learning community* rather than *church school* or *religious education program*. *Learning community* suggests a *mutual sharing* of faith rather than a classroom directed by a teacher; it also suggests that the faith is learned as it is *experienced* within the community.

For the liturgy to come alive, educators and liturgists must work together. There should be a parish liturgical committee composed of clergy, educators, musicians, writers, artists, dramatists, parents, youth, and other interested persons. For background the group should study the biblical readings that are coming in the weeks ahead. Then they should get together to plan the liturgy and other activities that will be offered in the learning community. See Appendix IV for a method of liturgical planning that may be helpful in the planning process.

As we work together in such groups, we can help each other focus on the power of the eternal story of Jesus Christ. The planning group will become a primary learning community of the parish as each of us discovers the presence of God revealed in our *individual* life story as well as in the biblical account of the salvation history of God's *people*. As we talk together in our planning sessions, we will translate the meaning of the liturgy for one another and for the parish at large. We will be taking time to get in touch with our own story so that we can enable others to get in touch with theirs. We will help people realize what the theme and the readings of the Sunday or feast should mean to them personally.

We will help our parishioners to identify their own story with the biblical story. And as we continue to meet and plan our liturgies and how to share our story with the learning community, we will come to see that we ourselves must live out the liturgy.

This book is designed to help the whole process of biblical-liturgical education happen in the assembled parish family and in individual homes. It is not a theoretical book of scholarly comments on difficult biblical or liturgical questions; it aims, rather, at showing parish educators and parents how to make the Bible and worship come alive in parish and home.

One of the most encouraging movements of our time is the ever-increasing tendency among Christians to stress the remarkable unity that already exists among them. I hope that this book on the Bible and Christian worship will give further impetus to that movement. I write as an Episcopalian pastor; but because of the deep-seated unity of belief and worship among Christians (shown, for example, in the use of commonly accepted versions of the Bible and of the three-year lectionary), I trust that this book will be a useful tool for all liturgically oriented churches—Episcopalian, Roman Catholic, Lutheran—as well as many other Christian churches. I offer it, then, in Christ's love, with the prayer that sharing it may hold for you some of the intense joy that writing it has held for me.

Introduction to the Second Edition

I am grateful to Morehouse-Barlow for the opportunity to offer a second edition of *Sharing our Biblical Story*. This edition reflects nine years of experience with the book in consultations, conferences and in my own preparations for worship and education. Margin notes written into my own tattered copy of *Sharing* are now

included in the text. Corrections that I longed to make have been taken care of, and new features have been added to make the book more helpful to you, the reader. They come from concerns and questions that people have raised with me about using the lectionary as the basis for the congregation's education program.

One of the major complaints about lectionary-based education programs is that the great sweep of the biblical story is missed when the lectionary dictates what will be studied week-by-week. The Old Testament suffers in particular because the lections are always chosen to be in harmony with the gospel or epistle reading.

Lectionary texts that we hear on Sunday do need to be seen in the wider context of their place in the Bible. Conversion and renewal happens most effectively when people are invited into the fullness of the Christian story revealed in the Word and in lives lived in faithfulness to the story. This was certainly an emphasis in the first century Church. But following the lectionary texts and sharing that larger picture are not mutually exclusive. Chapter Nine has been added to suggest ways of exploring the whole Bible with the congregation while staying in tune with the lectionary.

My approach to both preaching and teaching comes from the school of "narrative theology." The primary emphasis is on the stories from the Bible and from later history that shape our understanding of how God is perceived in history and in creation.

In narrative theology we do not look at doctrine and a conceptual understanding of the Christian faith, as important as that is, but rather at the stories that led individuals and communities of people to confess the one true God. Something happened to those people to call forth the response, "We believe!" That "something" is the story they told, a story interpreted and added to by later generations groping for their own understanding. Each story from the tradition contains the hidden stories of the people who interpreted and reshaped the earlier stories. Using the approach of narrative theology, stories are never used as illustrations to explain a theological concept. Rather stories are seen as the primary source of revelation. Narrative preachers and narrative teachers are storytellers. The sermon engages the congregation in the story found in the text. Participants are invited to step into the biblical drama; to experience the anguish, the hope and the tensions of the story told from the text. They are drawn into their own stories as they are led to reflect on how their story intersects with the biblical story. The narrative preacher will look beyond the doctrines of Paul's letters and ask what led Paul to make his statements. The story that lies behind the epistle may be of as much concern as the text itself.

"By recognizing that Christian beliefs are not so many 'propositions' to be catalogued or juggled like truth-functions in a computer, but are living convictions which give shape to actual lives and actual communities, we open ourselves to the possibility that the only relevant critical examination of Christian beliefs may be one which begins by attending to lived lives. Theology must be at least biography. If by attending to those lives, we find ways of reforming our own theologies, making them more true, more faithful to our ancient vision, more adequate to the age now being born, then we will be justified in that arduous inquiry. Biography at its best will be theology." (McClendon, James William, Jr., *Biography as Theology: How Life Stories Can Remake Today's Theology,* Nashville: Abingdon Press, 1974, pp. 37-38.)

The narrative preacher invites the congregation into the faith stories of the tradition. The narrative teacher invites participants to engage in conversation with the faith stories drawing out the participants' response in conversation, the visual arts, drama, fantasy or other means. The story is the thing.

As you use *Sharing* be aware of this story-centered approach, realizing that this is but one way to look at the task of teaching and preaching. Leading participants into a study of the doctrines of the faith, exploring the meaning of the sacraments, studying concepts that lead people to belief and action calls for the Church teacher to use a variety of teaching skills and methods.

Though no one approach to Christian education can ever satisfy the total needs of the congregation, Christians must know the salvation story and feel a part of it. Until we have a common story and a common language that reflects the faith of the Church, we will lack the bonds of understanding that enable us to truly be the Body of Christ. For many of us in the Church today, that story and language of faith are as alien as if they were written only in

Sanskrit.

At the moment of baptism let the congregation be drawn to the side of the Sea of Reeds (Red Sea) and feel again the Spirit of God moving before them to open up the possibilities of salvation. Let them stand with Jesus and John the Baptist knowing that God's favor rests on them. The dove descends in the touch of pastor's hand in the signing of the cross on their foreheads. But if the story is not familiar, then the baptismal font remains but a strange furnishing in a world where water is available at the turn of a tap and God's mystery passes before our eyes unseen. The stories that would give the mystery flesh go unheard.

E. D. Hirsch's, *Cultural Literacy, What Every American Needs to Know,* met with mixed reviews, but his thesis deserves attention. "No modern society can hope to become a just society without a high level of universal literacy. Putting aside for the moment the practical arguments about the economic use of literacy, we can contemplate the even more basic principle that underlies our national system of education in the first place—that people in a democracy can be entrusted to decide all important matters for themselves because they can deliberate and communicate with one another. Universal literacy is inseparable from democracy and is the canvas for Martin Luther King's picture as well as for Thomas Jefferson's." (E. D. Hirsch, Jr., *Cultural Literacy: What Every American Needs to Know,* Boston: Houghton Mifflin Company, 1987, p. 12). My twenty years as a Christian educator convinces me that there is a biblical illiteracy in the Church that is appalling. Sermons are preached into a vacuum. We offer conferences and church school courses to help people define Christian values because the values expressed in the struggles of our people through time are not a part of our awareness.

John Westerhoff writing in Religious Education Journal defines three areas of catechesis or teaching; formation, education and instruction. "Formation implies "shaping" and refers to intentional, relational, experiential activities within the life of a story-formed faith community. Education implies "reshaping" and

refers to critical reflective activities related to these communal experiences. And instruction implies "building" and refers to the means by which knowledge and skills useful to communal life are transmitted, acquired and understood. Formation forms the body of Christ, education reforms it, and instruction builds it up." (John Westerhoff, "Formation, Education, Instruction," *Religious Education Journal,* Volume 82, Number 4, Fall, 1987, p. 581.) Using Westerhoff's terminology, what I am most concerned with in the approach reflected in this book is the category of Christian formation. In John Westerhoff's descriptive language, "The aim of this formational process is to conserve the Church's catholic substance (tradition), to maintain its identity as the body of Christ, and to initiate persons over time into its faith and life." (Ibid.) Out of hearing the story, out of identifying the story happening in the life of the person and the community comes an identification with the story. When we can begin to say with conviction, "this is my story . . . these are my people . . . these are my values . . . I too have entered into Covenant with the God of Abraham and Sarah, Peter and Mary of Magdalene . . . Jesus the Christ is my Savior," then we know that formation in the Story has happened. Then the Nicene Creed recited week after week becomes more than mumbled word; it becomes an affirmation of life. Then education and instruction, (as John Westerhoff defines it), takes on added impact as people reflect on a real live story that is theirs.

An effective education program for the congregation will have all three aspects of teaching happening. In the small congregation, the formation can happen every Sunday as adults gather with their children before the liturgy to hear and relate to the story that is to be heard in the liturgy. Instruction and education opportunities may come as small groups of people gather in living rooms and in fellowship halls with two or three or half a dozen others to explore the meaning of their faith. In larger congregations a variety of opportunities can be offered Sunday morning, during the week and at weekend conferences. But from my experience I believe that formation around the story must be at the heart of the education program. And I believe that the lectionary of the Church and the annual round of feasts, fasts and festivals offers us the most natural way for that formation process to take place. Historically, that is how the early Church carried out the formation process. The church year grew up around the need to share the story with converts and coming generations.

Though Chapter four spells out ways to design education sessions using the lectionary as a basis, I want to stress that the Sunday morning process can really be done simply, especially in small congregations where life is naturally less structured. Do not let the planning process intimidate you. Sometimes the best experiences happen as adults, teenagers, young children and pre-schoolers gather before the liturgy to hear and respond to the biblical texts they will share in the worship service. They sing a couple of songs that express something of the lectionary texts. Then a storyteller shares one of the stories that will be heard in the Liturgy of the Word that morning. Where there is no story appointed in the lectionary, I offer suggestions for Bible stories that fit in with the lectionary theme. These suggestions are outlined in the week-by-week commentaries and in Appendix III. If you follow this book you will never be without a story to share Sunday morning.

After the story is shared, introduce a simple activity that can help participants experience something of the story. The activity can be a brief time of conversation about the story and about experiences the story brings to people's minds as they relate to it. For example, on the fourth Sunday in Lent, Year C, the lectionary story is the Parable of the Prodigal Son. Before the story is told, ask persons to form into groups of three persons. Ask one person in each group to listen carefully to the feelings and actions of the father. A second person identifies with the feelings and actions of the younger son while the third persons in each group identifies with the elder son. After the story is told each person talks about their character in the story. "What happened to your character? What do you think he felt like when . . ." The next step in the process is simple.

"Share a time in your life when you've had similar feelings and experiences." After fifteen minutes, persons are brought back together and encouraged to reflect on their experience of hearing and relating to the parable. Following the discussion, one of the liturgical leaders offers "program notes" about the service that everyone is about to share. The readings are outlined, a new hymn is rehearsed with an explanation of how it relates to the scripture readings, prayer concerns are gathered, announcements are made and refreshments are served.

There will be times when you will want to step out of the lectionary track and do some instruction/education units for a period of weeks. Prepare for the visit of your diocesan bishop or district leader. Study the Christian understanding of healing when illness is of particular concern to the congregation. Examine an issue of social injustice in the world or in the community so that people can make an effective witness. But always look carefully at the lectionary for ways of raising up issues of healing, social justice and other concerns as they are expressed in the lections. For example, Mark 8:34-10:52 is a teaching section of the gospel that outlined for the early Church and for us just what discipleship means. This section is heard from September 14th through October 26th (Propers 19 through 25) in Year B. Look at that block of time as an opportunity to study discipleship in the Church today. (There are similar sections devoted to the meaning of discipleship that can be applied in Years A and B.) As noted in the commentary chapters of this book, Lent and Easter are the times traditionally set aside to teach about the meaning of our baptism and our sacramental life in the Church. If we look to the lectionary, we need never ask again what program we can offer during Lent or Easter. The program is carefully outlined for us in the texts assigned for our study during those two great seasons of the year. The concepts and doctrines that we are called to teach are there. To ignore those texts and to go searching elsewhere for study material is to work at cross purposes with the lectionary that draws on the experience of the early Church to convert and renew.

An effective Christian education program will include a balance of what Westerhoff describes as formation, instruction and education opportunities over the course of the year. People always need to be formed in the story. They need to struggle with the story in light of present experience. Let the lectionary be the tool for formation and preaching. But the lectionary approach may not always be the most effective way to build a concept-centered program. Plan opportunities where instruction and education can happen using a variety of approaches and time frames to work in.

In addition to Chapter Nine, two new appendices have been added to this edition.

Appendix III answers the question so often asked; "But what do we do when there is no story appointed in the lectionary? How do we tell the story then?"

Appendix IV is offered as a way of encouraging more persons to enter into the process of planning the congregation's worship. Specific step by step guidelines are offered to help church teachers, pastors, musicians and others plan together so that the liturgy of the congregation is truly the work of the people.

Chapter 1
The Religious Educator as Storyteller

The Importance of Storytelling

Throughout the ages, the storyteller has performed the important function of handing down society's traditions, history, and vision of life to each generation. The stories we hear play an important role in shaping our lives.

Parents are the most important storytellers, for they are the ones who whisper and sing stories into their children's ears and consciousness. The children remember those stories because they were told to them with deep love and feeling. Each story is a gift given and received. Values and visions are shaped in the sacredness of that sharing.

Beyond the family a more official storytelling system has functioned in every community and society. In primitive cultures the shaman or ancient one of the village gathered the people together and narrated and interpreted the tribal stories that shaped their world view and understanding of life. The cathedrals and churches of medieval Europe told the stories in stained glass because acoustical problems and the use of the unfamiliar Latin tongue made it impossible for the people to understand the spoken word within the context of the liturgy. The roving minstrel sang the stories of the land in ballad and folk song. In their excellent storytelling guide, *To Tell of Gideon,* John and

Mary Harrell point to the cave dwellers of the Cro-Magnon period to show us how far back our storytelling roots go. Deep in the recesses of the caves are the pictures that told the tribal stories. It is evident that the tribe gathered in caves where the tribal storyteller literally traced their stories by pointing out the drawings that complemented the narrative.

Traditionally the Church has played the role of the shaman or tribal storyteller. The Church has been the steward of the stories that shape our consciousness as a people—stories that give life its shape and meaning. Traditionally, too, each family unit has reinforced the role of the Church by passing on the great stories from one generation to another.

But today, in all too many cases, television has replaced the personal sharing of the story with the impersonal broadcast. Though television is a powerful medium for communicating the story, it cannot replace the power of the story in which giver and receiver personally interact as the story unfolds. And because television provides visual as well as spoken image, it often stultifies the imagination of the receiver. Moreover, the love that is conveyed in a personal telling of the story is missing.

We who are the Church need to be aware of our role as storyteller for the faithful. The liturgist, musician, church-school teacher, dramatist, and craftsman are all storytellers in the ancient and time-honored sense of that title. We shape people's ideas, values, and world view by means of that ancient art of story sharing. Seeing our role in this light will point up for us the immense importance of our task in the Church. Our roots as religious educators go back to the cave dwellers!

How to Tell Bible Stories

The fact that the Bible and the liturgy come out of a storytelling culture makes our task within the parish and the family far easier. We have too often attempted to *teach* children the Bible as if it were a course in mathematics. But we can *share* the Bible the way it was shared for many generations before us. With this realization we can approach our task as parents and religious educators from a more enjoyable and relaxed perspective. We need not fear (as some do) that we will ruin a child's faith by failing to *teach* the right information or by answering a question the wrong way. Rather, we can view our task as a process of *sharing* the faith story with our people and helping them reflect on that story as it touches their lives. We can trust the Holy Spirit to do the rest! Our task is to celebrate and dramatize the story, to respond to it with music, visual form, word, and dance.

We need to share the story for the sake of the story rather than using it to nail down a theological or moral truth. We misuse the Bible when we attempt to force it to teach what we want to teach: "I will tell you this Bible story to show you how to behave." With that approach the story ceases to be a story and becomes a mere teaching tool whose power is limited to making one specific point. By contrast, the stories that Jesus told were open ended. Jesus knew that we never stop discovering truth in a story—that we can continually grow into new understandings of it.

Basically, then, we tell our story for the same reason we tell the story of our great-grandfather crossing the prairies in a covered wagon—not because we want to teach a moral lesson but because it is our family story. Abraham, Sarah, Jacob, Joseph, Moses, Ruth, David, and Elijah are *our* ancestors through

Jesus. As Paul wrote, ". . . if you are Christ's, then you are Abraham's offspring, heirs according to promise" (Galatians 3:29). That is why I like to preface Bible stories with "This is a story of our people. One day. . . ."

For many of us storytelling has become a lost art. Consult the Bibliography for storytelling resources. I recommend in particular *To Tell of Gideon* by John and Mary Harrell. This excellent booklet can give courage, conviction, and practical guidance. It is brief and includes a recording of persons telling stories with children. For your immediate study, however, here are a few suggestions about sharing stories with children.

The first step, of course, is to read the story you want to tell. Next, jot down on a note card the turning points and the details that help shape the story. Then let your mind go, and imagine yourself telling the story effectively to the group you will be sharing it with. Picture the best kind of response you would want from them. Then in your mind begin telling the story to the imagined group. Repeat the process until you can actually *see* the scene you are describing. When you say "And Moses stopped, for he saw a burning bush," you need to see Moses and that bush in your mind's eye and to picture the group's response. Go over the story in this way until you feel completely at home with it and can throw away your note card. If a detail escapes you or if you have to think about it so that you lose the picture in your mind, you need to go back to the source and pull the detail back into your consciousness.

Next comes the actual telling of the story. In telling stories to younger children, sitting on the floor with them gives an intimacy, a feeling of being together. If adults are included in the group, I like to have the children come and sit on the floor close to me and to let the parents sit behind the children. If the children are receiving the story, the parents will receive it too. On the other hand, if the child is blocked from receiving the story because of being too far away from the storyteller, the parent will be distracted by the child's inattention.

Felt boards and pictures have their place in helping the hearers respond to the story, but I discourage the use of any props or visual aids for a first telling. If you are to convey the story you love to someone you love, you must concentrate entirely on the story and the person. We do not need a felt board to tell our spouse we love her or him, and we do not need visual aids when we share a story with someone as a way of saying "I love you." (And that is what we are telling our people as we offer them stories: "I'm telling you this story as a way of saying I love you. This is a story I love because it's about our people. Because I love you, I want you to have this gift of our story." That is how sacred and special the role of the storyteller is!) Furthermore, visual aids are objectionable because we want the hearers to picture the story in their minds. We want them to be there and experience the feelings of Moses, Jesus, Peter, or Mary. If we use visual aids, the hearers see our picture rather than involving themselves in living into their own pictures.

Once we have told the story, we can sit back and share the hearers' responses, but at this stage we have to be very careful not to interpret the story for them or turn it into a teaching device. Let the hearers respond, and key your remarks to theirs. If this is a religious education setting, you may want to call forth a variety of responses. In dealing with children, let them cut out and mount felt-board figures and use them in telling the story. Encourage them to dramatize the story or to make up a taped presentation of it for their parents. Sing about the story. Respond with an art project. Have the older children or teenagers write a ballad and set it to a popular tune. There is no end of possibilities.

There are times, of course, when we will want to use biblical stories as "launching devices" for discussions with teenagers and adults. For example, we might tell the parable of the prodigal son to a group of senior-high students and adults to get them talking about their feelings as sons, daughters, and parents. In this case we would tell the story and then focus the discussion on how the three characters in the parable must have felt at various points in the narrative. Next we move into the more personal level of interpretation by asking if the participants can identify times in their own lives when they might have experienced some of those feelings. Then we can talk about theological implications for all of us: "Why do you think Jesus told that

story?" Lyman Coleman offers many resources that use this method of discovery. But note that we are still not using the story to *teach* with. We are using it as a means of helping people *discover* God's truth for themselves. If we look at what Jesus said and did as recorded in the gospels, we will see that this is the approach he consistently used as he related to people. When the rich man asked a question, Jesus responded with a story or question of his own. We have much to learn from this method. The Bible is the story of God's people; it is not a textbook on right behavior and response. Jesus told stories to shake the foundations of his hearers! He deliberately threw them off base to deepen their thinking, even though many people turned away from him because they wanted textbook answers. Our tendency to want neatly packaged answers is very human, but we must not make the Bible a *tool* for learning; it is rather our *source* for learning.

Some Difficulties Encountered in Telling Bible Stories

As we begin to look closely at the stories of the Bible, we may find some of their features difficult to understand. This may block us from sharing the Bible further. Here are some of the problems that persons have talked about with me as they began to share Bible stories.

Violence in the Old Testament
The Old Testament is filled with violence. For example, we hear that the entire population of Jericho was annihilated. ". . . the city and all that is within it shall be devoted to the Lord for destruction. . . . Then they utterly destroyed all in the city, both men and women, young and old, oxen, sheep, and asses, with the edge of the sword" (Joshua 6:17, 21). War and bloodshed were part of the life of these people as they came in from the wilderness and settled the land. War and bloodshed were also part of what it meant to be a great nation under Saul, David, and Solomon.

We need to realize that the Bible is the oral and written reflections of a community; it is a record of how they perceived God acting in their history. As the next chapter will make clear, the Bible traces a slowly evolving understanding of how God acts in his world. Our people only gradually came to understand that God acts not through armed might but through weakness, vulnerability, and love. We need to look at our own understanding of God's action in our nation's history before we judge our Old Testament ancestors too harshly. Our ancestors often justified the slaughter of American Indians on the grounds that this was our Promised Land, that the Indians were like the Canaanites, and that it was our duty to destroy them and cleanse the land for God. And how many times have we thanked God for clear weather so that our bombers could more accurately hit their targets during a raid? As a child I used to wonder whose side God had been on during our own War Between the States.

To avoid the stories that contain accounts of war and violence is to ignore large portions of the Old Testament. To "clean the stories up" by ignoring the actions of the people taken on behalf of God is to deny our hearers' own feelings of anger and desire for vengeance—feelings that they must deal with before they can appreciate the kind of vulnerable loving and giving that Jesus calls them to. Knowing our own history and our own inclinations, we can tell of the violence in a way that places the responsibility on the people rather than presenting it as a direct command from God. We can explain that Joshua ordered a massacre because he felt that the enemy was evil and therefore must be destroyed; he felt that this was what God wanted him to do.

God "Speaking" and Appearing to His People

If we literalize the Old Testament narrative we may end up wishing that God was still an active force in the world today as he was in biblical days, when he seemed to talk intimately and almost face to face with prophet and king. But we should look behind that literal language.

Many of the "conversations" occurred in dreams that were then explained by the dreamer or by a dream interpreter. We can still say that God speaks to us through dreams. If we get in touch with our dreams by training ourselves to remember them, our waking hours will be enriched. This is true whether one approaches

dreams from a psychological perspective or from a theological one.

In other places God is asked a direct question, and the questioner receives a direct answer. For example, in 2 Samuel 2:1 we read: "After this David inquired of the Lord, 'Shall I go up into any of the cities of Judah?' And the Lord said to him, 'Go up.' David said, 'To which shall I go up?' And he said, 'To Hebron.'" But what did this answer mean literally? One explanation is that it was the custom to cast lots in times of crisis to determine the will of God, and these lots were considered sacred. According to Deuteronomy 33:8 the tribe of Levi was responsible for the lots which were called the *Urim* and *Thummim* (see also Ezra 2:63). A clear indication of the use of the lots is found in 1 Samuel 14:41. "Therefore Saul said, 'O Lord God of Israel, why hast thou not answered thy servant this day? If this guilt is in me or in Jonathan my son, O Lord, God of Israel, give Urim; but if this guilt is in thy people Israel, give Thummim.'" According to the Jerusalem Bible footnote on this passage, the use of the Urim and Thummim died out after David, but their use explains why the Bible sometimes presents God as answering questions directly.

Visions are also recorded. Some of them were ecstatic visions such as those described in Isaiah 6. There, Isaiah is lifted up into the presence of God. "I saw the Lord seated on a high throne. . ." (Isaiah 6:1). Moses had a vision of a bush burning yet not being consumed by flame (Exodus 3:2). But visions are mystical experiences that are not limited to biblical times. We still hear of people having intense experiences, even to the point of seeing a person or scene before them. Whether one wishes to attribute this power to a "sixth sense" or to see it as a gift from God is determined by one's faith and understanding of such phenomena.

Finally, what we would call an inspiration is often presented in the Bible as direct conversation with God. But we ourselves often use this kind of language to describe an inspiring experience or thought. As I walk down the street feeling depressed, a thought comes to me. I suddenly feel inspired and joyful. I describe my experience to a friend and say "God touched me as I walked down the street. He told me everything was going to be all right. I feel great."

In some of the very ancient material found in the Bible, God is described as walking about upon the earth as a human person would have walked. The scene where he talks to Adam and Eve is the most obvious example (Genesis 3:8-19). And in Genesis 32, Jacob wrestled all night with a strange being who was supposedly God. Jacob called that place Peniel (meaning *the face of God*) because he believed that he had "seen God face to face" (Genesis 32:30). In Genesis 18, we find Abraham talking with three strangers. It becomes evident that one of them is God.

As the Israelites moved into the Canaanite lands, they adapted the ancient stories that were told in connection with some of the sacred places there. These stories were primitive accounts of gods who roamed the earth in the guise of strangers or who met face to face with people in their daily lives. The Israelites took these stories into their own heritage and adapted them to their understanding of how the one God was acting in their lives. These ancient stories are important to share, for they reflect the feelings and understandings of our people at that time in their history. Moreover, some of them touch deep roots in our consciousness and are helpful in telling our own personal stories. At the same time, however, they may confuse the hearer. In telling such stories, simply refer to the stranger or messenger as one who came bearing a message from God.

Miracles

We believe in a God who has infinite power. We will never be able to fully understand that power and the way it breaks into our lives. Jesus performed miracles of healing that we cannot explain medically. He demonstrated how powerful faith can be. If those stories were simply miracle stories about Jesus, however, they would be of only momentary interest. But they are far more than that. Jesus was not demonstrating *his* extraordinary powers as much as he was showing the power available to *us* as we open ourselves in faith. As we read the Book of Acts we discover that Peter, Paul, and the other apostles were endowed with the same power of healing that Jesus had. These, then, are faith stories. Jesus was not a magician. He was the living presence of God, meeting people in the flesh of human encounter. At Easter we proclaim that the risen Christ still meets us as the living presence of God within the flesh and blood of human encounter. Unexplainable miracles of healing and freedom still happen today. The act of faith acknowledges mystery and wonder in the midst of what we may otherwise consider an unexplainable existence. To speak of God is to speak of unknown, unlimited power.

If our children (or adults, for that matter) ask how these wonders could have happened, let us share with them the wonder of the mystery. We do not *know*, but we do *believe*. There is a mystery and a wonder to life. We can share the excitement and hope contained in that truth, and in doing so we share a priceless gift.

But some "miraculous" events described in the Bible are obviously natural events that were embellished in the course of many tellings. In the Book of Exodus, for example, the ten plagues are described as if Moses personally initiated each of them. "... take in your hand the rod which was turned into a serpent. And you shall say to him, 'The Lord, the God of the Hebrews, sent me to you, saying, "Let my people go ... I will strike the water that is in the Nile with the rod that is in my hand, and it shall be turned to blood"' " (Exodus 7:15-17). However the ten plagues are natural events that still plague Egypt. Frogs come and destroy crops. Disease causes death. The water grows red with mud and is unusable. As the story of those plagues was told over and over, however, the significance of the events became more apparent. Those events did not just happen. For Pharaoh and for the Israelites they were signs from God that the people should go free. Gradually the events took on the almost magic quality of the supernatural miracle; the people believed that it was Moses' rod that had turned the water red. The account of the crossing of the Red Sea or Sea of Reeds shows clear evidence of such embellishment over a long time.

Our people believe that God is active in the history of our people and of all creation. He gives us signs of his action in our lives. Our *description* of those signs, however, can be literal, or it can be a poetic, symbolic embellishment of the story that heightens its impact. As I look back at an event that changed my life or changed the course of history for my people, my description of that event will reflect my wonder.

As I tell stories containing this kind of miracle, I prefer to say something like "When Pharaoh saw his nation overrun with frogs, he too began to believe that God wanted the Israelites to go free just as Moses had told him." If we literalize that miracle, we leave our hearers with the impression that I had as a child: "God was active back in Bible times, but he isn't very active in our world today." However, if we help our hearers see that God works through the natural events of our time in the same way that he did in the biblical stories, we can help them find faith and hope in the present moment. Then they will feel themselves a part of the biblical story.

Poetry in the Bible

As we share the biblical stories, we may find ourselves using the poetic imagery that abounds in the Bible. We need to help our hearers develop their sense of poetry if they are going to understand the biblical language and story forms. Whenever we try to describe a feeling or a reality that is beyond our comprehension, we will inevitably find ourselves using the language of poetry or analogy. For example, since God is like a father to us, we call God our "Father." But if we literalize this analogy we lock ourselves and our hearers into the image of the bearded old man in the sky. Because the concept of God is beyond our comprehension, we do need to have images of God if we are to feel a sense of relatedness. Children may well picture God in the sky looking down at them, since that is the picture language of the Bible. There is nothing wrong with that, but we need to avoid locking anyone into that image. Always leave room for others to grow and discover new images and understandings. If a child asks where heaven is, we can safely say that we do not know. That is probably one of the safest theological statements we can make! There is much that our finite humanity does not know. It is not a confession of ignorance and weakness to acknowledge our humanity! But if we hear a little boy say "I believe that God is in heaven right over those clouds and that my pet puppy is there with him looking down at me," we need to appreciate that statement and affirm the child. We can respond

by saying "That is a beautiful thought, John. I like that." We affirm his self-image, but we allow him room to grow into a deeper understanding in the days and years to come.

Perhaps one of the most important things we can do for our hearers is to help them appreciate the nature of poetry. So many of our society's values are based on facts and scientific data that the beauty of the poetic word is all too often devalued, and we end up asking if a poetic statement is true. To ask the question is to destroy the truth. We need to explain that poetic language is a "stretched" use of language wherein we talk in images, comparisons, even exaggerations to convey a real, though not literal, truth. (If we say, "Joe's a regular beaver," we want to convey the truth of his industriousness. It would be foolish, then, for someone to claim that the statement is false because Joe doesn't have four feet, a broad, flat tail, and brown fur.)

Types of Stories Found in the Bible

Before we can share the power of a Bible story with our listeners, we ourselves must thoroughly understand the story. One of the basic approaches to understanding a story is to know the literary type to which it belongs. Such knowledge will help clarify what the author intended and how to interpret the literary techniques used. It will also help us to see what our ancestors had in mind when they repeated the story, and it can stimulate us to clarify our own purposes in sharing that story.

We share certain stories, of course, simply because they are part of our heritage—they help us feel in touch with "our people." In introducing the unedifying story of David and Bathsheba, for example, we can simply say "David is our forefather. We want you to know about him—to know his strengths and his weaknesses." But with many biblical stories it is crucial that we understand the characteristics of that type of story. The following pages discuss some of the more important types.

Myths

To understand myths, we must understand their origin and function. Myths are traditional stories (or themes or character types) that originate in preliterate societies. They deal with supernatural beings, ancestors, or heroes, and they sum up a people's cultural ideals and commonly felt emotions—their world view. (See *The American Heritage Dictionary of the English Language* for a precisely worded, packed definition.) Myths deal with ultimate origins, meanings, values. Beane and Doty point out that myth is "'living,' in the sense that it applies models for human behavior and, by that very fact, gives meaning and value to life. . . . Myth narrates a sacred history; it relates an event that took place in primordial Time, the fabled time of the 'beginnings.' In other words, myth tells how, through the deeds of Supernatural Beings, a reality came into existence, be it the whole of reality, the Cosmos, or only a fragment of reality—an island, a species of plant, a particular kind of human behavior, an institution. Myth, then, is always an account of a 'creation'; it relates how something was produced, began to be. . . . In short, myths describe the various and sometimes dramatic breakthroughs of the sacred (or the 'supernatural') into the World. It is this sudden breakthrough of the sacred that really establishes the World and makes it what it is today. Furthermore, it is the result of the intervention of Supernatural Beings that man himself is what he is today, a mortal, sexed, and cultural being."*

Myths, then, explain the unexplainable and establish for a society the basis for understanding origins, codes of morality, and life values. They tend to be the glue that holds a society together; they give the people a feeling of common origins and a common understanding of life.

Now, the Book of Genesis provided the Israelites with their mythic framework. Most of its stories were adapted from surrounding societies and reshaped to fit the theological understanding of Yahweh's people. For example, the myth of the fall of mankind in Genesis 3 shows marked similarity to the Greek Gilgamesh epic, to the Akkadian myth of Adapa, and to a Persian myth.** The story of Noah and the ark

*Wendell Beane and William Doty, eds., *Myths, Rites, Symbols*, pp. 3-4.

**Robert Graves and Raphael Patai, *Hebrew Myths: The Book of Genesis* (New York: McGraw-Hill, 1963, 1964), pp. 78-79.

also has counterparts in other ancient societies; a portion of that myth may simply have explained the origin of the rainbow. The Israelites modified stories of this kind so that they established a groundwork for understanding such important issues as the origin of pain and suffering, the establishment of a covenant between human beings and God, and other crucial questions of life and death. (Some other Old Testament myths simply explain the customs or landmarks of places in the land of Canaan where the Israelites settled. See Genesis 19:24-26, for example, where the pillars of salt found in that territory are put into a story to explain their origin.)

Why are these mythic stories so powerful? Bettelheim's remarks on the power of fairy tales (in *The Uses of Enchantment*) apply very well to myths also: They are profoundly symbolic, and as people identify with the characters they get in touch with feelings they might otherwise be afraid to acknowledge. It has often been pointed out, too, that some of these mythic stories are extremely powerful because they express the story of every individual; we "find ourselves" in them. Adam and Eve, for example, are each of us. We are all tempted to eat the forbidden fruit and become like God. Failing to accept the limitations of our humanity, we find ourselves separated from God and from creation; we feel as if we have been "kicked out of the garden." As we push against the authority and power of God, we find ourselves fighting wars of possession and conquest, misusing our natural resources, and bringing suffering into our lives.

The fact that myths are the stories of ourselves helps us answer the question "But are myths *true*?" Absolutely! Not, of course, true to literal historical fact, but true to the deepest meanings of life. The listeners, with the storyteller's help, can identify with the perennial truth of the ancient narrative. The story tells not of something that happened long ago but of something happening right now to each of us. When children hear us say "Once upon a time. . . ," they know we are in the realm of story, not the realm of scientific fact; we need not waste time explaining to them the difference between myth and science. It is enough, for example, to begin, "Today I want to tell you a story that our people told to explain why there are so many different languages in the world. Once upon a time, everyone spoke the same language. But then they decided to build a huge tower so they could be more powerful. . . .''

Fairy Tales

Though strictly speaking there are no fairy tales in the Bible, I mention this kind of story so that we can better appreciate the kinds of stories we do find there. Whereas myths deal with the primal relationship between gods and people and lay the groundwork for understanding cultural ideals, fairy tales—at least on the conscious level—are simply fanciful stories that appeal to the imagination. But Bruno Bettelheim and others feel that there is also deep unconscious significance to the fairy tales. Bettelheim "attempts to show how fairy stories represent in imaginative form what the process of healthy human development consists of, and how the tales make such development attractive for the child to engage in" (*The Uses of Enchantment,* page 12). Fairy tales lead the hearer through the struggles of the characters. These tales identify the truth that there is evil in the world and that one must engage in the struggle with that evil if one is to win the rewards of life. According to Bettelheim, it is in identifying with that struggle that the hearer attains a sense of integrity and freedom. Fairy stories usually include an element of fantasy, with talking animals and other extraordinary occurrences. Some of our biblical stories contain such elements. For example, read the account of Balaam and his speaking donkey (Numbers 22:22-35) and the whole Book of Tobit.

Legends

Legends are unverified stories about the heroes of a people. They are passed down from generation to generation, and though they may be partly historical, they have taken on fanciful details. Legends are an important type of Bible story, just as they are important in the story of a nation.

Anyone who has stood on the banks of the Potomac can realize that George Washington could not have thrown a silver dollar across it, but that story is deeply imbedded in our consciousness, as is the story of his chopping down the cherry tree. Though legends may not be literally true, they are an important part of the oral tradition of a people, for they help us appreciate the impact that a person or event made on the nation's understanding of its history. These stories are told partly to inspire the next generation and partly to explain the origins of traditions and the viewpoint of the people. We need heroes to admire and emulate. Our pride as a people grows as we think about those who helped shape our destiny. Some of the accounts of Elijah and Elisha and other Old Testament heroes are of this nature.

Bernhard Anderson sums up well the nature and the value of legend in discussing its relationship to history. "Often it is assumed that when something is 'legendary,' like say, the legend of Robin Hood, it has virtually no historical authenticity. What is legendary is opposed to what is historical—that is, according to our view, [to] exact sober history. Now it is quite true that legend lacks the precise accuracy demanded by a twentieth-century historian. In our sophisticated age no historian would think of writing history in the form of the story of Noah and the flood, or the legend of Jacob's dream at Bethel, or the Joseph cycle. But in a deeper sense these ancient popular forms tell us something about history that is sometimes ignored by the modern historian who is concerned only with giving a dispassionate report of wars, daily events, relations between nations, and so on. Legend is able to communicate to us out of the past history as experienced, the internal meaning of events and happenings. And if the deepest meaning of man's life is his relation to God, legend and poetry are exceedingly important ways of telling history" (*Understanding the Old Testament,* page 158).

A brief introduction can help to set the tone for receiving a legend. "It is said that our great prophet Elisha once. . . . How this happened or if it happened in just the way I'm going to tell it to you today, I don't know. I tell you this story so that you can know how our people felt about this prophet God had sent them."

Protest Stories or ''Underground Literature''

An oppressed people desperately needs to speak and write words of inspiration. The Book of

Daniel, for example, was written while the Jews were being persecuted by the Greeks (around 167 B.C.), although it *appears* to have been written much earlier. Daniel was a legendary figure associated with the period of the Babylonian captivity during the reign of Nebuchadnezzar, who ruled the Mediterranean world from 604 to 562 B.C. The first six chapters of the book describe the bravery of Daniel as he courageously clung to the principles of his Jewish faith. Because of Daniel's firm faith, the Lord protected him from a fiery furnace and from wild lions. The rest of the book describes Daniel's dreams and prophecies of the new age that God would bring in after evil had been defeated. Historical events from the time of Babylonian dominance up to the time of the Greek persecutions are described in mystical, symbolic language. The writing appears to foretell the future, since it *seems* to have been composed during the Babylonian captivity. Many biblical scholars feel, however, that the writer is looking *back* at history from the perspective of the Greek era.

To the suffering, persecuted Jew living under the shadow of the Greek ruler Antiochus Epiphanes, the message of Daniel was clear. If you keep the faith, God will protect you. Look at the faith your great forefather Daniel displayed. Nothing, not even the threat of fire or the lion pit, could force him to compromise his relationship with God. The more he was oppressed, the stronger he became. The winner in the end was our God, who showed his triumphant power through his faithful servant Daniel. Moreover, your God is in control of history. The suffering and oppression you are experiencing are not meaningless; they are part of God's plan. If you keep the faith, you too will see the great day of the Lord, when those who have been faithful will triumph and those who have oppressed you will be destroyed.

Again we may find ourselves questioning the truth of this kind of literature, and again we must distinguish between literal historical truth and truth expressed through various kinds of oral and written literary forms. Theologically, the Book of Daniel is true as an expression of the Jewish and Christian view of history—a view which proclaims that there is meaning in our struggle, that there is a purpose and direction to history.

The kind of literature that the Book of Daniel represents is very important. (The Book of Revelation is its New Testament counterpart. See the next chapter, pages 63 and 69, for a fuller explanation of this kind of literature.) The courage it inspires can mean the difference between despair and unshakable hope for a people in their suffering. For example, how many Jews must have thought about or read the Book of Daniel during the terrible persecutions in Nazi Germany!

So we need to share the Daniel stories with a sense of their importance, but we also must clearly indicate to our listeners the kind of story they represent. Say "For many generations our people have told this story about a man named Daniel so that they too could have courage when they were afraid."

Humorous Stories

Humor plays an important role throughout the Bible. Because of translation difficulties we may miss much of the subtle humor found in the wordplay used extensively in both the Old Testament and the Gospels. But plenty of other humor is within reach. Some of it is the more obvious kind found in stories told around the campfire. For example, the largely legendary tales of the strong man Samson would provide laughter at the expense of the Philistine enemy, such as when Samson tied torches on the tails of foxes to set the Philistines' crops on fire.

Humor is an important ingredient in many other tales, such as the whole Book of Jonah.

Remembering that humor would have been an effective device for heightening the attention of hearers seated around the campfire, we should try to be sensitive to the possibility of humor as we prepare to tell our stories. Besides reading commentaries on these stories we can learn a great deal about comic techniques by listening to good comedians like Bill Cosby. In his treatment of the Noah story, for example, Cosby finds humor in unexpected places and conveys it by such devices as appropriate pauses and vocal inflections. Analyzing and using comedians' methods would be a valuable way to enliven our telling of Bible stories.

Fables

A fable is "a concise narrative making an edifying or cautionary point and often employing as characters animals that speak and act like human beings" (*The American Heritage Dictionary of the English Language*). As Bruno Bettelheim points out, fables are moralistic tales that tell us what we ought to do or not do. This type of story has traditionally been used as a teaching device. There *is* a point to the story, and the storyteller tends to reinforce the teaching point as the story is completed. Jotham's fable (Judges 9:7-15) is a rare example of a biblical fable. Since fables are rare in biblical literature, I mention the type only to point up the differences in storytelling approaches.

Parables

The parable is a unique kind of story or saying. Whereas legends and myths *support* the world view and reinforce the moral conduct and thought patterns of a people, parables *confront* the accepted norms so as to open the people's minds to new understandings of truth and possibility. Parables are told, in a sense, to throw the hearer off base. We expect the story to end one way, but it ends in an entirely different, unexpected way. We are upset. Parables, then, confront the myths and systems we live by and force us to realize that truth as we know it may be truth only because we believe it. Parabolic religion, which Jesus represented, forces us out of our safe systems of accepted knowledge and understanding and confronts us with uncertainty and confusion so that we can move into deeper realms of reality that God is always opening up to us. In our religious quest we must never dare feel that we have arrived. God is always calling us into deeper communion and mystery. Thus parables make room for the mystery and transcendence of God by throwing the doors wide open to new possibilities for truth. No wonder Jesus' stories upset the Pharisees and Sadducees and caused people to turn away!

Read the parable of the laborers in the vineyard (Matthew 20:1-16). The ending is a surprise: Those hired last are paid the same as those hired first. The workers in the story grumble, and we can imagine the hearers grumbling too. It makes no sense economically.

We would never operate our business that way—but that is just the point. God's kingdom does not function the way our "kingdom" does. For Jews who had accepted their own preeminence in the Kingdom as a matter of course, this parable undermined the whole understanding of covenent relationship. Tell the parable of the prodigal son (Luke 15:11-32) and note the reaction. "Why, I'll bet the kid turned right around and did the same thing again" may well be the response of your hearers. God's mercy really makes no sense to our system of thinking.

Parables are dangerous to the established order. By the time the gospel stories were put into writing, the early Church was modifying the original parables of Jesus to make a system out of his teachings! We see evidence of this with the parable of the sower (Matthew 13:3-9). First there is the simple parable; then the parable is allegorized in verses 18-23 of the same chapter, where each type of ground is carefully equated with a certain type of listener. As the writer of the Gospel put the oral tradition into writing a generation after Jesus' death, it was natural for him to approach Jesus' words from the perspective of the growing Church and to place an interpretation on the stories that would grapple with current problems and help the people understand their new life in Christ.

I would call the book of Jonah an extended parable. For the Jewish hearer the story turns out in a shocking way: God shows care and love for the enemies of the Israelites. The prophet Jonah, who should have been the hero of the tale, ends up acting like a spoiled child; the heroes are the hated Assyrians living in Nineveh. This simple story shakes the foundations of understanding and knocks systems of thought awry.

Suggestions for telling the parables are made in A Guide to Stories of the Bible, pages 45-47. The main point to keep in mind is to avoid casting the parables in concrete and pretending that they are carefully worked out allegories (where every person, place, object, or event *actually* represents something else) or mere teaching tools with which to nail down truth. We do not tell the parables to answer questions or to resolve issues; we tell them with the deliberate intention of *raising* questions and of forcing the hearers to reexamine their assumptions about life and truth.

Actually, humor often plays the same role as the parable and can be parabolic in nature. We laugh at the clown or comedian and suddenly realize that we are laughing at all our own safe assumptions. That is why the role of the clown or comic in society is so important.

I have attempted in this section to offer a brief synopsis of the kinds of stories we will find in the Bible. If the words *myth, legend,* or *underground literature* make the Bible seem complicated, realize that there are many ways to express truth. I may not always tell my wife in a simple, straightforward way that I love her. Sometimes I give her a gift that says those words for me. Other times I will use the language of poetry: "You make the sun shine for me even though it's nighttime." To ask me if that statement is true would be an insult. Of course it's true! There are other times when I might tell her a story that helps us to laugh lovingly together. At still other times I may say something that will shake the foundations of our relationship so that we can come to a deeper level of understanding of what our love means. And so it is with the love story between God and his people that we find in the stories of the Bible.

A Guide to Stories of the Bible

We sometimes hesitate to tell Bible stories because we don't know which ones are most appropriate or because we find it hard to locate them in the Bible. This Guide will help you to become familiar with stories you can easily share in the parish learning community or at home.

Although this Guide lists stories from both the Old and the New Testaments, it is not an all-inclusive reference to Bible stories. You will no doubt want to add your own favorite Bible stories (from both Old and New Testaments) to this list. Many stories about Jesus have been omitted because they are so well known and because so much published material on them is available.

In *column 1* the Old Testament passages are listed in the order in which they appear in the Bible. The gospel passages present the life of Jesus chronologically, except that the stories of healing and Jesus' parables are each grouped together after the resurrection accounts. Some important stories from the Book of Acts are then listed. *Column 2* tells where the story is found in the three-year Episcopal lectionary *if* it appears among the readings for Sundays and greater feasts. Episcopalians, Roman Catholics, Lutherans, and many other denominations follow a three-year lectionary that assigns *many* of the same Scripture readings for a given Sunday or feast day. Despite this basic unity, however, *it is always wise to check with one's own worship planners* to see which Scripture readings will actually be used, because there is not total uniformity of assigned readings and because liturgy planners sometimes substitute other readings for the assigned ones. *Column 3* identifies the story's contents, and *Column 4* gives brief hints for the storyteller.

Selected Old Testament Stories

Passage	Lectionary	Story Content	Storyteller Hints
Genesis 2:4—3:24	First Sunday in Lent (Year A) Proper 5 (Year B) Proper 22 (Year B)	The epic account of "the fall" of the human race	This story is poetic in nature. Avoid destroying its poetry and mythic symbolism by literalizing it as an historic account. (Also keep these remarks in mind when sharing other readings from Genesis.) Adam and Eve represent all men and all women. The story of the Garden of Eden and of the fall are stories about ourselves. God creates us to live in harmony with him. We attempt to make ourselves gods (the symbol of the forbidden tree) and in doing so separate ourselves from God and from creation. As a result, we bring suffering into our lives and into the world.
Genesis 6:5—9:17	First Sunday in Lent (Year B)	The great flood—Noah and the ark	We deal here as much with legend and myth as with history. The ancient world did experience floods that encouraged stories about an epic flood covering the whole world. However, avoid literalizing the story by describing the drowning of the entire human race except for Noah and his family. Emphasize the covenant relationship between God and Noah,

Passage	Lectionary	Story Content	Storyteller Hints
			and Noah's great faith in following the command of God. Stress the rainbow as a continuing sign of this covenant. If the rainbow becomes a lifetime reminder of our covenant relationship with God, we will have sowed good seed as storytellers.
Genesis 12:1-9	Second Sunday in Lent (Year A)	The call of Abraham. Abraham (or Abram) feels the call to leave his homeland for the new land that God promises him and his descendants.	The strange incident of killing a heifer, a goat, a ram, a turtledove, and a young pigeon and of cutting all but the birds in half was a solemn and ancient sign that a covenant was about to be made. The fire that passed between the halves of the animals was a symbol that the covenant was being sealed by the Lord.
Genesis 15:1-21	Second Sunday in Lent (Year C) Proper 14 (Year C)	The divine promise to Abraham; God makes a covenant with Abraham.	
Genesis 18:1-15	Proper 11 (Year C)	The promise of a son to Abraham and Sarah	The three men are messengers from God. (With children, simply explain that God sent the messengers to bring good news to Abraham and Sarah. Children are accustomed to special messengers or superhuman beings in stories from other sources.) Notice the humor in this story. Sarah laughs because she cannot believe the message. The messengers confront her laughter.
Genesis 21:1-7		The birth of Isaac to Abraham and Sarah	
Genesis 22:1-19	Good Friday Second Sunday in Lent (Year B)	God tests Abraham's faith by asking him to sacrifice Isaac, his only son. Abraham proves his faith by starting to sacrifice Isaac, but God intervenes at the last moment to dramatize how he providentially rewards people of faith.	
Genesis 24:1-67		The marriage of Isaac and Rebekah	

Passage	Lectionary	Story Content	Storyteller Hints
Genesis 25:19-34		The birth of Esau and Jacob to Isaac and Rebekah. Esau sells his birthright to Jacob.	
Genesis 27:1-45		Jacob obtains Isaac's blessing by deceit.	A father's blessing was final and could be given only once. It was meant for the eldest son. Esau was the father of the Edomites; these stories were told to show (among other things) how much smarter the patriarch of the Israelites (Jacob) was than the patriarch of the Edomites.
Genesis 27:46—28:5		Isaac sends Jacob to his uncle Laban so that Jacob can find a wife among Isaac's own people.	
Genesis 28:10-22	Feast of St. Michael and All Angels	Jacob's dream of a ladder to heaven	The well-known account of "Jacob's ladder" tells of a dream, not of a literal happening. Our people told this story to explain the significance of Bethel as a center of worship and to express the sacred relationship that Jacob enjoyed with the Lord.
Genesis 29:1-30		Jacob's arrival at the home of Laban and his marriage to both of Laban's daughters; an amusing tale of how Laban tricked Jacob into marrying his less-attractive daughter first	
Genesis 29:31—30:24		The sons of Jacob	One need not go into a detailed account of the birth of Jacob's sons. The main point is that Jacob was the father of the twelve tribes of Israel. According to legend, each of the sons became the father of a tribe. (See Genesis 35:22b-26 and 35:16-18.)
Genesis 30:25—32:2		Jacob tricks Laban and escapes Laban's control.	Avoid telling the intricacies of cross-breeding Laban's herds. Simply indicate that Jacob was able to outwit Laban.
Genesis 32:23-33	Proper 24 (Year C)	Jacob wrestles with a stranger and is given the name Israel.	One reason for sharing this story is to establish that Jacob is the great forefather of the nation Israel. He receives a new name from the stranger (who is never identified—but the implication is that he is an angel or perhaps the Lord himself). According

Passage	Lectionary	Story Content	Storyteller Hints
			to The Jerusalem Bible's footnote on Genesis 32:28, the name Israel probably means either "May God show his strength!" or "He has been strong against God." An earlier footnote (at the beginning of the story) provides further help. "The author has made use of an old story as a means of explaining the name 'Peniel' ('face of God') and the origin of the name 'Israel'. At the same time he gives the story a religious significance: the patriarch holds fast to God and forces from him a blessing; henceforth all who bear Israel's name will have a claim on God. It is not surprising that this dramatic scene later served as an image of the spiritual combat and of the value of persevering prayer."
Genesis 35:16-18		The birth of Jacob's last son, Benjamin	
Genesis 37:2—50:26		The Joseph stories	Tell this extensive, exciting story in segments. The Joseph stories are filled with the details that a storyteller needs to make the story come alive. This would be a good place for the beginning storyteller to learn the art of sharing Bible stories.
Exodus 1:1-22		The success and then the slavery of the Hebrews in Egypt. We find out what happened to the descendants of Jacob.	
Exodus 2:1—6:1	Third Sunday in Lent (Year C) Trinity Sunday (Year B)	Moses' "call" by God. Crisis comes as Moses approaches Pharaoh and the Hebrews with God's message of freedom.	We begin the story of the exodus. God calls persons in every age to lead people into freedom. This is the key event in our Judeo-Christian understanding of what God is doing in our lives. The exodus account symbolizes each person's quest for liberation from guilt, oppression, fear, and prejudice so that each one is free to become a whole person, living fully the life God has given. The story is crucial for understanding the New Testament, especially the meaning of death-resurrection, baptism, and the Eucharist.

Passage	Lectionary	Story Content	Storyteller Hints
Exodus 7:14—12:14	Maundy Thursday	The ten plagues and the Passover	We may hesitate to tell this story because it indicates that God willed suffering and death for the Egyptians. However, the plagues and Passover are very important stories in the Judeo-Christian tradition. We can overcome some of our objections if we preface the stories with a statement such as "In those days our ancestors felt that God caused the death of the firstborn. When the Egyptians became sick, our ancestors saw it as a sign of God's power. Because of Jesus and the prophets, we know now that God is a God of love." All of the plagues were natural phenomena, but the Hebrews interpreted those natural events as signs of God's power working for them. So we could preface the story of the first plague, for example, with "When the water turned red from the mud, the people saw this as a sign of God's power." Emphasize that it was the *people's understanding* of events rather than God's direct intervention that makes up the Bible narrative. Our understanding of events is shaped by our understanding of our relationship with God. Today we see different signs of God's presence because we have a different understanding. Chapter 2 of this book further explores this truth.
Exodus 12:29-42		The tenth plague and the departure of the Israelites from Egypt	
Exodus 13:17—14:31	Easter Vigil	Israel's departure, Pharaoh's pursuit, and the crossing of the Sea of Reeds or Red Sea	This earliest description of the passing through the Sea of Reeds mentions "a strong east wind (blowing) all night" and says that God "made the sea dry land." Later narratives interspersed with the earlier ones show signs of legendary additions such as walls of water on either side of them. Many scholars think that the Sea of Reeds was more of a marsh than a sea. In storytelling I follow the marsh theory. Children especially can appreciate the wind as a sign of God's presence happening in their lives right now,

Passage	Lectionary	Story Content	Storyteller Hints
			whereas walls of water place the narrative in the world of make-believe. Baptism is our "walk through the waters of the Red Sea" in which we become aware of God's power and presence in our lives.
Exodus 16:1-36	Proper 13 (Year B)	The manna and the quails	Again note the natural phenomena here. A substance like the manna described in the Bible is still found in the Sinai. The manna could have been either tree sap, plant resin, or a substance left by insects. Any of these could provide nourishment for the desert nomad. Quails flying over the desert become exhausted and can easily be caught for food.
Exodus 19—20	Pentecost Proper 6 (Year A) Third Sunday in Lent (Year B)	The giving of the Law and a description of Moses' vision on Mount Sinai	Preface conversations between God and Moses with a statement such as "In a vision Moses saw or heard God say. . . ." Particularly in dealing with children, this approach leaves the child open to grow in understanding how God approaches people. We don't want to fix images in children's minds that will freeze their understanding in years to come. These passages express the idea of covenant. The people of God agree to an absolute bond with God. This covenant establishes their relationship with God and with each other. We relate to God in community as well as individually. And relationships within the human community are based on our relationship with God. The Ten Commandments, though only a small portion of the covenant, are symbolic of the whole covenant. Four of the commandments deal with our relationship with God; six deal with our relationships with one another. We relate to our neighbor in love and service not simply out of desire but out of a covenant commitment to do so. Christians have the same kind of covenant relationship with one another as they do with God—a relationship based on the New Covenant realized through Christ.

Passage	Lectionary	Story Content	Storyteller Hints
Exodus 24:1-18	Last Sunday after Epiphany (Year A)	The covenant is ratified; Moses goes up the mountain to receive the stone tablets.	The ceremony in which the covenant is ratified is a strange one to us but interesting when we reflect that the blood of Christ we share in the Eucharist marks our New Covenant with God.
Exodus 32:1-24	Proper 19 (Year C)	The Israelites make a golden calf while Moses is on the mountain. Moses intercedes with God to have mercy on the people. He breaks the stone tablets in anger.	
Exodus 34:1-5	Feast of the Holy Name	Moses returns to the mountain and receives two stone tablets like the first.	
Exodus 34:29-35	Last Sunday after Epiphany (Year C)— Feast of the Transfiguration	Moses comes down from the mountain, his face glowing.	Read Luke 9:28-36 and note similarities to Exodus 34:29-35, including the brilliance of Moses' and Jesus' faces.
Numbers 11:4-35	Proper 21 (Year B)	The people complain in the wilderness. Seventy elders are appointed to help guide the people. Quails fall in a miracle of feeding.	
Numbers 13:1—14:38		Spies are sent on a reconnaissance mission into the land (Canaan) that God promised to the people. On their return they report that the land is full of giants, and the people are afraid. In a vision Moses is told that the people must wander in the wilderness for forty years as punishment for their lack of faith in God's promise. Caleb and Joshua will enter the land, but even Moses will die without entering the promised land.	This story explains why the Israelites had to wander in the wilderness for an entire generation.

Passage	Lectionary	Story Content	Storyteller Hints
Numbers 22:1—24:25		An amusing story in which Balak, the king of Moab, attempts to pay a soothsayer to curse the Israelites as they try to pass through his nation on their way to attack Jericho after their years of wilderness wandering. Instead of cursing the Israelites, the soothsayer Balaam blesses them on four occasions. He has no choice, he says, but to follow the words the Lord has placed on his lips.	
Joshua 1:1-9		At Moses' death Joshua becomes the new leader of the tribes of Israel.	
Joshua 2:1-24		Joshua sends spies into Jericho.	
Joshua 3—4		Crossing the Jordan	The Jordan stopped flowing as the Israelites entered it. This story is similar to the Sea of Reeds crossing. Remarks made concerning the crossing of the Sea of Reeds (page 24) can be applied to this narrative, too. You might preface this story with "We do not know how this strange and wonderful story happened. Perhaps part of it is legendary. I only know what I have been told, and I pass this story on to you the way I heard it." This allows the hearer to accept the account literally or to interpret it as legend. In any case, it is a powerful memory for the people of God. As we pass through the waters of our own baptism, we know that God is with us and that we are his people. Passing through the water has long been a sign of covenant between God and the faithful.
Joshua 6:1-25		The taking of Jericho	We do not know how "the walls came tumbling down." Legendary material may have crept into the story as it was retold. We do know that the walls

Passage	Lectionary	Story Content	Storyteller Hints
			of the city were taken and victory secured. The remarks about the ten plagues (page 24) apply to this story as well.
Judges 6:1—7:24	Fifth Sunday after Epiphany (Year C)	Gideon is called and leads his first battle.	This is a very beautiful and amusing story. Gideon, the "least of the sons of Joash," is chosen by God to lead an army of three hundred against the mighty Midianites. The impossible victory is to be a sign that it is God's might that brings peace to the people. The sequel to this story is in Judges 8:22-27. Though Gideon refuses to be named king, he asks that an ephod (religious emblem used to worship Canaanite gods) be created and placed in his city. "And Gideon made an ephod of it and put it in his city, in Ophrah; and all Israel played the harlot after it there, and it became a snare to Gideon and to his family" (Judges 8:27). We see in this story the tragedy of Gideon—and of much of human history as well. After humbly acknowledging his dependence before the Lord, Gideon rejects the Lord in the next moment with an act that leads his people into idolatry.
Judges 13—16		The stories of Samson	The Samson stories need not be taken literally. They are the kind of stories told to give a sense of pride to the people. The enemies of the Israelites are made to look foolish. The unusually powerful folk hero, despite mistreatment by his enemies, is able to overpower them. As with previously mentioned materials, preface these stories with a remark that sets the tone: "I tell you a story today that has been told by our people for hundreds of years. We don't know how some of these events happened or if they happened in the way that we were told, but I want you to know the tales of Samson so that you will sense how strong our people were when they believed they were God's people."

Passage	Lectionary	Story Content	Storyteller Hints
Ruth	Proper 23 (Year C)	The Book of Ruth is a charming story about King David's great-grandmother.	
1 Samuel 1:1-28		The birth of the great prophet Samuel	
1 Samuel 3:1—4:1	Second Sunday after Epiphany (Year B)	The call of Samuel	
1 Samuel 9:1—10:16		Saul is called by Samuel and anointed as the first king of Israel.	Notice the ancient practice of anointing the servant of God with oil. Jesus is God's anointed in this sense. The word *Christ*, taken from the Greek word *Christos*, means *anointed one*. The Hebrew word *Messiah* means the same. Thus the ancient practice of anointing the one who is to speak and act for God is the origin of Jesus' title, Christ. It explains why in the Episcopal and Roman Catholic tradition persons are anointed with oil at baptism. Like Saul and David they are chosen to speak and act for the Lord. In fact, they share the priesthood of Christ, *the* Anointed One.
1 Samuel 13:7-15; 15:1-31		The prophet Samuel rejects Saul as king.	Saul is rejected because he showed a lack of faith in failing to obey the directives of Samuel, God's prophet. Despite Samuel's orders, Saul did not wait until Samuel arrived to offer sacrifices to God before battle. He acted out of fear when he saw the enemy mass for battle and his own men deserting. After winning the battle, he failed to place all of the enemy under "the ban" (that is, failed to destroy the enemy completely). Samuel ordered the ban, but Saul spared King Agag "with the best of the sheep and cattle, the fatlings and lambs and all that was good. They did not want to put those under the ban; they only put under the ban what was poor and worthless" (The Jerusalem Bible, 1 Samuel 15:9). Although we may think this was merciful, we must understand the culture of the times. To spare the life of the enemy was to fail to destroy evil

Passage	Lectionary	Story Content	Storyteller Hints
			in the sight of God. The important thing to stress is Saul's lack of faith and his disobedience to orders spoken in God's name. In 1 Samuel 15, Saul makes explanations which are countered by Samuel's accusations. We can all identify times when we have felt the way Saul did when he was confronted with Samuel's accusations. As you tell the story, get in touch with those feelings.
1 Samuel 16:1-23	Fourth Sunday in Lent (Year A)	There are two accounts of how David came to the attention of King Saul. In this first account Samuel seeks out the successor to Saul and secretly anoints him as the next king. David then enters Saul's service as armor-bearer and minstrel.	
1 Samuel 17:1—18:5		The second, better-known account of David's recognition by Saul: David slays Goliath.	
1 Samuel 18:6-16; 19:1—24:22		David as an outlaw. King Saul became more and more jealous of David's popularity and power as David's reputation spread throughout the kingdom. The fact that Saul felt God's rejection undoubtedly added to his insane jealousy.	The stories in this section are adventure stories and are fun to share. David became an outlaw, living a life not unlike Robin Hood's. He roamed the country with a band of followers, raiding the Philistines and avoiding King Saul's efforts to trap him. The stories could be told in installments.
2 Samuel 11:1— 12:25	Proper 6 (Year C)	David's sin with Bathsheba; his repentance	This story contains the elements necessary for understanding confession and absolution. 1) David was confronted with his sin. He became aware of the wrong he had done. (In dealing with children, simply explain David's sin as that of wanting another man's wife and then having her husband killed.) 2) He confessed his wrong and showed sorrow.

Passage	Lectionary	Story Content	Storyteller Hints
			3) He was forgiven but was made aware of the irreversible consequences of his actions. He could be sorry for what he had done, but there was no way he could erase the effects of his actions. This powerful story shows the weakness of David as well as his strength. What made him a great leader was not perfection but his willingness to acknowledge his weakness and repent. The prophet Nathan was able to confront David with his sins by telling a story. The power of a story can draw us into a confrontation with our life situations.
2 Samuel 13:23—19:24		David's son Absalom leads a revolt against his father. For a time David is driven out, and Absalom reigns in his stead. Absalom is killed, and David returns to take his place again as king over the united tribes.	Tell this extended narrative in installments. Many details show the intrigue within David's court and his feelings toward his defiant son.
1 Kings 1:1—2:25		The last days and the death of David. Solomon's consecration as king. Rivalry between David's sons Solomon and Adonijah.	
1 Kings 3:1-28	Proper 12 (Year A)	Solomon gains power. In a dream he asks God for wisdom, and his request is granted.	The account of how Solomon judged a situation in which two women claimed the same infant as their own illustrates his legendary wisdom.
1 Kings 7:51—8:21		Solomon's Temple is built; the Ark of the Covenant is placed in it.	
1 Kings 10:1-29		The Queen of Sheba's visit to Solomon; his fabulous wealth	
1 Kings 12:1-33		The nation is split between the ten northern tribes and the two southern tribes. Jeroboam becomes king over the northern tribes	Talk about our War between the States to describe people's feelings about the separation of a country.

Passage	Lectionary	Story Content	Storyteller Hints
		and introduces idol worship. The northern kingdom is called Israel; the southern kingdom, Judah. The northern tribes rebuke the house of David, which originated from a southern tribe: "What share have we in David? / We have no inheritance in the son of Jesse" (The Jerusalem Bible, 1 Kings 12:16). Rehoboam's belligerence is the last straw for the northern tribes.	
1 Kings 16:29— 19:21	Last Sunday after Epiphany (Year B) Proper 8 (Year C) Proper 27 (Year B) Proper 5 (Year C)	Encounters between King Ahab and Elija, the great prophet of God; the calling of Elisha as successor to Elijah	Some legendary material is found in this narrative. The remarks in connection with legends (page 16) apply here.
1 Kings 21:1-29		Elijah confronts King Ahab after Ahab murders Naboth over the purchase of Naboth's vineyard.	
1 Kings 22:1-38		Ahab and the battle against Ramoth-gilead	This story provides an interesting contrast between "state prophets," who speak what the king wishes, and the prophet of God, who in this case speaks against the king's plan.
2 Kings 2:1-15	Proper 12 (Year B) Ascension Day (Year C)	At Elijah's death his spirit goes to Elisha.	Tell this story as a great legend of our people that helps to express the awe of this moment in our people's memory.
2 Kings 2:19-22; 2 Kings 4:1—8:6	Fifth Sunday after Epiphany (Year B) Sixth Sunday after Epiphany (Year B) Proper 1 (Year B)	A series of stories about Elisha; some of them reflect the earlier tales told about Elijah.	The stories of Elijah and Elisha will help the listeners appreciate how our people felt about these great prophets. The stories are also important because they are reflected in some of the stories told about Jesus. To appreciate the impact that Jesus had on the people of his time, we must have an appreciation

Passage	Lectionary	Story Content	Storyteller Hints
			for the stories they were familiar with. Elijah became associated with hope for restoration. The great prophet would return to usher in the new and victorious day of the Lord. At the Passover meal celebrated by Jews to this day, a place is always set for Elijah in case he returns during the meal. See Matthew 16:13-14 and 17:9-13 for references to the Jewish hope for the return of Elijah.
2 Kings 18:18—20:21		The reign of King Hezekiah in Judah. During Hezekiah's reign the Assyrian king's armies invade Judah and threaten Jerusalem. The prophet Isaiah reassures Hezekiah that Judah will withstand the siege.	This is a story of faith overcoming fear. It will also help people appreciate the role of Isaiah.
Ezra 3:6—6:18		The rebuilding of the Temple after the return from exile; Samaritan hostility delays the rebuilding. Our people lived in Babylonian exile from 586 to 538 B.C. King Cyrus of Persia finally defeated the Babylonians and released the Jews from their captivity. He seemed to be the answer to years of prayer, for he encouraged the Jews to return to their land and rebuild the Temple, even arranging for the return of all the treasures removed from it by the Babylonians (see Ezra 1:1-8).	This story lacks the action necessary to tell it in an extended form. Share the details *briefly* to help persons have a feeling for the struggle of our people as they returned from exile.
Nehemiah 1:1—2:20		In exile, Nehemiah asks the king for permission to return to his homeland and rebuild Jerusalem. His request is granted.	The stories of Nehemiah are filled with the details a storyteller needs. For example, notice the nervousness of Nehemiah as he approaches the king.

Passage	Lectionary	Story Content	Storyteller Hints
Nehemiah 4:1-17		Opposition from the Samaritans leads Nehemiah to post guards during the rebuilding of the wall. The Jews' efforts are ridiculed.	This story lends itself to dramatization.
Nehemiah 6:15—7:3		At last the wall is finished, but the opposition heightens.	
Nehemiah 8:1-18; 9:1-3; 10:1, 28-39; 12:27-30	Third Sunday after Epiphany (Year C)	With the completion of the wall, Ezra and Nehemiah turn to the rededication of the people to their covenant with Yahweh. The people again hear the Law of the covenant read and recommit themselves to being the people of the covenant. Hearing the covenant, the people become aware of their sinfulness; this moves them to a deeper commitment. The story ends with the dedication of the wall.	Nehemiah 8 recounts a liturgical celebration not unlike the ritual we share as the gospel is proclaimed at the Holy Eucharist. Ezra stood up above the people. The people themselves rose to their feet. As Ezra began the reading he gave a blessing to which the people responded in acclamation. After the reading Ezra interpreted the law as a pastor would give a sermon interpreting the gospel. The roots of our ritual go very deep in our heritage! Note that the people celebrated the Feast of Booths, an important Jewish festival celebrated in our own day. Notice, too, the exclusive nature of the covenant: Jewish men may not marry foreign women.
The Book of Tobit		Tobias is sent on a quest by his father, Tobit, to restore the family fortune. Part of his adventure includes marrying Sarah, whose previous husbands have all died on the wedding night.	The Book of Tobit is part of the Apocrypha. It is a short novel that combines Oriental folklore with Jewish piety and wisdom sayings. Note the fairy-tale-like details. It is an exciting story that also edifies.
The Book of Esther		A folktale about the bravery of Esther during the Babylonian exile	This tale is not historical, but it is the type of story that is shared by a people to give them a sense of pride in their nation and history. To introduce it say "This is a story told by our people so that when we face frightening times, we may have courage and faith in God. This story is in the Bible because it is a part of our heritage and has strengthened the faith of God's people

Passage	Lectionary	Story Content	Storyteller Hints
			for generations.'' There is no need to relate the revenge story found in the ninth chapter.
1 Maccabees 2:1-70		During the period of Greek domination the Jews successfully re-volted for a time and regained control over their own land. This passage describes the beginning of the rebel-lion. Mattathias and his sons refuse to offer sacrifice to the pagan gods, and they kill the guards in protest.	Notice the subversive nature of the Greek domination. All the Jews need to do to be the king's friends is to sacrifice to the pagan gods.
1 Maccabees 4:36-61		Judas, the son of Mat-tathias, took over the leadership of the rebellion after his father's death. In this story, Judas and his men purify the Temple after they capture it from the Greeks.	Tell this story at Hanukkah time in December, as this story tells the origin of that Jewish holiday. The call for an annual eight-day observance is found in verse 59.
The Book of Job	Holy Saturday (Years A, B, C) Proper 7 (Year B) Second Sunday of Easter (Year C) Proper 27 (Year C)		This story is far too complex to tell in detail, but the principal points of the narrative need to be shared in the learning community, since Job is an extremely important book both in the Church and in Western literature. Tell the action points of the story. With adolescents and adults, do a dramatic reading of parts of the Lord's response to Job (Job 38—41).
Isaiah 36:1—38:8		Jerusalem is threatened by the Assyrian army but rescued by God.	See 2 Kings 18:18—20:21 for an explanation of this story.
Jeremiah 11:1-23		Jeremiah preaches doom to the people.	We get a glimpse in this passage of the kinds of speeches Jeremiah gave that turned the people against him.
Jeremiah 12:14— 13:14; 16:1-18; chapters 27, 28, 32	Third Sunday of Easter (Year C)	Here we see the kinds of symbolic actions Jeremiah did to dramatize the word of the Lord that came to him in judgment of the people.	Can participants think of similar symbolic actions taken in our own history? The Boston Tea Party was a dramatic symbol of defiance in Revolutionary times. Some of the protests of the 1960s were of this

Passage	Lectionary	Story Content	Storyteller Hints
			nature. Hunger strikes on the part of revolutionary leaders including Gandhi are another example.
Jeremiah 19:1— 20:18	Proper 7 (Year A)	Jeremiah is placed in the stocks as punishment.	Tell the story of Jeremiah's punishment and then do a dramatic reading of a portion of his cry to the Lord (Jeremiah 20:7-18). His words of pain to the Lord are important to share. The prophet had his doubts, as we often do.
Jeremiah 26:1-24		Opposition to Jeremiah continues to mount because of his prophecies that the city and Temple must fall to the enemy. Jeremiah is threatened with death until some of the princes rise to his defense. Uriah, another prophet who speaks similar words, is not so fortunate and is killed by order of the king.	
Jeremiah 36:1-32		Jeremiah dictates a message of warning to the people; his secretary Baruch writes it on a scroll. As the scroll is read before King Jehoiakim, he cuts off segments of the scroll and casts them into the fire. Jeremiah promptly dictates the same message to Baruch to be placed on a second scroll.	
Jeremiah 37:1—40:6		The Babylonians (Chaldeans) besiege Jerusalem. Jeremiah continues to urge surrender. His words bring him imprisonment and mistreatment. Many of the people are sent to Babylon, leaving only the poor behind in the land. Jeremiah is freed by the Babylonians but	Jeremiah's words to surrender to the enemy may seem as traitorous to us as they did to the princes of Judah. But to him the Babylonians were Yahweh's instruments to chastise his people for their unfaithfulness.

Passage	Lectionary	Story Content	Storyteller Hints
		chooses to remain in Judah. (See also chapter 52—the destruction of Jerusalem.)	
The Book of Daniel		The first six chapters contain folktales about Daniel and his companions during the Babylonian exile.	The stories show that by keeping faith in God, one can withstand the worst trials. These stories strengthened the will and faith of the Jewish people in times of persecution. Introduce them as you would introduce folktales.
• Daniel 1		Daniel insists on maintaining traditions despite the temptation to compromise them.	"This is a story told by our people during a time of persecution. I tell it to you just the way it was handed on to me." The truth of the story lies in the power and vision received when faith in God is expressed. Stories do not have to be literally true to express deep truth.
• Daniel 2		Daniel interprets Nebuchadnezzar's dreams.	
• Daniel 3		Daniel and his companions withstand the fires of the furnace; their canticle of praise and thanks.	
• Daniel 5		Daniel interprets the handwriting on the wall.	
• Daniel 6		Daniel survives the lions' den.	
• Daniel 14		Daniel confronts the priests of Bel.	In *The New American Bible* and *The Jerusalem Bible* the story is included in the Book of Daniel, Chapter 14. In other translations of the Bible you will find the story in the Apocrypha under the title "Bel and the Dragon."
The Book of Jonah	Proper 14 (Year A) Proper 20 (Year A)	The well-known story of Jonah's mission to Nineveh	This is a good example of how fantasy can express religious truth. Jonah is called to speak the word of the Lord, although he agrees with neither the mission that the Lord sends him on nor with its outcome. This amusing story was originally told to counter the racial exclusivism of the Jews after their exile to Babylonia. The story shows the mercy of God toward all people, not just toward the Jews. Be sure to emphasize the humor and irony inherent in the tale.

Selected New Testament Stories

Listed first are passages in the gospels where the storyteller can locate the narratives of Jesus' birth and youth, beginning of public life, suffering, death, burial, resurrection, and postresurrection appearances. Passages on his healings appear next, followed by his parables and by stories from the Book of Acts. Remember that many of the passages mentioned in one gospel can be found in one or more of the other gospels, too. Many Bibles have references indicating such parallel passages.

Jesus' Birth, Youth, and Public Life

Passage	Lectionary	Story Content	Storyteller Hints
Luke 2:1-20	Christmas	The birth of Jesus	
Matthew 2:1-12	Feast of the Epiphany or Second Sunday after Christmas	The visit of the Magi	
Luke 2:41-52	Second Sunday after Christmas	Twelve-year-old Jesus in the Temple	
Mark 1:1-8	Second Sunday of Advent (Year B)	John appears in the wilderness baptizing new followers.	
Matthew 3:13-17	First Sunday after Epiphany (Year A)	Jesus is baptized by John.	The descending dove and the voice from heaven could be interpreted as a poetic way of describing how Jesus felt at that moment.
Matthew 4:18-22; Luke 5:1-11	Third Sunday after Epiphany (Year A)	Jesus calls his first disciples. (Luke's account offers two added details: Jesus talking to the crowds from Simon's boat, and the miraculous catch of fish.)	
Matthew 9:9	Proper 5 (Year A)	The disciple Matthew is called.	
Matthew 10:1-4	Proper 6 (Year A)	The twelve apostles are listed.	
Matthew 21:1-11	Palm Sunday (Year A)	Jesus enters Jerusalem.	This and the following six passages from Matthew are Holy Week readings.
Matthew 21:12-16		Jesus drives the money changers out of the Temple.	

Passage	Lectionary	Story Content	Storyteller Hints
Matthew 26:1-35		The conspiracy against Jesus deepens as Judas betrays him. Jesus talks of Peter's denial. The Last Supper.	
Matthew 26:36-56	Palm Sunday (Year A)	Jesus prays in the garden of Gethsemane; his arrest there.	
Matthew 26:57-75	Palm Sunday (Year A)	Jesus is taken before the Sanhedrin (the court presided over by the high priest Caiaphas). Peter denies him.	
Matthew 27:1-66	Palm Sunday (Year A)	Jesus is brought before Pilate, is mocked, crucified, dies, and is buried. (From the cross Jesus cries out: "My God, my God, why hast thou forsaken me?"—Psalm 22.)	
John 13:1-20	Maundy Thursday	The Last Supper	The Gospel of John describes washing the disciples' feet as a symbolic act of complete love that they are to live out in their own lives. The passage is an excellent launching device for a discussion of the meaning of discipleship. It replaces the description of sharing bread and wine as reported in the other gospels, since John has already dealt with this theme in chapter 6.
John 13:33-35	Fifth Sunday of Easter (Year C)	Beautiful, poetic commission of the disciples: "...even as I have loved you,...love one another."	

Jesus' Burial, Resurrection, and Postresurrection Appearances

The concept of resurrection, which is difficult for most adults to understand, is even more difficult for young children. Most of the passages mentioned in these sections will be heard in the liturgy during Holy Week and Easter. Many parishes will have liturgical experiences that dramatize the readings. Talk with the children about what they hear, and then deal with their fears and feelings about death and their questions about the mystery of the resurrection. *Hope for the Flowers* is a beautiful book about caterpillars and butterflies; it will help the children appreciate the concept of dying in order to become fully alive.* C.S. Lewis's *Last Battle* is also very helpful for children nine years old and older.†

Passage	Lectionary	Story Content	Storyteller Hints
Matthew 27:57-61	Palm Sunday (Year A) Holy Saturday	Jesus is buried by Joseph of Arimathea.	
Mark 15:42-47	Palm Sunday (Year B)	Jesus is buried by Joseph of Arimathea.	
Matthew 27:62-66	Holy Saturday	The guard at the tomb	
Matthew 28:1-8	Easter Sunday	Mary Magdalene and the other women see the tomb with the stone rolled away. In a vision they are told "He is not here, he has risen."	
Matthew 28:9-10	Easter Sunday	Jesus appears to some of his followers saying "Do not be afraid; go and tell my brethren to go to Galilee, and there they will see me."	
Matthew 28:11-15	Easter Monday (Years A, B, C)	The chief priests pay the (tomb) guards to lie and say that Jesus' disciples have stolen the body.	
Matthew 28:16-20	Trinity Sunday (Year A)	Jesus appears to the disciples on a mountain, where he commissions them "Go and make disciples of all na-tions.... And lo, I am with you always, to the close of the age."	

*Trina Paulus, *Hope for the Flowers* (New York: Paulist Press, 1972).

†C.S. Lewis, *Last Battle* (New York: Macmillan, 1970). This is the final volume of *The Chronicles of Narnia*.

Passage	Lectionary	Story Content	Storyteller Hints
Luke 24:9-11		The apostles refuse to believe the women who claim to have seen Jesus; Peter goes to the tomb and finds it empty.	
Luke 24:13-35	Third Sunday of Easter (Year A) Easter Wednesday (Years A, B, C)	Jesus appears to two disciples on the road to Emmaus.	This account is a good discussion starter for discovering how we "meet Christ" in our lives today. It is particularly good as a meditation or as part of Liturgy of the Word in a liturgical celebration. Note that before the disciples can recognize Jesus they have to be exposed to an understanding of how God encountered man in the past: "And beginning with Moses and all the prophets, he interpreted...." Their mood changes from despair to a vision of hope and new life as they enter into searching dialogue with the man on the road. In a sense they have opened themselves personally to experience the Good News. Finally they experience the presence of Christ in the breaking of the bread with the stranger. This reminds us that we encounter Christ in the Eucharist and in sharing the "daily bread" of our lives.
Luke 24:36-49	Easter Thursday (Years A, B, C)	Jesus appears to the the disciples. To emphasize the reality of his presence, he eats with them. He then "opens their minds" to give them new understanding of his continual presence in their lives and in the world; he orders them to remain in the city until they are "clothed with power from on high."	
John 20—21	Easter Tuesday Easter Friday Second Sunday of Easter (Years A,B,C) Third Sunday of Easter (Year C)	The resurrection appearances of Christ. The empty tomb is discovered by Mary Magdalene and the woman (20:1-2); Peter and "the other disciple discover the empty tomb (20:3-10);	

| | | when Christ appears to Mary Magdalene near the tomb, she mistakes him for a gardener (20:11-18); Christ appears to the disciples and commissions them "As the Father has sent me, so I send you"; he breathes on them; they receive the Holy Spirit and the authority to bring wholeness and forgiveness and to confront evil as they encounter it (20:19-23). Christ appears to the disciples on the shore of the Sea of Tiberias; they share bread and fish with him; Jesus commissions Peter to "feed my lambs" and warns Peter of the consequences of following him (21:1-19). | |

Gospel Stories of Healing

See the fourth through seventh Sundays after
Epiphany (pages 210-211) for a discussion of
healing.

Passage	Lectionary	Story Content	Storyteller Hints
Matthew 8:1-4		Jesus cures a leper.	The leper is brought to wholeness through faith in the power of God.
Matthew 8:5-13		Jesus cures the centurion's servant.	The centurion's servant is healed because the centurion has faith. The centurion acknowledges a need that lies beyond his power to give orders.
Matthew 8:14-15		Jesus cures Peter's mother-in-law.	
Matthew 9:18-26		Jesus cures the woman with a hemorrhage and raises to life the official's daughter.	
Matthew 9:27-31		Jesus cures two blind men.	The healings remind us of the importance of faith in finding wholeness. As we "faith in" the power to be made whole, we are in touch with the source of wholeness and our "dis-ease" may be alleviated or eliminated.
Matthew 9:33-34		Jesus cures the mute demoniac.	The people of Jesus' time had strong feelings about being possessed by demons. One would lose the capacity to act, they felt, as the power of evil took possession. These accounts of exorcism of demons remind us of the central message of the Gospel: The power of love and creation does overcome the power of evil and separation. How do we explain demonic possession and exorcism, especially to younger children? *One* way might be this: In times of fear or anger we say we have "lost our tempers." We have lost control of ourselves in that moment. At other times we may become so distraught in grief or guilt that we can no longer make decisions or act normally. To regain control of ourselves, it is necessary to face fully

Passage	Lectionary	Story Content	Storyteller Hints
			the feelings that are causing us such intense "dis-ease." Though we may not use the term "demon" for such feelings, they give us an idea of how possessed persons felt who came to Jesus. Jesus faced the demon, and the demon left the person, who now could speak normally.
Matthew 15:29-31		Jesus cures many persons on the shores of the Sea of Galilee.	This is a summary statement mentioning the many persons who came to Jesus for healing. It is a good passage to use in a liturgy dealing with healing and wholeness.
Matthew 17:14-20		Jesus cures the epileptic demoniac.	Jesus shows frustration with the lack of faith among his own followers. Without faith, wholeness is not possible.
Mark 2:1-12	Seventh Sunday after Epiphany (Year B) Proper 2 (Year B)	Jesus cures a paralytic.	Notice that the man was paralyzed by a sense of guilt. Jesus' words of forgiveness bring him wholeness. As we become more aware of how much physical illness is caused by emotional distress, this passage carries great impact. A doctor cannot cure a person simply by "repairing" the physical body; one must heal the whole person. If the patient is still suffering from guilt and stress, the ulcer or heart condition will be a continuing problem.
Mark 7:31-37	Proper 18 (Year B)	Jesus heals the deaf man.	
Mark 8:22-26		Jesus cures a blind man at Bethsaida.	
Luke 17:11-19	Proper 23 (Year C)	Jesus cures the ten lepers.	Only one of the ten lepers returns to Jesus to express thankfulness. Note that the one who does return is a Samaritan. This was a pointed reminder to the Jews that it was the outcasts of society who were often the most open to receive the word and healing of God made known through Jesus and who therefore were most apt to express thanksgiving. How often do we praise God for healing that we see taking place in our own lives?

Some Parables of Jesus

An explanation of *parable* has been given on page 18. Though many parables are found in more than one Gospel, the version of the parable that is most suitable for the story teller is listed in this section.

Passage	Lectionary	Story Content	Storyteller Hints
Matthew 13:3-9	Proper 10 (Year A)	The sower	The thought of this parable is "Don't despair when God's word seems to have little effect. His will is done, though sometimes we aren't aware of it." This simple parable was later made into an allegory (see verses 18-23), which was not part of the original saying.
Matthew 13:31-32	Proper 12 (Year A)	The mustard seed	The Kingdom of God may be barely discernible in our world, but it grows and spreads just as the tiny mustard seed grows into a mighty bush.
Matthew 13:33	Proper 12 (Year A)	The yeast	Makes the same point as the mustard seed parable: The Kingdom, almost unnoticed, grows much the way that yeast works in the vastness of the dough.
Luke 14:7-14	Proper 17 (Year C)	Choosing one's place at the banquet table	
Luke 14:15-24	Proper 17 (Year C)	"The Great Supper"	This is one of the parables Jesus told as a warning that in the reign of God things will be reversed. We cannot assume that we are the righteous ones in the eyes of God. In this parable, the invited guests end up being excluded from the banquet by their own excuses while those who may have been considered outsiders end up sitting at the table.
Luke 15:1-10	Proper 19 (Year C)	The lost sheep and lost coin	God cares for all creation. When someone returns to God after breaking the covenant relationship, God rejoices as the good shepherd does when he finds the lost sheep.
Luke 15:11-32	Fourth Sunday in Lent (Year C)	The prodigal (or lost) son	This is a beautiful parable about God's grace and forgiveness. Note the very negative feelings expressed by the elder son. You may find yourself identifying with him, which could lead to some interesting discussions about God's love and mercy.
Luke 18:9-14	Proper 25 (Year C)	The Pharisee and the tax collector	
Matthew 13:44	Proper 12 (Year A)	The treasure buried in the field	The Kingdom of God is like a treasure someone joyfully discovers.

Passage	Lectionary	Story Content	Storyteller Hints
Matthew 13:45	Proper 12 (Year A)	The merchant finding a precious pearl	Makes the same point as the parable of the treasure. These short parables can be made into posters or banners.
Matthew 18:21-35	Proper 19 (Year A)	The unforgiving debtor	Grippingly illustrates "Forgive us our sins as we forgive those who sin against us."
Matthew 20:1-16	Proper 20 (Year A)	The laborers in the vineyard	This was the way Jesus dealt with the Jews who felt they had earned special favor with God. A shocking concept to his listeners.
Matthew 21:28-32	Proper 21 (Year A)	The two sons	The righteous one *does* the will of God rather than simply *saying* he or she will do it. Jesus pointed out that those sinners who believed and repented were far more righteous than the so-called faithful Jews who spoke of righteousness but did not practice it.
Matthew 21:33-43 and Luke 20:9-19	Proper 22 (Year A) Fifth Sunday in Lent (Year C)	The tenants	Read the "Song of the Vineyard" (Isaiah 5:1-7) for background. This parable is a poignant reminder that we have a responsibility to use in a positive way the resources that are given us. This is a good tie-in to stewardship. We are tenants, not owners of our property. We give our tithes in thanksgiving for our gifts.
Matthew 24:45-51		The conscientious steward	We "stewards" may also be asked at any moment to give an accounting of what we have done.
Matthew 25:1-13	Proper 27 (Year A)	The ten bridesmaids	
Matthew 25:14-30	Proper 28 (Year A)	The talents	
Matthew 25:31-46	Proper 29 (Year A)	The last judgment	The time will come when persons will be separated. Those who responded to Christ as they met him among the hungry, the thirsty, the naked, and the suffering will enter the Kingdom.
Mark 4:26-29	Proper 6 (Year B)	The seed that grows by itself	Once the seed is planted, it grows by itself; once the Kingdom of God has been planted, its growth is inevitable.
Luke 10:25-42	Proper 10 (Year C)	The good Samaritan	Deals with "Who is my neighbor?"
Luke 12:13-21	Proper 13 (Year C)	The rich fool	This parable confronts us with our goal of building up possessions to obtain happiness and fulfillment.

Passage	Lectionary	Story Content	Storyteller Hints
Luke 11:1-8	Proper 12 (Year C)	The Lord's Prayer and the Persistent Friend	The parable of the persistent friend is an amusing story that adds impact to the teaching of the Lord's Prayer. If persistence leads to a person getting out of bed in the middle of the night to provide bread for a friend, surely God will respond to our persistence in praying for the "daily bread" of our lives.
Luke 16:1-8	Proper 20 (Year C)	The crafty steward	An example of Jesus' humor. If an unjust servant has sense enough to get things in order for himself in the face of judgement, surely the followers of Jesus ought to be smart enough to do the same.
Luke 16:19-31	Proper 21 (Year C)	Lazarus and the rich man	This parable is a vivid warning that when the reign of God comes into our lives there will be a dramatic reversal of values and status. The poor and oppressed will be raised up. The insensitive wealthy will be brought low. The same point is made in the "Magnificat" or "Song of Mary." "He has cast down the mighty from their thrones, and has lifted up the lowly. He has filled the hungry with good things, and the rich he has sent away empty."
Luke 18:1-8	Proper 24 (Year C)	The Widow and the Unjust Judge	This parable makes the same point as the parable of the persistent friend noted above. In telling the story, emphasize the humor of the situation. If even a crooked judge will grant the woman's request because he can't stand her constant demands for justice, surely God will respond to our prayers.

The Book of Acts

The Book of Acts really forms the second part of the Gospel of Luke. It continues with the good news that the power and presence of Christ have spread throughout the Mediterranean world. It records how the disciples received the Holy Spirit (the "power from on high") and how it helped them spread the word and the presence of Christ. Peter's and Paul's roles in the early Church are emphasized.

Passage	Lectionary	Story Content	Storyteller Hints
Acts 2:1-13	Day of Pentecost	The disciples experience the power and presence of the Holy Spirit.	This passage is the basis for the Church's celebration of Pentecost.

Passage	Lectionary	Story Content	Storyteller Hints
Acts 2:42-47; 4:32-37	Third Sunday of Easter (Year A) Fourth Sunday of Easter (Year B)	Descriptions of the early Christian Church	Notice the cornerstones of the early Christian community: instruction, breaking of bread, prayer, awe at the signs of God's power, sharing of all property, worship at the Temple, care and support of each other.
Acts 3:1-10		The disciples find that they can bring wholeness to persons just as Jesus did.	
Acts 4:1-22; 5:17-42	Easter Friday (Year A)	The disciples encounter the opposition of the Temple authorities.	
Acts 9:1-30	Third Sunday of Easter (Year C)	Saul is confronted by Christ on the road to Damascus and is converted. He escapes the Jews.	
Acts 16:16-40	Seventh Sunday of Easter (Year C)	Paul and Silas are imprisoned at Philippi.	The extraordinary love shown by Paul and Silas when they refuse to escape converts the jailer and his family.
Acts 17:1—18:11	Fifth Sunday of Easter (Year A)	Examples of Paul's preaching	

Chapter 2
An Overview of the Historical, Literary, and Theological Development of the Bible: Implications for the Religious Educator

In chapter 1 we looked at the role of the parent and the religious educator as the storytellers of the faith community. We looked at ways of telling the biblical story and at the kinds of problems encountered in sharing Bible stories. Then we pointed out the types of stories to offer in the home and in the parish learning community.

In this chapter I want to approach the storyteller's task from another perspective. If I am going to have a feeling for the story I am sharing, it is essential that I understand the ideas of the people from whom the story came. This means that I need a grasp of how the people of the Bible perceived their lives and their relationship with God over the many generations reflected in the biblical story.

As Bernhard Anderson has observed, Blaise Pascal long ago pointed out that the God of the Bible is the God of Abraham, Isaac, and Jacob—in other words, not the God of the philosophers and the sages. Anderson explains: "This is true in the sense that Biblical faith, to the bewilderment of many philosophers, is fundamentally historical in character. Its doctrines are events and historical realities, not abstract values and ideas existing in a timeless realm" (*Understanding the Old Testament,* page 8).

The Bible is the story of how our people have understood their relationship with God and how they have seen God working throughout their history. It is important for us as religious educators to appreciate this truth as we share this faith story with our children. Note the word *relationship.* When I say that I "know" John, I am really saying that I know John through our relationship. This sense of knowing him will change and deepen as our relationship goes on. If you were to ask me to describe John after our first meeting and then ask me to describe him after I had known him for a year, my responses would undoubtedly be very different. Furthermore, if someone else were asked to describe him, the description would reflect that person's relationship with him and might be very different from mine, depending on the kind of relationship each of us had with John.

In the Bible we see a record of how the Israelites' understanding of God changed as their relationship to him deepened over many generations. Thus the Bible does not present *an* understanding of God but evolving and changing views of God. Furthermore, the relationship is based on a deep and abiding faith that our people's experiences with God reveal a caring and loving God. A non-Jewish person experiencing the wind blowing across the Sea of Reeds or experiencing the ten plagues or the finding of water and manna and quails in the desert might report seeing natural events. The people were lucky it happened, this witness might say. But our people have seen in these same events a God who acts in our story, revealing himself in wind, in word, in manna, in the dawn and in the darkness of life's story. To our people, the inspiration and the words that "came to Moses" were direct communications with "the God of Abraham, the God of Isaac, and the God of Jacob." To someone else those words were simply a personal "inspiration" that led Moses to assume leadership in setting a band of slaves free.

How our people have described God's action in their lives reflects their understanding of biblical events. When a thought comes into my mind I can say "I had an inspiration," or I can say "God spoke to me this morning on my way to work." If the thought is life-changing for me, I might go on to describe its impact by expanding the image of the conversation: "When God spoke to me this morning I could hear the sound of thousands of voices singing for joy. I could see his hand reaching down through the clouds to offer me strength and hope. I could see him striking down my earthbound fears with a sword in his right hand. It was as if heaven descended upon earth and a new world was created just for me." This description would let you know how I *felt* about the impact of God's word. As a sharer in my faith story you might well respond "You must have felt the way Moses did at Mount Sinai" or "There have been times when I've felt that way too." But while you and I shared our hope and vision in the language and poetry of faith, our neighbor might say "I was walking right next to you that day. I didn't see anything like that happen!" Whose statement is true? Mine, of course. I experienced the presence of God in the word he "spoke" to me and in the feeling that I tell you about. But my neighbor's view is also true, of course. He too expresses the truth of my morning's experience, but as he understands it.

This is important to keep in mind as we share the faith story of our people. As we read the Bible's descriptions of God's dealings with our people, we can easily begin to wonder when God stopped acting in the world. The opening of

seas, the trembling of mountains, and the literal seeing of God are not usually a part of our experiences. But the experience of discovering God's action in our daily routine, in our "inspired" moments, in our relationships and in our group's history is a common one for each of us once we begin to reflect on our story in the light of the story expressed in the Bible. We may even find ourselves writing and speaking poetry as we describe these experiences. As we do so, we may indeed find that we too have stood upon the trembling mountain and walked dry-shod across the water. We too have seen the vision of God through the window of our deepening faith-filled experience of daily life.

With these thoughts in mind, let us trace the developing, evolving understanding of our people's relationship with God throughout their history.

Patriarchal Religion

The patriarchal view of our ancestors' relationship with God is reflected in the Book of Genesis. In that view God is like the great father of the tribe. Other gods play the parent role for other tribes, but *this* god controls *our* destiny, the fertility of *our* crops, and *our* relationship with the peoples around us. He walks among his people, sometimes to help them, sometimes to test and punish them. God's actions can be induced by following prescribed rituals at the holy place he has set apart.

This very simple anthropomorphic understanding of God is found in such stories as the one in Genesis 18 in which three strangers visit Abraham and Sarah. One of them promises that Sarah will give birth within a year. Abraham then accompanies the strangers toward Sodom; on the way he talks with one of them about saving the city from destruction by an angry God if there are even a few just people living there. This ancient story reflects the primitive anthropomorphic view of God as a person who would eat and drink with a man and woman and then rise from the meal to go and destroy a decadent people living in a neighboring city.

Other Genesis stories tell about the origins of certain holy places or recount legends surrounding those places. As was mentioned earlier, the Israelites inherited these stories connected with the Canaanite territory they were settling, but they shaped the stories according to their understanding of the God of their fathers.

Genesis is a fascinating book, for it reveals the seeds of our ancestors' understanding of how God calls his creation into being and into response. To read Genesis is to be in touch with the deepest roots of our Judeo-Christian faith.

Wilderness Religion

In the patriarchal theology reflected in the Book of Genesis, God is a God of place and tribe. We go to this place to worship our God. We do these things to encourage fertility in our fields that surround this place. We bow to this rock or figure to put us into touch with our tribal God.

In the Book of Exodus we move to a deeper understanding of our relationship with God. When Moses experienced "the God of Abraham, the God of Isaac, the God of Jacob" at the burning bush in the wilderness (Exodus 3), he became aware of an entirely new relationship with his creator. This God who spoke to Moses identified himself as "I am who I am." In Exodus 3:14-15, Moses asks the voice in the midst of the burning bush for the name of this God who calls and receives an answer. "God said to Moses, 'I AM WHO I AM.' And he said, 'Say this to the people of Israel, "I AM has sent me to you.... The Lord, the God of your fathers, the God of Abraham, the God of Isaac, and the God of Jacob, has sent me to you": this is my name for ever, and thus I am to be remembered throughout all generations.'" The New American Bible explains that this "I am who I am" title is apparently the source of the name Yahweh (or Jehovah) that is commonly used in the Old Testament (note on Exodus 3:14).

There are various understandings of this unusual name. One way of interpreting it is to realize that the God who identified himself to Moses was the "God of what is happening." In other words, "I am who I am" is "I am what is happening to you" or "I am your story or history."

The reality of this name became more and more evident to Moses and the Israelites as their relationship with this God deepened in the wilderness wanderings. Now God is understood in a far more powerful and direct way than as a god of place or tribe. God is seen as the source of our people's story. He is "in" their history. They realize his power and presence by what is happening to them. To know that his power now is to recall his power shown in the story of the past. Our God is now a God of history. Our people become a story-sharing people.

At first no one believed Moses' tale of the God-encounter of the wilderness. But then things began to happen. The water turned a bloody red, boils broke out on the Egyptians, and finally in the tenth plague the firstborn male child in each Egyptian family died a horrible death. Next our people found themselves saved at the Sea of Reeds. The wind blew, and the marsh or sea dried up so that they could cross. By the time Pharaoh and his chariots arrived, the wind had stopped and the body of water was impassable. Then as the Israelites struggled across the wilderness, their thirst was quenched with the water that Moses discovered, and they were fed with manna and with the quails that fell at their feet. As each event happened, their consciousness of a God who acts in their story was heightened, even though they repeatedly forgot the story and fell back into their fears. All these wonders were natural events that happen in that part of the world to this day. But how one views them determines whether one responds to a God of history or to the chance whim of nature.

To recall and reexperience this mysterious God of history, it is essential to have an "outward and visible sign" of the continuing presence of that God. The Ark of the Covenant served as that sign. The Ark was probably a chest supported on poles so that it could be carried with the tribes as they moved through the wilderness. King David brought it into Jerusalem when he captured the city and made it his capital; it was placed in the Temple during King Solomon's reign. To see the Ark was to feel the powerful presence of Yahweh. The tribes stood back in awe as Moses went into the Tent of the Meeting, or the Tabernacle, where the Ark was kept when the tribe was not moving.

Mount Sinai became another point in the story where our people's understanding of their relationship with God deepened: God was not only a God of history but a God of covenant. They were to be his people; he was to be their God. The covenant made with Moses at Mount Sinai still forms the basis of our understanding of our relationship with God. As John Westerhoff has said, we are called out by God to be his history makers in the world. God is "in" our history, and we act with justice and power in his world in order to bring about his purpose and will in creation. We must be just because God is just. We must be faithful and forgiving because God is faithful and forgiving. As people experience faith, forgiveness, power, justice, and love through God's people, his presence is made known. In other words, we live to point beyond ourselves to God's presence. This is the unique role of God's people in the world. This is the exciting concept that gives life meaning, direction, and purpose for Jew and Christian, and the covenant serves as the guideline for this to happen. God commands that I keep the Sabbath, for in keeping it I witness to his presence and am re-created during that day of rest, praise, and reflection. I am called to love my neighbor as myself because in my loving I reflect and witness to the loving God who is the source of that love.

To break the covenant is to bring destruction on myself and on my society, for I separate myself from the power of God and from my awareness of him. To act unlovingly or uncaringly is to cause pain and separation. To live without praising and without being re-created is to become dry and unresponsive to the creativeness welling up within me and all around me. I lose touch with the blue sky, the song of the bird and the wind, and the love of my wife, my child, and my friend. (See Deuteronomy 11:13-17.)

This understanding of God as the God of history and covenant is a striking theological development in the story of our people. Their awareness of a need for social justice and their feeling of stewardship for all that they have and use in this world sets our people apart at a very early date.

This wilderness God of history and covenant was also a God of war. Yahweh destroyed the enemies of his people, but he also punished his people with defeat if they lost faith in him. For example, during the battle with the people of Amalek, so long as Moses held up his hands the battle went well for the Israelites, but if he let his hands drop the battle went against him. At the end of the battle God promised that he would " 'utterly blot out the remembrance of Amalek from under heaven.' And Moses built an altar and called the name of it, The Lord is my banner, saying, 'A hand upon the banner of the Lord! The Lord will have war with Amalek from generation to generation' " (Exodus 17:14-16).

Here is where we often deal with a question raised by child and adult alike. How could God have destroyed the infants in Egypt, the Amalekites, and the other enemies of the Israelites? How can the psalmist write such bitter words asking God to rain down destruction and suffering on the psalmist's enemies? The response can be more easily made if we can see that what we are dealing with is a people's *understanding* of God's action—an understanding that grew out of their historical situation. Rather than saying that God did these things, we might more appropriately say "This is the way our people *understood* God as working in their lives." The all-merciful and all-loving God expressed in later Old Testament writings and in the New Testament is the same God that we know in the whole Old Testament, but our people's experience of their relationship with this God—and hence their understanding of him—deepened over the generations and most especially through their personal relationship with Jesus of Nazareth. The God they met on the cross is the same God that led Moses and our people through the wilderness, but our understanding of how God works in our individual lives and in our collective history has deepened.

"Landed" Religion— The Period of the Judges

As our people entered the land of Canaan and settled there under Joshua's leadership, their understanding of God as a God of history and covenant and war was modified by the religious understandings of their Canaanite neighbors. As the Israelites danced and wailed around the walls of Jericho, they knew the wilderness God of war and history and covenant. But as they settled down in their newly acquired fields to plant and care for crop and vine, they found themselves drawn to the idol in the corner of the field. Their Canaanite neighbor went there every morning to pray and offer sacrifices. His crops seemed to prosper when he did this, and he warned them that they had best do the same if they wanted to prosper in the new land. When it came time for the spring planting, the Canaanite might go to the holy place on the nearest hill (a "high place") and have sexual intercourse with a priestess to insure the fertility of his fields. It all seemed like a part of what it meant to be a farmer and vinedresser. Our ancestors' feelings of relationship with the wilderness God of history and covenant and war were tempered by a new understanding of a God of field, vineyard, and high place. The God of the wilderness influenced them, for they were called to live in covenant. But they thought they could influence the God of their field if they made the right sacrifice or carried out the right ritual at the proper time. No wonder there are such strong prohibitions against worshiping idols and having other gods before "the Lord your God who brought you out of bondage."

Each time the enemies of the Israelites threatened their existence, a leader came forward to recall the wilderness experience for the people. "When the people of Israel cried to the Lord on account of the Midianites, the Lord sent a prophet to the people of Israel; and he said to them, 'Thus says the Lord, the God of Israel: I led you up from Egypt, and brought you out of the house of bondage; and I delivered you from the hand of the Egyptians, and from the hand of all who oppressed you, and drove them out before you, and gave you their land; and I said to you, "I am the Lord your God; you shall not pay reverence to the gods of the Amorites, in whose land you dwell." But you have not given heed to my voice' " (Judges 6:7-10). In the same chapter we read of Gideon being called by God to lead the people back into battle in the Lord's name and with the Lord's power. We learn that after uniting as in the days of the wilderness, the tribes would forget the gods of the fields and once again remember the covenant and the God of the wilderness. But when the threat was over, they would drift back to the practices of their Canaanite neighbors until the next threat came and another judge rose up to recall them to the covenant.

Despite the decadence of the field-and-vineyard God relationship, there is a growing realization during this time that Yahweh is a God of creation as well as a God of history and covenant and war. Though there may have been a good deal of turning away from Yahweh to worship Baal, there was also a growing consciousness that Yahweh *was* Baal in the sense that God was the God of field and vineyard as much as he was the God of history and battle. In Judges 6:25-28, Gideon rips down the altar to Baal and replaces it with "an altar to the Lord your God on the top of the stronghold here, with stones laid in due order." He places the altar to Yahweh on the same hill that the altar to Baal was on. (In time the legends and stories of Baal, the god associated with that high place, were often adapted by the Israelites to reflect the story of Yahweh's early interaction with their ancestors. As mentioned above, some of the stories of Genesis have their origin in the tribal traditions of the Canaanites and other neighboring peoples.) Yahweh now becomes the God of this *place* as well as the God of history and covenant and war.

When the Israelites moved into the land of the Canaanites, they found the people celebrating festivals of planting and harvesting. The agricultural life of the people was framed by the annual round of festivals that marked the passing of each stage of the agricultural year. Thus in the Feast of Booths the booth was simply the shelter erected in the field for the convenience of the harvesters. Rituals became a part of the life lived in the booth. As the Israelites inherited those traditions from their Canaanite neighbors, they added the *historical* level of understanding. The booth came to represent the years of wilderness wandering and was a vivid reminder to each new generation of the mercy and love of the God of history as he led their people from Egypt to the promised land. The assimilation process that went on within the religious festivals expresses also the assimilation that was going on in terms of how the people understood their relationship with the God of history-covenant-war-field-vineyard-high place.

We Christians have inherited the Jewish understanding of God and the agricultural/historical festivals that go with that understanding. Hence at Easter we celebrate the resurrection as a historical reexperiencing and recalling of the resurrection events. But we also celebrate that historical event with Easter eggs and the planting of seeds, with Easter lilies and new clothing. These latter ways of expressing the historical event come out of our understanding of new life and new growth as it is expressed in creation around us. So the new-birth aspect of Easter is celebrated at the new birth occurring in the agricultural season of planting and blooming.

God-and-Country Religion

The time came when the people wanted a more stable and permanently visible form of government, so they approached the prophet Samuel and begged him to appoint a king to unite the tribes into a nation. Samuel was hesitant to grant the request, for he could see that the Israelites might come to consider the king a god, as many peoples did. Such a king could easily enslave his people. The Israelites might forget where their ultimate loyalty and response lay and might forget the covenant of their wilderness wanderings. (Samuel's concern was well founded, for this is precisely what happened.)

Up to this time in Israel's history nothing had been written down. The stories of Israel's relationship with Yahweh were handed on orally from generation to generation. They were memorized and shared at the campfires of the wilderness, in the festivals, and within each family. With the introduction of the kingdom, however, it became essential to preserve the story and the traditions in writing and to adapt them to the new situation, for people feared that with the change in world view the heritage would not be handed on in the way it once was. Thus the first writings came from this period. The ancient story was written on scrolls along with the legends, songs, and ballads of the people.

During the bicentennial year, two members of our congregation published the history of our parish. They spent considerable time going through old scrapbooks, newspaper clippings,

letters, and official records. They interviewed some of the older members of the parish so that they could be in touch with the oral tradition that had been handed on. Gradually they were able to piece all of these sources together into a written history of our parish.

This is the kind of process that happened when the oral traditions of the tribes were first written down on scrolls. Even though the writers pieced together a wide variety of sources and traditions, they still left their trademark on their work. In this first written history, God was usually referred to as Yahweh or Jehovah, so this writing has come to be called the J source.

As a result of public pressure, Samuel sought God's guidance in choosing a king. He was led to Saul, whom he anointed as the first king of the tribes of Israel. The story of Saul's appointment as king is found in 1 Samuel 9:14-26; in chapter 10, Saul's anointing is recounted. "Then Samuel took a vial of oil and poured it on his head, and kissed him and said, 'Has not the Lord anointed you to be prince over his people Israel? And you shall reign over the people of the Lord and you will save them from the hand of their enemies round about' " (1 Samuel 10:1). The Hebrew word for one who is anointed as king or spokesman for God is *messiah.* The Greek word for the same title is *christos.* Saul became the first messiah or christos of the Lord. His anointing expressed his special relationship with God. When he spoke, he spoke the word of the Lord; when he acted, he acted for the Lord. This is what separated the king of Israel from the kings of the surrounding kingdoms. All the kings spoke sacred and powerful words, but the words of the king of Israel point beyond himself to Yahweh.

When Saul fell from God's favor, Samuel was led to choose David and to promise David that he would be father of a line of kings. This is an important shift of understanding. Now for the first time we see a special relationship conferred not only on one person such as Abraham or Moses or Saul but on that person's family. "Moreover the Lord declares to you that the Lord will make you a house. When your days are fulfilled and you lie down with your fathers, I will raise up your offspring after you, who shall come forth from your body, and I will establish his kingdom. He shall build a house for my name, and I will establish the throne of his kingdom for ever. I will be his father, and he shall be my son. When he commits iniquity, I will chasten him with the rod of men, with the stripes of the sons of men; but I will not take my steadfast love from him, as I took it from Saul, whom I put away from before you. And your house and your kingdom shall be made sure for ever before me; your throne shall be established for ever" (2 Samuel 7:11-16). So this "messiahship" is now passed from father to son, from generation to generation through the whole house of David.

From this theological viewpoint, God and country are synonymous. God's kingdom is the nation Israel, presided over by an anointed king and his heirs. This God-country relationship was deepened when David captured the city of Jerusalem and made it the "city of David." It became both the political and religious capital of the people. The ancient Ark was brought into the city as a sign that God dwelt with his king and his people in the midst of his nation. After David's death his son Solomon built the Temple and placed the Ark within its inner recesses. With a temple of stone, God becomes localized; he can be "seen" on the hill of Jerusalem. He is no longer a wandering God of the wilderness, "carried" from here to there. The prophet Nathan foresaw this problem when he told David "Thus says the Lord: Would you build me a house to dwell in? I have not dwelt in a house since the day I brought up the people of Israel from Egypt to this day, but I have been moving about in a tent for my dwelling. In all places where I have moved with all the people of Israel, did I speak a word with any of the judges of Israel, whom I commanded to shepherd my people Israel, saying, 'Why have you not built me a house of cedar?' " (2 Samuel 7:5-7).

Years later when the remnant of the kingdom was about to fall, first to the Assyrians and then to the Babylonians, the people held on to the hope that God would not allow "his" city or "his" dwelling to be destroyed. They felt that because God "dwelt" in Jerusalem, that great fortress was impregnable. If Jerusalem should fall, then Yahweh himself would fall. God and country, God and king, God and Temple become synonymous in this understanding of our relationship with God.

In this God-country theology, though God is the "one God" of the Israelites, there are other gods for other peoples. If Jerusalem fell to the enemy, Yahweh would fall to the enemy gods. Who could conceive of such a thing? Furthermore, it can always be assumed that the enemy of the people is by definition the enemy of Yahweh. God *will* destroy our enemies and preserve us because we are his people and his nation.

Prophetic Religion

With the death of Solomon came also the death of the united tribal kingdom under the house of David. The northern tribes rebelled against Solomon's son Rehoboam in about 922 B.C. to form the northern kingdom of Israel, set apart from the southern kingdom of Judah. The house of David continued to govern Judah, but in the kingdom of Israel a whole new political and religious system arose to replace the house of David and the Temple in Jerusalem. The sanctuary at the northern city of Bethel became the religious center for the northern tribes, replacing Jerusalem in their allegiance. A new temple priesthood arose, with cult prophets, festivals, rituals, and a liturgical calendar to provide the framework of faith response for the now-separate nation of Israel. The dynasty of the northern kings was never very stable. First one family ruled and then another, and there was frequent civil strife and maneuvering for leadership.

Of more importance to us than the political history is our people's growing awareness of their relationship with Yahweh. The great prophets of the Old Testament were heard in the town squares and along the roadsides stating that God was "whistling up the Assyrians," the enemies of Yahweh's people, to punish them for their constant breaking of the covenant. So Amos spoke in the northern sanctuary at Bethel:

"They do not know how to do right," says the Lord,
   "those who store up violence and robbery in their strongholds."

Therefore thus says the Lord God:
"An adversary shall surround the land,
and bring down your defenses from you,
and your strongholds shall be plundered."
(Amos 3:10-11)

"I hate, I despise your feasts,
and I take no delight in your solemn
assemblies.
Even though you offer me your burnt offerings
and cereal offerings,
I will not accept them,
and the peace offerings of your fatted beasts
I will not look upon.
Take away from me the noise of your songs;
to the melody of your harps I will not listen.
But let justice roll down like water,
and righteousness like an ever-flowing stream."
(Amos 5:21-24)

". . . therefore I will take you into exile
beyond Damascus,"
says the Lord, whose name is the God of hosts.
(Amos 5:27)

In these powerful words we see a significantly deeper understanding of Israel's relationship with God. Yahweh is no longer synonymous with the nation of Israel or Judah. Yahweh will not protect "his" city or even "his" Temple. When his people break covenant with him, God will raise up enemies to chastise them, even to destroy the Temple. The people's relationship with God is maintained not by where they live or by what festivals they keep in the Temple but by how they live by the covenant or, to put it another way, by how they "keep history" with the Lord. Furthermore, Yahweh is not an agricultural god who can be influenced by what is sacrificed at a certain time of the year. The festivals are profanities to the Lord when they are not accompanied by the true sacrifice of justice and goodness that lies at the heart of the covenant.

The prophets' concept of God shows great maturity in theological thinking. Needless to say, however, many were shocked at it, and the prophets were not very popular in the halls of the king and Temple! Amos was exiled from Bethel. In a later generation Jeremiah was imprisoned.

The prophets give a distinct flavor to our Judeo-Christian understanding of faith. On the one hand we talk of the kings of Israel as being anointed to speak and act for God. On the other hand we talk of the prophets as receiving a direct vision or call from God. (Before the great prophets whose writings are found in the prophetic book we have stories of Elijah, Elisha, Nathan, Samuel, and other prophets who acted under the guidance of God's spirit.) The prophets, as well as the kings, spoke the word of God. They felt the spirit of God within them, placing words in their mouths and giving them courage in the face of opposition. Often they confronted the king and the institution of the Temple.

The prophets stressed that Yahweh is a God of justice and goodness and that he demands the same kind of justice and goodness from his people. He controls the destiny not only of his own people but of other peoples. Hence the ruler of Assyria can be an instrument of God's will just as much as a king of Israel or Judah can.

In 721 B.C. the northern kingdom of Israel fell to the Assyrians, leaving only the small and weak kingdom of Judah, whose faith and political ambitions still centered on the city of Jerusalem. The prophets had warned the people of the north in vain.

We need to look at another aspect of the prophet's word. The prophets said that once the nation was chastised for straying from the covenant, God would restore his now-purified people. Out of the darkness would dawn a new day. There would be a new exodus from the bondage of darkness and evil, an exodus far more powerful and beautiful than the first exodus out of the slavery and bondage of Egypt. Parts of the closing chapter of Amos point to this hope.

"Behold, the eyes of the Lord God are upon
the sinful kingdom,
and I will destroy it from the surface of the
ground;
except that I will not utterly destroy the
house of Jacob,"
says the Lord.

"For lo, I will command,
  and shake the house of Israel among all the
    nations
as one shakes with a sieve,
  but no pebble shall fall upon the earth."
                                        (Amos 9:8-9)

"In that day I will raise up the booth of David
    that is fallen
  and repair its breaches,
  and raise up its ruins,
  and rebuild it as in the days of old . . ."
                                        (Amos 9:11)

  "Behold, the days are coming," says the Lord,
    "when the plowman shall overtake the reaper
    and the treader of grapes him who sows the
      seed;
the mountains shall drip sweet wine,
  and all the hills shall flow with it.
I will restore the fortunes of my people Israel,
  and they shall rebuild the ruined cities and
    inhabit them;
they shall plant vineyards and drink their wine,
  and they shall make gardens and eat their fruit.
I will plant them upon their land,
  and they shall never again be plucked up
  out of the land which I have given them,"
    says the Lord your God.
                                        (Amos 9:13-15)

In Isaiah 35:1, 2b, 5-6a we also read of the new
exodus that is to come in the day of restoration.

The wilderness and the dry land shall be glad,
  the desert shall rejoice and blossom. . . .

They shall see the glory of the Lord, the majesty
  of our God.

Then the eyes of the blind shall be opened,
  and the ears of the deaf unstopped;
Then shall the lame man leap like a hart,
  and the tongue of the dumb sing for joy.

    Thus in the prophetic books of the Old
Testament we see another stage in theological
understanding. There is meaning in suffering and
adversity. God works through our history and
story. Suffering often comes because we have
broken covenant and faith with creation. A
nation that strays from justice falls by the weight
of its own injustice and oppression. It becomes

weak inwardly and is prey to the first enemy that
comes over the hill. As we reflect on our
adversity, however, we are led to return to the
ways of covenant and in doing so are restored as
God's people. God always holds out a promise at
the same time that he allows us to fall into
adversity.

    When the northern kindgom fell, a second
source of historical writings was added to the Old
Testament, for it was essential to preserve the
stories and traditions of the northern tribes as the
people were sent off into exile. The northern
tribes, of course, had some of the same stories as
those already recorded in the J source, though the
perspective from which they were told often
differed. Other stories, however, were unique to
the northern tribes.

    Just as editors had pieced together the J
source to offer a written history of God's people,
an editor also pieced together the stories of the
northern tribes. Rather than writing two separate
histories, a later editor put both sources together,
weaving one account into the other. This process
explains why in the Old Testament we sometimes
find two stories about the same event. Despite the
interweaving process, scholars can identify the
northern tribal source because in its version the
name given God is *Elohim*. For this reason the
northern history is called the E source.

Deuteronomic Religion

The Book of Deuteronomy was part of a scroll
found in 621 B.C. in the Temple during the reign
of King Josiah in the kingdom of Judah. The
scrolls found in the Temple contained not only
the present Book of Deuteronomy but also a
summary of Israel's history from the time of
Joshua to the time of Josiah. In a sense this
Deuteronomic writing (called the D source) is a
stylized history of the Israelites from the
prophetic viewpoint. This viewpoint stresses that
when the people have lived by the covenant, they
have prospered; when they have broken covenant,
they have suffered. It is that simple. The present
Book of Deuteronomy purports to be a sermon
by Moses given just before he died. He reminds
them of the covenant he had proclaimed in the

wilderness, a covenant that calls them to fear and serve the Lord. "And now, Israel, what does the Lord your God require of you, but to fear the Lord your God, to walk in all his ways, to love him, to serve the Lord your God with all your heart and with all your soul, and to keep the commandments and statutes of the Lord, which I command you this day for your good? . . . For the Lord your God . . . executes justice for the fatherless and the widow, and loves the sojourner, giving him food and clothing. Love the sojourner therefore; for you were sojourners in the land of Egypt" (Deuteronomy 10:12-19). The people must be just and loving because their Lord is just and loving. The Deuteronomic writings express this demand for justice in ringing tones.

On the negative side, however, these writings tend toward a simplistic theology. We do right so that we can prosper. If we follow the Law exactly, nothing can happen to us. The "doing" of justice, mercy, and love became codified in the minds of many. This understanding led to overreliance on a legalistic following of the covenant—a legalism that Jesus condemned among the Jews of his time—and to a false reliance on God's protecting his people. Since part of the purpose of the writings was to strengthen the cultic Temple practices at Jerusalem, emphasis was placed on God's favor of the city and the Temple. Part of keeping the covenant was following the Temple rituals. How, then, could God allow the Temple to be destroyed? If the Temple were gone it would be impossible to keep the ritual side of the covenant.

We have now seen three layers of writings unfolding in the history of our people. The J writings came at the time of the establishment of the kingdom. The E writings came when the northern kingdom fell, and the Deuteronomic or D writings were added to the Old Testament scrolls during the reform movement of King Josiah. The Deuteronomic history, with its distinct historical viewpoint, was interspersed among J and E where the same episodes were recorded. Thus in one chapter we might find portions of all three writings, with each one reflecting the viewpoint of the original tellers of the story.

The theological perspective of Deuteronomy is similar to that of the great prophets in that it called upon God's people to exercise justice and righteousness and warned that if they failed to do so, their decadent society would fall at God's hands. However, the prophets had far more depth of feeling and of perception than the Deuteronomic school did. Jeremiah, for example, wrote at the same period as Deuteronomy and at first agreed with the reform movement that stemmed from the discovery of the scroll. However, he soon parted company with Josiah and the reform movement. He proclaimed that God could not be boxed into the Temple and that the people must not rely on God's love of the Temple to protect them from disaster. Moreover, Jeremiah could see the legalistic carrying out of the Law replacing the intent of the Law as the guideline of the people.

Religion of the Exile

In 587 B.C. the southern kingdom, Judah, fell to the next wave of invading armies, the Babylonians. Again the cream of the people were sent into exile, leaving a remnant behind to pick up the pieces of a lost nation.

What does one do in exile when one can no longer worship Yahweh in the Temple of Jerusalem and therefore cannot follow the ritualistic prescriptions of the covenant? How does one relate to a national God of Judah when one can no longer live in that land? What do we place our hope in when our nation lies desolate and we are sent as captives to a strange land among a people with alien beliefs and customs? Of even greater importance, how can we maintain our identity as Yahweh's people in this foreign land when we have lost our national identity? As children are born to us in this land, how will they know their identity as Yahweh's people? What will keep them from drifting into the customs and world view of the Babylonians, especially since our captors treat our people well? These are the kinds of questions that faced our people in exile. In responding to them out of the painful realities of an ever-unfolding history, our people gained new insights into our relationship with God.

Several ways of understanding this exile relationship are possible. Hence there was also a variety of responses to the same questions during the exile.

Despair

Psalm 137 beautifully reflects the pain of an exile who felt separated from God in a foreign land.

By the waters of Babylon,
   there we sat down and wept,
when we remembered Zion.

How shall we sing the Lord's song
   in a foreign land?

O daughter of Babylon, you devastator!
   Happy shall he be who requites you
   with what you have done to us!
(Psalm 137:1,4,8)

Away from Jerusalem, this person could not sing or be in touch with Yahweh. In anger and anguish he calls for revenge on those who would separate him from God.

Relating to God in Ritual and in Keeping Oneself Unspotted by the Surrounding Culture

During the exile some persons felt that their survival as a Jewish people depended upon remaining entirely separate from the non-Jewish culture. "Keeping the faith" meant following intricate ritualistic prescriptions for living out each day in this separation. If my children are to know Yahweh, they reasoned, they must know him in the ritual of the family and of the synagogue. Though we cannot make the pilgrimage to Jerusalem, we can make the pilgrimage of faith each day in a ritualistic acting out of our faith in God.

In this view the whole life of the people is a response to God. In a sense, every minute of every day is seen as a liturgy or living service to God. It is as if we Christians were to see every day of our lives as a continuing living into the liturgy of the Holy Eucharist. Upon rising in the morning we would say to one another the greeting from the liturgy, "Blessed be God: Father, Son, and Holy Spirit." At breakfast we would sing hymns of praise that would be an

extended "Glory to God in the highest" acclamation. Later on we would read the Scripture, as the Church does in the Lessons of the Holy Eucharist. Our whole day would be lived as an expression of the Eucharist.

This kind of ritualitic relationship demands a total commitment of the people, and by definition it does set them off from all who do not share their faith. Out of this understanding comes a new insight into our relationship with God. If we are not to be a political kingdom set apart by political boundaries and by kings, court and Temple, then what we can and will be is a "kingdom of priests," a people consecrated for service and praise to the Lord. One of the sources of our Christian understanding of the Church is found in this developing Old Testament understanding that came during the Babylonian captivity. In line with that understanding, we believe that by sharing the sacraments and by accepting the way of Jesus the Christ as our way of life, we set ourselves apart from the world at large. In doing so we act as a "kingdom of priests" by pointing beyond ourselves to the living presence of God in the world.

Since the people in exile did not have access to the Temple, they began gathering in other meeting places for the Sabbath worship and festivals. The synagogue as a meeting place for studying the biblical word, hearing it, and responding to it in prayer probably got its start during this exile.

To enable a people to move into this new understanding of their relationship with God, there must be authority for what is proclaimed. Out of this need grew the fourth strain of Old Testament writings, which scholars refer to as the priestly or P source. As the priestly writers traced the story of the Israelites, they emphasized the establishment of the priesthood by Moses at Mount Sinai and the importance of the priestly authority and of the ritualistic prescriptions of the Torah. The Holiness Code of Leviticus 17—26 says "And the Lord said to Moses, 'Say to all the congregation of the people of Israel, you shall be holy; for I the Lord your God am holy' " (Leviticus 19:1-2). Observing the ritual demands of the covenant helped to reinforce its ethical demands. The one is not to be separated from the other. "You shall not hate your brother in your heart. . . . You shall love your neighbor as yourself: I am the Lord" (Leviticus 19:17-18). Loving one's neighbor becomes part of the "living liturgy" of the Jew, as do keeping the Sabbath and other ritual acts.

Thus as the priestly writers traced Israel's story, they did not emphasize the establishment of the nation Israel but the establishment of Israel as a priestly line instituted by Moses to be the responsive sign of Yahweh's presence in an alien world. In other words the priestly writings establish the authority for the Jewish "church."

This does not mean that the writers made up a body of material to support their view. Rather, they reflected on their own story and realized a new significance in their relationship with Yahweh. Looking back through history, they began to discern a different pattern in their story than had been discerned by others who had traced the record of Yahweh's relationship with his people.

To look forward in history for a moment, we can note that a similar variety of perspectives among New Testament writers sheds further light on what happened in Old Testament times. As the writer of the Gospel of Mark reflected on the gospel message, he wrote from the perspective of one awaiting an imminent return of the risen Lord. Paul's early letters reflect the same high expectation; they were not interested in the long-range survival of the Christian in an alien world but were concerned with preparing people to hear the good news of Jesus' life, death, resurrection, ascension, and imminent return to bring in the Kingdom of God. By the time Luke and John wrote and by the time the later epistles were written, there was an awareness that the proclamation of the good news must be supported with structure, authority, and rules for ethical conduct, for it was obvious that the Lord was not going to return in the very near future, as had first been thought. The later writers reflected on the same story as the early writers did, but from their new historical perspective they point up different understandings. In addition, a generation of living into the reality of the gospel had provided these later writers with more story to write about and reflect on. They too had to concern themselves with establishing a church in addition to spreading the gospel.

The priestly writers of the Old Testament likewise demonstrated how a variety of approaches is possible. The priestly writings, however, were not separated from the previous writings as later New Testament writings were separated from earlier ones. Instead, they were inserted directly into the narrative and woven into the J, E, and D material. It is as if the four Gospels were combined into one account, with portions of Matthew interspersed among John, Mark, and Luke. In fact, the priestly account of creation is the very first chapter of the Old Testament. The priestly writer provided a beautiful poetic description of the creation, but his main concern was to establish the authority for keeping the Sabbath: On the seventh day God rested, and so must we.

We can certainly see the dangers in the priestly writings. They can, and often did, run into blind legalism. Jesus' repeated confrontations with the legalistic authority figures of his day are a vivid reminder of this danger. On the other hand we dare not condemn the priestly understanding of our relationship with God. The film and play *Fiddler on the Roof* provides us with an insight into this way of living. Tevye could find joy in the midst of persecution. His suffering and the suffering of his family and people became a "living liturgy." Tevye praised and responded to the one God in his suffering as well as in his dancing. In the priestly writings we discover the same impressive concept of holiness described above. Perhaps many of us would attribute the words "You shall love your neighbor as yourself" to Jesus, but he was actually quoting the priestly writings as he reflected with the lawyer on what the most important commandments were.

Out of the priestly writings comes another development in our people's awareness of their relationship with God. We can relate to God not only in the Temple or in the political nation of Israel and Judah but wherever and whenever we worship together. For example, it is as if God said "When you reenact the Passover in the seder meal, I am with you in an outward, visible sign of my presence. And when you recall that I rested on the seventh day and do likewise, you will know that I am with you." The commandment to celebrate the Passover meal each year comes from the priestly writings. "Tell all the congregation of Israel that on the tenth day of this month they shall take every man a lamb according to their father's houses, a lamb for a household. This day shall be for you a memorial day, and you shall keep it as a feast to the Lord; throughout your generations you shall observe it as an ordinance for ever" (Exodus 12:3,14). Thus Jesus' prescription at the Last Supper to "do this as a remembrance of me" has a long history behind it. As Christians we believe that we experience the presence of God when we gather as his people in acts of dramatic remembrance. As we recall and reenact the events of the Last Supper, those events become our contemporary experience of the Lord's presence celebrated in the community of God's people.

So we owe much to the insights of the priestly writers. Their understanding of God's relationship with his people directly influences our own understanding of how in our daily lives we might see God as Father, Son, and Holy Spirit.

Hope in a Mysterious Direct Intervention of God

When we lose hope of political restoration and when we suffer one calamity and persecution after another, we tend to hope in divine intervention and miraculous restoration for ourselves and in punishment for our enemies. Prior to the Assyrian invasion the prophet Amos wrote that God would intervene directly to punish the people of Israel.

". . . on the day I punish Israel for his
    transgressions,
  I will punish the altars of Bethel,
and the horns of the altar shall be cut off and fall
    to the ground."

(Amos 3:14)

In the Book of Ezekiel we see further writings that point to a mysterious direct intervention of God. Chapters 38 and 39 describe in strange poetic terms a classic battle between the forces of evil and the forces of God. Though the evil forces, called Gog, appear to triumph at first, God then utterly banishes evil from the earth by helping his people win a glorious victory. This style of literature is called *apocalyptic writing*.

The poetry and symbolism of apocalyptic writing lifts one from despair to hope in a God who can and will act outside history as well as within history. God's power is not restricted to the natural course of human events. God has the power to intervene at any time to reward the righteous and punish the wicked. There is another world and another age coming that will right the balance of injustice and prove God's power over all evil. Apocalyptic writing, therefore, is a distinctive form of literature arising out of times of suffering and persecution. In a sense it is underground literature. Written from within an alien, hostile culture, it must be understandable to the faithful but confusing to the enemy. The extensive symbolism hides the true identity of the adversary while proclaiming a message of hope to the faithful.

Ezekiel's writings come from the period of the Babylonian exile. Ezekiel, with his unique historical perspective, deepened the people's understanding of God. He tells us that in our finiteness we cannot know the full scope of God's power or wisdom. What may appear to be injustice must be weighed in the light of a knowledge and understanding far beyond ours. The suffering of the moment has meaning in the overall divine plan. We can find meaning in that suffering as we contemplate the glory that will come out of our struggle. There is hope in the unknown kingdom to come that exists far apart from the world as we know it now. Whether we want to speak of heaven, eternal life, or new kingdoms to come in the world as we know it, this hope in the extra-historical gives a sense of power even in the face of an unjust and otherwise meaningless death.

Here we see another huge step in theological understanding. And again there is both positive power and negation in this understanding. On the positive side, this apocalyptic awareness opens the faithful to the sweep of the mystery of God in creation. There are worlds and kingdoms beyond the known and the provable. God cannot be tagged and boxed into what we can rationally figure out. The mystery of creation constantly tantalizes us and sends us back into the world as far more humble persons praising the mystery that is beyond the visible, tangible creation so familiar to us.

At the same time that we recognize the power of apocalyptic literature, we also need to recognize its limits. We are not dealing with literal truth but with poetry and symbolism—with poetic truth—to express hope in a hopeless world. Since its inception, apocalyptic literature has been misused to prove when the new age is going to dawn. Or its extensive symbolism and poetry have been literalized to prove that this or that predicted event has already happened. Such an approach to apocalyptic literature can in effect encourage us to be emotionally absent from God's world as we await the coming of the new world. As we await God's coming we can lose sight of him as he meets us each day in history. We can also become self-righteous in our waiting period, feeling that we are the ones who will be saved and that those who disagree with us will be damned.

The new kind of awareness that apocalyptic literature brings, then, marks another beautiful step in discovering our many-faceted relationship with God. But like all the other steps we have made in our pilgrimage, it must be seen in full context. Our relationship to a God of mystery and of future victory is only one kind of relationship. As we have seen, we also meet God in history, in our neighbor, in the story of the past, and in our present struggle.

Seeing Power and Meaning in Suffering

The Book of Isaiah actually contains the writings of three prophets. The prophet referred to as Deutero-Isaiah (meaning Second Isaiah) wrote during the time of the Babylonian exile. His writings constitute chapters 40 through 55. He saw the suffering of the people not as a sign of God's rejection but as a sign of their calling and their being chosen by God. Read the four Servant Songs to get the flavor of this understanding of our relationship with God: 42:1-4; 49:1-7; 50:4-11; 52:13—53:12.

In the third song the message is that God's suffering servant, his people in exile, must respond to their suffering with bravery and trust. The writer sets the example.

The Lord God has opened my ear,
    and I was not rebellious,
    I turned not backward.

I gave my back to the smiters,
    and my cheeks to those who pulled
        out the beard;
I hid not my face
    from shame and spitting.   (Isaiah 50:5-6)

The reason for holding fast in the face of suffering becomes clear in the fourth song. God has called upon his people to suffer so that they can bear the sins of the surrounding nations. His people must not only atone for their own breaking of the covenant; they must suffer vicariously for the sins of the nations of the world. Seeing the Jews suffering for them, the nations will be brought to God in humility and repentance. Finally, the Jews will be restored and exalted by God and by those nations that have been led to God. Through pain and suffering comes exaltation for the servant, the nation of God. In a sense, the nation in exile becomes a sacrament for the world. It becomes the "outward and visible sign" of God's judgment, forgiveness, and power. Through that sign people are moved to respond to God. This "sacrament" becomes their means of reaching oneness with God.

An analogy may be helpful here. Let us say that a family of Vietnamese refugees moves into our city. As the children enter the school system with their strange customs and language, they are ridiculed and rejected. The school actually has been filled with hostility and anger before the children arrived, but now all of this anger is projected onto them. Gradually violence builds up, and the children are pushed and shoved throughout the school day, but they never seem to respond in anger. They receive the hostility with a sense of calm that infuriates their antagonists. One day during the lunch period the children are severely beaten, and two of them have to be rushed to the hospital. As they are carried down the halls of the school they wave good-bye to their classmates. Suddenly the whole building becomes hushed. The students are now confronted in "an outward and visible way" with the results of their hatred and pent-up anger. Visitors to the school a week later wonder about the change of attitude; they sense a new feeling of respect and caring as they walk through the once-hostile halls.

The Suffering Servant Songs may well have given courage to the Jews who suffered under the Nazis. The songs were certainly in the minds of those disciples who experienced the passion of Jesus with him and of those who suffered later for proclaiming the gospel. As these latter followers looked back at Jesus' suffering and death, they could see a fulfillment of all that Deutero-Isaiah had written. The passion narratives and Jesus' own words reflect the Suffering Servant Songs. The Servant of God had come. He had suffered vicariously for the sins of the whole world. As a result, people's lives were changed; they felt as if they had been born again when they moved from repentance to an awareness that God dwelt within them through the Holy Spirit. And when they found themselves facing a hostile world, they could see their lives as "sacraments" of God's grace and his confrontation of evil. When they recalled Jesus' words calling them to be servants, when they recalled the words of the Sermon on the Mount about the blessings of those who suffered, they knew the exaltation of being God's instruments in his world.

We have moved to a whole new level of understanding our relationship with God. In an earlier age, being God's chosen meant success and victory in battle. Now it means being open to the possibility of suffering, and in that suffering seeing oneself as a sign of God's action in the world among his people. We can remember with amusement Tevye's comment in *Fiddler on the Roof*: "Lord, we are your chosen people. Why don't you choose someone else for awhile?"

Notice how our understanding of relationships changes with our history and our story. The understanding comes out of the story; or to put it another way, *our story leads to our theology.* In adversity and suffering, our ancestors were forced to come to grips with a new understanding of their relationship with God. The same thing happens in our own lives. Turning points and crises (times when we have to adjust physically or emotionally to changes) often lead us to a new understanding of our relationship with God and with one another. Crises such as moving to another city, changing schools, getting married, giving birth, or going back to school—any of these can lead to a

deepened awareness, a new understanding. To trace our own story in that way is to trace our own developing theology.

Finding Hope in Future Restoration as a Nation

The Jews did not suffer physically in Babylonia; they were treated quite well. Losing hope in Yahweh could easily lead to adopting the ways of their captors. So hope in the power and promise of Yahweh needed to be stressed daily. That is what Deutero-Isaiah did (as did other prophets and spokesmen of the time). He promised a new exodus from bondage even more glorious than the exodus from Egypt. This exodus would disgrace their captors.

Thus says the Lord:
"In a time of favor I have answered you,
    in a day of salvation I have helped you;
I have kept you and given you
    as a covenant to the people,
to establish the land,
    to apportion the desolate heritages. . . ."

(Isaiah 49:8)

Deutero-Isaiah stood as a new Moses reminding people of their enslavement, but pointing toward the exodus and the Promised Land.

From such writing comes the awareness that our relationship with God is always filled with promise. We may not realize that promise in the present moment, but the promise points to the dawning of a new day. God has not forgotten us. We can absolutely count on his faithfulness and love for us even when we have initiated the separation.

The Individual Within the Community

The prophet Ezekiel also wrote during the Babylonian exile. Part of his concern was to help the individual within the community of God's people understand his or her own fate at the hands of the Babylonians. Our Judeo-Christian religion is a faith of the *people* of God rather than an individualistic religion in which each person seeks his or her own place in creation. Ours is a collective story and a collective vision of wholeness. Paul, for example, later described Christians as the "Body of Christ." We are all integral parts of that Body, he explained. No one is more important than another. We all have unique gifts that contribute to the whole. We find our salvation, our wholeness, in relating to the community. Separated from the community, we are alone and alienated. The covenant deals with life in that community of the faithful. This sense of community, however, can also lead to a sense of helplessness. What my parents have done binds me in the present punishment. What the people around me do keeps me locked in corporate guilt from which there is no escape.

Ezekiel gave us a deeper awareness of our relationship to God as individuals and as members of the community of God's people. He tells us that we are not inextricably bound by the sins of past generations or of the people around us; we are individually responsible for our own actions. If we find ourselves suffering, we must look into our own personal life and see what we must change. God will know us in our individual quest for change and wholeness as well as knowing his people collectively in their prilgrimage as a nation.

Israel as a Light to the Nations, as the Chosen Instrument of God to Bring All Peoples into a Relationship with the One God

The exile, painful though it was, brought deep insight to the Jewish people. Perhaps the very fact that they were forced into a different geographical setting made them better realize God's action in history. In any case, we discover in Deutero-Isaiah a new awareness that God is the creator of *all* things and *all* peoples. God is found not only in the history of Israel and Judah but also in the history of the whole human race. He is "I AM" to Jew and Gentile alike. It is a great theological breakthrough for a struggling, suffering people to see itself as having a divine mission to bring salvation or wholeness to the whole human race and even to think of its own suffering as contributing to God's plan. That loving plan is good news to be proclaimed from the housetops. The writer of the Gospel of John would much later state the good news this way: "For God so loved the world that he gave his only Son, that whoever believes in him should

not perish but have eternal life. For God sent the Son into the world, not to condemn the world, but that the world might be saved through him" (John 3:16-17).

Without imposing New Testament thinking on the Old Testament, we can see New Testament universalist theology already taking shape within the pages of the Old Testament.
We get a hint of this universality in Genesis, where God sends Abraham forth to settle the new land. "I will bless those who bless you, and him who curses you I will curse; and by you all the families of the earth shall bless themselves" (Genesis 12:3). Abraham is seen as the father of *all* peoples. In Deutero-Isaiah we hear the ringing words reaching out to us across the generations:

"Turn to me and be saved, all the ends of
 the earth!
 For I am God, and there is no other."
(Isaiah 45:22)

This universal hope had also been expressed by First-Isaiah and by Micah, both of whom wrote in Judah around the years 742 to 687 B.C.

. . . many nations shall come, and say:
"Come, let us go up to the mountain of the
 Lord,
 to the house of the God of Jacob;
that he may teach us his ways and we may walk
 in his paths." (Micah 4:2)

In this theological outlook, then, God is the creator, sustainer, and liberator of the whole human race. He calls into relationship a people who cannot earn or deserve that calling. He calls because he is creator and lover of his created beings. This is another way of stating the doctrine of grace as we know it from the New Testament. The creator's power and insight soar high above any limited plans and power of ours. Our worst fear or most frightening enemy is but dust in the sight of God. Judah, even in exile, even in the face of death, you can take heart!

Postexilic Religion

Wisdom Writings

Most of the writings of the Old Testament seek the wisdom implicit in the *story* of God's relationship with his people as a *people*. It is the wisdom of the story told by the historian, the teller of legends, the prophet, and by the priest as he recalls the story in ritualistic acts. But after returning from exile, the Jews came to appreciate a type of writing popular in other nations around them—wisdom literature. This kind of writing does not deal with the *story* and its interpretation, and it does not focus on the community of God's *people*. Rather it uses *non-narrative* forms and seeks for truth as it applies to the *individual* who wishes to live a happy life.

The Book of Proverbs comes out of this postexilic time. Paging through it, the reader can quickly see that it is filled with short proverbs not unlike the "Confucius say" style familiar to the joke teller. But underneath these proverbial sayings is the unique Jewish understanding that the heart of all wisdom is awe and worship ("fear") of the Lord. To seek after wisdom is to seek after the Lord.

Two other wisdom books come out of this historical period. The Book of Job deals with the question of suffering, and the Book of Ecclesiastes calls into question assumptions about the meaning of life. Both of these books are radical in that they shake the foundations of faith upon which the people have based their answers to life's questions. Job is an extended narrative poem. The writer refuses to accept the principle that suffering always comes as a direct result of breaking the covenant. As noted above, this assumption lay at the heart of the Deuteronomic writings and had permeated Jewish thinking. Nonsense, says the writer of Job; sometimes the reason for suffering remains a mystery. We may, and sometimes do, shake our fist at God and question why, but God's wisdom far surpasses ours, and it is not our lot to understand everything under the sun. In the face of this frustration, Job can still express hope in a creative mystery.

"For I know that my Redeemer lives,
    and at last he will stand upon the earth;
whom I shall see on my side,
    and my eyes shall behold, and not another."
                                        (Job 19:25,27)

Job's closing speech concludes with a statement of awe, wonder, humility and repentance.

"I know that thou canst do all things,
    and that no purpose of thine can be thwarted.
'Who is this that hides counsel without
        knowledge?'
Therefore I have uttered what I did not
        understand,
    things too wonderful for me, which I did not
        know.
'Hear, and I will speak;
    I will question you, and you declare to me.'
I had heard of thee by the hearing of the ear,
    but now my eye sees thee;
therefore I despise myself,
    and repent in dust and ashes."
                                        (Job 42:2-6)

In similar fashion Ecclesiastes questions all the assumptions of Jewish faith and finds them wanting. One can *never* get to the bottom of God's wisdom, he writes, so there is little point in attempting to categorize the wisdom we seek and think we have found. All we can do is live from day to day and try to make the most of what happens. Furthermore, despite all pious words to the contrary, nothing really satisfies the searcher. Whatever we try soon loses its flavor and turns to dust.

As the seeking after wisdom became a more dominant theme in Jewish writings, wisdom itself began to be seen as a personification of God. Wisdom is that aspect of God that reaches out to the people to reveal and guide.

Happy is the man who finds wisdom,
    and the man who gets understanding,
for the gain from it is better than gain from silver
    and its profit better than gold.
She is more precious than jewels,
    and nothing you desire can compare with her.
Long life is in her right hand;
    in her left hand are riches and honor.
Her ways are ways of pleasantness,
    and all her paths are peace.
                                        (Proverbs 3:13-17)

This understanding of wisdom deepens in the writings of the Apocrypha.

(Compare the following poetic statements with the preface to the Gospel of John: "In the beginning was the Word, and the Word was with God, and the Word was God.")

"I came forth from the mouth of the Most High,
    and covered the earth like a mist . . . .
From eternity, in the beginning, he created me,
    and for eternity I shall not cease to exist."
                    (Ecclesiasticus 24:3,9)

She is a breath of the power of God,
    pure emanation of the glory of the Almighty;
hence nothing impure can find a way into her.
She is a reflection of the eternal light,
    untarnished mirror of God's active power,
    image of his goodness.
         (The Jerusalem Bible, Wisdom 7:25-26)

Through handing on and living out the story of our people comes an ever-evolving awareness of our relationship with God. At this stage of Jewish history we find our people uncovering new aspects of their relationship with Yahweh. They felt that the simplistic answers of the previous generations could not settle all life's questions; that though we shake our fist at the heavens and raise the agonizing questions, we must be ready to hear the response of God in the whirlwind, as Job did. All the answers are not ours to know; God is all-encompassing.

Furthermore, our people came to see that God's word or wisdom itself is power; to seek wisdom is to seek the Lord. (Later, our people would see in Jesus the "enfleshment" or "incarnation" of the Word. To know Jesus was to know the Word or Wisdom "in the flesh.")

The wisdom writings helped to broaden the historic faith of a people in pilgrimage to include the individual's own personal quest for wholeness as well.

Continuation of the Priestly Outlook

The priestly outlook in Old Testament writings continued as the people drifted back to their own land and rebuilt the Temple in Jerusalem. It soon became obvious that Israel was not going to be a great nation, at least for the present. So hope lay in a "church" centered around the restored Temple. It was essential that this hope have some foundation in Israel's history if the life of the people was to center on Temple rather than nation. Thus during this period we see another level of writings added to the sacred scrolls—the work of the "Chronicler" who wrote First and Second Chronicles and the books of Ezra and Nehemiah.

The Chronicler traced Israel's history and saw in it a clear indication that Israel was called to be a "church" in the sense that God's people were called out to worship and praise him in their Temple worship, in the way they led their lives, and in their total dedication to the principles and discipline of the Torah and covenant. Putting it into more familiar Christian terms, Israel was to be a sort of lay monastic order of people totally dedicated to living a separated life that would witness in worship and in action to God's glory and presence among all peoples.

As was true during the exile, this emphasis meant both separation of the people from the surrounding peoples and a strict, unwavering allegiance to the rituals and legal precepts of the Torah. The people were called to renew the ancient Mosaic covenant and to live by the way of life it laid down for them.

Exclusivism and extensive ritual rules of conduct can take their toll in a people's ability to spread the good news of God's love and compassion for all people. Deutero-Isaiah's grand vision was lost momentarily at this stage in our people's story. Nevertheless, just as the Word and the culture of the past were preserved in the dark recesses of medieval monasteries, so in Judah's time of trial and weakness, this narrow priestly understanding of our people's relationship with God preserved the ancient roots of faith for Jew and Gentile alike.

Parenthetically, we should recall that over the centuries the land of the Jews had been overrun first by one invading army and then by another. (James A. Michener's book *The Source* gives us an idea of the tragic story of the area.) The Assyrians had invaded the northern kingdom of Israel and exiled its rulers and leaders. The Babylonians had claimed the southern kingdom of Judah and exiled the cream of the leadership from that area. The Persians had restored the people of Judah (now called the Jews) and allowed them to build the Temple, but the nation was terribly weak. No longer could our people accept that their relationship with God was based on their being the great nation of David. In their adversity they saw a new role. They were to be a "church" of God, a kingdom of priests whose role was modeled after the priestly role of King David, who had instituted the city of Jerusalem as the sacred center of Israel. They would be a "light to the nations" as they lived by the Torah and literally lived a continuing "liturgy" of praise and thanksgiving. But another wave of domination was yet to come, that of the Greeks.

Religion of Hellenistic Times

Alexander the Great conquered our people's territory in the fourth century before Christ. Greek culture was strong and attractive; to many Jews, Judaism looked pale by comparison. So even though at first the Hellenistic practices were not forced upon the Jews, many of them adopted Greek customs and thought patterns. The result was syncretism and a turning away from Judaism. Even faithful Jews accepted many Greek ideas, as we can see in the Apocrypha. The wisdom of Solomon, for example, shows Greek influence, though it maintains a strong tie to the concepts of the Torah.

Hellenistic philosophy was concerned with the way of light or life and the way of darkness or death. The personification of wisdom mentioned above was further developed in Greek philosophy. Though Greek culture could endanger the message of Judaism through syncretism and distortion of ideas, it could also serve as a powerful vehicle for transmitting the ancient story through new symbols and language patterns prevalent in the Hellenistic world. The ideas of the Greek or Hellenistic world added new insights to the Jews' understanding of their relationship with Yahweh, the Holy Other, the source of wisdom and light. To jump ahead to the New Testament for a moment, we can notice, for example, how the darkness-and-light theme appears in the Gospel of John. "The light shines in the darkness, and the darkness has not overcome it" (John 1:5). The concept of light overcoming darkness in a powerful struggle for dominance in creation had often been expressed in Greek philosophical writings, but the writer of the Gospel of John adapted this powerful thought to express the meaning of the Christ event.

Apocalypticism: A Kingdom of God Outside History

Apocalyptic literature became more important during the Hellenistic era as the Jews struggled to make sense of their continuing adversity. Some apocalyptic writings said that a cosmic figure, the "Son of Man," would appear in the heavens to usher in a new extrahistorical age. Throughout apocalyptic literature there was a general expectation of the coming of this Son of Man. Mixed in with this figure was the hope for the coming of the Messiah. (The term *messiah,* as we have seen, was the title given to the kings of Israel, anointed as God's spokesmen.) With the fall of the northern and southern kingdoms, the Jews looked for a Messiah who would usher in the new political Kingdom of God. But the apocalyptic writings saw this Messiah as one who would usher in the Kingdom of God *outside of* history. Hope for a Messiah was also influenced by Persian philosophical thought patterns in which the world was locked in battle between the distinct forces of good and evil (though the religion of the Torah speaks of God as creator of the whole realm of life). As this Persian philosophy finds its way into later Old Testament writings and into the New Testament, we see increasing mention of Satan and the powers of evil. In apocalyptic thought the Messiah will usher in the age in which the powers of Satan are destroyed and God's rule is made secure.

(At the time of Jesus both connotations of the word *messiah* would be prevalent: the Davidic figure who would restore Judah's political fortunes, and the heavenly, extrahistorical figure who would usher in the Kingdom of God from the heavens to replace the decadent kingdom of fallen people.)

Closely allied to belief in a kingdom of God outside history is belief in a resurrection of God's people. We must now trace the rather complex interconnections of these two beliefs.

The Concept of Resurrection in Late Old Testament Times

In Isaiah 26:19, a late postexilic addition to the Isaiah scroll, comes the first (though not clear) mention of a resurrection of God's people:

O dwellers in the dust, awake
  and sing for joy!
For thy dew is a dew of light,
  and on the land of the shades
    thou wilt let it fall.

The dead will rise so that they can participate in the great day in which the Kingdom of God is inaugurated. And from the Book of Daniel comes this statement: "And many of those who sleep in the dust of the earth shall awake, some to everlasting life, and some to shame and everlasting contempt. And those who are wise shall shine like the brightness of the firmament; and those who turn many to righteousness, like the stars for ever and ever" (Daniel 12:2-3).

The concept of the resurrection of the dead helps the person of faith deal with the painful question of what happens to those who die before the Day of the Lord or the coming of the Son of Man. What of those who have witnessed and died for the faith but who have experienced only pain and suffering in that witnessing? Surely they will not go down into the shades of non-being. And what of those who have done evil? Surely they cannot be allowed to go unpunished by a just God. We find ourselves dealing again with the meaning of suffering and the search for some hope that ultimately those who have borne the pain of life will personally find their consummation in God's kingdom. It is all very well to talk of the Suffering Servant as an instrument of God's divine will; I can die with the hope that in the generations to come my death will be seen in perspective as a necessary prelude for the new age. But when we come right down to it, I find myself groping for a more solid assurance of hope and restoration.

The Daniel passage quoted above is the first *clear* Old Testament mention of hope in the resurrection. (The Isaiah passage quoted previously is a less-clear indication that the concept of the resurrection was finding its way into Judaic thinking toward the close of the Old Testament period.) Surrounding cultures had no clear doctrine of a resurrection, although the belief in gods who died in the fall season to be released again with the spring blooming was common, as were other beliefs touching on life after death. Even Egyptian culture, with its elaborate burial of the dead, was not a belief in the resurrection as the Jews gradually came to conceive of it; nor, as we shall mention below, was it akin to the Greek concept of the immortality of the gods.

Our topic again makes it necessary to look forward to the New Testament. By the time of the Pharisees of Jesus' day, belief in the resurrection would be well established. It was one of the major doctrines that separated the Pharisees from the Sadducees; the latter refused to accept the resurrection because it was not mentioned in the Torah.

When we speak of the resurrection as understood by the Jews and then by the early Christians, it is important to distinguish it from the Greek approach to the body-soul relationship. In at least some Greek schools of thought, the material world is the prison of the soul or is merely a reflection of the true picture of reality. Thus, they said, our historic bodies will pass away and leave our soul, which is that part of us that is eternal and tied to the ultimate knowledge or creator. Gnosticism, a serious Christian heresy, was the child of this Greek thought pattern. Within each person, it said, there is a divine spark entrapped in evil flesh. Jesus, therefore, was not really a man, it argued, for it was inconceivable that God would assume real flesh. Moreover, Jesus did not really suffer and die on the cross, for that too was inconceivable to the Gnostic. We can see why the Nicene Creed speaks so vehemently of Christ as being born of a woman, really suffering, and dying to rise again.

In any case this Greek thought pattern has permeated our Christian thinking down through the generations. What many of us mean when we talk about the resurrection is that at death our soul will be released from our decaying body; the soul will go to heaven, and the body will decay in the earth. But this is Greek thinking that is alien to the Judeo-Christian understanding of the resurrection as a historic, bodily life in the age to come.

As mentioned above, the "day of the Lord" was first conceived of as the day when Israel's political power would be supreme and the people of God would live out the covenant as they related to each other in the kingdom of Israel. The prophets, we have seen, put a new twist to that day of the Lord. It would be a day of destruction for the nation; out of it would come restoration resulting from Israel's returning to the Lord, humbled in chastisement. Thus the day of the Lord in this political historic sense was to be a time of trials and tribulations and the shaking of the foundations for the nation Israel. These images were taken up by the apocalyptic writers of both Old and New Testaments, who talk of the day of the Lord that would be ushered in by the Son of Man outside the normal course of history. God would intervene in history to institute his new reign. The covenant would be fulfilled, people would be restored to wholeness in mind and body (the lame would walk, and the deaf would leap for joy), and all nations of the world would process to the hill of Jerusalem, recognizing in this new Jerusalem the true light to the nations.

To this picture is added in late Old Testament times the concept of the resurrection. Those who had died would be raised up to participate in the new age. Those who had done evil in the sight of the Lord would receive punishment. In this view the new age, including the resurrection, is *historical,* even though instituted by God outside the normal course of history. It culminates and fulfills history. It opens up a new story. The people of the story are brought into the new story with their whole being. Since the world is a good world created, sustained, and redeemed by God, *all* of it is brought to full flower. Hence not just my soul or "spark" is redeemed; my whole being as a person living in historical time is called into the new age.

To complete the picture of Old Testament belief in the resurrection, we need to mention again the influence of Persian wisdom. Under this influence our people conceived of God and the forces of good as engaged in battle against Satan and the forces of evil. At the final time Satan and evil will finally and eternally be defeated. This idea still does not negate the world and the things of the world, however. The world and the flesh are not bad. Satan, who has invaded God's world, is what is evil.

(For a beautiful poetic understanding of this concept of resurrection, read to yourself and your children C. S. Lewis's *Last Battle,* the final book in the *Chronicles of Narnia* series.)

Understanding the trials and tribulations that are to come as the prelude or dawning of the new age gave courage to those living in painful times. We see here another explanation for suffering, and another comfort arising out of it. If the world seems to be falling around me, this view says, it is really the birth pangs of God's new age. With this thought in mind, I can live through the beatings and the stadium filled with lions and can even conquer death itself.

We have traced now the full sweep of our people's understanding of their relationship with God as it unfolds in the Old Testament, with some brief anticipations of its effect on the New Testament. There is an evolving understanding that grows out of the historical situation of our people in each age. When crisis comes I raise questions about my faith. When the old answers fail to fit the new situation, I am thrown first into discouragement and then into deeper awareness that opens up a whole new spectrum of my relationship with God, his creation, my family, and myself. This process of questioning, probing, and deepening our faith relationship must never stop for the individual or for the people of God gathered in story and response. When the old world view no longer fits, we must push our thinking out to see new perspectives. Our theology grows out of our history, our struggle, and most of all, out of our dreams and hopes.

Before leaving the Old Testament we should notice that there are always counterunderstandings that arise to balance out the probing and discovering that always goes on. For example, to balance the exclusivism of the postexilic times, the books of Ruth and Jonah were written. Despite all the cries for racial purity being issued as the official "party line" of the time, the story of Ruth was circulated to show that this ancestor of David came from outside the covenant people. Jonah, a humorous short story, was written during this postexilic time to show God's love for *all* people, including the people of Nineveh, the hated enemies of the Jews.

These "counter" writings are a reminder that we can never pin down our relationship with God any more than we can pin down our understanding of our relationship with our spouse, child, or friend. The longer we live together in love, the more we discover in each other and in our relationship. But the moment we think we have arrived in our understanding, something else comes and sends us seeking to comprehend the new vista that has opened up. And always balancing the viewpoint from one side comes a countering viewpoint from the other. One might say, then, that our understanding of God as well as of each other comes out of dialogue. We talk back and forth, taking both sides of the issue, to arrive at a new balance. To lose this creative tension in the search would be to miss finding the truth. The universalism of Deutero-Isaiah had to be countered by the exclusivism of the priestly writers if Judaism was to be maintained and carried down to the present day. But in postexilic times the exclusivism of the Temple cult had to be countered by the wider vistas of Ruth and Jonah and the apocalyptic writers if Judaism was to survive the destruction of the Temple. We will see this same process happening in the writings of the New Testament. We turn now to those writings as they reflect the impact of Jesus on our quest to relate to God.

Religion of the New Testament Writers

The Old Testament, and the journey in history with God recorded there, is an integral part of the New Testament. The New must always be read with the Old so that the whole story can be seen in perspective. The much wider use of the Old Testament in the lectionary readings is a recognition of this fact, and we have already noted some of the unity of the Bible in mentioning how the Old Testament apocalyptic writings and the theme of resurrection would be continued in New Testament times. Now I want to discuss more fully how our understanding of the relationship between God and his people deepened because of the birth, life, suffering, death, and resurrection of Jesus of Nazareth.

The writer of the Gospel of John states the new understanding in dramatic terms. "In the beginning was the Word . . . And the Word became flesh and dwelt among us, full of grace and truth; we have beheld his glory. . . . No one has ever seen God; the only Son, who is in the bosom of the Father, he has made him known" (John 1:1,14,18).

Jesus of Nazareth, his followers began to realize, revealed God in the sense that to know Jesus was to know the living presence of God in their midst. Jesus did not speak *for* God. He *spoke* God's word or wisdom. He spoke with a new authority. Everywhere he went, God's kingdom came alive in that moment and in the story of that person or people. In him God is now known not only in history, creation, hope, suffering, in biblical word, Temple, teaching, and searching. He is also known *personally* through our relationship with Christ. Jesus did not talk about the covenant with God; he was a walking fulfillment of the intent of the covenant. He was what Israel was called to be in the wilderness: a living "liturgy" of response, offering, and praise to the Creator. To respond to Jesus was to respond to God. To respond to God was to know ultimate wholeness or holiness. It was like being "born again" into the ultimate relationship our people had talked of for generations. The Kingdom happened at that moment. Jesus was the Moses of the Sea of Reeds and wilderness. He was the covenant. He was the Suffering Servant. He was the Son of Man or Messiah announcing the day of the Lord. He was the Paschal Lamb that took away the sins and separation of the people. He was the Temple standing within the midst of the people, pointing to the ultimate glory of the Father. He was the fulfillment of all that had been written, memorized, talked about, and dreamed of. In him, God becomes personally accessible. The Law, the forgiveness, the healing, and the hope are no longer mediated through Temple priest, sage, or prophet. We receive them ourselves, his followers now realized, from the hand of Jesus.

Let's take this realization a step further. At the Last Supper Jesus celebrated a new seder or Passover meal. He might well have said "Whenever you gather in my name and rehearse our story together, I am with you. Take this bread; it is my body. A new paschal lamb dies for you by choice and not by lot, and in that death you will know the mercy and love of God seeking you out even before you ask to be forgiven. By my death you will know your forgiveness and your relationship with God. It is a relationship as close as that of a parent and child, a husband and wife. Take this wine. May it be a foretaste of the wine we will share at the banquet celebrating my Father's reign. This wine is my blood that is to be shed for you. My blood, given in love, will be the mark of the new covenant written on your hearts and not on stone."

Jesus' resurrection three days after his death sealed for the disciples the reality of what they had experienced. Jesus *was* the embodiment of God. He was the Son of Man ushering in the new age. But then faith took a further step. Acts 2 describes in symbolic terms what the apostles and followers of Jesus experienced after the resurrection. They realized that in a very real way God dwelt within them. The prophets had spoken of the spirit of God placing words in their mouth. But now the disciples felt this spirit in a more direct, personal way. As they gathered and broke bread and passed the cup, they recognized that God was present with them at that moment just as he had been when they had gathered at the Last Supper. Their lives together were now the embodiment of God. The covenant was written on their hearts rather than on tablets of stone. Moreover, they found themselves empowered to speak the word, heal the sick, and proclaim the Kingdom in the same way that Jesus had done. They became the tabernacle or "tenting place" of the Lord among his people.

We speak of Jesus as being the incarnation of God. The word *incarnation* comes from a Latin word meaning *in the flesh*. God came to his people "in the flesh" of Jesus of Nazareth. With the coming of the Holy Spirit the people of the New Covenant realized that they still met God "in the flesh" of their lives together. "God is love, and he who abides in love abides in God, and God abides in him," wrote the author of 1 John (4:16). The people of God now knew that God is embodied in the love we share, is as close as the touch of our hands held out in love.

This realization that we have inherited from early New Testament times is a radical step in understanding our relationship with God. It frees us from the bondage of separation, guilt, and despair. We know that in baptism we too

move through the waters, as did our ancestors at the Sea of Reeds, and in doing so we mark our liberation and our birth into a new reality with God.

The viewpoint of the priestly writers and the postexilic Jewish leaders enters into the Christian's understanding of Church. The apostles saw themselves as set apart to become a "kingdom of priests" in the sense in which we used the term earlier in this chapter. But the shaping of the Church as an institution came only with time. The earliest New Testament writings point to an imminent culmination of God's kingdom which Jesus' life, death, and resurrection had inaugurated; the Christian's mission would be to spread the Good News and to prepare for the day of the Lord.

Later New Testament writings temper impatience for the day of the Lord with the realization that Christians must survive in a hostile environment as a Church with authority and conviction; to survive, the Church must become an institution. But the Church is none the less God's holy people who therefore must lead their lives as a living liturgy of praise, offering, thanksgiving, and celebration of the story and the vision.

The sacraments of this Church become the way we telescope the story and find continuing power in it. As we tell the story of the exodus we realize the exodus happening in our lives, and we act out that realization with the waters of baptism. As we tell the story of the Last Supper we share a Christian seder or Passover meal and experience the Lord leading us in our own Passover with Christ. We are a storytelling people who together find power for the present and vision for the future in celebrating the story together in sacrament and in daily life.

The ultimate vision of the Kingdom of God always calls us beyond history into mystery. As Christians we proclaim that God acts in history. If we proclaim God as the God of all creation, we respond to a creator of the universe, of stars and galaxies. Only poetry, the language of symbolism, can adequately say what we mean by the Kingdom of God, eternal life, resurrection, or heaven and hell. But the relationship with God that we proclaim through Jesus Christ is an eternal one that includes our history as individuals and as a people and that calls us into "continual growth in thy love and service."* The relationship uncovered in the Old Testament comes to flower in the writings of the New. When speaking of this eternal life it is always important to keep the full sweep of Old Testament theology in mind. Our resurrection is the resurrection of the *people* of God, not of isolated individuals. I am brought into the Kingdom as an integral part of the whole people of God. My story is a part of their story; we find salvation or wholeness together.

The Ongoing Story

The story of this growing understanding of our relationship with God does not stop with the last writings of the New Testament. It is important for religious educators to have a grasp of the sweep of Church history down through the ages since that time too, because our relationship with God is understood in each age in the light of the history of the people who live that relationship.

For example, notice the fluctuation between an emphasis on meeting God in the world each day, on looking forward to God's intervening in this world at the close of the age, and on finding God outside this world in the heavenly realm. During the Middle Ages, emphasis was on the heavenly kingdom; for people in this evil world the only hope came from the promise of eternal life. The Reformation years emphasized that we ourselves must bring about the Kingdom of God in this world; Church and State would legislate out the vices of evil and bring in the day of the Lord. After World War II the emphasis was similar: We should rearm the world morally to combat sin, poverty, and warfare; we can make the world a better place if we all live more Christian lives. Our relationship with God centered on the here and now. The sixties brought this dream crashing down around us. Disillusionment with the Church led many to leave in sorrow, disappointment, or disgust. The new day had not happened. Today, many Christians emphasize the

Second Coming. They look again for God's intervention in the world to bring in the new Kingdom. Passages in the Book of Daniel and in the Book of Revelation are anxiously scanned to literalize the symbolism in order to pinpoint the trials and tribulations leading to the final age. Frustrated with the world and our own efforts, many people look beyond history for hope.

And so our theology, our understanding of our relationship with God, is influenced by our history. The same process that we find in the biblical writings continues in each age. We condemn the psalmist or the Israelites for calling down God's wrath upon their enemies; we are shocked as we ask how God could possibly want to kill all the Egyptian infants. Yet in time of war we find ourselves praying to a God of war, a wilderness God who fights for us when we go forth in his name and with his chaplains in the front lines; we thank God for good weather that helps our planes destroy enemy cities. In time of peace we reach out for a relationship with a God who loves all people; we become ecumenical and less provincial about how we see God acting in our history. In times when our hope for fulfillment in this world grows dim, we tend to look outside history for meaning. When the old answers no longer seem to fit the questions we raise, we, like the people of the exile, find ourselves following many divergent paths in our quest for a relationship with the Holy Other.

This process also happens for us individually; our own individual religious development or journey follows along the lines of understanding we have seen in the biblical writings.

The preschooler exemplifies a "Genesis" faith. God is a parent who watches over the child and answers the right prayers or punishes the one who forgets to pray. The child who gets sick asks what he or she has done wrong.

Then we come to the "Exodus" and "Judges" stage. God is with me as I walk to school if I whistle a certain tune or wear a cross around my neck. He will protect me from the big kids down the block just as he protected the Israelites in the wilderness. When the football players come out on the field they huddle for a prayer with the chaplain or local minister; God and team are synonymous. We are in touch with a relationship expressed during the time of the kingdom: "We'll carry the Ark onto the field of battle and win against the enemy. God is on our team because his minister prayed for us."

When things don't go the way we would want, we too are forced into the crisis of having to seek new understandings, for our old world view no longer fits our situation. Sometimes we fall into depression or despair, seeing no way out of our new situation. With the old answers shattered, we lack the courage to seek and probe with new questions. At other times we find ourselves lifted up, realizing that as painful as this groping is, we can see our life's journey from a whole new perspective as we reflect on what we have been through.

And then the day comes when a spouse, close friend, parent, or sibling helps us to see in their love and forgiveness that there is a dimension to our relationship that points beyond us to creation itself. We know in that moment and in that person the incarnate presence of God in the flesh and blood of our life together. Then the ringing words from the First Epistle of John will become our words: "God is love, and he who abides in love abides in God, and God abides in him" (1 John 4:16). We begin to feel the eternal dimension of that love when someone close to us dies. The presence of that person is felt in a very real and personal way as we share moments of bread-breaking with others who know him or her. Gradually, our story is caught up in The Story. The Christ experience has touched us, and we know the covenant that is written in our hearts. We feel the Spirit within. We feel the enthusiasm, the inspiration, the spiritedness, and we know that that too is eternal, a gift of the Creator.

This, in simplest terms, is my story and my pilgrimage. The exciting thing is that it goes on and on; there is no arriving. There are the anticipation, the glimpses, the deeper realities, the entrance into new rooms in the mansion, the unbelievable uncovering of love and acceptance; there is the realization that my story is an integral part of The Story as it too becomes uncovered for me every time I open the Bible or express the story in liturgy, song, prayer, and praise.

But there are many times when I slide along the scale of theology. When I am anxious,

I can find myself right there in the wilderness carrying my "Ark" into the conference or meeting. I mouth a prayer that I realize later was more of a good-luck omen than an honest prayer. Or as I pray for victory in the championship game, I find myself in the God-and-country relationship with God, cocksure that God is on our side. And in times of crisis, depression and doubts fill my mind. I feel like the psalmist of the exile who sang the sad lament "How shall we sing the Lord's song in a foreign land?" (Psalm 137:4). In a time of pain my wife and I sit and look at each other with deadened eyes and wonder where all our dreams and feelings went. And then the insight of the prophet comes in the words of a friend or in thoughts and feelings that come to us. Pain leads to reflection, and reflection leads to a new revelation of what forgiveness, acceptance, and love mean after all.

Each book of the Bible has its own special meaning to me, for each one expresses stages along my journey. Moses becomes my leader; Job, a reflector of my angry questions; Mary, my moments of saying yes; Peter, a friend and partner; Jesus the Christ, my constant meeting place with God in the body and blood of my life's struggle. I can think of no more important function for religious educators than to tell the story of our people and to reflect on our own individual stories as members of God's people.

But if we are to be liberators and guides along the way for one another, we must constantly reflect on our stories so that we can move into ever-deepening understandings of our relationship with God. Our temptation is to seek to arrive at the final revelation and stay there. As religious educators we need to gently and lovingly move one another off balance so that we can enter more deeply into our relationship with God and with one another. That is why Jesus told parables and answered questions with questions. He was not interested in nailing down truth but in helping each person discover ever-unfolding truth. In human relationships, as with our God relationship, it is tempting to stay on the plateaus, to fear to ask the probing question of friend or spouse because we may not like the answer. But the religious educator needs to be a question raiser and a parable teller as well as a storyteller. The religious educator needs to know the story of each participant as well as his or her own story in order to be sensitive to the times, to raise questions, to nudge gently, to encourage, and to enable birth to happen. This is a sacred and exhilarating trust for each of us.

The following chart may help you keep the evolving theology of our people in mind as you hear the readings from the lectionary and as you share the faith story of our people at home and in the parish.

The Bible's Evolving Understanding
of Our Relationship with God

Historical Stage	Book of the Bible	Theological Perspective
2000-1500 B.C.:		
Patriarchal times The Hurrian invasion settles the Upper Euphrates. (The Hurrians and Habiru peoples are the ancestors of the Hebrews.)	Genesis	God is a god of nature who controls fertility and the destiny of the people. God's actions can be controlled by ritual. God is a god of place. To leave the place is to leave the territory of that god. Legends and folklore explain local phenomena, customs, and ideas. (Bethel, Beersheba, Hebron, Schechem, and Jerusalem are important holy places from earliest times.) Individual families may have their own gods.
1500-1350 B.C.:		
Wilderness times	Exodus, Leviticus, Numbers	God is "I am what's happening to you." He is a god of story or history. God is a god of war and a deliverer, leader, physician, provider, victor. God is a god who takes the initiative with his people. God is an awesome god who places demands upon his people. Israel is accountable to this god. The people are destroyed when they disobey. Ethic and religion are inseparable. God is a god who demands animal sacrifice as a way of sealing covenant or making peace with his people.

Historical Stage	Book of the Bible	Theological Perspective
		God is a god who covenants with the people: They are to be holy as God is holy.
1350-1030 B.C.:		
The taking of the land of Canaan, and the period of the Judges	Joshua, Judges, 1 Samuel 1—7	God as a god of history and a god of "this place" tend to become mixed. When enemies come, our people relate to the god of war. In time of peace, they relate to the god of the vineyard and field (Baal). This synthesis helps our people to see God in creation as well as in history.
		Israel's victories are Yahweh's victories, but Israel's defeats are *not* Yahweh's defeats. Israel fails because she has defied Yahweh.
		The Spirit of the Lord empowers leaders to act. The Judges, Samuel, and Saul are charismatic leaders.
1030-936 B.C.:		
United monarchy	1 Samuel 8 through 1 Kings 11	The anointed king (*messiah* or *christos*)
		God-and-country relationship with God develops.
		The Temple is built, and the Ark of the Covenant is placed in it. (Temple architecture reflects more Canaanite and Syrian influence than Hebrew influence.)
		The first of the prophets appear. Samuel confronts Saul in a way that sounds like the later prophets. (See 1 Samuel 15:22-23.) Beginning of the struggle between "Church" and State. Cult or ecstatic prophets important. King Saul influenced by them. (See 1 Samuel 10:6.)

The J or Yahwist epic is written. The first full interpretation of history is recorded for later generations.

936-721 B.C.:

The divided kingdom: Israel in the north, Judah in the south

1 Kings 12 to 2 Kings 17

Amos—prophet to the north; condemns the decadent ways of the people. The wealthy forget the covenant in their life of ease. Amos demands justice.

Hosea—northern prophet; compares his marriage with the prostitute Gomer to the relationship between Yahweh and Israel. He expresses hope for Israel because of the forgiving love of God; love will triumph.

The early prophets oppose the God-and-country relationship felt by Temple and court. God will raise up our enemies to chastise us for not following the covenant, the prophets warn. God confronts his people when they forget his ways. God and country are *not* always synonymous.

Elijah anoints Jehu King of Israel to overthrow King Ahab.

Elijah is the first to mention the "faithful remnant" who will survive God's chastisement of the people.

Elisha replaces Elijah. He, too, shows sympathy to those in trouble and confronts the king with God's word.

Micaiah refuses to prophesy for Ahab when Ahab wants assurance from the prophets that he can win in a battle.

Being Yahweh's chosen people means accepting more responsibilities to live in justice according to the covenant.

After God has chastised his people in defeat and suffering at the hands of the enemy, his people will be restored. The "remnant" will inherit the covenant relationship. The people of Israel tended to absorb more of the religious understanding of surrounding peoples than Judah did. Judah was more conservative in following traditional ancestral practices.

Historical Stage	Book of the Bible	Theological Perspective

721-586 B.C.:

Fall of Israel; survival of the Kingdom of Judah	Isaiah 1-33, "First" Isaiah's call came before the fall of Israel and extended to about 701 BC. 2 Kings 18-25 describes this period.	God-and-country concepts oppose statements of the prophets. Our people begin to question their continued suffering. Why does God let these things happen? Habukkuk's answer: Live in faith now. The unjust will be punished in time.
The leaders and wealthy in Israel are sent into exile by the Assyrians.	Isaiah is native of Jerusalem. Unlike Amos and Hosea, he is a sophisticated city dweller and is faithful to the Davidic monarchy and nation. Isaiah 6 gives a vivid picture of his call. The "fullness of the earth is his glory." God's justice and righteousness revealed through history are signs of his holiness. Yahweh calls for faith, not reliance on military might. (See Isaiah 30:15 and Isaiah 7.) A remnant will survive. Survival of that remnant will be a sign of God's continued power.	The E, or Elohist, epic is written. It contains folklore and history from the viewpoint of the northern tribes. The role of Moses is emphasized more than in the J epic.
	Micah—written during the same time as First Isaiah. He bitterly judges the cities. The Temple and Jerusalem will fall.	
	Zephaniah—written during King Josiah's reign preceding the Deuteronomic reform. A remnant will survive, but a day of doom lies ahead. He blasts the corruption of Temple priests, princes, the rich, the illustrious.	
	Book of Deuteronomy and the Deuteronomic writings that are scattered throughout the Torah—written about 621 B.C.; contain the *Shema* or statement of faith: "Hear, O Israel. . ." (Deuteronomy 6:4-9). Worship must be concentrated in Jerusalem. Presents the theme of love: Yahweh's love for Israel demands a loving response from people (see also Leviticus 19:18); Israel must love the alien as well as the neighbor (Deuteronomy 10:19). Presents the theme of election and covenant with Israel. Israel must avoid	"Deuteronomic religion" develops. Deuteronomic Reform too simplistic: Success and failure depend only upon following or failing to follow covenant. It fails to explain the plight of the just person or nation that suffers and tends to absolutize the cult in Jerusalem. Easy to substitute cultic purity for the demands for justice.

Historical Stage	Book of the Bible	Theological Perspective

entanglement with surrounding religious practices. Love demands justice. Even animals and trees are to be loved.

Nahum—written in Assyria in 612 B.C. (Babylonia begins to replace Assyria as a world power during this time.)

Habakkuk—written about 597 B.C., just before the fall of Judah during the rise of Babylonian power. Our nation is falling, he writes. We cannot rely on pat answers or false hopes. We must be patient and wait for the Lord.

Jeremiah—written from the time of King Josiah's reign to the fall of Judah and the Babylonian exile (about 628-586 B.C.). Jeremiah remains behind in Jerusalem and continues to speak and write during the early days of exile. He confronts the drift away from the covenant and sees Babylonia as God's judgment on the people. Therefore he advocates surrender to the enemy. This is all part of God's reign, a working out of God's plan. The Temple and Jerusalem will fall. The old covenant is gone. A new covenant, written on the heart, will come (Jeremiah 31:31-34).

Jeremiah begins to question the Deuteronomic reform of King Josiah. He sees the people relying too heavily on the Temple and ritual practices to save them from God's judgment.

586-538 B.C.:

Babylonian exile

The P or priestly writings.

Ezekiel writes in Palestine at the time of the fall. He is the son of a Temple priest. Is carried off into exile with King Jehoiachim; has an ecstatic vision in Nippur

Despair at being separated from God in not being able to worship in Jerusalem. (See Psalm 137.)

The priestly writers (P source) find God in ritual and in keeping in 592 B.C. Judah and the Temple must be destroyed, for they are evil, he says. Judah is responsible for her sin in breaking the covenant. Thus the nation must fall "in order that you may know that ! am Yahweh."

After the fall of Judah, Ezekiel writes that God wants to turn the wicked back to him rather than destroy them. From words of doom, the prophet turns to words of hope of restoration. Ezekiel 37:1-14 records the well-known vision of the valley of the dry bones. God will be like a shepherd to his people and will not allow his honor to be profaned. The nation will become a "church." Israel is a temple community (see Ezekiel 43:1-9).

"Deutero" or Second Isaiah (Isaiah 40—55)

Lamentations is written after the fall of Jerusalem.

the Law precisely. Judah is to be a kingdom of priests or a "church." The people themselves are to be outward and visible signs of God's activity in history. Moreover, God is present whenever we worship together, following the prescribed ritual and tradition.

The synagogue develops.

Apocalyptic ideas develop: God will intervene outside of history.

Suffering is a sign of that divine intervention coming.

The concept of the suffering servant appears. Our suffering redeems the world, and all nations will be healed.

God-and-country feelings continue. God will restore us as a great nation.

Ezekiel realizes a personal, individual relationship with God. We are not bound to the sins of our people. If we suffer, we need also to look at our personal faithfulness to the covenant (Ezekiel 33:10-20 and chapter 18). We cannot just blame our ancestors or the rest of the nation for sin's evil effects on us. We are individually responsible for our sins.

Deutero-Isaiah (Second Isaiah) points to a new awareness of God's *universal* role in creation. God acts in the history of all peoples. The Jews are to be the "light to the nations," bringing *all* people to the mountain of God (Isaiah 55). A new exodus will come; God's people will be redeemed.

Historical Stage	Book of the Bible	Theological Perspective
538-332 B.C.:		
King Cyrus of Persia allows the Jews to return home; postexilic times of restoration in Judah.	Proverbs, Job, Ecclesiastes Third Isaiah (Trito-Isaiah) Chapters 56-66 Jonah Haggai (urges people to rebuild the Temple)	The wisdom writings. God is in wisdom. Wisdom is personified as an aspect of God. This viewpoint sees God acting in wisdom as well as in history, in place, and in ritual. To seek wisdom is to seek the Lord.
Second Temple is built in Jerusalem.	Zechariah Malachi Book of Psalms Ezra Nehemiah Ruth 1 and 2 Chronicles	The priestly influence continues from exilic times. Jews must remain apart from non-Jews in order to keep the faith and witness intact. Tradition is preserved. Stories are told not for the sake of the stories but to tell people how to conduct themselves. Examples: Creation stories, to set Sabbath apart as sacred; Noah story, to set forth diet restrictions in Genesis 9:4.
332-167 B.C.		
The Greek or Hellenistic Period	Daniel Joel—written at the dawning of the Greek period Obadiah	The resurrection of the people by direct intervention of God Apocalyptic writings important. The new age of God is coming. God will intervene in history to restore his people in an extrahistorical way. The resurrection concept is tied to the age to come: A Son of Man or messiah will usher in this new age of God.
167-70 B.C.		
The Maccabean Age	Writings of the Apocrypha: 1 and 2 Esdras Tobit Judith Additions to the Book of Esther The Wisdom of Solomon Ecclesiasticus or the Wisdom of Jesus, the son of Sirach Baruch Additions to Daniel	

Historical Stage	Book of the Bible	Theological Perspective
	The Prayer of Manasseh 1 and 2 Maccabees The letter of Jeremiah (in some versions this is included as Baruch 6)	
ca. 50 A.D. — 96 A.D. Formation of the Christian Church	The New Testament Books	The Word (or Wisdom) has become flesh and dwells among us. God is known personally in Jesus of Nazareth, who is the fulfillment of the covenant. The "Suffering Servant" of Isaiah is Jesus. All the writings of the Old Testament that pointed towards the new age and the coming Messiah point to Jesus. God is Love. Whenever Christ's people gather together and "do this in remembrance of me," Christ is with them. Through the Holy Spirit the covenant is now written on people's hearts. The resurrection of God's people is assured. God "dwells" with us "in the flesh" and within us through the Holy Spirit who "inspires" us. The Church is the "outward and visible" sign of Christ's continuing presence in the world. The Church, as the "Body of Christ," is called to be a "light to the nations" and to spread the good news in word and healing action.

Chapter 3
Sharing Our Story in the Liturgy:
The Liturgy as Dramatization

We Christians are the people of the story. The biblical story shapes our understanding of life: creation, joy, suffering, death, eternity. This is why sharing the story of our people is so crucial for us. In the first two chapters we have looked at the story we have to tell from the Bible. In this chapter I want to look at how the liturgy and rituals of the Church *dramatize* the faith story of our people.

Liturgy is a dramatic proclamation, a dramatic participation in the faith story of a people. The ritual expresses in the deepest way the story that shapes our world view; that is why active participation in the liturgical life of the parish is so crucially important. Liturgy (from the Greek word meaning *the work of the people*) by its very nature calls for the active participation of all the people in the act of worship. Liturgy includes ritual acts and symbols that help, as John Westerhoff puts it, to "telescope our understandings and ways, giving meaning to our lives, and provide us with purposes and goals for living" (*Will Our Children Have Faith?*, page 55).

Westerhoff also reminds us that liturgy and ritual are the most powerful means we have of participating in and handing on our faith story (pages 54-60). At the heart of the parish religious education program, then, is the central act of worship, the Eucharist.

Let us look at the celebration of the Holy Eucharist through the eyes of the storyteller of faith. As we do so, we see that the whole act of celebrating the Eucharist is a dramatization of our Judeo-Christian faith story. The first half of the liturgy is given the title The Word of God or The Liturgy of the Word. We begin with a greeting and a prayer that remind us of the sacred nature of our gathering. Then we sing a hymn that praises God. Next we sit to hear the great stories of our people as related from the Old and New Testaments. The story is read and then interpreted in a sermon or homily. Having heard the story, we stand and respond by repeating the story in poetic form as our creed or statement of faith. The creed repeats the story of God's creation, our fall, the salvation brought by Christ, and our eternal hope. Next we kneel or stand in an act of prayer that expresses our faith in a creator who listens and cares for his people. Since confession is a part of our dramatic liturgical life together, we speak in the general confession (which comes next in the Episcopal liturgy) of our failures and guilt; this leads, in turn, to the proclamation of the good news that we are forgiven and healed by the Lord's love made known to us on the cross.

We have broken covenant with God, but God remains faithful to us as we acknowledge our separation. In prayer and confession we have been in touch with our own personal stories. These are our concerns. These are the painful realities that we must acknowledge. These are the hopes that we express as Christians. We share this personal story within the common words of the liturgy, but in doing so we realize that we are not alone in our concerns and hopes. The words of prayer and confession include every situation that is a part of our life story.

Having heard the story of our people proclaimed and having responded with our own story expressed in prayer and confession, we turn to the celebration of the Holy Communion or Liturgy of the Eucharist, the second half of the Sunday eucharistic liturgy. In the spirit of Deuteronomy (see Deuteronomy 26:10-11, The Jerusalem Bible), at the offertory or preparation of the gifts we "bring the firstfruits of the produce of the soil" to God and then at Communion time "feast on all the good things Yahweh has given (us)" as we are nourished with the "bread of heaven" and with the "cup of salvation." Listen carefully to the Prayer of Consecration that proclaims the significance of the Eucharist; notice that it is a *story*. "In your infinite love you made us for yourself; and, when we had fallen into sin and become subject to evil and death, you, in your mercy, sent Jesus Christ, your only and eternal Son, to share our human nature, to live and die as one of us, to reconcile us to you, the God and Father of all. . . . On the night he was handed over to suffering and death, our Lord Jesus Christ took bread. . . . After supper he took the cup of wine. . ." *(The Book of Common Prayer,* page 362).

The story is told in shorthand; it is telescoped, as John Westerhoff would say. We are brought together in this powerful story, and our faith and the faith of the community is intensified in the process. But these words of the liturgy are not only read; they are *dramatized*. The participants stand, kneel, sit, move forward to the altar to receive the Sacrament, hold up their hands to receive it, make the sign of the cross at various points, join in the prayers and responses, and do other actions that involve them in the dramatic redoing of the Judeo-Christian story. The priest at the liturgy takes the role of Christ at the Last Supper, breaking the bread, blessing the wine, and offering the Sacrament. This is a drama in which there is no audience; everyone participates as an actor in this divine dramatization of our eternal story. Even the vestments of the ministers at the altar are part of the drama and help the other participants to enter more deeply into the faith story.

The Influence of Jewish Festivals

This dramatic sense that pervades Christian worship comes out of the Jewish concept of worship. As faithful Jews recall every year at the Passover the exodus from Egypt and the journey across the wilderness into the promised land, they become a living part of that exodus experience. It is each person's story just as much as it is the story of his or her ancestors. In recalling how God acted for his chosen people in the past, Jews become aware of how God is still working in their lives in the present moment. The past event of power and wonder becomes the contemporary experience whenever it is recalled. In a very real sense, then, every moment of God's saving history is brought into the present moment as it is remembered from the past. This profound truth has been the core of Jewish life and worship for many centuries, and its influence on our eucharistic worship is one of Judaism's richest gifts to us.

Because history is a living tradition for the Jew, the events of the past are a part of the present. Therefore it is very important for the Jew to recall the great stories of Scripture. A yearly round of festivals and holy days brings the people together to "tell the story" of faith year after year. Our Christian liturgical calendar, with its seasons, holy days, and festivals, grew out of this ancient Jewish calendar. Christianity and Judaism are not based on an abstract, philosophical understanding of God but on telling and acting out the story of God's past actions so that we can see his wonders in our lives today and have hope for the future.

Throughout the centuries the Jews have told their story around the family table, in the formal retelling of Temple and synagogue worship, and in their annual round of festivals and holidays. The festivals and holidays became, and still are, dramatizations of the story. Great portions of the Bible were revealed and rehearsed as the folk gathered to dance, sing, process, take part in ritualistic acts, feast and fast in their active participation in the dramatic act of storytelling. For example, the story of the Torah is dramatized every year with the Jewish festivals of Passover, Pentecost, and Sukkot. Passover remembers the exodus from Egypt. Pentecost celebrates the making of the covenant at Mount Sinai fifty days after our people had left Egypt. The celebration of Sukkot (or Tabernacles or the Feast of Booths) recalls the wandering of our people in the wilderness. By the time the Jewish family has celebrated those three festivals year in and year out, it has *experienced* the first five books of the Old Testament. It has dramatized the faith story that lies at the heart of the Jews' understanding of God's action in their lives.

Theodor H. Gaster, *Festivals of the Jewish Year* and Siegel, Strassfeld, and Strassfeld, *The Jewish Catalog* (see the Bibliography) contain a wealth of material on Jewish feasts. As the Jewish festivals come up in the calendar, you may want to include some of the ancient Jewish customs in your own parish celebrations. The Passover celebration is an example of how this dramatization of the story happens for the Jewish people every year in their festivals.

In the spring, Jewish families gather at the family table to eat a ritualistic meal that recalls for them the story of their people as they left the slavery of Egypt for the promise of freedom in their own land. The meal is called the seder ("*say*-der"), which means *order of service*. They share *matzah* or unleavened bread along with other symbolic foods. The story of the exodus is narrated as the meal is eaten. Psalms are said or sung, prayers and blessings are offered, and the family enjoys the experience of telling the story in the context of a dramatic meal.

This meal grew out of ancient customs associated with the Temple in Jerusalem. During Jesus' time the Passover was a pilgrim festival in which people journeyed from all over the nation to participate. As pilgrims arrived in the city they purchased an unblemished lamb. It was slaughtered by the priests of the Temple, and the sacrifice of the lamb took away the sins of the people. As the family gathered in rented quarters

for the sharing of the Passover meal, the head of the household presided as the lamb was eaten along with unleavened bread, wine, and other symbolic foods. The lamb was the Passover sacrifice which was given for the sins of the people.

A Christian Passover: The Christian Easter and the Eucharist

According to Matthew, Mark, and Luke the Last Supper was the Passover meal that Jesus shared with his disciples. "Christ *our* Passover is sacrificed," we say in the liturgy. Through Christ we recognize that God is calling us out from slavery into freedom. In our present struggle for wholeness we can identify with the Israelites as they left their days of slavery behind to move into the unknown wilderness towards the promised land. We too find ourselves enslaved by fear, prejudice, and in some cases, outright oppression. We too are called to leave that slavery and seek the freedom and life that God would lead us into. We too pass through the waters of our baptism into our days of wilderness wandering. We fall back in fear and lack of faith even when we have the signs of God's presence all around us. The Book of Exodus is our story as much as it is the story of the Israelites of old. In fact, the Passover story, in which the persons seek freedom from enslavement to guilt, anxiety, fear, prejudice, oppression, and sickness, is everyone's story. Christ is our Moses leading us out of slavery into freedom. Christ is our Passover lamb. His death is an *eternal* sign of God's love and of God's call to all people in all times. Jesus might well have said, "Here, take this bread as you would take the Passover lamb . . . this is my body which is given for you."

While Holy Week and Easter are the *annual* "Christian Passover" celebration in which we recall Christ's sacrifice, death, and resurrection into the new covenant and promise, the celebration of the Holy Eucharist becomes a weekly (or daily or monthly) celebration of that same Passover. The Eucharist is patterned after the Jewish Passover meal and follows the same ancient customs that included (and still include) the sharing of wine before and after the meal, the washing of hands, and the blessing, breaking, and sharing of bread. Extensive prayers of "remembrance" were offered, with the understanding that as the faithful remembered the great acts of God in creation, in history, and in covenant, God was "remembering" the faithful at the present moment in his active participation in their lives. This remembering, in turn, pointed to a final consummation when Jerusalem would be fully restored and the Messiah would come. We have only to read over and listen carefully to the Prayer of Consecration at the Mass or Eucharist to see the Jewish context out of which our liturgy of Holy Communion comes.

At the Eucharist, as we recall the mighty acts of Jesus we become aware that he is acting in our lives this very moment, leading us from bondage and slavery into freedom. Jesus takes bread *now,* and through the power of the Holy Spirit it becomes his body. He takes wine *now,* and through the power of the Holy Spirit it becomes his blood. The Eucharist is a reexperiencing of the event so that we can realize the living presence of Christ feeding us at his table in this moment. And so in the Episcopal liturgy the priest can say as the people approach the altar to receive the sacrament, "The Gifts of God for the People of God. Take them in remembrance that Christ died for you, and feed on him in your hearts by faith, with thanksgiving" (*The Book of Common Prayer,* pages 364-365).

The celebration of the Holy Eucharist, then, dramatizes our life in Christ. Drawing on our common memory of the past, it points to a vision of what is to come—a vision that gives shape, meaning, and purpose to the present moment. The Holy Eucharist dramatizes the story of our people and of our own individual quest for wholeness in God's kingdom. No aspect of our lives is left untouched by what we share together at the Eucharist. As a priest celebrating the Eucharist with the people of the parish, I am reminded of this time and again. No matter what the Scripture reading and sermon have been about, we come to some point in the ritual of the Eucharist that touches on that theme. There are times when I want to stop in the middle of the

consecration prayer and say "See! This is what I was talking about!" Our whole life is lifted up and made holy as we participate in the dramatization week after week. Often in counseling sessions I will find myself coming to the same realization. No pain is left untouched by what we say and do at the Eucharist. So the Eucharist not only dramatizes the story of our people in the past; it also dramatizes our own personal stories as God's people in the present. Through the power of the Holy Spirit, the past becomes present and future. The dramatization of the story becomes the active presence of the risen Christ in our lives.

We see the same beautiful proclamation of our life's story unfolding in the round of the church *year.*

The Liturgical Year as Dramatization

Though there is always a historical significance to the feasts and festivals, there is also a contemporary application for the person and for the faith community. For example, Advent not only recalls a past expectation of Christ's coming and a present expectation of his coming again; it also touches and symbolizes all the times of expectation in our lives. From birth to death, joy to mourning, the liturgy of the Church supports us and directs us into a deeper experience of life made known through Christ.

Each of the days and seasons has actions, symbols, and words that express the meaning of that celebration which has developed down through the centuries. For example, think of the words and symbols associated with Christmas. One needs no caption to tell that a picture of the inside of a building was taken at Christmas; the symbols and colors speak for themselves.

Obviously, we do not experience anticipation just during Advent or new life just at Christmastime, but the Church sets aside these special seasons to celebrate and to make holy all those times in our lives when we do experience those feelings. By celebrating events from the past we are more apt to recognize and experience such moments in our present and future. Thus the

Church takes every aspect of what it means to be alive and proclaims it holy (leading toward wholeness).

This concept of sanctifying and celebrating all that makes us alive has had deep meaning for thousands of years, for it taps the roots of our very *being* by giving us life-giving symbols through which we find meaning and hope. We are empowered as we participate in life-giving symbols that touch the roots of our struggle for life in its fullness. The actions and words of the liturgy help us identify the feelings within us that inhibit or enable our growth. They provide growing roots for our dreams, courage for our quest, support in times of failure. They tie us to the eternal quest for life. "Psychologists have helped us to see that there is a level of human understanding—vital for growth into maturity—that is nonverbal and nonrational. We now know that this unconscious level responds to a reality as it is conveyed by symbolic forms and actions. We know that such an unconscious response begins at birth, if not earlier" (*Holy Baptism with the Laying-on-of-Hands; Prayer Book Studies 18 on Baptism and Confirmation,* page 15). A simple example will suffice: Even the one-year-old can appreciate the feeling of being sung to, receiving gifts, and blowing out the traditional candle on his or her birthday. These are all simple ritualistic actions that become significant in the life of even the very young child. Try offering the birthday cake without the candles if you want to test the power of ritual!

Harvey Cox, a theologian from the Baptist tradition, has said: "A liberating ritual is one that provides the formal structure within which freedom and fantasy can twist and tumble. It provides the person with a series of movements in which he is given access to an enormous wealth of human feeling. But these feelings now become the material for his own ... creativity" (*The Feast of Fools,* page 75).

With these thoughts in mind, let us look at the seasons of the liturgical year as they apply to telling the story of our people in the past and to seeing that story happening in our own lives today. The liturgical year helps us to identify our story with the story of God's people as told in the Bible and throughout history. Our own personal, individual quest for wholeness is of course a part of our people's common struggle. This personal quest for wholeness is caught up and celebrated in the annual round of the church year. But we must always remember that the Bible is the story of a people. The Bible tells the story of a community, a nation, a people called out uniquely to proclaim the coming reign of Christ in the face of the present reign dominated by human rebellion against God's intentions. Thus the church year calls us back to God's agenda. It confronts us with creation and history as God sees it; a far different vision of the world than we are accustomed to. The church year, by definition then, is radical. It shakes the foundations beneath our feet. As we live out the round of seasons, feasts and fasts, let us keep in balance the personal quest of the individual with the social call to do God's will "on earth as in heaven."

The following brief chart summarizes the more detailed discussion of the church seasons found in chapters 5, 6, and 7.

The Season	Recalls the Past	Celebrates the Present
Advent	We recall how our people waited for the coming of the Messiah. After the death of Jesus, the Christians waited for Christ to come again.	We express our dreams and hopes for this life and for life at the Second Coming. This is a time of sharing our visions of that life in Christ. We experience anxiety as we face the unknown, and expectant hope as we share our dreams of life to come.
Christmas	We recall the birth of Jesus in Bethlehem.	We celebrate all those times of new birth that have come into our own lives. We are called to look for Christ in the child who walks by our side, and in the oppressed peoples of the world who cry out for justice.

The Season	Recalls the Past	Celebrates the Present
Epiphany	We recall how Jesus revealed himself to the world. (The word *Epiphany* means a *revealing* or *manifesting*.) We recall the stories of • the visit of the Magi • Jesus' baptism • his first miracle at Cana • the calling of the disciples • Jesus' going forth into the world to proclaim the good news, to heal, and to call people into the Kingdom of God.	We realize *our* responsibility to reveal or manifest Christ's love and power to the world. We recognize *our* calling as disciples. We are to carry the light of the Gospel into the world. This is the season in which we get in touch with our own mission and vocation. We celebrate Christ's continuing revelation in the world today.
Lent	We recall Jesus' forty days in the wilderness and his temptations. Looking back to the Old Testament, we remember the Israelites' forty years of wilderness wandering. They succumbed to temptation, but Jesus did not.	This is a time to be in touch with our own "wilderness wandering" as we prepare for new risen life in Christ. We look at our temptations and failures as individuals and as a society. As we dare to reflect, we discover things about ourselves we dislike and cannot accept. "Lord have mercy," we cry out. But the wilderness was also the place where our people made covenant with God. This is our time of either preparing to make covenant at our baptism/confirmation or to reaffirm our covenant with God after realizing how far we have strayed in our pilgrimage of faith.
Holy Week	During Holy Week we dramatize the last week of Jesus' life, including his arrest, trial, and crucifixion.	We walk with Jesus, the disciples and generations of pilgrims on the road to the Cross. We stand cheering with the crowds on Palm Sunday. We kneel in anguish and without hope at the foot of the Cross on Good Friday. We are buried with Christ on Holy Saturday so that we can be raised up new with Christ on Easter Sunday. On this anguished walk we face our own trials and inevitable death with the realization that God shares with us these moments of pain and the unknown. In Holy week we are also in touch with those times when we have to "die" to lost relationships and dreams about ourselves and our world.
Easter	We proclaim Jesus' resurrection.	At Easter (a season of seven weeks) we proclaim our own hope in the resurrection and our hope for those who have died. We live for seven weeks as if the reign of God has fully come; a time of joy and wonder at God's gift of grace revealed in Jesus' resurrection and in the reality of resurrection that touches us today.

The Day of Pentecost	We dramatize in word, act, and symbol the Apostles' receiving the gift of the Holy Spirit, the seal of the New Covenant (or New Testament) in Christ.	We acknowledge and celebrate the Holy Spirit who comes to *us* through the sacraments of the Church and in our experiences of power and inspiration.
The Season after Pentecost/ Ordinary Time	After the Day of Pentecost, the lectionary leads us chapter by chapter through the sections of the Gospel that have not been read during the seasons of Advent through Easter. Several epistles are also read sequentially during this half of the year. Old Testament readings are chosen in thematic harmony with the Gospel texts.	Roman Catholics call this period "Ordinary Time." We recognize God in the ordinary moments of our lives as well as in the times of intense revelation and celebration.

Thus the church year provides us with a structure in which we tell the story of Jesus and of the people of God again and again. It is a familiar story, and the more familiar it becomes, the more power we find in it. We gradually discover that we are in that story ourselves. As mentioned earlier, each season touches aspects of our lives that we experience all year long but celebrate at a particular time. A friend of mine calls these the "seasons of the soul," and I like the feel of that phrase. So now we find ourselves telling *our* story within the framework of the Christ story. Gradually in our life's journey we discover the deep and wonder-filled truth that Christ is with *us* in our struggle and our moments of revelation as we are with him. Our stories meld together so that they become The Story.

Bob Haertig of the United Church of Christ has developed the following guide for telling our story within the framework of the Christ story.

As I reflected on my own life, using this guide, I found myself thinking back to the hopes my parents had for me as a child. This brought mixed feelings of appreciation and disappointment. My rebellion against some of those hopes had caused feelings of guilt and regret. But on the positive side, I was thankful that my life was shaped by an environment in which others had voiced expectations and dreams for me. My thoughts then moved to the dreams I had for myself in youth and in later years. I shared those dreams and expectations with the other members of my small group, and they

shared theirs with me. In bringing out feelings that fitted the seasonal theme of Advent, I got in touch with my roots, my own yearnings, my feelings of guilt, anticipation, and hope. I found I had feelings and experiences in common with others in the group, and we grew closer together in the process of sharing. We did this kind of reflecting and sharing at each season of the church year.

As time goes on, we may find ourselves using the seasons as symbol words for our own experiences. If someone says to me "I had a real Lenten time last night," I can know exactly what he or she is feeling. We may use all kinds of biblical symbols to convey the meaning at a deeper level. "My golden calf was the temptation to refuse the promotion," my friend may go on to say. Christmas times are not restricted to the middle of winter. I can say "Merry Christmas" to my Christian friend in the middle of July if I have had an experience of new birth and wonder. Then as Christmas time comes on the liturgical calendar, my year's experiences of Christmas are lifted up and celebrated. Christ has been born into my life this year on countless occasions, I realize as I sing the familiar carols and share in the Eucharist. The church year tells my story in Christ, and I begin to realize the holiness of my life. My story becomes one with my people's story.

One of the most important gifts we can share in our parish life is to help persons sense, tell, and celebrate their stories. In their storytelling they will gain that sense of power and affirmation that comes when we realize the eternal significance of our lives as the people of God.

As we share the yearly round of Judeo-Christian festivals, feasts, and seasons, our people can begin to find their unique individual story within the great biblical story of God's people. We too are searching for the freedom and fulfillment of the "promised land." Jesus comes and heals us within the flesh and blood of our human relationships. The Holy Spirit touches us as with "tongues of fire" at Pentecost. If we can feel that story happening within us and see ourselves on an internal quest for wholeness, then we can see our struggle and our hopes within a framework of power and hope. If we feel that even in crisis we are on a pilgrimage in faith, we may realize that even tragedy has meaning. On the other hand, to feel that our life in aimless is to taste despair.

And so as liturgists and educators we help persons to realize and share with others the significance and the power of their story. We support them in their journey, and we celebrate that journey together as the people of God. There *is* real power in sharing our life stories. Each one of us feels that we are the only one who has felt a particular way. Everyone else can love and forgive us except ourselves. Or we carry guilt and anxiety around for years. Ironically, others assume that we have everything under control; we seem so calm and "with it," and so they think that they are the only ones who feel anxiety and fear.

As you begin to hear one another's story, watch the faces in the circle. You will see people identifying with pain; you will see looks of relief and wonder; you will hear laughter and perhaps some crying. People are being released from bondage in that moment of storytelling; they are finding freedom and liberation as they begin to discover the common touching points of their story. ("I didn't know you felt that way too! I thought you were always on top of things. Now, that gives me some hope!") As we begin to uncover and unravel those things about us that we dislike and cannot accept, we begin to realize that the other persons *do* accept us. We were sure we would blow our image and that everyone would get up and leave us in disgust. Instead,

people are reaching out to say they are there too.

Then we need to return to the Bible and hear again the stories we have been hearing perhaps all our lives. God has called people just like us to be kings, prophets, and apostles. We do

---

Seasons of the Soul

Each and every one of you is a storyteller. Your lives are your stories and you share your stories with each other.
 —Pleasant de Spain

You have four tasks:

1. Chart your own life story. (Do this individually. Draw this chart out as a trail or chart it on a straight line on the paper you have been given.)

Your Hopes (your Advent times):
The hopes of your parents before you were born. The hopes you have for yourself. The hopes in which you were nurtured.

Your Births (your Christmas times):
The ways you have experienced the fulfillment of those hopes. Your own literal birth date, place, circumstances.

Your Journey (your Epiphany times):
What you have done with the life you have been given.

Your Suffering (your Lenten times):
Your setbacks, losses, struggles, pain.

Your Experiences of Resurrection
(your Easter times):
Your glimpses of wholeness. Insights gained through your sufferings. Religious experiences that have changed your life.

Your Mission (your Pentecost time):
How you see your unique mission in life.

2. Share your personal journey (story) with your group.

3. Affirm one another and thank God for each person in the group. Name them, bless them, hug them, and pray for them.

4. Offer the total group's journey to God and thank God for it.

not look back at St. Peter as the great apostle because he was perfect. We look back to him with love and honor because he was able to acknowledge and accept his weakness and his failures. With his acknowledgment came the understanding that Jesus had accepted and forgiven him. Without the story there would have been no acknowledgment. Without the acknowledgment there could have been no awareness of forgiveness. And so it is with us.

We often feel that we must see Jesus as the perfect model whom we must emulate. But God comes to us not in perfect strength but in weakness—open to pain, frustration, and temptation. God does not work out his plan in history through perfection but through the struggle of his people as they deal with agony, temptations, and so-called failures. This is certainly the biblical story that we dramatize in the liturgy.

This does not mean that God condones or encourages sin or weakness. Rather, it means that he understands our struggle and is with us at every stage of our journey. God *is* with us in our struggle. He is with us in the Advent times of our lives, in the Christmas and the Lenten times. Knowing that, we can experience his presence with us in the Easter and the Pentecost times when we proclaim resurrection and the indwelling of the Holy Spirit. We do have a story to tell!

After this overview of how our story is dramatized in liturgy and in the seasons of the church year, we go on in the remainder of this book to look at the specific seasons, Sundays, and festivals of the church year to see how the biblical story and our own story are expressed in our life together that we celebrate at the Eucharist.

Chapter 4
How to Design a Parish Religious Education Program Based on the Church's Liturgy; Three Model Programs

From this chapter on, we move from general ideas about sharing the biblical story to specific suggestions for using our common Episcopal, Roman Catholic, and Lutheran lectionaries as the basis of our religious education program. (A lectionary is a collection of Bible readings that are assigned to be read on particular days of the church year.) There are many lectionary commentaries published for the preacher, but this commentary is offered for religious educators who are interested in looking to the lectionary for the theme and focus of the religious education program in the parish and for parents wanting to share ideas with their children during the week at home. Having heard a Bible story in the liturgy on Sunday, what can we do during the week to help our family apply the concepts of the story to our daily life? What can we do in the learning community of the parish to reinforce the story for our people and to help them *experience* that story happening in their lives? As you look to this section as a resource, it is important to realize that you are using a commentary, not a curriculum. This book is meant to help you in your parish and home setting to move from reading and discussing comments about the weekly readings to designing *your own* curriculum. This chapter provides guidelines for designing your own curriculum. As a further aid

to your planning, I have worked out three specific designs based on the lectionary: one for the season of Epiphany in Year A, one for the Easter season of Year B, and one for the summer Sundays of Year C, so that you can see how the homegrown design process works in practice.

Though this commentary is tied to the common lectionary of the Episcopal, Roman Catholic, and Lutheran churches, persons from other denominations will find it helpful also. The broad seasonal ideas will stimulate your thinking, and you can work out your own congregational lectionary of readings to use in common with the preacher during the various seasons of the year. If a published lectionary seems restrictive, remember that many denominations use uniform Sunday School lessons based on a common reading of the Scriptures, so in effect they are already accustomed to using a "lectionary." Here we simply extend the idea to include the readings shared in the worship so that there is one common theme and approach used in both worship and Sunday School.

The custom of the lectionary is a very ancient one that goes back to Jewish synagogue practices; particular sections of Scripture were read at various festival times. By the fourth century the growing Christian Church adopted the practice of emphasizing certain portions of Scripture suited to the seasons and festivals of the year.

Our lectionaries, then, come out of a rich and ancient heritage. Our present lectionary consists of two major divisions. The first is a three-year cycle of readings appointed for the Sundays and holy days of the church year. From the First Sunday in Advent (the beginning of the church year) through the last Sunday after Pentecost (the last Sunday of the church year) we are led through the books of the New Testament and great portions of the Old Testament. During the first year's cycle (Year A) we follow the Gospel of Matthew. During the second year we follow Mark; during the third year we read Luke. The Gospel of John is used in all three years during the Easter season and at other points in the church year.

The second major division is a daily lectionary for use by individuals in their daily devotions or by communities of people who gather to worship together during the week. In the Episcopal and Roman Catholic churches this daily lectionary follows a two-year cycle so that the person following it will read through the Bible once every two years.

Chapter 3 of this book outlines the major themes of the seasons of the church year. Under the umbrella of the seasonal theme, each week of the church year has its own theme based on the gospel appointed for that week. The Old Testament reading is chosen to parallel or add a dimension to the theme expressed in the gospel. The selection from the epistles *sometimes* follows that theme, but in many cases the epistle reading is part of a chapter-by-chapter reading of a particular letter; in these situations, the epistle has its own independent theme not related to the Old Testament and gospel readings. Psalm responses to the readings are also appointed for each Sunday and add to the richness of the thematic expression. (Many of the psalms have been set to music, and our hymns frequently reflect the influence of the psalms. This rich heritage of music can add a great deal to expressing the theme of the lectionary. For example, Martin Luther received his inspiration for the well-known hymn "A Mighty Fortress Is Our God" from Psalm 46. If this psalm is appointed for the week,

the singing of Luther's hymn will carry the theme in both the sung and spoken word. See Appendix I for comments on some psalms that are especially appropriate in the religious education setting.)

In addition to the three Bible readings and the psalm response, each Sunday has an assigned prayer called a Collect. (The word *collect* comes from the Latin expression *oratio ad collectam* meaning *prayer of the congregation*.) The Collect may express the theme of the gospel or of the season, but most often it simply gathers the congregation in prayer before they hear the biblical readings and sermon.

Taken together, the Collect, Old Testament selection, responsorial psalm, and selections from the epistles and gospels appointed for each Sunday are called the Proper of the day. (Roman Catholic liturgy has a Prayer over the Gifts and a Prayer after Communion which are also "proper" to the day. Many churches also have "proper" prefaces for certain feast days and seasons.) The Proper gives us the theme that needs to be expressed by liturgist, preacher, musician, religious educator, and parent. In coordinating all the elements of church celebration, we are doing what we do in our celebrations at home. At a birthday party, for example, everything we do emphasizes and reinforces the theme and spirit of the occasion, from the table decorations to the songs we sing and the games we play. Keep this in mind as you plan your liturgical celebrations, because each week of the church year also has a theme and a spirit that needs to be emphasized by everything we do together, from choosing hymns to placing posters on the walls of the parish learning center.

Time will not always permit such planning for every celebration of the liturgy, but we should hold this goal out as an ideal for liturgist and educator. As we grow more accustomed to working together and have more history to draw on, we may find ourselves increasing the number of times when we can reach that ideal.

Three Planning Steps

In our constant grasping for time we are always tempted to take shortcuts to program designs.

But good programs do not come from shortcuts. Even if we purchase the best curriculum published, we must still make it our own by walking through the suggested designs with a planning group made up of committed persons who meet regularly to coordinate the religious education and liturgical life of the parish. Persons responsible for the liturgy—musicians, dramatists, storytellers, parents, youth, artists, and other persons with particular talents or interests—should be on the team in addition to the persons we normally think of when we talk about teachers or religious educators.

Planners should follow three basic steps in designing a program: first, a preliminary meeting and the subsequent "homework" assigned at it; second, a brainstorming session after the "homework" has been done; and third, a number of regular meetings to plan the week-by-week programs or events.

The sample program for the Epiphany season of Year A will illustrate these three steps in concrete detail. But for now, some comments on the brainstorming session, step two, are in order. This session, like any good brainstorming session, should encourage participants to submit all ideas that come to mind—anything even remotely applicable to the theme—with no initial attempt at organizing or evaluating them. Are there films, television series, filmstrips we can draw on? What about that curriculum that has been used in past years and now lies carefully stored in some upstairs closet? What about current published curricula? You may want to adapt ideas from such published sources or use the curricula in their entirety to explore certain seasons, concepts, sacraments, or biblical stories. Go through a published curriculum and make it your own by exploring each suggested step and by brainstorming changes or additional ideas. Because brainstorming your own program ideas does take time, you may want to use a published curriculum as the basis of your year-long program but intersperse your own "homegrown" ideas for specific times of the church year or for particular events in the life of the parish.

After brainstorming general ideas about a seasonal program, we brainstorm the specific design that will form the substance of each session within that program. The following form,

Essential Points in Planning an Event

Purpose of the event

When and who

Background information for leaders

How will we
open or launch the event?

present the story or concept?

help participants to explore and experience the story or concept?

help participants to respond creatively?

conclude and/or evaluate the event?

adapted from Donald L. Griggs, *Teaching Teachers to Teach*, outlines the essentials for planning a session. It helps us make sure that all the bases of design planning are covered in the brainstorming session. (Notice that this chapter's three sample programs follow this format, with minor variations.)

The following comments on certain items in this form may be helpful.

Purpose of the event: It is important that the group have in mind a definite purpose. What do we want to do today, this weekend, this session? We can easily get caught in the trap of coming up with many good ideas but then finding ourselves frustrated because the ideas don't seem to go anywhere. Midway through the planning session, or worse yet, at the end of it, we find ourselves asking why we did what we did.

When and who: The planning team must decide when the event will be offered and for whom. Many times during the planning you will have to ask whether your plans are appropriate for the intended group and for the allotted time.

Background information for leaders: If there is specific information essential for the leaders, write down what it is so that they can be prepared for their task.

Launching device: Each session needs something that launches the participants into experiencing the session. The launching device sets the stage for what is to follow by generating interest, curiosity, or immediate emotional participation. The launching device may be as simple as an Advent wreath set out on a table on the Sundays of Advent. It may be a film, role play, record, brief game, or any number of other devices. If it is successful, it will draw the participants together with a common interest and soon be forgotten as the group goes on to explore the story or concepts to be shared.

Presenting: From the launching device we move to the specific presentation to be made to the group. This is the input, the actual material we want to share. If we are following the lectionary, the material will be either the story

told within the readings appointed for the day or the concepts behind the readings. If we are focusing on a rite of passage or something growing out of the life of the congregation, we will present the ideas associated with that passage point or event (see Appendix II). For example, say "Next Sunday during the liturgy the McAllisters are going to celebrate their fiftieth wedding anniversary by renewing their wedding vows during the offertory. So we want to talk about Christian marriage in our time. How many of you have been to a wedding?" Some time is then spent in presenting the concept of Christian marriage.

Exploring: If what is presented is to take root with the participants, they must have a chance to explore the story or concepts shared. This is the time for them to begin to experience in their own ways the ideas presented. What does Christian marriage mean to them in their families? What does it mean to the many children who live in families where the parents are divorced? What various kinds of covenants and commitments have adults and children made?

Responding creatively: After raising questions the participants need to be encouraged to experience the concept or story themselves by getting down inside the feelings that grow out of what has been shared. A group of teenagers, for example, could design their own wedding liturgy, or they could role play a counseling session where a couple faces divorce. Response can come from painting, role playing, filmmaking, writing, puppet shows, "radio shows" taped on a cassette recorder, or from other ideas brainstormed by the group.

Concluding: The session should close in a definite way. What has been experienced needs to be shared, however briefly. If participants have risked being vulnerable in a discussion and creative response, that participation should be recognized and affirmed. The theme and the experience should be tied together before persons leave the group. The conclusion can be a simple prayer of thanksgiving that mentions in a personal way the experience of the session. It can be a brief time of sharing in which everyone has a chance to offer a closing thought. Or the closing can be tied to the concluding words of the liturgy. For example, the leader says "Let us go forth rejoicing in the power of the Spirit." And the group responds "Thanks be to God."

Evaluating: Persons participating and leading the session need to have some measure of how the session went. Simple written evaluation sheets usually generate more honest feedback to the leadership team than the spoken word. The team should gather as soon as possible to go over the evaluations. Then what we consider as mistakes or failures or frustrations can become learning experiences rather than defeats. This is where having a clearly stated purpose is important. If we don't know what we set out to do, we have no way of knowing if we have accomplished it! For mature participants an evaluation might include questions and statements such as
• What was most meaningful to you during our session today?
• What was least meaningful?
• In a future session, I wish we could....
(Complete the sentence with your idea or need.)
• I feel free to express my ideas and feelings in the group. (Rate your feelings on this scale.)

Low 1 2 3 4 5 6 7 8 9 10 High

Or the evaluation may simply be a question or two asked of the group at the end of the event. "What did you learn today?" "How do you feel about what we've done together?"

Working with a planning sheet will assure you that you have walked through the design and have considered what is necessary for your design to work smoothly. The group may have filled sheets of newsprint with good ideas, but if the ideas are not presented well or do not fit the purpose or context of what you are trying to do,

they will fall flat in the actual carrying out of the design. Walking through the design in the order in which the design needs to unfold will also help the leaders as they administer the design in the learning community setting. Leaders need to have a clearly defined direction in mind as they begin an actual event. They need to have worked through it emotionally and intellectually before attempting to share it with a group. Even if you are using a published curriculum that shows the steps of the design process, it is still essential to put that design into your own words and talk it out with the rest of the planning team. In this way the published design will become your own personal design by the time you come to share it.

With these ideas in mind, we will now walk through the actual planning for three seasonal designs. For the balance of this chapter, assume that we have been commissioned by the parish religious education committee to design events based on the lectionary. We are a part of a team whose members come with the varying backgrounds suggested (see page 99). The religious education committee wants to try out this idea and introduce it gradually over a period of three years. We are commissioned to design one program for the season of Epiphany in Year A, one for the season of Easter in Year B, and one for the summer Sundays of Year C. For the balance of the year the parish will continue using a published curriculum and age-grouped classes. We have been given free rein during these three seasons to brainstorm, recruit, publicize, and administer the religious education program. The pastor will be meeting with us from time to time to insure a coordinated effort between us and those responsible for the liturgy. We will use the material in this book as the basis for our program design.

We are now meeting for the first time to lay the groundwork for our Epiphany program. Imagine yourself sitting around the table with me and with others as we begin. Are you ready? Here we go!

Three Model Programs

Designing a Program
for the Season
of Epiphany, Year A

The first step for each member of the design
team is to do some "homework." At a
preliminary meeting you should agree to read the
Scripture passages appointed for the season, and
chapter 5, pages 156-162, for my comments on
those readings. Above all, agree to read and
reflect on the lectionary readings themselves,
especially those for Year A. Before the first
regular meeting, members should also check the
parish library and other libraries for books
dealing with the Epiphany season. Ask friends
from other liturgical churches about traditions
they have followed—including traditions their
ancestors brought with them from their
homelands. Ask older members of your own
parish and of other parishes to share their
memories with you. Do they know folktales or
legends associated with the season? At this
preliminary meeting or at the brainstorming
meeting the pastor may want to give some
theological background on the Epiphany season
and share some reflections on the readings to
supplement the ideas found in this book.

Step two consists of a brainstorming
session about the "homework" done and about
how to use the results in designing a program for
the Epiphany season. Share the fruits of your
Bible reading and reflection and other study as
well as firsthand information gathered about
Epiphany traditions. Draw on your own
childhood memories and the memories of persons
you have talked to. Record ideas as they are
shared; newsprint is ideal for this, since everyone
can see and recall what has been discussed.

Here are some random brainstorming
ideas that grew out of such a session. Notice that
these *are* random ideas; no attempt was made to
place them in any order or to evaluate them; we
simply recorded ideas as they came up. Since the
readings of this season focus on discipleship, we
centered our brainstorming on two questions:
Whom did Jesus call as disciples, and what does
it mean to *be* a disciple?

Brainstorming Ideas for the Epiphany Season

• The disciples were ordinary people. As we look
at the people God has called to be leaders, we
find that this is often the case. He doesn't seem
to choose the people we might ordinarily think of
as leaders in society. Our readings from
1 Corinthians during the Epiphany season also
remind us that the first-century Church was
composed of people struggling to achieve faith.
They were not perfect Christians living wholly in
the light of Christ. They bickered, argued, often
lost their sense of vision, and caused Paul many
problems. As we talk about those early Christians
and as we think about the important persons of
the Bible, we may be able to see that we too can
be instruments of God's love and healing power
even in the midst of our own struggles as
individuals and as a church. We are not perfect,
and neither were they. There is hope for the
Church today!
• St. Peter is the apostle we know the most
about. Even Peter did not realize the full
significance of the Gospel that was to be
proclaimed to *all* people. In Galatians 2:11-14 we
learn that Cephas (Peter) took sides against Paul
and broke the unity of the Church by not eating
with the uncircumcised Christians.
• God demanded a radical faith from the people
he called. To follow the Word of the Lord meant
taking stands and facing persecution, anger, and
hatred. Apostleship today, then, may mean going
against the norms of our society and thereby
facing rejection from our neighbors.
• Let's begin our confirmation class on the first
Sunday of Epiphany. On that Sunday we recall
the baptism of Jesus, and we can offer the
sacrament of baptism to those desiring it for
themselves or their children. Everyone can renew
their baptismal vows as a part of the celebration
of the sacrament. At offertory time, those
wanting to become part of the confirmation class
can commit themselves to their quest for
apostleship, and the congregation can bless them
on their way.
• The mention of the Spirit of God descending
like a dove at Jesus' baptism can lead us into a
study of the Holy Spirit. Answering our call to
discipleship is impossible unless we realize the
power of the Holy Spirit dwelling within each
of us.

• We need to help persons appreciate the difference between a disciple and an apostle. A disciple is one who follows a master and learns the master's ways. The word comes from the Latin word *discipulus*, meaning *student*. The title *apostle* comes from the Greek word *apostolos*, meaning *messenger* or *envoy*. The titles denote the change in role of the twelve men who surrounded Jesus. Before his death they were merely his students or followers. They learned his ways. But after his resurrection they received the gift of the Holy Spirit and became apostles. They now went out in Christ's name and acted on their own with the power of his living presence.

• Participants need to identify their own role as disciples and apostles. What are we all called to become as Christ's apostles? Part of our understanding of discipleship or apostleship is that we live our lives in such a way as to point beyond ourselves to Christ. We witness with our lives to Christ's presence in the lives of his people. How *do* we witness to that faith and presence?

• Let's study Peter during the Epiphany season. Look closely at his strengths and weaknesses so that participants can identify with him as a real person who struggled in much the same way as we do. Look at the whole season of Epiphany through the eyes of Peter. What were his thoughts when he heard Jesus' Sermon on the Mount? How do you think he felt when Jesus told him to leave his fishing nets and follow him? Role play the conversation Peter might have had with his family when he went to tell them he was leaving to follow Jesus. How do you think his family felt? Would they have understood him?

• One way of looking at the Sermon on the Mount is to see it as a job description or guidelines for the apostle. This is what we might expect in our life as apostles: Blessings come to us through our struggle even in the face of rejection and persecution. We are apostles when we help bring peace, when we struggle for what is right, when we can somehow understand our enemies.

• Make a slide show of Peter's life or a home movie of his experiences.

• Tie in the Matthew 5:14-16 ("You are the light of the world") passage with the Feast of Lights service. Light a candle at the beginning of the

sessions during Epiphany and encourage families to light candles at their dinner table and to recall the sayings of Jesus.

• With older participants, study persons we might consider apostles in our contemporary world, people who have taken stands and have faced the rejection of their own people. The films *A Man for All Seasons* and *Becket* would also provide opportunity for good reflection.

We have now recorded our scattered brainstorming ideas about the Epiphany season. Many of these ideas will never find their way into the program, but they will influence our thinking and will be there to draw on this year or in future years when we focus on these same readings or themes. (Be *sure* to keep a file of all your ideas and completed designs, along with an evaluation of how the designs actually worked out. This information will be invaluable for future planners.)

At this meeting we also brainstorm about which of our ideas will actually go into the program—which ones we might emphasize during the whole season.

At this meeting we also brainstorm the overall seasonal objective and discuss which ideas will fit in with that objective. (In the sample program given below, several of our preliminary ideas found their way into the final design, and the emphasis on St. Peter was even carried over into our plans for Easter of Year B.)

The rest of the planning meetings will be devoted to the third step, the planning of week-by-week programs. In these meetings we use our planning sheets and go through the disciplined process of organizing our scattered ideas into a coherent seasonal program. Regular meetings should begin about in July—approximately six months before Epiphany.

The following week-by-week design is an example of what we might have come up with in designing our program.

Celebrating the Feast of the Epiphany: Twelfth Night

The term *Twelfth Night* may be familiar to us as the title of a Shakespearean play. The term is an old one in our English heritage; it is another name for the Feast of the Epiphany, which falls twelve days after Christmas. A Twelfth Night party can be fun for the parish family, and the Epiphany story is told very effectively through such a celebration. Because this event is so informal, I will describe it without going through the more detailed planning outline given above.

(If a Twelfth Night party is planned, you may want to tone down your parish Christmas programs. With all the pressures of the pre-Christmas season, holding off the major effort for Twelfth Night can be a welcome change. It also serves to remind us that Christmas, after all, is not just one day. Preparations for the Epiphany celebration can be a part of the celebration of the twelve days of Christmas.)

The Twelfth Night party begins with the people of the parish gathering for refreshments. At the appointed time the King's cake is brought out. Hidden within the cake are three beans or three coins. The persons who find the beans or coins in their piece of cake are crowned kings or queens for the evenings. While they are being outfitted for their high and majestic office, the rest of the guests are following the custom of stripping the parish tree of all ornaments. (German Lutherans call this "plundering the tree.") Candy canes on each branch entice the children to participate in the stripping process. Then the tree is ceremoniously removed from the room and saved for the Lenten season, when it is stripped of its branches and made into a cross that can be carried in procession or hung somewhere in the parish building.

The kings and queens, now in their costumes, are ushered back into the parish hall with great fanfare and pomp and are seated on thrones befitting their office. (Properly speaking, it was wise men or astrologers who came seeking Jesus, but the well-known hymn "We Three Kings" influences the party motif, as do some of the traditions that have accompanied the feast.) An officially appointed storyteller or court jester then gathers the people together before the thrones to tell the story of the three kings or wise men who went seeking the infant Jesus. The legendary names from the hymn are used to identify the travelers, and the story is narrated from Matthew 2:1-12. If there is a creche in the parish hall, the youngest child present can place the kings at the creche. (In our parish we move

the figures of Mary and Joseph closer to the sanctuary creche each Sunday of Advent. During the twelve days of Christmas the figures of the wise men are also gradually moved toward the creche and are finally placed at the creche on Twelfth Night.)

Now that the kings and queens have been duly crowned and their authority established in the telling of their story, they must be entertained royally. Party participants are divided into groups and given pantomime skits to perform before the royalty. The planning group may have other ideas for entertaining royalty. There are several traditional Twelfth Night plays that can be obtained from your library. *Amahl and the Night Visitor* is probably the best known.* Henry Van Dyke's story, *The Other Wise Man*, also offers an excellent reading for the occasion.† (It is out of print, but consult libraries.)

We conclude our evening's celebration with the Feast of Lights liturgy. The group enters the darkened nave. The Paschal candle is lit to denote the light that came into the world with the birth of Jesus. John 1:1-18, which speaks of Jesus as light, can be read during the lighting of the Paschal candle. Then we sing "We Three Kings," and as the kings' names are mentioned, the kings enter, bearing gifts for the Christ child. As each king arrives at the Paschal candle, he takes a small candle, lights it, and remains in the sanctuary with his lit candle. Then the names of the apostles are called out, and one by one children come forward to take the place of the apostles. They too light a candle from the Paschal candle. Several more children walk down the aisle to take their place in the sanctuary; they represent the bishops, priests, deacons, and lay persons who have carried the Christ light to us throughout the generations. Then each person in the congregation receives a small candle. Now the nave and sanctuary are filled with candle light. When people leave they carry their lighted candles into the night. Some make a game of seeing if they can get home without their candle going out. When they arrive home, they place the candles on

Amahl and the Night Visitor (New York: Whittlesey Publishers, 1952).
†Henry Van Dyke, "The Other Wise Man," *The Blue Flower* (New York: Charles Scribner's Sons, 1902).

the table and say a prayer of thanksgiving for the Christ light before the children go to bed.

The actions of this brief but moving liturgy are interspersed with the final singing of some of the familiar Christmas carols.

Note: The Roman Catholic name for the post-Epiphany time differs from that of Episcopalians and Lutherans. Below, **E, L,** and **RC** designate the three churches.

First Sunday after Epiphany   E, L
Baptism of the Lord   RC
Today we hear the story of Jesus' baptism. This would be an ideal time for a parish celebration of the sacrament of baptism. It is very important to make baptism a major celebration of the church family. Not only does this practice reinforce the communal nature of baptism, but it also serves as a valuable time of recommitment and sacramental learning for the entire congregation. The sacrament should be centered around a preparation time that emphasizes commitment and teaching. The liturgy of baptism, with its rich symbolism, is perhaps one of the greatest teaching opportunities we have in the parish, so we should make every effort to take advantage of this opportunity.

Purpose of the event: To expose participants to the theological concepts expressed in the sacrament of baptism.

When and who: This design can be used in age-grouped classes or in an intergenerational setting before the liturgy.

Background information for leaders: Read ideas under "launching device" and "presenting" below.

Launching device: Tell the story of the exodus as it is outlined in A Guide to Stories of the Bible. This is *the* key story for understanding our Judeo-Christian picture of life in covenant with God. Emphasize that it was in being led through the waters of the Sea of Reeds (or the Red Sea, depending on the translation) that the Hebrews realized they were God's people, called into freedom through their covenant relationship with God. Jesus is *our* Moses who leads us out of our enslavement to guilt, fear, anxiety, sin, and oppression into the wholeness known through God's healing love. It is in being "led through the waters" of our baptism that we realize we too

are God's people, called into freedom through our covenant relationship with God.

Presenting: Talk about the water of baptism as an "outward and visible sign" of our life in Christ.

1. In our exodus story the water of baptism is related to the water of the Sea of Reeds. As we "pass through the waters," we become aware that we are called out to be God's people. Actually, the origin of baptism is this epic act that predates John the Baptist by many generations. Proselytes to the Jewish faith were immersed in water so that they too could say they had passed through the waters as God's people. Children raised in the Jewish faith had passed through the waters by virtue of their ancestors' experience, but proselytes had to incorporate themselves into the story by physically moving through the waters.

2. Water expresses new life. An infant is born out of the water of the mother's womb. It is probable that all life evolved out of the waters over eons of time. And so we are born into the Church out of the waters of baptism. The term *born-again Christian*, used by some persons to denote their conversion experience, expresses this idea. Baptism marks our birth into the Body of Christ just as the breaking of the water in the mother's womb marks the beginning of the child's birth into the world. Jesus' conversation with Nicodemus in John 3:4-5 expresses this theological understanding poetically.

3. Water is necessary for the origin and survival of plant and animal life. In John 4:13-14, Jesus promises the woman at the well that she will never thirst again if she knows him. In John 7:37-39, Jesus speaks of the thirsty person coming to him and discovering "living water." We too speak of "thirsting for knowledge." The waters of baptism express the reality that to know Jesus is to have one's thirst quenched eternally. Jesus is our source of life, growth, and sustenance.

4. Water is a symbol of cleansing. Frequently we use the word *clean* or *dirty* to express how we feel about what we've done. "You can forget about him in your investigation. He's clean," says the police officer on the television detective show.

We should get in touch with the feelings of "being dirty" in the sense of feeling badly about ourselves. Then read what Jesus says to Peter as he is about to wash his feet: "He who has bathed does not need to wash, except for his feet, but he is clean all over; and you are clean...(John 13:10). Think of those words as the baptismal waters touch the person at baptism. Christians will inevitably become "stained" with a thousand marks of guilt and wrong in a lifetime, but baptism is the "outward and visible sign" of the cleansing forgiveness that is always known through Jesus.

5. Water is a symbol of death. To those of us who do not swim well, water can be frightening. When someone is totally immersed at baptism, this feeling of dying in order to experience new life is felt more fully. In order to be born again into our relationship with Christ, we must first die to our old way of approaching life. Thus part of baptism involves touching death. St. Paul reminded the Galatians that in a sense he had participated in Christ's crucifixion in order to be born into life with him. "I have been crucified with Christ; it is no longer I who live, but Christ who lives in me; and the life I now live in the flesh I live by faith in the Son of God, who loved me and gave himself for me" (Galatians 2:20). Again we see an allusion to dying to our old self so that we may be born into our new life with Christ.

At a deeper level of death/birth is the Christian understanding of resurrection. "I am the resurrection and the life; he who believes in me, though he die, yet shall he live, and whoever lives and believes in me shall never die..." (John 11:25-26). The waters of baptism help us express the deep truth that in dying we find new life in Christ, both in this age and in the age to come.

6. Water is an expression of covenant. As a result of passing through the waters of the Sea of Reeds, the Hebrews were led to Mount Sinai and the covenant made there. As a result of our passing through the waters of baptism, we are led into our baptismal covenant with God. Simply to be released from bondage does not lead to freedom. To live in freedom, a people must live with a sense of responsibility toward one another and toward creation. The covenant made at Mount Sinai pointed to a way of freedom and justice. The Ten Commandments or Decalogue are only a very small portion of the total covenant. Thumb through the books of Exodus, Leviticus, and Numbers to get an idea of what keeping the entire covenant meant for the Israelites. Actually there are 613 separate ordinances contained within that covenant. Still, the Decalogue gives us an idea of what Christians, as well as the Jews, are called to live out. Three of the commandments speak of the relationship between God and the people. One of the commandments deals with keeping the ritual code of Israel, and the remaining six are directed at relationships among people. The Mosaic covenant is concerned that justice be done. God is a God of history who meets the people in their struggle for that justice.

As we talk about living in the covenant, we need to point to the Baptismal Covenant in *The Book of Common Prayer* (pages 304-305). After affirming the Apostles' Creed, those persons being baptized are asked

- Will you continue in the apostles' teaching and fellowship, in the breaking of bread, and in the prayers?
- Will you persevere in resisting evil, and, whenever you fall into sin, repent and return to the Lord?
- Will you proclaim by word and example the Good News of God in Christ?
- Will you seek and serve Christ in all persons, loving your neighbor as yourself?
- Will you strive for justice and peace among all people, and respect the dignity of every human being?

These baptismal questions, like the Ten Commandments of the Old Testament, provide us with a constant guide to what is involved in our covenant relationship with the risen Christ. Finally, in John 13:34 we hear the basis of this covenant that we are called to live. "A new commandment I give to you, that you love one another; even as I have loved you, that you also love one another."

We cannot comprehend the Christian faith without an understanding of covenant. As

Christians we have a calling to *be* God's word in the world. What we do as we act in covenant speaks of God's love and healing. We accept a life-changing vocation in this act of baptism, but we do so with the realization that the Holy Spirit guides, strengthens, and empowers us for this vocation. To break covenant is to turn from our vocation. Of even deeper concern, it is to participate in evil and bring darkness instead of light into the world.

Exploring: Hold a mock baptism, with different persons acting as priest, parents, acolytes, and so forth. Talk about the meaning of what we are doing.

Ask persons if they remember their own baptism or the baptism of their child. What feelings did they have at the moment? What understanding of their life in Christ did they have then? How has that understanding grown over the years?

Responding creatively: As we have seen, the sacrament of baptism is rich in life-giving symbols. Encourage parishioners to participate in the celebration of the sacrament by
• making the bread for the baptismal Eucharist.
• creating simple garments to be offered to infants or young children being baptized. This baptismal garment comes from St. Paul's references to clothing oneself with Christ and putting on "the new nature" (Galatians 3:27-29 and Colossians 3:10). The traditional white garment denotes purity and the dignity of our new life in Christ.
• decorating a candle for each person being baptized and presenting it during the baptism. The candle represents the light of Christ.
• taking part in the liturgical procession at the baptism. Different persons could carry candles, the Bible, the parish register (to symbolize the placing of the names of those baptized into the "family book" of Christ), and other symbols associated with the sacrament.
• learning a song to sing to the newly baptized.
• planning and hosting a party or reception following the baptism.

Concluding: Participating in the celebration of baptism and reflecting on the experience afterward will be a fitting conclusion for this event.

Second Sunday after Epiphany   E, L
Second Sunday in Ordinary Time   RC

Purpose of the event: To share the stories of the calling of Jesus' disciples.

When and who: A one-hour Sunday morning graded program following the Sunday liturgy. This suggested design is for third- and fourth-grade children.

Background information for leaders: See chapter 5, pages 157-158, for an overview of the readings.

Launching device: As children enter, they see twelve candles set up on a table in the middle of the room. The Feast of Lights liturgy is recalled. How many of the apostles can the children remember? As each name is mentioned, one of the candles is lit. (See Acts 1:13 for a listing of the apostles—except Judas Iscariot. Acts 1:15-26 tells us that Matthias replaced Judas Iscariot.) The leaders add whatever names the children miss. The names are then shown in print, and the children repeat them together. A brief prayer is said, thanking God for the light that the apostles and *all* of Jesus' disciples spread to the world.

Presenting: The stories of the call of the disciples are now told. We know very little about most of the disciples, and the stories of how Jesus met and called them are limited to just a few of the men. Perhaps the children can make up stories about the background of the rest of them. Though the twelve apostles and many other disciples were men, it is important to include the women disciples too. Read the following passages in order to tell the stories of the disciples' calls:
• Luke 5:1-11: the call of Simon Peter, James, and John
• Matthew 9:9-13: the call of Matthew (in the Gospels of Mark and Luke he is known as Levi)
• John 1:35-51: John's version of the calling of the first disciples
• Matthew 10:2-4: a listing of the twelve apostles
• Luke 8:1-3: mention of the women who followed Jesus: Mary Magdalene, Joanna, Susanna "and many others, who provided for them out of their means"
• John 20:1-10, Mark 16:1-8: Mary Magdalene, Mary the mother of James, and Salome (see also John 20:11-18)

- Luke 10:38-42, John 12:1-8: Mary and Martha
- Matthew 26:6-13, Mark 14:3-9, John 12:1-8: the woman who anointed Jesus at Bethany
- Matthew 28:1-8, Mark 16:1-8, Luke 24:1-10: the women at the tomb

Exploring: Have the children role play Simon and Andrew telling their families about their decision to follow Jesus. (We know that Peter was married, because Jesus healed his mother-in-law—Mark 1:29-31).

Responding creatively: Using a cassette tape recorder, have the children tape a "radio show" for their parents and the children in the other classes. Use sound effects, background music, an announcer, and even commercials if the children want to include them. The scenes would include

- Luke's account of the calling of Simon Peter, James, and John.
- The scene at the home of Peter and Andrew when they told their families about going off with Jesus. The script for this scene would grow out of the role play mentioned above.
- The healing of Peter's mother-in-law (Matthew 8:14-15). This is a very brief account in the gospels. Have the children expand the account by imagining what took place. Base the script on how the children perceive the scene and what might have been said.

Concluding: Gather around the twelve candles on the table, light them, and repeat the names of the twelve apostles. Offer a brief prayer of thanksgiving for the apostles and all disciples of Jesus and for our time together this morning.

Evaluating: At the end of the event, ask the children what we mean by an apostle and a disciple. How many can they name?

Third Sunday after Epiphany   E, L
Third Sunday in Ordinary Time   RC

Purpose of the event: To explore the role of the prophet so participants can appreciate the radical nature of God's Word.

When and who: A senior high, adult, or confirmation group meeting in a twenty-four-hour retreat setting, with participants returning Saturday evening to share in the parish liturgy on Sunday morning. The retreat would begin Friday evening with a time for community building and presenting and would continue during the day on

Saturday to give time for participants to explore and respond to the ideas presented Friday evening. The creative response of the participants would be incorporated into the Liturgy of the Word at the parish liturgy on Sunday.

Background information for leaders: See chapter 5, pages 158-159, for an overview of the readings. Clarence Leonard Jordan has written paraphrases of the books of the New Testament in which the characters are contemporary people living in the Southeast. For example, Paul's Letter to the Romans became the Letter to the People of Washington. The Christians became the oppressed peoples of the South who have turned to God for guidance in their quest for freedom. In this setting, the words and implications of the Gospel take on a whole new meaning. Ideas that have become so familiar to us that we accept them unthinkingly now threaten the most basic assumptions we make about our society. Jordan's paraphrased New Testament came out of his lifetime quest to enable the poor Blacks of the South to express their freedom as God's people and to understand modern agricultural methods. In 1942 he helped organize a cooperative farm in Georgia where Blacks and Whites owned and shared everything in common, in line with the description of the first-century Christian community in the Book of Acts. The farm was to be a model for Christian community and modern agricultural methods. In its some twenty years of operation, Jordan and his friends were denounced by the Church, harrassed by neighbors, boycotted by suppliers, and threatened with violence. Jordan's work and writings give us insight into a man who attempted to live the life of an apostle. Amos's words "The Lord has spoken;/who can but prophesy?" (Amos 3:8) summarize the spirit of Jordan's work.

A brief background of Jordan's life and viewpoints can be found in James McClendon's *Biography as Theology.* Jordan's *Cotton Patch* versions of the books of the New Testament are still in print.*

Launching device: The conference opens with participants gathered around a table. The room is lit by candles on a table. The Old

---

*Clarence Jordan, *The Cotton Patch Version of Paul's Epistles* (New York: Association Press, 1968).

Testament and gospel readings appointed for the Third Sunday after Epiphany are read. The participants read Psalm 139:1-12 in unison. Following the lectionary readings, a reading from Acts 2:42-47 sets the stage for the rest of the conference. This reading describes the Christian community of the apostles' time, in which all property was shared in common. Ask the participants to take a moment and think about the possession they value the most right now. Hand out small slips of paper and pencils. Have each person write on the paper a description of what he or she has been thinking of. Now place the slip of paper in a common container as a symbol of giving up our valued possession to the total community. Say "For the balance of this retreat, let us hold our possessions in common as did our ancestors in the faith."

Presenting: Share with the participants a brief overview of Clarence Leonard Jordan's life and of his understanding of theology that came out of his story. Think about the events of Jordan's life that influenced his thinking and actions. His intense study of the Bible meant that it deeply influenced his life. The Bible was not just a comforting book; it inspired action as Jordan attempted to make his life congruent with the Word of God revealed there. James McClendon's theories about the biblical images that shaped Jordan's life could lead conference participants to think about the images and words that have shaped their own understanding of life. Then read portions of Jordan's *Cotton Patch* versions of various New Testament writings. Compare his paraphrase with the biblical writing so that participants can see how Jordan understands the New Testament message. Duplicated copies of the sections under consideration would be helpful. Close the formal part of the evening with discussion, questions, and worship.

Exploring: The next morning divide participants into pairs. Give each pair one chapter of Jordan's "The Letter to the Christians in Washington" (Epistle to the Romans) from his *Cotton Patch Version of Paul's Epistles* and ask participants to list on newsprint the major ideas and feelings expressed in that chapter. Why might the members of the local church that excommunicated Jordan's group from

membership respond negatively to the writing? How might a new member of the cooperative farm respond to the ideas? How do the participants themselves react? Briefly list the participants' answers on the newsprint. Next examine the same passage from the Epistle to the Romans as it is originally written (that is, from St. Paul's point of view). Why do we think the Jews responded negatively to Paul's writings? How might a new convert to the Christian community have felt? How do we react? After the research time, bring the entire group together to share what has been discovered. What are some common points between Peter's and Paul's lives and Jordan's struggle for freedom? A brief overview of the writings of the prophet Amos could lead to a similar comparison. (Participants could be sent back into dyads to do a chapter-by-chapter study of the prophet's writings.)

Responding creatively: Now we need to move these words of prophet and apostle into our own setting. All too often we keep the words of the Bible at a safe distance from ourselves and nod in casual assent to words of radical power that should dramatically change our lives. Have participants return to their morning dyads. Ask them to write their own paraphrase of the chapter or chapters they studied earlier. How would the group paraphrase the epistle so that it would apply directly and immediately to their personal situation in the nation, the community, and the home? What makes the words of the New Testament radical for us? What might separate us from neighbor or even from a member of our own family? A similar treatment of Amos's writings could be done if time permits.

Get together again with all the participants and share the group's thoughts and paraphrases. If possible, shape the paraphrases into a reading for tomorrow morning's liturgy—as a homily or as a reflection on the biblical readings. For example, the group writings could be introduced with words from the biblical readings for the day.

- The Lord spoke to the prophet Amos and said: "The lion has roared; who will not fear?/ The Lord God has spoken; who can but prophesy?" (Amos 3:8)
- Jesus went about Capernaum and proclaimed: "Repent, for the kingdom of heaven is at hand" (Matthew 4:17).

- He called disciples, . . . "Simon who is called Peter and Andrew his brother. And he said to them, 'Follow me, and I will make you fishers of men.' And going on from there he saw two other brothers, James the son of Zebedee and John, in the boat with Zebedee their father, . . . and he called them" (Matthew 4:18-21).
- The Lord called St. Paul in a vision on the road to Damascus, and Paul spoke and wrote words of power that confronted people with their enslavement and pointed to the way of freedom in Jesus Christ.
- And the Lord calls *us* to follow him and to speak words of reform and words of freedom.
- Today we come to speak in ways that we feel Christ may be speaking through out own story: words of enslavement, words of reform, words of freedom. Though we speak not with the authority of a Paul or a Peter, we speak as members of Christ's Body, the Church, of which we are all a part as we gather in his name this day.

If an adult class is to meet after the liturgy, the retreat participants can help lead the class in dealing with some of the issues raised by the liturgy; or the adult class can be the setting for the entire session.

Evaluating: Hand out evaluation sheets and ask participants to respond in writing. (See page 101 for an example of the kind of questions you may want to raise.) In designing your evaluation questionnaire, think about the kind of information you need to judge how well the design accomplished its purpose. What kind of feedback would be helpful to future designers of a similar event?

Fourth through Eighth Sundays after Epiphany   E, L
Fourth through Eighth Sundays in Ordinary Time   RC
Purpose of the four-week focus: To explore the Sermon on the Mount as it applies to our understanding of what it means to be a disciple of Jesus.

When and who: An intergenerational experience on Sunday mornings for one hour following the liturgy.

Background information for leaders: See chapter 5, pages 159-162, for an overview of the readings.

Fourth Sunday
Purpose of the event: To expose participants to the Beatitudes and their significance for the Christian.

Background information for leaders: See chapter 5, pages 159-161.

Launching device: Launch the overall study with the solemn reading of the Ten Commandments during the morning liturgy. *The Book of Common Prayer* gives provisions for sharing the Ten Commandments as a part of the liturgy of the Word. To each commandment the congregation responds "Amen. Lord have mercy." When the gospel reading is offered, it should be read in the same solemn cadence. Just as the Ten Commandments frame the world view of the Jew, the Beatitudes frame the world view of the Christian. We could respond "Amen. Lord have mercy" after each of the Beatitudes. By doing so, the participants might capture the implications for the Christian life-style. The sermon should deal with the meaning of the Beatitudes for the Christian.

Presenting: In this design we will be keeping families together in the learning community. Single persons may become adopted aunts, uncles, or grandparents in the family unit or may become members of their own family grouping composed of other single persons. Open the session with everyone gathered in the parish hall. Have a storyteller relate the story of St. Peter from the time of his call by Jesus to the legend of his death. (There is no historical evidence of Peter's death, but tradition states that he was crucified upside down during one of the Christian persecutions in Rome.) The storyteller will naturally need to exclude some stories about Peter so that the presentation will not be too long, but the story needs to be told with enough detail to give participants a feel for Peter and for his struggle as a disciple and later as an apostle.

Exploring: Now send the families off to meet with two or three other families and a leader. In each small group meeting area there should be a newsprint reproduction of the Beatitudes. How does Peter's story express the

Beatitudes? Can children remember parts of the story that show how Peter's life reflected the Beatitudes? Have members of the families play charades, with participants guessing which Beatitude is being acted out. As we talk about Peter, we will see times when he did not reflect the life-style of the Beatitudes. He was not always a peacemaker, for example. As we read Galatians 2, we realize that Peter was at the center of a major controversy with Paul. Peter struggled just as we do. The Beatitudes describe the Kingdom of God. Only when God's will is fully done "on earth as in heaven" will the blessedness of God's people be fully realized. Meanwhile we struggle for that reality as pilgrims on a journey, catching only glimpses of such wholeness.

Responding creatively: Each family group could create a collage showing pictures of persons who seem to be fulfilling the principles of the Beatitudes. This may help us to see the persecuted and the hungry more distinctly. These are the people, we need to remind ourselves, who are most clearly reflecting God's love and compassion in the world today.

Concluding: Have the entire community reassemble in the parish hall. Share the collages and reflections from the small groups. Repeat the solemn reading of the Ten Commandments and of the Beatitudes from the morning liturgy.

Evaluating: Leaders should listen carefully to ideas in the conclusion to gain insights into how the session went for the participants.

Fifth Sunday

Purpose of the event: To explore with participants the concept of light and darkness as it is used in the Bible and in our liturgical life.

Background information for leaders: This Sunday the gospel reading talks of disciples being the "salt of the earth" and the "light of the world." Disciples are to give the flavor of God to his creation, or, in the words of the *Interpreter's Bible*, ". . . keep the world from spoiling or being tasteless."* The song "This Little Light of Mine" expresses the feeling of the gospel reading. The light of Christ begins to be seen in a dark world because of the actions of his disciples.

*Sherman E. Johnson, "The Gospel According to St. Matthew," *The Interpreter's Bible*, vol. 7 (Nashville, Tenn.: Abingdon Press, 1951), p. 288.

Launching device: Begin the learning community experience with a recalling of the Twelfth-Night Feast of Lights festival. If there is any way to darken the parish hall, repeat a portion of that liturgy, with everyone being given a candle and passing the "Christ-light" on to his or her neighbor. The children's song "This Little Light of Mine" can be sung as the candles are lit.

Presenting: If possible, move back into the same small groups that met last week. The community will change from week to week, but whenever possible keep the same families and individuals together over the whole four-week experience.

A more intimate launching can be introduced into the small group if it is possible to darken the meeting room. As participants arrive, have the room in darkness. Let them grope about the room and then, on the basis of their experience of the environment in the dark, describe what is there. Then light candles or turn on the lights and compare descriptions. Have members of the families brainstorm thoughts that come to mind when we concentrate first on the word *darkness* and then on the word *light*. What do we think of when we contemplate *darkness*? There are good things to do in the dark, including sleep, but generally speaking we like to have light. Why? What can we do in the light that we can't do in the dark? Can participants tell stories that express this dark-and-light theme? Grandparents or "adopted" grandparents might recall the rigors of living without electricity. Others can talk about camping trips and the welcome beam of the flashlight as we crawl into the tent. What does the comic-strip writer mean when he puts a light bulb in the balloon over the character's head? What did St. Peter do that brought light to people? What did Jesus do that brought light to Peter? What did Peter do that brought darkness? How might he have felt at such times? What gave him the sense of light again?

Exploring: Talk about people we know who bring light to us. How do they do it, and how do we feel? If time permits, give each participant materials to make greeting cards for those light bringers. The materials can include a good quality of heavy paper, felt-tip markers, magazines to find pictures in, and other art supplies. The message on the card is "Thank you for sharing the Christ light" or some other greeting of appreciation. Give persons time to create the card, and encourage them to hand or mail the cards to their special people. Provide envelopes for convenient mailing. This kind of project could be extended to include making gift candles to be presented to those special friends at Easter time or at the Feast of Pentecost. After the candle is made, one can attach cards or pictures around it by dipping the candle and card in hot wax, pressing the cards or pictures in place, and allowing them to dry. The greeting "Thank you for sharing the Christ light" would then become a permanent part of the gift.

Concluding: Gather the entire community again for a sharing of the morning experience. Ask participants what they gained from the experience and how they can apply their discoveries at home. An Order of Worship for the Evening from *The Book of Common Prayer* (pages 109-112) would make a fine concluding liturgy if curtains can be drawn, since it *is* meant as an evening service. (Be sure to mention the significance of the candles used in the liturgy. As we light the candles on the altar, we think of the Christ light in our lives.)

(All stand.)
(Officiant) Light and peace, in Jesus Christ our Lord.
(People) Thanks be to God.
(Reader) Jesus said, "You are the light of the world. A city set on a hill cannot be hid. Nor do men light a lamp and put it under a bushel, but on a stand, and it gives light to all in the house. Let your light so shine before men, that they may see your good works and give glory to your Father who is in heaven" (Matthew 5:14-16).
(The Officiant then says the Prayer for Light.)
Let us pray.
Grant us, Lord, the lamp of charity which never fails, that it may burn in us and shed its light on those around us, and that by its brightness we may have a vision of that holy City, where dwells the true and never-failing Light, Jesus Christ our Lord. *Amen.*
(The candles at the Altar or table are now lighted, as are other candles and lamps as may

be convenient. During the candle-lighting, an appropriate anthem, such as "O Gracious Light," or a psalm may be sung, or silence kept.)

O Gracious Light *(Phos hilaron)*
O gracious Light,
pure brightness of the everliving Father in heaven,
O Jesus Christ, holy and blessed!

Now as we come to the setting of the sun,
and our eyes behold the vesper light,
we sing your praises, O God; Father, Son, and Holy Spirit.

You are worthy at all times to be praised by happy voices,
O Son of God, O Giver of life,
and to be glorified through all the worlds.

Evaluating: The questions asked during the conclusion will serve to evaluate this session. "What insights did you discover together? What can we do in our homes to reinforce this idea?"

Sixth Sunday
Purpose of the event: To explore the significance of Jesus' words about anger. To enable participants to become more aware of their own way of handling feelings of anger in their relationships.

Background information for leaders: See chapter 5, page 161. This Sunday would be a good time to focus on how to handle anger within our families and in other daily relationships. Each family group will need to be led in this exploration so that feelings expressed can be handled openly and creatively.

Launching device: We need a launching that will stimulate participants to think about ways they handle their anger. Have the community meet in the parish hall. After reading the gospel appointed for this Sunday, have several persons put on brief skits that reflect the different ways we are apt to handle our anger. For example:

Act One: Mrs. Cool portrays the person who is never really angry. "I'm not angry. What do you mean, angry? Just because I haven't said anything to you in thirty days doesn't mean I'm angry!"

Act Two: Mr. Hot storms about the house, kicking and screaming and making life generally miserable for everyone. His anger goes out in so many different directions that it is hard to pin down the cause of his anguish. Questions to help the family understand Mr. Hot's anger only bring on more evidence of anger.

Act Three: Jumping Jill displays the typical temper tantrum when things don't go just her way.

Act Four: Sam Sidestep yells at his wife about keeping him waiting for ten minutes, but he is really angry with his boss. His wife knows that his level of anger is way beyond the ten-minute wait at the station, but he refuses to get to the heart of the situation until she has probed extensively.

Act Five: Mr. and Mrs. Rightway give examples of dealing with anger assertively, creatively, and directly. For instance, "We need to talk because I'm really feeling angry at you and I'm not sure why," says the wife to her husband. This open sharing of feelings allows the couple to release their feelings and to move into a deeper understanding of each other and their relationship.

Presenting: In this initial input it is important to express that anger is a normal and creative part of our life together as Christians. We often tend to deny our hostile feelings because we think we should not be angry, but suppressing the anger only deepens it. The feelings we think we are dealing with by ignoring them are actually being shared just as clearly as if we were dealing with them openly. There is no way, ultimately, that we can deny our feelings. If a feeling is suppressed long enough, our physical health suffers along with our mental health.

The skits should be offered with some loving humor so that the session is not too heavy. If we can laugh lovingly at ourselves, we can handle the self-examination and move to more creative ways of behaving.

Exploring: As participants move into their family groups, have newsprint posted in each family area with these or similar reflections:

I can remember a time when I was
Mrs. Cool: "I'm not angry!"

Mr. Hot: Kicking and screaming
Jumping Jill: Having a temper tantrum
Sam Sidestep: "I'm telling you I'm angry at *this*, but actually. . . ."
Mr(s). Rightway: "I think I did a good job of handling my anger when. . . ."

Give persons five to ten minutes to think about ways they have handled anger lately. Young children will need to think out loud about this with their families. The leaders should open the group sharing time by reflecting on their own experiences, modeling for the group an ability to confront oneself with humor and self-love rather than self-negation. Talk briefly about the effects of your behavior on others. You might talk about how you wish you had handled the situation. What did you learn from the experience? Not all the examples are going to be negative. We need to affirm those times when we feel we have dealt creatively with a situation. How the leader models the sharing for the rest of the group will make a great deal of difference in the degree to which others are able to share openly and supportively.

Responding creatively: Let participants make up their own skits about Mrs. Cool, Mr. Hot, Jumping Jill, Sam Sidestep, and Mr. and Mrs. Rightway. Separate adults from children, and have the children put on a puppet show for the adults. Silly skits reflecting the same ideas could be offered back to the children by the adults.

Concluding: Gather the families together for a closing time. Have group leaders share their reflections gained from the group life. Be sure to acknowledge that we *all* fall into the trap of Mrs. Cool, Mr. Hot, and the rest of the gang. A brief general confession shared by the group would reinforce this common failing, and the proclamation of the good news that God accepts and forgives us as we recognize our need for change and growth would help participants accept themselves in their own struggle.

Evaluating: Ask each person to respond to a brief evaluation questionnaire. Young children can be interviewed by their parents. This more extensive evaluation will give you a check on how participants are feeling about the entire Epiphany program and will help you decide whether you need to do some reshaping of the design for the remainder of the program.

Questionnaire

I (we) have participated in _____
sessions of the Epiphany program. Insights
I've discovered so far in this program are

In future, I wish we could

One idea I'd like to try in our home as a
result of this program is

I (would/would not) like to participate in
another program involving children and adults.

I found myself feeling (free/uptight) about
expressing myself in a group composed of
children and adults. (Rate your feeling on this
scale.)

Free 1 2 3 4 5 6 7 8 9 10 Uptight

The most helpful part of this experience for
me has been

The least significant experience has been

Seventh Sunday

Purpose of the event: To share the stories
and words of the Bible that guide us in relating to
other persons, including our enemies. To enable
participants to look at their own behavior toward
friend and enemy alike and to compare that
behavior with the behavior called for by Jesus.

Background information for leaders: See
chapter 5, page 161. Jesus spoke of relating to
others in such a way that our behavior witnesses
to his kind of love. Where we would retaliate in
kind to insult or anger, or where we would
respond minimally to someone's need, Jesus
always pointed to a greater love and a higher
standard of relationship. Responding with this
kind of love becomes our witness to Christ's
presence in our lives.

Sometimes humor is a way of dealing with
a question that is loaded with feelings and long-
held prejudices. Humor helps us let down our
guard, and in the process we discover deeper truth.

Launching device: After the liturgy, gather
the participants in the parish hall. Have two
persons dressed as clowns offer the typical
slapstick routine in which one clown acts
aggressively toward the other and the second
clown retaliates in kind. A paddling by one
results in a paddling from the other; a pie-in-the-
face from one results in a pie-in-the-face from the
other. If you can rent the typical slapstick silent
movie for the occasion, so much the better. The
Three Stooges are classics for this kind of humor
in a slightly later era of filmmaking. "Spy vs.
Spy" in *Mad Magazine* is a contemporary
example of retaliation humor. The two spies in
the series are on opposite sides, and they
constantly try to outwit each other. The White
spy designs an intricate trap to destroy the Black
spy, only to be caught up by an even more
intricate trap sprung by the Black spy. The
humor comes from the subtleties of the mutual
entrapments.

Presenting: Read the gospel for the day
immediately after the films or skits. Then have a
storyteller offer one or more of the following
stories from the Bible:
- Jesus' words of forgiveness and his death on
  the cross (Luke 23:32-34).
- The story of Paul and his coworkers
  imprisoned in Philippi. When an earthquake

shook the foundation of their prison and made possible their escape, they chose instead to stay where they were. This strong witness of loving faith in Christ led to the conversion of the jailer and his family (Acts 16:25-34).

- The death of St. Stephen (Acts 7:54-60).
- How David spared Saul's life on two occasions during the time when Saul was attempting to find David and kill him (1 Samuel, 24 and 26).

Exploring: After drawing out feelings about the skits, the gospel, and the stories, the leader should be ready to offer a personal story that reflects a time when Jesus' words had an effect on a relationship in the leader's own life. A bishop shared an experience in the context of a sermon that I have never forgotten (a reminder of the power of a story; we tend to remember stories far longer than theoretical presentations). The bishop was waiting in a long line at the cleaners. Since he was tired, the long wait was irritating. His feelings of frustration were heightened by the woman behind the counter. She would greet each customer angrily and then discourteously demand the cleaning ticket. The bishop felt words of caustic retort coming into his mind as his turn came closer. But as he stepped up to the counter, a different feeling came over him. Instead of the cynical retort he had framed in his mind, he heard himself say to the woman "It must be a tough day for you today." Suddenly the woman's whole attitude changed. Tears came into her eyes, and she began to pour out a story of continuing frustrations. The bishop's day changed, and so did hers.

I find myself thinking of that story every time I am confronted by the same situation, though my urge to retaliate in kind often wins out, I must confess. The "other cheek" response is harder to offer, but the response is worth the effort.

After the leader's sharing, other participants can be encouraged to offer their stories. Someone may have influenced them by a higher standard of behavior, or they may have exemplified it themselves. Or humility may lead us to share a time when we've blown it too!

Responding creatively: Using clay or "play dough," have the families and individuals create simple sculptures that reflect the higher standard that Jesus calls us to. For example, one child may want to model a few figures that go with one of the stories we have shared; others may want to sculpt an abstract design that speaks to them of love, forgiveness, and compassion.

Concluding: Two persons who represent the slapstick characters of retaliation call the people back into the parish hall. They begin to strike each other with paddles but then stop in mid-act; they light two candles, then hold each other's hands as the Gospel lesson for the day is again read. They send the people home with the words of dismissal from the liturgy: "Go in peace to love and serve the Lord." The people respond: "Thanks be to God."

Evaluating: Leaders get together after the event and reflect on the participants' comments and creative responses.

Eighth Sunday

Purpose of the event: To explore the significance of Jesus' words about true riches.

Background information for leaders: See chapter 5, pages 161-162. On the Sabbath, Orthodox Jews must set aside all routine activities as a witness of their covenant with God. From sunset Friday to sunset Saturday the people of God are called to contemplate the beauty and the mystery of Yahweh (God). This is a built-in "Look at the birds in the sky" day for Orthodox Jews. They are prohibited from doing anything that would keep them from this contemplation. Their own reputations and attempts to build kingdoms for themselves must be suspended so that they can center on the true kingdom of God. To the outsider the customs of the Sabbath may seem stringent, but to the Jew the Sabbath can be a great joy. It is like a day of enforced vacation for everyone, including those who bear the responsibility for preparing meals in the home. (Many of us structure our vacations in such a way that life is just as hectic and work-oriented as our everyday lives. We can learn from our Orthodox Jewish friends!)

Launching device: The total learning community gathers in the parish hall and shares ideas about the Sabbath and its customs. If possible, show a short film that studies the actions of birds, the waves of the ocean, or other natural phenomena. It should be an uncomplicated film that simply absorbs the attention of the participants in the beauty and serene wonder of God's creation. If a film is not practical, a record or tape of the sea or other sounds of nature will suffice. Or the picture can be offered in words of prose or poetry.

Presenting: In small groups, have the leaders share the thoughts from today's lectionary commentary, chapter 5, pages 161-162.

Exploring: Ask participants to tell about the things they do that make them feel most at peace with God and with one another. When do they feel the greatest sense of thanksgiving? We live in a society where possessions are important, and there is no point in discounting the feelings of thanksgiving that we all have over possessions. But let's see if we can get underneath the "thing" to see a more personal, gospel-centered response of thanksgiving, like that of the little boy who thanks his grandparents for a toy truck because it reminds him that they love him.

Responding creatively: As noted above, the Sabbath is a sacred day for the Orthodox Jew. All normal routine activities must stop so that the faithful can be raised up from the dailiness of life to realize the eternal, sacred nature of all creation. No phone calls can be made, no work can be done, cars cannot be driven, and a host of other guidelines set the pace for the day. What is left is a day spent in the enjoyment of the Lord, of each other, and of nature.

The assignment for each small group is to design a "Sabbath" experience for the participants. How could we spend a day living the reality of Matthew 6:24-34? How can we help each other pull back from the usual pressures and temptations of our daily lives to experience together the wonder of creation and the humbleness that goes with our awareness? Can the group actually set aside a day or a part of the day to spend such a time together? If they can, the designing takes on real significance. If time or circumstances do not allow such direct participation, have the cluster create a "Sabbath book" filled with suggestions for an experience of the Sabbath.

One of the beautiful gifts my parents offered me as a child was an exposure to art. Museums were a regular part of our family life. My appreciation for the beauty of creation comes

in no small part from this early exposure to what is beautiful and mysterious in the world. How about a Sabbath in the museums and parks of the city? Remember that no one in the family can cook this day! Food should be prepared the day before. Make a game of carrying out some of the traditions. Light the Sabbath candles at the evening meal the night before. (Episcopalians are provided with such a home liturgy in *The Book of Common Prayer,* pages 108-114.)

"Consider the lilies of the field, how they grow" (Matthew 6:28) on a nature walk or at a museum of natural history. Plan a day or an evening of playing family games. Be sure to include the single folk in the group in any activities that are planned by the family. Some of us work-oriented creatures of habit can relax more effectively if we see our leisure time as a duty. The concept and practice of the Sabbath may help the "birds-in-the-sky" times become more a part of our lives. In the process we will have moved closer to the Creator of all that is beautiful and life-giving.

Concluding: Bring the entire learning community back together. Share some of the ideas that came out of the small groups. (A parish "Sabbath-keeping" may be an outgrowth of today's activity.) Close by reading the gospel lesson, and let the descriptive sounds from tape, film, or spoken word send us forth to appreciate God's creation.

Evaluating: Ask participants to share their assignment of designing a "Sabbath experience." How do they feel about actually doing the experiment? Their responses will help you evaluate the session.

Last Sunday after Epiphany   E, L
(Transfiguration of Our Lord   L)

The Roman Catholic lectionary does not include this Sunday; the transfiguration story is read each year on the second Sunday of Lent.

Purpose of the event: To explore the story and concept of the Transfiguration so that participants can appreciate moments of transfiguration in their own lives.

When and who: An intergenerational experience preceding the liturgy.

Background information for leaders: See chapter 5, page 162.

Launching device: The learning community gathers before the liturgical experience. This means that what we begin here together can be expressed and carried out in the parish family's sacramental life that follows the religious education meeting. The people can participate far more fully in the liturgy because they have been prepared for the experience by what they have already done together.

If possible, the room in which the people gather is darkened. A figure representing St. Peter enters; we can barely see him move about the room. Then a single bare bulb in the middle of the room is lit as the call of Peter (Luke 5:1-11) is read; Peter stops and listens. The light goes out after the reading, and the person representing Peter moves slowly across the room. Then the light is lit again as the healing of Peter's mother-in-law is recalled (Matthew 8:14-15). The room is again darkened, and the figure moves on. Other "seeing-the-light" experiences in Peter's life are recalled with the same light-bulb ritual. The person portraying Peter stops each time in his wandering about the room as the light is lit. The experiences are

- Jesus calming the stormy waters of the lake (Matthew 8:23-27)
- Jesus feeding the five thousand (Matthew 14:13-21)
- Jesus walking on the water (Matthew 14:22-33)
- Jesus healing the people (Matthew 15:29-31)
- Peter recognizing Jesus as the Messiah (Matthew 16:13-20)
- Jesus' announcement of his passion and death (Matthew 16:21-23)
- The transfiguration (Matthew 17:1-8)
- The Last Supper (Matthew 26:26-30)
- Peter's denial (Matthew 26:69-75)
- The resurrection (Matthew 28)

At the announcement of the resurrection, the lights are left on.

Presenting: A very brief input should outline the concept of the transfiguration. Our lives are transfigured as we see Christ fully revealed in our own personal stories.

Exploring: Using the same kind of family groupings mentioned in connection with the fourth through seventh Sundays after Epiphany, have the group talk about the story of Moses. They will be hearing a small part of that story in the Old Testament reading later in the liturgy. The leader can bring a flashlight, and every time a "seeing-the-light" anecdote about Moses is told by one of the participants, the light can be lit and passed to the person telling the story. If the group is not familiar enough with the story of Moses to participate, let the leader tell the story in brief form. When participants hear those parts of the story where they feel the light was being revealed, have them reach into the middle of the circle and turn on the flashlight.

Then shift from the story of the Bible to the story of the people present. The leader, taking the light back, tells a couple of stories that reflect his or her own "seeing-the-light" times. To hold children's attention, we must share all these accounts as stories; that is, we must share them in such a way that the participants can *experience* them with us. Other members of the group can now be encouraged to share similar stories of their own lives, keeping in mind the need to be brief and yet intense enough to hold the interest of children as well as of adults. Children, of course, need to be included in the story-sharing time. A walk in the woods to look for a Christmas tree may have been a "seeing-the-light" experience for a child in discovering the stillness of God's world.

The leader can also mention "seeing-the-light" experiences of other persons in history. What did Martin Luther King, Jr., mean when he said on the steps of the Washington Monument "I have been to the mountain"?

Responding creatively: Have families come back into the central meeting area where your "resident artists," musicians, and creative writers have set up several optional centers where people can express the concepts and stories they have shared. Whatever is created can be placed in the nave of the church or shared as a part of the liturgical experience.

Concluding: The people rehearse the music for the liturgy. The choir director or organist explains the significance of the songs or hymns to be sung. The preacher may want to give a brief preview of what is to be shared at the sermon time. For example, "Today I'm going to be telling the story of a contemporary Christian saint. As you hear the story, turn on your imaginary flashlight at those points where you think this person is having an experience of the transfiguration." Psalm 99 is appointed for this Sunday in the Episcopal lectionary. The psalm reflects some of the symbolism found in the transfiguration account. (Verse 7, for example, says "He spoke to them in the pillar of cloud.") The liturgy can begin with the recitation of the psalm. The words are majestic and awesome. The psalm concludes with these words of power:

Extol the Lord our God,
and worship at his holy mountain;
for the Lord our God is holy!

If the psalm is immediately followed by the liturgical greeting between priest and people and then by a grand and triumphant hymn, some of the feeling of the transfiguration can be experienced at the outset of the liturgy.

Evaluating: Ask participants to write on a small piece of paper a word or phrase that expresses the transfiguration for them.

The Epiphany Program:
Conclusion

The above suggestions for education during the Epiphany season in Year A are meant to stimulate your own brainstorming ideas. Notice that a religious education program involves far more than an hour on Sunday morning. It can include a family trip to the museum, a day in the park, life in the home. But the liturgical life of the parish is the focus of the whole-life experience of the people. The direction your program may take will be shaped by the environment and the people involved in the parish. It will be a unique expression of your own life together and yet tied to the life you share with every Christian who feels the call of discipleship.

Be sure to get the planning team together for an evaluation session at the conclusion of the whole Epiphany season program. Record the conclusions of the planning team so that future planners can benefit from what you learned in reflecting on the feedback about the design.

Three Model Programs

Designing a Program for the Season of Easter, Year B

Let us say that your design team has carried out a program for the Epiphany season in Year A. After the last Epiphany session the team got together to evaluate the design and administration of the program. Someone took detailed notes which were placed in a permanent file for future reference. Now we draw a new design team together. Some of last year's persons are anxious to get involved again, and we invite newcomers as well. We may also have some volunteers. "I enjoy telling stories to children," someone might say. "I'd be glad to serve as storyteller if you do another intergenerational program." This year's homegrown liturgical program will be the Easter season, we decide. That means we should get the team together for the first time very early in January at the latest. (Be sure to check the variable date of Easter.)

To get under way we follow the procedures used in planning the Epiphany program (see pages 102-103). At a preliminary meeting we ask the members to do "homework" before the next meeting. They will read and study the Bible readings assigned for this season, as well as this book's commentaries on them (see chapter 6, pages 215-217). They will get additional information on the season's meanings and traditions from older members of their own families, from friends, neighbors, nearby churches, and libraries.

In step two, the brainstorming meeting, the pastor or someone else may wish to offer some specific insights into the season and its lectionary selections. But basically this meeting is a sharing of the results of their "homework"—the information, ideas, and feelings generated by their own study and reflections on the Bible readings, the meaning and spirit of the season, and the traditions learned from family, friends, neighbors, and other churches.

At this session, as with Epiphany preparation, we bring out the sheets of newsprint and first brainstorm general ideas about the Easter season, paying no attention thus far to order or suitability of ideas—simply recording

them. Then we brainstorm the overall seasonal objective and discuss which ideas might fit in with that objective.

Future meetings will be devoted to the third major step, planning the week-by-week programs.

Here are some ideas that came out of the brainstorming meeting.

Brainstorming Ideas for the Easter Season

• Focus on Paul in the Book of Acts the same way we thought about Peter during the Epiphany program. How might Paul have understood Jesus as the Good Shepherd? How did he experience and respond to the appearance of the risen Christ?

• Have the learning community publish a weekly newspaper during the Easter season and call it "The Good News." Pull out the adventure stories in the Book of Acts and report them in the paper.

• Take the children on a nature walk and point out the evidence of resurrection in nature. See the new birth growing out of the decaying matter on the forest floor. Using brown twine, hang weathergrams on the trees of the church property. (These are 3″ x 5″ strips of kraft paper on which sayings about nature are written in calligraphy.)

• Study the life cycle of the caterpillar and butterfly. Read *Hope for the Flowers,* by Trina Paulus, and talk about the new understanding of birth and discovery expressed there.*

• The miracle of birth can and often does lead to belief in God.

• When we see the lives of people transformed by a powerful experience, we begin to realize the power of the resurrection as it applies to the life to come. We need to point to situations in history or in our own lives in which we have felt as if life had ended then discovered that the crisis actually led to a rebirth. For example, someone loses his or her job, and the whole family feels as if their world has collapsed. Years later the family looks back to that event and realizes that it was the beginning of a beautiful change in their lives. They all grew and were transformed through the experience.

*Trina Paulus, *Hope for the Flowers* (Paramus, N.J.: Paulist Press, 1972).

• The book *Passages,* by Gail Sheehy, reminds us that we all move through crises or death-and-rebirth experiences.* In going through those passage points, we may discover a whole new world. How we handle those crisis points determines whether the death experience will be growth-producing or stunting, whether it will be a resurrection experience or an experience of hell.

• The road-to-Emmaus account of the resurrection (Luke 24:13-35) serves as a prototype or symbol story of how we encounter the resurrection experience of Christ. The risen Christ appeared to two disciples as a stranger along the road. He recalled for them "the things concerning himself" in Old Testament passages. He then sat with them and "took the bread and blessed, and broke, it and gave it to them." At that point the disciples recognized the risen Christ and went quickly back to Jerusalem to spread the news. Similarly, it is in hearing the stories of God's activity in the past that we are made aware of his activity in our own lives today. The risen Christ becomes "visible" for us as we share the bread and wine of the Eucharist.

• We need to let our children experience setbacks if they are to have a sense of self-worth. It *is* all right to fail, and we need to have the freedom to fail. In a sense, the Bible is a book of failures. God allows each of us to fail, and we often do. The Bible is filled with the sense of this freedom to fail and with our people's response to it. But God also knows that we have the strength to survive failure and to be "resurrected" from it. Whether we grow or whether we are destroyed is determined by how we perceive the crisis. Without faith in the possibility of new life, we might live in despair. If we perceive even the "failure" experience of death as a threshold to new life, we can live in the hope that comes out of a life of faith.

At the next planning meeting the group should look back at what they talked about and brainstormed at their previous session. In the following suggested design the thought of focusing on St. Peter and St. Paul led to thinking about making a film about the Book of Acts. The weekly newspaper idea became the weekly

filming. As was true in the Epiphany program, we will save all our notes for future generations of program designers.

Program for the Season of Easter: An Overall View

Purpose of the Easter program: To enable participants to feel themselves a part of the Easter story proclaimed by the Church.

When and who: Junior-high or middle-school children sharing a common program before and/or after the liturgy on Sunday mornings and/or during the week.

Reflections on the design: The whole Book of Acts is a story that reflects the power of the resurrection in the lives of the disciples. The continuing unfolding of the story week by week in the context of the liturgy will help to hold the children's interest. We call this a story in seven parts and dramatize the Book of Acts as a serial. We involve the children during this seven weeks in the making of an 8mm film. Their varied interests can be met in making sets and costumes for the production, acting out the parts, and literally getting into the story. The film is also a learning device that can be shared by the parish at large and enjoyed by other children in years to come. With home movie cameras that include sound tracks we can even have "talkies." If such cameras are not available, tie the movie together with a tape-recorded narrative of the action, using only limited speaking parts.

This kind of program will obviously involve more time than the usual one hour scheduled for religious education. Therefore we suggest a midweek meeting after school or in the evening or on a Saturday. If the group meets before and/or after the liturgy on Sunday morning, participants hear the stories and work on scripts and ideas for the action. The midweek session would consist of the filming. Thus the participants would be introduced to the story on Sunday and would experience the story during the week.

Launching, presenting, exploring, responding creatively to the readings of the Easter season: In this Easter program it will not be necessary to go into the details of each segment of the design. Each week the *launching* of the event will be the telling of the story from the

---

*Gail Sheehy, *Passages: Predictable Crises of Adult Life* (New York: E. P. Dutton, 1974, 1976).

gospel or the Book of Acts. Segments chosen for filming do not necessarily follow the lectionary, but the entire project will add meaning to the lectionary readings from Acts. *Presenting* the story will consist of giving the background information necessary for filming the event. *Exploring* the story will consist of discussing how the scenes will actually be filmed. *Responding creatively* will be the actual filming.

Concluding and evaluating: We conclude and evaluate the program with the presentation of the completed film to the whole parish. Asking the participants how they felt about their project will help the planning team with their evaluation. A pizza party or other event would give a sense of celebration after the ''premiere'' showing of the film.

Second Sunday of Easter

Today in the gospel reading we hear cf Jesus' resurrection appearance to his disciples in the upper room. Thomas is not there at the first appearance and therefore does not believe the story until Jesus comes again and asks him to place his hand in Jesus' side. This story, or the story of the disciples on the road to Emmaus, could be dramatized along with the scene at the empty tomb. You will need to be prepared to talk about just how the disciples perceived the resurrection of Christ. How did he walk through doors and yet be a solid-enough vision to demand that Thomas place his hands on Jesus' glorified body?

Obviously we have no pat answers for this. We need to encourage questioning and even doubting if the youth are to grow in the faith. They will grow with the stories as they grow in the faith. Some will take the accounts as symbolic poetry; others will accept the literal facts of the story. The important point to make is that something dramatic happened to those frightened people to send them out into the streets to proclaim the resurrection. A very good brief study of the resurrection appearances is outlined in *Twenty Ways of Teaching the Bible,* by Donald L. Griggs.* You may want to spend the first

*Donald L. Griggs, *Twenty New Ways of Teaching the Bible* (Livermore, Calif.: Griggs Educational Service, 1978).

study session on a comparison of all the resurrection appearances. Then decide how to film the scene.

Third Sunday of Easter

Acts 2:1-13 tells that the apostles were empowered by the Holy Spirit. Then in Acts 3 and 4 we begin to see the results of the indwelling of the Holy Spirit on the lives of the apostles. In the beginning of chapter 3, Peter and John heal a crippled man, and the crowds witness the miracle. Peter then addresses the crowd and tells them the story of Jesus. Because of this public preaching they are arrested and taken before the Temple court. Chapter 4 describes the scene before the court. Peter, a common fisherman, finds words of power to address the court; this amazes the interrogators. Finally they release Peter and John with the warning that they must not publicly proclaim the name of Jesus.

The courtroom scene could include a mock trial, with the members of the group role playing the members of the Sanhedrin and Peter and John. The actors will need to identify with the concerns of the Sanhedrin. These disciples are disturbing the public order and the faith of the people. If they arouse too much attention, the Romans may be drawn into the situation, and the stability of the Jewish hierarchy that was allowed to function under Roman domination may be threatened. The students need to realize that these are real concerns that we can identify with today. How would we feel if two persons we considered radical and irrational came into our lives and threatened our stability? Remember that Peter and John have only recently received the gift of the Holy Spirit; this experience of healing and speaking is new to them. Notice that in the readings appointed for the next Sunday, Peter and John return immediately to the Christian community that by now is a close-knit communal group who share their possessions. But the two prisoners had to stand alone before the Sanhedrin. We can identify with the feelings of exhilaration mixed with fear that they may have had as they stood before the court. The scene of Peter and John returning to their Christian friends following their release could be included in this week's shooting.

Fourth Sunday of Easter

We introduce Paul (or Saul) in this week's filming. In Acts 7:54-60 we first meet Paul as he witnesses the stoning of the first Christian martyr, Stephen. Acts 8:1-3 indicates that Saul was one of the leaders in the first general persecution of the Christians. Our next glimpse of Paul (or Saul) comes in Acts 9:1-31. Paul became a follower of Christ as a result of a vision he experienced on the road to Damascus — a vision in which the risen Christ called him into the apostolic life. His subsequent baptism and introduction to the apostles in Jerusalem are described in this section. Paul had to escape from Damascus by being lowered over a wall with ropes because the Jews were determined to kill him after his conversion.

Fifth Sunday of Easter

Acts 16:16-40 describes an adventure that offers possibilities for filming. In the town of Philippi, Paul exorcised a girl who had earned money for her masters by telling fortunes. The exorcism infuriated her masters because she was not able to tell fortunes after her exorcism. So her masters stirred up the citizens against Paul and his companions and had them arrested. The jailer placed them in maximum confinement and chained their feet. Undaunted, the Christians spent the evening singing and praising God. At about midnight an earthquake hit the city and broke down the walls of the jail. Instead of escaping, as they could have done, Paul and his companions remained. The jailer was so moved by this witness of love and confidence that he was converted on the spot, and he and his family were baptized that very night. This episode would end with Paul's official release the next morning. Perhaps embarrassed that they had arrested the Christians on such loose evidence, the magistrates tried to get Paul to leave town quietly. He refused to do so, demanding a show of justice as a Roman citizen.

Sixth Sunday of Easter

Acts 21:15—23:35 is another adventure story about Paul that would offer possibilities for filming. After Paul's three missionary journeys in which he proclaimed the good news among the Gentiles, he and his companions returned to Jerusalem. Paul's presence there caused concern among the Christians because he had become so controversial during his missionary travels. Many Jewish Christians felt that to be a follower of Christ one must also be a follower of Moses, observing the full ritualistic code of the Mosaic law, including circumcision. Not so, said Paul, and the apostles in Jerusalem had agreed with him. Instead, they had set down four simple conditions that Gentile converts were required to follow after conversion: "...they should abstain from what has been sacrificed to idols and from blood and from what is strangled and from unchastity" (Acts 21:25). This agreement had been made at the council of Jerusalem after Paul's first missionary journey. But rumors in Jerusalem were saying that Paul had encouraged Jewish Christians who had remained faithful to the Mosaic covenant to abandon their Jewish practices. This caused concern for the Jewish Christians and infuriated even more the Jews who had rejected Paul's preaching of Christ. To counteract the rumors, the apostles in Jerusalem urged Paul to go to the Temple and take part in a purification ritual to show his continued obedience to and respect for the Mosaic Law as a Jewish Christian. But while Paul was in the Temple, he was recognized by some Jews from the province of Asia. The ensuing riot led to Paul's arrest by the Romans and his subsequent protective custody in the Roman prison. The next step in the plot came when four Jews vowed to kill Paul. He was secretely transferred to Caesarea at night.

Seventh Sunday of Easter

The last installment for filming could be the shipwreck described in Acts 27, the winter spent in Malta, and the final arrival in Rome described in the last chapter of Acts. A basement room in the parish center could be fitted to look like the hold of an ancient ship. Actors in the film would pass boxes out the door to indicate the attempts to lighten the ship in the storm. The crew would act as if they were being tossed to and fro about the room. Then film the scene as they struggle ashore in an outside setting. (Paul was sent to Rome because, as a Roman citizen, he had the right to appeal to the Emperor for justice. His appeal is described in the first part of chapter 25.)

Three Model Programs

Designing a Program
for the Summer Sundays, Year C

Many parish programs become dormant during the summer. Though a quiet vacation time is important, the parish can stimulate discovery and growth in the Spirit during the summer. If several churches cooperate in a summer program, new leaders can be drawn into the activities, and persons who have been involved during the winter can take a much-needed rest.

The summer Sundays are called the Sundays after Pentecost (or Sundays in Ordinary Time or Sundays of the Year, in Roman Catholic terminology). The feast of Pentecost celebrates the gift of the Holy Spirit. The Holy Spirit inspires us to respond in wonder to the beauty that God continues to create all around us. Thus summer is the season of the Spirit, both in the liturgical calendar and in nature. All nature praises God. If we feel depressed, just observing the birds or watching the water flow over the rocks of a quiet stream can lift us up out of ourselves to a Spirit-filled praise of God. We return home renewed after such a simple summertime experience of the Spirit. Psalm 96 is typical of this kind of response.

Let the heavens be glad, and let the earth rejoice;
> let the sea roar, and all that fills it;
> let the field exult, and everything in it!
Then shall all the trees of the wood sing for joy
> before the Lord, for he comes,
> for he comes to judge the earth.
> (Psalm 96:11-12)

Such can be the nature of the summertime experience. As we walk along the hot pavement of the city, we may see a sprig of grass struggling up through a crack in the cement. "Life will be," we think to ourselves. Nature has provided us with a meditation. Summertime gives us vacations and time for art museums and libraries, concerts, outdoor camping experiences, walks and hikes, and many other opportunities for growth and discovery in the Spirit. Let the parish church be the center for this kind of discovery during the summer months. We need not compete with what the city park departments, YMCA and YWCA,

and other organizations are doing; we can join with them and share our facilities with them. But we come with another purpose that we need to make sure is heard and experienced: We come to proclaim that in our summertime discoveries we are touching the mystery and wonder of God who is Creator. And we want to tie our experiences to the experience of the worshiping community, to express and celebrate our discoveries together in the context of the Sunday liturgy. In turn the Sunday liturgy sensitizes us to how the Spirit may be touching us in the unfolding week.

In the following sample program, we begin with suggestions for many informal, outdoor activities; then we return to a more formal analysis of the lectionary readings, but we emphasize *activities* rather strongly; at the end we celebrate with a parish fair.

The following ideas are offered with the hope of stimulating your own program ideas. As is true with the other suggestions made in this chapter, my assumption is that you will meet with a planning group to develop your own program based on your resources and interests. Remember that your best resources are the people of the parish; their enthusiasm and commitment is the most important ingredient in anything you plan.

I'm convinced from my own experience that one of the greatest gifts we can share as adults is the ability to relax and play together. Jesus' admonition to become like little children in order to enter the kingdom of God (Matthew 18:3) is an apt one. We discover a great deal about ourselves and others as we play. In our relaxed moments of complete surrender to enjoyment, our guard is down, and like children we can see the world in all its wonder and joy.

Summer Leisure Activites

A Weekend of Play
> One of our growing traditions in our parish in western Oregon is the annual adult weekend at the diocesan conference center on the Oregon coast. The purpose of the weekend is simply to relax and enjoy one another and the beauty of our environment. Arriving Friday evening, we have a party and settle in for the weekend. Saturday is a play day for everyone. In the morning, people offer to share their talents

with whoever is interested. Groups can be found on the beach engaged in weaving, wood carving, beachcombing, writing, reading, or just talking. In the afternoon, groups play golf, tour the surrounding area, or go to a nearby beach resort. The latter choice leads to bumper car and more exhilarating rides, tandem bicycle rides, and strolling. The evening is devoted to an amateur night program in which various persons share their silliest talents with the group. On Sunday we celebrate the liturgy together. The power of that liturgical experience convinces me that a valid religious experience is happening beneath the surface of our playtime together. Our summertime experience has begun. We can feel the difference when we return home. Strangers have become friends. The Christian community feels a common bond from having shared an experience in the Spirit.

Children can easily be added to make this same event a family experience. The enjoyment of watching children relate to adults is exciting for everyone involved. We gain new insights into our own family life as we observe other families relating together. A further benefit comes as children see their parents acting like children! This weekend together reminds us of the importance of regular family times to play. We can easily fall prey to the temptation of letting television be the focus of learning and experiencing. For some, this weekend may be a learning experience in family play.

Weekend Family Camps

Another variety of family weekend is a more structured conference. In the diocese of Oregon we have designed family weekend conferences that use fantasy as a means of discovering religious concepts.

C. S. Lewis's *Voyage of the Dawn Treader* was the vehicle for one of our family weekends recently. *Voyage* is one of the seven books written by C. S. Lewis to help children understand Christian theology through the use of fantasy. (The seven books are offered in paperback. See the Bibliography.) Aslan the lion is the Christ figure in the series. He created the mystical world of Narnia that the heroes and heroines of the stories enter by miraculous means. In *Voyage of*

the Dawn Treader the children are sitting in the bedroom of their aunt's home looking at a picture of the Narnian ship *Dawn Treader*. Suddenly they find themselves literally drawn into the picture. The next thing they know, they are being fished out of the water by their Narnian friends and are on an adventure to the very end of the Narnian world. Their pilgrimage takes them to mysterious islands where they must survive various crises. In the process their obnoxious cousin Eustace Scrubb is confronted with the destructive nature of his behavior. He is cleansed in the presence of Aslan with a baptism that removes the scales of the dragon form that he had assumed in his selfish greed, and he becomes the person he was created to be. On the surface the book is merely an enjoyable adventure for children. Beneath the surface it is a powerful conveyor of the gospel.

As participants arrived at the retreat center, they drove their cars through a huge picture of the *Dawn Treader* that had been painted on canvas and hung across the road. Once "in the picture" they found themselves in a shower of water being sprayed from a hose. Greeted with cries of "Men and women overboard!", they were directed to "swim" across the grass field to the waiting *Dawn Treader*. Their destination was the large dining hall that had been decorated to look like a ship. As they arrived at shipside, they were helped up the rope netting and greeted by the costumed crew.

The weekend consisted of dramatizing life aboard ship, with personal family experiences planned to help participants internalize the Christian theology expressed in the story. On Sunday afternoon we shared a liturgical experience with Aslan in Narnia and then stepped back through the picture to discover a table set with bread and wine. A celebration of the Eucharist helped to translate the Narnian terms into Christian concepts.

This kind of experience grows out of the same kind of brainstorming mentioned earlier in this chapter. For the family camps we chose to use books or stories that expressed Christian theology in completely different terms because by stepping outside the familiar we can often add new insights to what we may have come to accept as commonplace. It is like flying over the city where we have lived all our lives and seeing an entirely different environment from the air.

Christian Day Camps

The Bible itself, of course, offers plenty of stories and adventures to experience in play and drama. For several years we have offered an experience called Adventure Week. A city park is the environment. Children from preschool age through the sixth grade gather for five days from ten o'clock in the morning until two in the afternoon. Junior- and senior-high students have helped as leaders along with adults.

The children and their adult or teenage guides gathered in the morning for a presentation of the day's theme. In the case of the exodus experience we told a portion of the story of Moses and the Israelites as the launching device for the activities. To hold the children's interest we dramatized the story in what we called the "Sesame Street style." Repetition and humor were the ingredients of the skits, as were litany-style responses from the children. After the common sharing time the children were divided into age-grouped tribes and spent the next three hours in their small groups experiencing concepts of the story. The last half hour of the day was spent together as we talked about the day that was closing and began to set the theme for the next day's adventure. The fifth and sixth graders spent one night in the park, which added to their "wilderness" experience.

I will always remember our last day together with the children. With the blowing of "ram's horns" and the shouting of the leaders, we gathered all the tribes of Israel together and formed a grand procession to move into the Promised Land. Nothing could be left behind. All the possessions of the tribes had to be loaded into wagons or carried into the new land. Once in the new land, we gathered around a central place and shared a liturgy that included drinking milk and eating honey and bread.

This kind of experience could of course be offered in an overnight conference setting just as easily. The day-camping arrangement opened the experience to many children who might not have been able to leave home for a longer time, and it enabled us to use the natural resource of the nearby city park.*

A Parish Communal Garden

A parish community vegetable garden can be an enjoyable and productive summer experience. In our community the city offers garden plots for minimal rent. If you can locate a little land, offer garden-size plots to parish families. Tie the garden planting to a rogation celebration (see chapter 8, pages 276-277). The rogation procession can take place at the parish garden. Crosses for the garden will be blessed and placed at each plot, and the day can end with a picnic supper shared in the midst of the freshly planted and blessed gardens. At harvest time have a parish celebration as the fruits of field and vine are gathered. Remember to give a tithe of the "first-fruits" and offer the fresh vegetables to persons in need.

Summer Program Ideas Based on the Lectionary

If the summer program is going to be effective, we need to draw together that all-important planning group. The suggestions just made might help to launch the summer season in the parish family. Now we look at some ideas that may form the basis for your own summertime planning around the reading of the lectionary. We will cover only selected Sundays because the previously-suggested activities will form a large part of the summer program.

Proper 6   E
Eleventh Sunday in Ordinary Time   RC
Fourth Sunday after Pentecost   L

Purpose of the event: To share the stories of God's forgiveness made known to King David through the prophet Nathan and to all people through Jesus. To explore with the participants the Christian understanding of God's forgiveness.

When and who: An intergenerational experience prior to the Sunday liturgy.

* The curriculum from one of our summer adventures based on the exodus experience of the Israelites was published in 1975. See the Bibliography.

Background information for leaders: See chapter 7, page 258, for an overview of the readings.

Launching device: A storyteller relates the story of David and Bathsheba and the gospel story. The David and Bathsheba story may seem a bit risque for younger children, but we need not go into detail about David's sin. "He treated Bathsheba as his wife so that she was no longer faithful to her own husband" would be enough explanation for old and young alike. The gospel reading should probably be told in much the way as it was told before the gospels were put into writing. "This is a story Jesus told one day as he entered a home."

After sharing the Old Testament and gospel stories, separate the families and individuals into small, intimate groups. The leader of each small group can then tell a story that illustrates the biblical theme of the day. The following is an example of such a story. (I heard it told many years ago but have been unable to discover a published version of it. My thanks and apologies to the unknown author and publisher.)

The young girl watched her mother's face light up with appreciation as her grandmother placed the beautiful vase on the table in the living room. It was a very old vase, Sarah could see just by looking at it. Then her grandmother looked at her. "This vase was in my home when I grew up, and your own mother remembers it from her childhood. Now I want you to have it in your home. Maybe you can give it to your child someday."

Tears came into her mother's eyes, and it was obvious that she did indeed remember that vase from her own childhood. It had stood on the hall table. Secret letters to special friends and even to Santa Claus were placed in it. If the old vase could talk, it would tell a lot of stories about her family!

The girl's mother walked toward the front door. "I'm going to take your grandmother home now. I'll just leave the vase here for the time being. We'll decide what place of honor we'll give it when I get back. For heaven's sake be careful of it. Don't play rough with the dog in this room as you sometimes do. I just can't stand

to think about what I would do if something happened to that vase," she said as she went out the door.

No sooner had the door closed when Jumping Jack, the puppy, came bounding into the room. Forgetting her mother's words, the little girl started playing with the dog. The more she played, the sillier and wilder Jumping Jack got. It was fun to watch the dog race at full speed all around the room. At one point the dog almost ran into the wall. It looked as if he put brakes on as he almost literally screeched to a halt a fraction of an inch from the wall.

And then it happened. Jumping Jack didn't screech to a halt fast enough this time. In his racing about the room he hit the small table that the vase was sitting on. Frantically Sarah reached out to grab for the table and steady it, but instead of saving the vase her hand brushed against it and the beautiful vase went crashing down to the floor.

Now, you know that sick feeling that comes into the pit of your stomach when you realize that you have done something just awful. It's like the feeling you get when you see a police car coming up behind you with the red lights flashing. Well, that's the way Sarah felt as she looked at the vase lying on the floor, smashed into a hundred pieces.

"I'll glue it back together," she shouted out, and ran to get the glue out of the kitchen. She tried frantically to fit one piece to another, but the two pieces only fell apart in her hand and shattered into more bits of broken china. She knew it was hopeless.

"Jumping Jack! Come here! I'm going to spank you so hard you'll never run around this room ever again!" But as she began to chase after the poor sulking little puppy she realized that after all it wasn't his fault. She was the one who had egged him on to his wild running. And besides, he was just a puppy, and puppies naturally love to chase and run.

"I could say it was his fault," she thought to herself. "I was just sitting here reading and minding my own business when that silly dog came running into the room and hit the table." But Sarah knew that she couldn't stand the deep questioning look in her mother's eyes if she told that story. Her mother had a way of knowing—really knowing—what she was thinking about.

And then she heard it. The car was coming back up the street. It stopped out front on the street. Another car passed, going in the opposite direction. Then the car pulled up into the driveway and stopped. The door of the car opened, then closed with the sound of metal meeting metal. Footsteps in the driveway. Footsteps on the front porch. Footsteps at the door. Her mother stood in the hall. A million words of excuse, apology, anger, flooded into her mind.

"Mother," she heard herself saying as if she were someone else listening to this whole agonizing scene. "I broke your vase. It was my fault. Jumping Jack came into the room, and I egged him on and he hit the table. Oh mother, I'm *so* sorry. Please forgive me!" Tears flooded her eyes and flowed down her cheeks. If only her mother would say something! She heard first a gasp, then loud sobs, and then the sound of her mother's own anger in words that made no sense.

But then something strange happened. Her mother was hugging her. "I've got so many feelings of grief, anger, hurt flooding through me right now, Sarah, I can hardly think straight. But there's another feeling that's getting stronger, and it's the one I want to share with you now. That's my love for you, Sarah. You've said you're sorry, and I know just by looking at you and holding you that you are. I also have a memory, Sarah. A memory of a time when I was playing in our family car and released the brake and ran over my brother's brand new tricycle. He had been sitting on it a moment before, and I could have hurt or even killed him. Oh, Sarah! I remember how I felt, and I feel that feeling now. I forgive you, Sarah. We can't put the vase back together. We can't undo what either of us has done, but we can both grow from this, and we can be closer together because most of all we both know what it feels like to be loved. And you know something else, Sarah? The next time I receive something valuable and fragile I'm going to place it on a shelf that's solidly connected to the wall and not on an end table!"

With this both Sarah and her mother started laughing. There really wasn't anything to laugh at. But the laughter came from a sense of love and identity that only very special people feel when they know that they are very, very close to each other because they understand each other perfectly.

The leader may want to share this story, but a personal anecdote might carry more impact and encourage others in the group to be open themselves.

Exploring: Ask members of the group to share stories of their own. As children hear their parents or other adults relate their own times of feeling guilty, it helps build a bond between parent and child. As with the mother and the child in the story of the vase, a sacred sense of identity develops.

You may find yourself discussing the role of punishment. Why didn't the mother in the story spank the child? In some situations we find the painful reality that forgiveness is not offered and that guilt and resentment remain. From such a perspective the story may be hard to identify with. Some of Jesus' parables, including the parable of the prodigal son that we will share at the close of this experience, may even anger people. "I'll bet the kid ran off and got in trouble again. The old man was crazy to take him back" is an oft-expressed feeling at hearing the story.

Jesus' words of forgiveness from the cross speak to each of us of forgiveness from God. Like the mother in the vase story, Jesus knows us perfectly, since he shares our human nature. He is like the mother holding us in her arms, the father by the side of the road watching for us.

Responding creatively: On a large sheet of butcher paper or newsprint have the members of the group draw pictures, write sayings, create symbols, or just scribble to make a group mural that expresses the theme of forgiveness.

Concluding: Have the entire learning community gather again in the parish hall. Mount the murals on the wall so that the environment reflects our life together. The storyteller who shared the David and Bathsheba account now offers the parable of the prodigal son. The celebrant of the liturgy enters the circle and leads the people in a general confession. Urge participants to use a period of silence now to get in touch with those times when they have felt like the prodigal son or like David or like any of the people in the story. Repeat the confession together. Then the priest can announce the absolution. Again keep silence and ask the group to reflect on those who have to come to us seeking forgiveness. Let the people all join in saying the absolution. Close this session with the passing of the peace and a procession into the nave for the liturgy. If possible, the preacher should include remarks in the sermon that incorporate some of the morning's experience. At the formal confession and absolution, refer back to the parish hall experience so that the liturgical confession will have more impact.

Evaluating: Ask participants to share their feelings and discoveries of the day. This can be done briefly at the close of the event.

An Independence Day Parish Picnic
(July 4)

Purpose of the event: To celebrate Independence Day in a way that proclaims God's presence in the history of our nation.

When and who: A picnic for the parish family that incorporates the celebration of the Eucharist.

Background information for leaders: The appointed readings for Independence Day are as follows:

Episcopal:	Deuteronomy 10:17-21
	Hebrews 11:8-16
	Matthew 5:43-48
Roman Catholic:	Isaiah 9:1-6 or 32:15-20, 18, 20
	or 57:15-19;
	Philippians 4:6-9
	or Colossians 3:12-15
	or James 3:13-18;
	Matthew 5:1-12
	or Matthew 5:38-48
Lutheran:	(The Lutheran lectionary does not have specific propers for Independence Day. Readings are provided, however, for "A National Holiday.")
	Jeremiah 29:4-14
	Romans 13:1-10
	Mark 12:13-17

In addition to studying the readings so that they can be offered with eloquence at the outdoor liturgy, the planning group may want to do some background study on Independence Day traditions that have characterized our celebrations over the years.

Further suggestions: Because of the informal nature of this event, we will not follow the remainder of our planning outline. But here are some suggestions for planning the day.

In the parish newsletter advertise an old-fashioned Fourth of July picnic. Encourage parishioners to come dressed in period costumes. Make the event a potluck picnic so that participants will have more of a feeling of sharing with the parish family at large. Plan a time for games that can involve persons of all ages playing together. The water balloon toss is a favorite with us. *The New Game Book,* edited by Andrew Fluegelman, is filled with ideas for non-competitive intergenerational games.* If the environment permits, plan for a grand Fourth of July parade that will include everyone in a procession so that they can enjoy seeing one another's costumes. Find fife and drum players to lead the procession. Encourage other instrumentalists to join in the band. Some of the old-timers might be willing to tell a few stories about the Fourth of July celebrations they remember from childhood. You may even find someone who is willing to give a Fourth of July political oration in the grand old style.

But the high point for this day is the celebration of the Eucharist. If we follow the ancient traditions of our forebears in the first-century Church, the Eucharist will precede and yet be a part of the meal itself. Call the people together with the recitation of Psalm 145. The "band" from the parade could set the theme for that beautiful reading. The theme for the day's experience is expressed in the fourth verse of Psalm 145: "One generation shall laud thy works to another." These words can be repeated as a refrain and can be incorporated into the greeting between priest and people. "This is what we are here to proclaim this day. All generations together shall praise your mighty works in our

* Andrew Fluegelman, ed., *The New Game Book* (Garden City, N.Y.: Doubleday, Dolphin Books, 1976).

nation's history this day. Blessed be God, Father, Son, and Holy Spirit. And blessed be his kingdom now and forever. Amen.'' The music for the liturgy can be national hymns and songs that everyone knows and can sing with enthusiasm.

Then comes the proclamation of the Word of God. The readings should be read with a sense of power and proclamation. In lieu of or as a part of the sermon, read portions of the Declaration of Independence and other documents that remind us of the dream our ancestors had for us. Lincoln's Gettysburg Address, Martin Luther King's ''I have been to the mountain'' speech, President Kennedy's inaugural address could be offered by readers who stand before the group to proclaim the words of our own people. Little more need be said. By the end of the day one generation will have praised God's works to another and declared God's mighty power. The political speeches, memories of past celebrations, games, and other festivities can follow the picnic potluck.

Proper 10   E
Fifteenth Sunday in Ordinary Time   RC
Eighth Sunday after Pentecost   L

Purpose of the event: To share the parable of the good Samaritan and to explore the concept of loving our neighbor.

When and who: A Sunday morning program preceding the liturgy. The whole group meets in the parish hall for an initial presentation. Then participants are separated into an adult/senior-high group, a junior-high or middle-school group, and a grade-school group. The program continues with the Sunday liturgy and with a midweek tour of places where ''loving your neighbor'' is happening.

Background information for leaders: See chapter 7, page 259, for an overview of the readings.

Launching device: As people arrive at the parish hall, highway signs direct them toward the road to Jericho. (Some children can have prepared both the skit and the signs the week before this event.) Highway markers, speed-limit signs, and even billboards advertising the fine motels and shops in Jericho surround participants on their way into the parish hall. A ''state policeman'' directs participants to their seats in the parish hall, and after a very brief introduction the dramatization of the parable of the good Samaritan begins. Let the children expand the story if they want to. What do they think the priest and Levite might have said as they came upon the stranger? Why did they hurry on by?

Presenting: Participants are now divided into the age groupings:

For adult/senior-high participants, read in dramatic fashion:

Deuteronomy 10:17-21—''For the Lord your God is God of gods.... He executes justice for the fatherless and the widow, and loves the sojourner, giving him food and clothing. Love the sojourner therefore; for you were sojourners in the land of Egypt.''

Matthew 5:43-48—''You have heard that it was said, 'You shall love your neighbor and hate your enemy.' But I say to you, Love your enemies and pray for those who persecute you.'' In both these passages we hear our higher calling as God's people. We respond in ways that go beyond the normal call of duty. We respond as God responds in love and mercy to *all* people.

Matthew 25:31-46—This is the well-known passage in which Jesus says to his followers: ''For I was hungry and you gave me food, I was thirsty and you gave me drink.'' When we respond to the person in need, we respond to the risen Christ.

1 John 4:7-21—'' ... for love is of God, and he who loves is born of God and knows God.'' Later we are reminded that '' ... he who does not love his brother whom he has seen, cannot love God whom he has not seen.''

For younger participants:

Tell the story *The Other Wise Man* by Henry Van Dyke. (The book is no longer in print; check your library or used-book store.) This story powerfully expresses the idea of Matthew 25. A fourth wise man, unknown to history, made the trek to find the Savior, the story tells us. He left his homeland with three very valuable jewels. On the way to his rendezvous with the other three wise men, he was delayed as he cared for a dying Jew on the road. This act of caring caused him to just miss the meeting with the other three wise men. He spent years attempting to find the Savior, only to miss those opportunities because he stopped along his way to offer assistance to persons. His jewels went to help people in crises. The tale ends with the realization that the "other" wise man had indeed met the Savior in every person he had helped.

Exploring:
For adults/senior high:

Putting ourselves in the place of the priest and the Levite, what practical concerns would have kept us from responding to the man by the side of the road? Have there been times when we have chosen not to respond to a need? How do we feel about having responded or not responded? Is there an outcome to our own good Samaritan story?

Talk about cases where people have been killed in front of witnesses but no one stepped forward to intervene or even to call the police. Many of us dislike being involved in the process of caring even to the extent of serving on juries or voting in elections.

It is easy to convince ourselves that people should take care of themselves or that the State will take care of those in need.

We may run into some strong feelings in this discussion. All of us have turned away from our "neighbor" at various times. Guilt may cause us to be defensive over the whole issue. We may hear ourselves saying "Well, we can't be responsible for everyone in this world, or we won't have the energy left to take care of ourselves." Are Jesus' words impractical? What *do* we think he is calling us to do on our roads to Jericho?

For younger participants:

We can ask the children to identify with the priest and the Levite as was suggested with adult participants. Picking up the hitchhiker at the side of the road may be one of the concerns raised. "How come my mom never picks up hitchhikers?" a child may ask. It is important to balance the call of the Gospel with a concern for our own safety, but how can we determine when we are using our heads and when we are making excuses to ourselves? Talk with the children about *The Other Wise Man*. What feelings did the children have when they realized that he was probably going to miss his meeting with the other

wise men as he stopped to care for the old Jew on the road?

Responding creatively:
For adults/senior-high participants:

Since the liturgy follows the religious education event, we can deepen the liturgical experience with the discoveries we make in the learning community. Ask the group to design and offer a brief presentation at the time of the offertory. Call it "The Unknown Words." Basing it on dialogue in the group, write up a rough script of what the injured man, the priest, and the Levite might have said. Go on to make up a list of our typical responses when we fail to respond to Christ as we meet him in a stranger, in a neighbor, or in the agonizing social problems that grip our world. The congregation can respond "Lord, have mercy" in litany fashion after each statement. For example:

"World hunger is such a vast problem, there is really nothing I can do about it."
Lord, have mercy.
"If you get involved with someone in trouble, you're apt to get sucked into their problem and get hurt yourself."
Lord, have mercy.
"I know I should do something about that, but I'm afraid to speak out because it might hurt my business."
Lord, have mercy.
"I know it's wrong, but if I say anything about it in my sermon, it might make some of our important people in the parish angry."
Lord, have mercy.

This liturgical offering could be made at the time of the general confession or penitential rite as a meditation leading the congregation into their own personal awareness of Christ's call to love our neighbor.

For younger participants:

Make simple puppets of the characters in the good Samaritan parable, and put on a puppet show. Have the children act out through the puppets what the priest, Levite, and injured man might have said. This too could be offered as a part of the liturgy if conditions permit.

Concluding: The litany-type response during the liturgy can conclude this portion of the program. The sermon can include some of the thoughts shared if the preacher was a part of the learning community experience. Since people need to be affirmed as well as confronted in their neighbor role, the sermon should include examples of how people are responding to Christ's commandment to love one another.

Evaluating: Ask for written or spoken reflections from the participants.

Midweek program: This theme can be continued with a midweek tour of places where the good Samaritan principle is happening. For example, take the children to the emergency room of the hospital. Talk with the ambulance drivers who respond to crisis calls, and see the equipment they use. Visit other volunteer or professional helping organizations and ask the persons to share their stories.

Proper 12   E
Seventeenth Sunday in Ordinary Time   RC
Tenth Sunday after Pentecost   L

Purpose of the event: To expose participants to the concept of Christian prayer and to the traditional forms of liturgical prayer. To encourage participants in their own life of prayer.

When and who: A Sunday morning program, preceding the liturgy, for children or for adults, youth, and children meeting together.

Background information for leaders: See chapter 7, pages 259-260, for an overview of the readings. See also the discussion of liturgical prayer found in connection with Proper 24, chapter 7, pages 265-266.

Launching device (for all participants): Traditionally, the Church has recognized seven kinds of prayer: adoration, praise, thanksgiving, penitence, oblation, intercession, and petition. This morning, introduce the whole concept of prayer and the specific kinds of prayer with a series of Bible stories that will illustrate each kind of prayer. Have a different storyteller come forward for each story. Tell the story as one would share an ancient tale of our people. End each story with the statement "Let us pray to

God in adoration . . . in praise . . . " (and so forth).

Use the suggested stories to illustrate each kind of prayer.

- Intercession—Genesis 18:20-23: Today's Old Testament lesson is an ancient folktale that can be introduced in the learning community so that it will have greater impact as the people hear it read in the liturgy later in the morning. The storyteller may want to read over the remarks in chapter 1 regarding the telling of folk stories. Avoid literalizing the story. Let it stand as a reminder that from very early times our people have felt free to intercede with God for others. From reading chapter 2 we can realize that God was once considered by our people to act without mercy when anyone transgressed his commands. The story reflects this harsh understanding of God, but it may also express the deep feeling we have when we cry out "O God, have mercy on her. She didn't mean to do it!"

- Petition—1 Samuel 9:28: Hannah prays to the Lord for a son. Her prayer is so fervent that the priest of the Temple thinks she is drunk and warns her to sober up! Part of her prayer is a promise to offer a son to God if one is born to her. She later does conceive and give birth to Samuel, who anointed both Saul and David as king in the Lord's name.

- Confession or Penitence—Luke 15:11-32: The younger son returns to the father with a prayer of confession on his lips. "Father, I have sinned against heaven and before you; I am no longer worthy to be called your son."

- Oblation—Luke 22:39-46: An oblation is an offering; a prayer of oblation is one in which we offer ourselves to God as a servant of the Lord's will. Part of the prayer of Consecration is a prayer of oblation. In Rite One of *The Book of Common Prayer* we read "And here we offer and present unto thee, O Lord, our selves, our souls and bodies, to be a reasonable, holy, and living sacrifice unto thee. . . ." In Rite Two, the prayer of oblation says "Sanctify us also that we may faithfully receive this holy Sacrament, and serve you in unity, constancy, and peace. . . ."

  The prayer of Jesus in the garden is a perfect prayer of oblation. "Father, if thou art willing, remove this cup from me; nevertheless not my will, but thine, be done'' (Luke 22:42). Jesus offered himself to God completely and fully even in the face of his dread. Tell the story of his agony in the garden. The disciples could not stay awake to pray with him. He faced the ordeal alone, and in the power of fervent prayer he found the strength to offer himself.

- Adoration—2 Samuel 6:1—7:29: David arranged to have the ark of the covenant brought into Jerusalem after his capture of the city. This was a tremendously exciting time for David and the people. The ark's presence in the city signified God's presence in the nation and solidified David's authority to reign over the people as God's own king. He thought of building a temple to place the ark in, but the prophet Samuel warned him that this would not be the proper time. (It was David's son Solomon who built the Temple.) Beginning at 2 Samuel 7:18, we read the prayer of praise and adoration attributed to David. The prayer is delightful, for it reminds us of a child who has received a wonderful gift from a parent. "Who am I, O Lord God, and what is my house, that thou hast brought me thus far?" As a part of the prayer, he prays for God's blessing on the house of David that his family "may continue for ever before thee." In one sense it is a selfish prayer for power, but in another sense it is a prayer that David's family may do God's will in the generations to come. Out of David's great sense of awe and gratitude came a deep desire to respond to the gift in love and service to the Lord.

Many of the psalms are attributed to David. They contain similar words of praise and adoration which lead to a response from the people, an outburst of song.

In telling this story, describe the dancing and singing of David and the people as the ark was brought into the city. This is described in 2 Samuel 6. An amusing sidelight to David's family life is provided in his wife Michal's disgust at his display of joy before the ark. David's disdain for Michal after his confrontation with her is painful to recall and is not an essential detail of the story, but it provides us with insights into David's nature as a far-from-perfect servant of God.

- Praise—Luke 1:26-56: In a vision Mary sees an angel stand before her to announce that she will give birth to Jesus. The beautiful canticle called "The Song of Mary" or the "Magnificat" is attributed to Mary. It is a song of praise and awe of God.
- Thanksgiving—Psalms 105, 106, 135, 136, 138: These psalms summarize all the gifts that the Lord has given to the people. They are joyful prayers of thanksgiving for the mighty acts of God made known in the Israelites' history. Conclude the storytelling by having the people shout out the refrain of thanksgiving, "Hallelujah!" Note the litany response in Psalm 136, "for his steadfast love endures forever." Psalm 136 would be particularly appropriate for this occasion, since the refrain can be dramatically repeated over and over. Psalm 138, appointed for today's reading, is a beautiful prayer of thanksgiving for one who called on God for help and felt God respond. If we share this psalm in the learning community it will have far more impact as our people gather for the liturgy.

Presenting: Talk with the children about the stories they heard that help to define the kinds of prayer that Christians are called to offer God. The leader should then give personal examples of situations in which the different kinds of prayer have been appropriate. Share these examples as stories out of your own life. Tell the story and ask the children to identify the kind of prayer being expressed.

Remember that we often offer simple prayers of thanksgiving or petition. "Thank God we made it through the snow," we might say as we arrive home after a trip. "God help me face this test" and the brief, plaintive cry "O God" are prayers. While on the one hand we are presenting the concept of prayer in a rather formal way by discussing the traditional seven kinds of prayer, we also need to help the children appreciate that we can commune with God through the simplest expression of God's presence with us. The very act of praying affirms our faith in a creative power that responds in love, much as a parent responds to the cry of a child. That is why the Church has traditionally called God by the intimate names of Father-Brother-Spirit.

Exploring: Encourage the participants to share their understanding of prayer. Can they offer their own stories of prayer? Do they offer prayers in their home at meal times or on other occasions?

Responding creatively: A seven-year-old friend wrote the blessing used in her home: "God, the greatest of them all, thank you for the waterfall. Thank you for the flowers so sweet. Thank you for the food we eat." The prayer was written during a summer vacation several years ago and still has meaning to the child and her family. Form several "response centers" that will enable children to experience liturgical or formal prayer. One center can be for artistic response. Explain that many artists have offered prayers of praise to God by means of their artistic creations. Show examples of such art. A picture of a child's pet cat becomes a prayer of thanksgiving if offered in the spirit of prayer. Mosaics, finger painting in joyful response, or any number of other art forms can be experienced.

Another center can be for a musical response in prayer. The psalms and canticles of the Bible and the hymns and songs of the Church are prayers. Sing a few hymns for the children, and ask them to identify the kind of prayer that the hymn expresses. Teach them one of the song-prayers, or better yet, help them write their own. A banner that sometimes hangs in the nave of our parish church proclaims "He who sings, prays twice," a reminder of the beauty of the sung prayer.

Another center can be for the writing of prayers. Help the children express their joy, thanks, petitions, and various feelings in words of prayer and praise.

Prayer can be in the form of dance and body movement. Indeed the whole dramatic flow of the liturgy is one continuous act of prayer in which the simple acts of standing, sitting, kneeling, moving forward through the nave, raising the hands in supplication to receive the Sacrament, and all the other movements of worship become a physical act of prayer in adoration, penitence, petition. Let the children get in touch with their prayer feelings by ritual, dance, and body movement.

Concluding: The liturgy that follows this learning community experience is the natural place to celebrate what the participants have created. The adult/youth program as well as the children's offerings can be incorporated into the prayers, music, and dramatic action of worship. For example, include the written prayers as a part of the formal prayers of intercession at the liturgy. Have the children bring forward the offering after helping them see in their learning center that this is, in itself, an act of dramatic prayer. When the Bible lessons are read and the Lord's Prayer is shared, children and adults may have a whole new appreciation of the power of their worship experience together. Because parents have focused on the same ideas as their children, we have a much better chance of seeing some of the impact of this Sunday's experience carried into the home. A child's prayer that was written this Sunday and then offered at dinner will never be forgotten. As friends of the child join the family for dinner, the homespun prayer will be a witness to them of the Lord's presence. This is where evangelism begins!

Propers 13 and 14   E
Eighteenth and Nineteenth Sundays in Ordinary Time   RC
Eleventh and Twelfth Sundays after Pentecost   L

Purpose of the event: To expose participants to the contrast between the persons who base their lives on amassing power and wealth, and the persons who place their complete faith in the Lord. To enable participants to experience the simple life of faith.

When and who: An intergenerational experience, preceding the liturgy, for families and individuals in the parish.

Background information for leaders: See chapter 7, page 260, for an overview of the readings. These propers form a two-week focus on the same theme. This allows us to develop the theme in more detail and still stay with the focus of the lectionary. During the first week we can introduce the ideas; in the second week we can explore some of the ramifications of the theme. A parish "survival fair" in which parishioners explore the possibilities of making their own essential items and sharing their survival skills with others would be a way of helping persons experience the theme.

Launching device: Have parishioners meet in the parish hall for a common presentation. The parable of the rich fool can either be told or read and dramatized, using the Arch Book* account of the story mentioned in the commentary. St. Francis of Assisi offers a powerful contrast to the parable. Francis gave up the wealth of his family for the simple life of faith and service to the Lord. He relied on the natural resources of creation for survival. A rather romanticized but effective film was released several years ago on the life of St. Francis under the title *Brother Sun, Sister Moon.* The legends of Francis are appropriate to tell. Even if not historically accurate, they give us an idea of how people have felt about this great saint over the centuries.

The story of Abraham can also be shared in storytelling fashion. Though Abraham did not give up his wealth, he did move into unknown lands and faced the attendant risk with simple and complete trust in the Lord. He gave up the security of what he knew for an unknown risk in following God's call.

This launching process will probably take the major part of this first week's session. Move from the parish center into the nave for the liturgy.

Presenting: Continuity in weekly programming is risky at best, and summertime. attendance is apt to be sporadic, with persons going on vacation and returning. You will need to repeat the launching device from last week in briefer form both to renew the experience for those who were there and to introduce the theme for the newcomers.

After the initial presentation, form smaller groups of three or four families and several single persons. The leader of each group can offer a simple presentation of the theme of this two-week focus. Wealth and possessions are not in themselves destructive. It is the love of possessions or money that is evil. ("For the love of money is the root of all evils"—1 Timothy 6:10.) Also read James 4:1-10 for the feeling of the early Church regarding wealth and power. The envy that comes out of the desire to acquire wealth leads to strife and bickering among God's

people. Read the words of Jesus in the Sermon on the Mount regarding riches (Matthew 6:19-24).

Exploring: In small groups, ask persons to think about how they would feel if they were to follow the steps of St. Francis. How hard would it be to give up what they have now to follow the simpler way? Would it make sense to do so? What do we value most in our life right now? Be sure to include the children in this discussion; they need to hear their parents grapple with the issue.

Let's pretend that we are going off into a survival situation for the next three months. All the stores in our State are going to close. Electricity will be turned off. We will have to live like the settlers of yesteryear. How long could some of us survive in such a situation?

Responding creatively: Move from the discussion groups to several optional learning centers set up for the purpose. Each center is a place where persons can experience a survival skill. For example, one center will have directions and an assigned leader to help persons learn how to make their own soaps. A candle center would be handy in a blacked-out home. Food drying and canning techniques can be offered in another center. With no television to watch we'd better include a center that can introduce simple folk games and crafts that persons can enjoy during this three-month period. If we make this experience attractive enough, some of our families may want to try a week or two of "survival" in camping or at their home. If there is not time for the learning centers, send participants home with directions for the various activities and encourage them to try some of the ideas at home during the week. A community garden clinic can form the basis for another center.

Concluding: As mentioned above, this unit can conclude with a parish survival fair. Those who have learned to make candles, soap, and other items can now teach others and display their creations. The survival fair can simply be an enlarged version of the learning centers just described, but the learners in the first situation can become teachers and sharers at the fair. Open the event to the community at large, and enjoy the experience and opportunity for Christian witness. Include folk music, games, and dance as

* Janice Kramer, *The Rich Fool*, Arch Book Series (St. Louis, Mo.: Concordia, 1964).

an added attraction and for an air of festivity.

Naturally, the feelings and discoveries of this learning experience should find expression in the liturgy. Some of the input into the liturgy may not come until the fall harvest or rogation procession, but prayers, preaching, and the offerings of the people will be influenced by the life the people experienced in the learning center. One of the centers can teach bread- and wine-making techniques. Let the parish be its own source of supply for sacramental needs.

Proper 17   E
Twenty-second Sunday in Ordinary Time   RC
Fifteenth Sunday after Pentecost   L

Purpose of the event: To expose participants to stories that express the need for humbleness. To explore the concept of humbleness as it is expressed in our Judeo-Christian heritage.

When and who: An intergenerational experience prior to the liturgy.

Background information for leaders: See chapter 7, page 262, for an overview of the readings.

Launching device: Gather the community and share the story of Gideon. See A Guide to Stories of the Bible, chapter 1, page 28. The story is found in Judges 6:1-7,22, with the sequel in Judges 8:22-27. If a group wants to dramatize the story, this can be done. Be sure to include the humor inherent in the story.

Presenting: A brief input is offered to the community after the story of Gideon. The story really is a reflection of the whole biblical narrative. It would seem that God has constantly chosen the humble and weak to be instruments of his will. Israel, after all, is a very small nation in terms of territory. Jesus, born in a stable, chose the weak and powerless to be his disciples. He himself died in humility at the hands of the greatest power of the Western world. The language of the New Testament is the Greek spoken by the poor and laboring class. But the people of the Bible constantly went the way of Gideon. Once they felt the power of God working in their lives, they tended to forget that it was the Lord who brought them life, and they made themselves and their possessions their gods

instead. (See Deuteronomy 8:1-3,6-10,11-16, and 17-20 for an expression of this concern attributed to Moses before the people's entrance into the land of Canaan.)

Exploring: At this stage, break the community into smaller groups to share more intimate responses. The leader in each small group needs to rehearse, not retell, the story of Gideon with the participants. At each turning point in the story the leader should stop and ask what feelings Gideon might have had at that point. "Gideon was alone working at the winepress when suddenly he saw an angel. How do you think he felt?" Record the answers on newsprint, and note the point in the story where the feelings fit. "God told Gideon to reduce the number of men in his army by taking them to the stream to drink. How do you think he felt?" The last point in the story would be the sequel. "And Gideon made an ephod of (the gold) and put it in his city in Ophrah; and all Israel played the harlot after it there, and it became a snare to Gideon and to his family" (Judges 8:27). Now go back over the events and the feelings associated with the events. At what times in the story was Gideon closest to God, and at what times was he most able to be an instrument of God's action in the world?

Responding creatively: Have each family or group of three to four persons think up a sequel to the story of Gideon. He drops out of sight as far as the Bible is concerned. But we can write another chapter of his story. The ending of the story is that Gideon returns to God and again becomes a man of faith and humility. Have the families or individuals dream up the details of what happened between the golden ephod and the return to the Lord in humbleness. Give the families about fifteen minutes to talk about it and make up their story; then have them regroup to share their stories. The newsprint "feeling line" could be extended by having the rest of the group identify the feelings of Gideon at each stage of the sequels being shared.

Concluding: As participants return to the parish hall to gather again as a whole community, they find the chairs arranged as if set around a large banquet table. A head table has been set up marked with a large plaque saying "The Place of Honor." After people are seated, the gospel of the day is read in which Jesus commands the people "...when you are invited, ...go and sit in the lowest place, so that when your host comes he may say to you, 'Friend, go up higher....' For every one who exalts himself will be humbled, and he who humbles himself will be exalted" (Luke 14:8-11).

After the gospel reading, the celebrant at the liturgy steps forward and invites the participants to the banquet of the Lord to be celebrated in the sanctuary of the church. The people can respond with the words from Rite One of *The Book of Common Prayer:* "We do not presume to come to this thy Table, O merciful Lord, trusting in our own righteousness, but in thy manifold and great mercies. We are not worthy so much as to gather up the crumbs under thy Table. But thou art the same Lord whose property is always to have mercy. Grant us therefore, gracious Lord, so to eat the flesh of they dear Son Jesus Christ, and to drink his blood, that we may evermore dwell in him, and he in us. *Amen*" (page 307). (In the Roman Catholic liturgy, similar words of humility are said before the receiving of the Sacrament.) Then the people can process into the nave to celebrate the Sacrament together.

An End-of-the-Summer Festival
The end of the summer has arrived. We have shared events and experiences during the season, from planting our parish garden together to making soap; from seeing a film of St. Francis' life to writing prayers for the liturgy. Now we are getting ready for the big seasonal change. School will open soon. Labor Day weekend will mark the official turning of the secular season that so strongly influences our lives. Some of us are busily harvesting the fruit of our labor in the garden. Canning, drying, and freezing are under way. There is a wistful feeling about the summer vacation time being over. Long faces on the children greet us at breakfast as they count down the few days of vacation left and remember the fun times in the warm summer sun. But there is also a great feeling of anticipation. Who will be my teacher this year? All of us are caught up in preparing to start new programs and to reinvolve ourselves in organizations that have been dormant during the summer.

Well, let's celebrate the turning of the season. Look back at what we've done during the summer season and bring it all together. A medieval festival adds color, pomp, banners, and costumes of ladies, lords, and court jesters. Get the teenagers to create simple folding booths. Display the homemade soap, the canned fruit from the garden, the puppets the children made in their program earlier in the summer. Encourage other persons in the parish to share their hobbies, from stamp collecting to wood working. A quarter gets you booth space on the grand castle grounds. Invite some strolling minstrels to sing and dance along the avenue of booths. Recorder music adds a medieval sound to the festivities. Ask your artists to display their latest summer creations. Have a poetry reading for those who create with words. The family that came back from their trip excited about the Revolutionary War history they discovered in New England can enthusiastically share their adventures and make history live again by way of slides, maps, battle plans, and routes of march. The skits or puppet shows created during the summer program can be repeated on the staging ground at advertised intervals. The fair crier can make sure everyone is aware of the next event by announcements made with bell and shouts of "Hear ye...."

In the late nineteenth century, the Chautauqua was an exciting event for any community. Speakers and artists of renown spent the week in the community offering lectures, plays, and concerts at stated times during the day and helping folks of the community learn skills at workshops. The Chautauqua idea started as a religious education event and then broadened out to include all kinds of entertainment and cultural enrichment. Let's take the idea back and share it again. Invite a well-known speaker or artist to share talents with us in the evening. Follow the main event with a workshop in which the "headline" speaker or artist can give participants an opportunity to go deeper into the art form or topic of interest.

Invite the community to your festival. This is a time for evangelism. As parishioners are caught up in the excitement of proclaiming Christ's living, creative presence in their lives, the community becomes infected with the same enthusiasm. The day or days of festival can end with a candlelight sharing of Evening Prayer (Vespers) in the nave. But it won't end for the children. Tell them the traditions of the Feast of Booths (Sukkoth) shared by our Jewish friends and ancestors in the faith. As night falls, decorate the booths from the fair with harvest stalks, branches, and the fruit of the vine; let the children sleep in them in accord with the ancient tradition described in chapter 3, page 89. If the same children are willing to help strip down the fair the next morning, their parents can offer them a special treat of a huge breakfast with pancakes, sausages, and other delicacies.

Banners are a part of any fair, especially one that follows the medieval motif. Bring out the banners used in the nave and around the parish house. Create new ones for the occasion, and then include them as liturgical or parish house banners for the remainder of the year. Banners will bring the story of this summer back again in midwinter. Have some of the prayers written by the children done in calligraphy and displayed as paper banners or even offered for sale as devotional cards. These prayers will be included in the evening liturgy. Collect the prayers written during the Sunday when we focused on prayer. Have them printed, and offer a parish prayerbook filled with your unique expressions of prayer and praise.

Oh yes, a hot-air balloon. Some persons are taking up this old-fashioned flying technique as a hobby. Others offer the hot-air balloon ride as a commercial venture. Whether the balloon flies along or just hovers over the festival, it adds a note of color and wonder to the environment.

Folk dancing is a storytelling form in itself. That is partly what makes folk dancing such fun. In a sense it is a form of liturgy. The movement of the dance and the words to the songs that go with it express the people's story and their quest for wholeness. (The dances of Native Americans are an example of this.) Folk dancing is also joyful because it includes everyone in a common expression of joy and creativity. It is community-building activity at its best. Even very young children can take part in the simpler dances and feel at one with their parents and other adults of the community. Folk dancing and square dancing (the latter a uniquely American expression of folk dancing) are becoming increasingly popular. Learning the steps, of course, is essential to enjoyment. So hire a teacher for the evening, if necessary; a good teacher is crucial.

Invite theater or mime or folk-dance groups from the community to join the festival. If you have a professional group in mind, see if you can find persons in the parish who will subsidize the cost of performances. A small admission to view the event can also be charged, of course.

Celebrating an end-of-the-summer medieval festival on the "village green" is a way to end the summer and welcome the fall. It is one way of proclaiming the Lord's presence in every season, in every creative act, in every moment of solitude, and in every moment of gathering in the Lord's name.

The ideas just shared may sound overwhelming to the small parish, but we need not try everything. A simple Sunday-after-church sharing in the church yard is a start, and a good one at that. The summer festival may simply be an extended coffee hour with displays, singing, and the sharing of goodies created for the occasion. But brainstorming is fun. Don't limit yourselves at first when you plan. Let all the ideas flow out, as wild and impractical as they may seem. The "reality check" comes at the next stage. What can we actually do in this space, with these resources, in this time, with these persons? As we shape our ideas to the reality, we need not despair about not having done everything. If we had not let our minds go free, we wouldn't have come up with the simpler ideas we can enjoy together.

Chapter 5
A Commentary
on the Eucharistic Lectionary,
Year A

Use the following list to see which Bible passages the commentary is referring to in discussing a given Sunday or feast day. To discover the *calendar* date of a day, consult your own church calendar or liturgy expert.

Despite minor differences and occasional local variations, there is now substantial agreement among Episcopalians, Roman Catholics, and Lutherans (and some other churches as well) on the scriptural readings assigned for Sundays and greater feast days. In the following list, then, assume that the readings are the same for the three churches unless variants are noted. (Notice how minor many variants are—simply a few verses added or omitted.)

Terms for a day or a season may differ. For instance, what Episcopalians and Lutherans call the Sundays after Pentecost are called Sundays in Ordinary Time (or Sundays of the Year) by Roman Catholics; Episcopalians designate the readings and prayers proper to those Sundays as Proper 1, Proper 2, and so on, indicating in *The Book of Common Prayer*

that Proper 11, for instance, is used on the Sunday nearest to July 20. In the following list, terms or observances peculiar to Episcopalians, Roman Catholics, or Lutherans are designated **E, RC,** or **L.**

A sample entry, 1 Cor 10:16-17(18-21), refers to First Corinthians, chapter 10, verses 16-17, with verses 18-21 optional.

Note that the psalms assigned as responses to the readings are not listed here, since this book deals primarily with the readings themselves. Nevertheless, the psalm responses are an important part of the total worship experience, and every effort should be made to familiarize our congregations with them. See Appendix I for comments on psalms that are particularly appropriate for the religious education setting.

The following abbreviations are used for books of the Bible. Note carefully the difference between books such as Ecclesiastes (Eccles) and Ecclesiasticus (Ecclus), Zechariah (Zech) and Zephaniah (Zeph).

Key to Abbreviations

Acts	Acts	1 K	1 Kings
Amos	Amos	2 K	2 Kings
Bar	Baruch	Lam	Lamentations
1 Chr	1 Chronicles	Lev	Leviticus
2 Chr	2 Chronicles	Lk	Luke
Col	Colossians	1 Mac	1 Maccabees
1 Cor	1 Corinthians	2 Mac	2 Maccabees
2 Cor	2 Corinthians	Mal	Malachi
Dan	Daniel	Mic	Micah
Deut	Deuteronomy	Mk	Mark
Eccles	Ecclesiastes	Mtt	Matthew
Ecclus	Ecclesiasticus	Nah	Nahum
Eph	Ephesians	Neh	Nehemiah
Est	Esther	Num	Numbers
Ex	Exodus	Ob	Obadiah
Ezk	Ezekiel	1 Pet	1 Peter
Gal	Galatians	2 Pet	2 Peter
Gen	Genesis	Phlp	Philippians
Hab	Habakkuk	Phm	Philemon
Hag	Haggai	Prov	Proverbs
Heb	Hebrews	Ps	Psalms
Hos	Hosea	Rom	Romans
Isa	Isaiah	Ruth	Ruth
Jam	James	Rev	Revelation
Jer	Jeremiah	1 Sam	1 Samuel
Jn	John	2 Sam	2 Samuel
1 Jn	1 John	1 Thes	1 Thessalonians
2 Jn	2 John	2 Thes	2 Thessalonians
3 Jn	3 John	1 Tim	1 Timothy
Job	Job	2 Tim	2 Timothy
Joel	Joel	Titus	Titus
Jonah	Jonah	Tob	Tobit
Josh	Joshua	Wis	Wisdom
Jdt	Judith	Zech	Zechariah
Jude	Jude	Zeph	Zephaniah
Judges	Judges		

Lectionary Readings for Sundays and Greater Feasts in Year A

Sunday or Feast	Episcopal*	Roman Catholic†	Lutheran‡
1st Sun. of Advent	Isa 2:1-5 Rom 13:8-14 Mtt 24:37-44	Rom 13:11-14 Mtt 24:37-44	Rom 13:11-14 Mtt 24:37-44 or Mtt 21:1-11
2nd Sun. of Advent	Isa 11:1-10 Rom 15:4-13 Mtt 3:1-12	Rom 15:4-9	Rom 15:4-13
3rd Sun. of Advent	Isa 35:1-10 Jam 5:7-10 Mtt 11:2-11	Isa 35:1-6,10	Isa 35:1-10
4th Sun. of Advent	Isa 7:10-17 Rom 1:1-7 Mtt 1:18-25	Isa 7:10-14 Mtt 1:18-24	Isa 7:10-14(15-17) Mtt 1:18-25
Christmas Vigil **RC**	* §	Isa 62:1-5 Acts 13:16-17, 22-25 Mtt 1:1-25	* §
Christmas Day I **E**; Mass at Midnight **RC**; Option 1 **L**	Isa 9:2-4, 6-7 Titus 2:11-14 Lk 2:1-14(15-20)	Isa 9:1-6 Lk 2:1-14	Isa 9:2-7 Lk 2:1-20
Christmas Day II **E**; Mass at Dawn **RC**; Option 2 **L**	Isa 62:6-7,10-12 Titus 3:4-7 Lk 2:(1-14)15-20	Isa 62:11-12 Titus 3:4-7 Lk 2:15-20	Isa 52:7-10 Heb 1:1-9 Jn 1:1-14
Christmas Day III **E**; Mass during the Day **RC**; Option 3 **L**	Isa 52:7-10 Heb 1:1-12 Jn 1:1-14	Isa 52:7-10 Heb 1:1-6 Jn 1:1-18	Isa 62:10-12 Titus 3:4-7 Lk 2:1-20

1st Sun. after
  Christmas **E, L**;
Sun. in Octave of
  Christmas (Holy
  Family) **RC**
	Isa 61:10—62:3
	Gal 3:23-25;4:4-7
	Jn 1:1-18
		Ecclus 3:2-6,12-14
		Col 3:12-21
		Mtt 2:13-15,19-23
			Isa 63:7-9
			Gal 4:4-7
			Mtt 2:13-15,19-23

Holy Name (Jan. 1) **E**;
Mary, Mother of
  God **RC**;
Name of Jesus **L**
	Ex 34:1-8
	Rom 1:1-7 or
	   Phlp 2:9-13
	Lk 2:15-21
		Num 6:22-27
		Gal 4:4-7
		
		Lk 2:16-21
			Num 6:22-27
			Rom 1:1-7 or
			   Phlp 2:9-13
			Lk 2:21

*The Book of Common Prayer and Administration of the Sacraments and Other Rites and Ceremonies of the Church (New York: The Church Hymnal Corporation and The Seabury Press, 1979).
†Lectionary for Mass (New York: Catholic Book Publishing, 1970).
†Lutheran Book of Worship (Minneapolis, Minn.: Augsburg Publishing, 1978).
§Episcopal and Lutheran lectionaries do not have this service.

Sunday or Feast	Episcopal	Roman Catholic	Lutheran

2nd Sun. after Christmas	Jer 31:7-14
	Eph 1:3-6,15-19a
	Mtt 2:13-15,19-23
	  or Lk 2:41-52
	  or Mtt 2:1-12
		Ecclus 24:1-4, 8-12
		Eph 1:3-6,15-18
		Jn 1:1-18
			Isa 61:10—62:3
			Eph 1:3-6,15-18
			Jn 1:1-18

The Epiphany	Isa 60:1-6,9 Eph 3:1-12 Mtt 2:1-12	Isa 60:1-6 Eph 3:2-3,5-6	Isa 60:1-6 Eph 3:2-12
1st Sun. after Epiphany E, L; Baptism of the Lord RC	Isa 42:1-9 Acts 10:34-38 Mtt 3:13-17	Isa 42:1-4,6-7	Isa 42:1-7
2nd Sun. after Epiphany E, L; 2nd Sun. Ord. Time RC	Isa 49:1-7 1 Cor 1:1-9 Jn 1:29-41	Isa 49:3,5-6 1 Cor 1:1-3 Jn 1:29-34	Isa 49:1-6 1 Cor 1:1-9 Jn 1:29-41
3rd Sun. after Epiphany E, L; 3rd Sun. Ord. Time RC	Amos 3:1-8 1 Cor 1:10-17 Mtt 4:12-23	Isa 8:23—9:3 1 Cor 1:10-13,17 Mtt 4:12-23	Isa 9:1b-4 or Amos 3:1-8 1 Cor 1:10-17 Mtt 4:12-23
4th Sun. after Epiphany E, L; 4th Sun. Ord. Time RC	Mic 6:1-8 1 Cor 1:(18-25) 26-31 Mtt 5:1-12	Zeph 2:3;3:12-13 i Cor 1:26-31	Mic 6:1-8 1 Cor 1:26-31
5th Sun. after Epiphany E, L; 5th Sun. Ord. Time RC	Hab 3:1-6,17-19 1 Cor 2:1-11 Mtt 5:13-20	Isa 58:7-10 1 Cor 2:1-5 Mtt 5:13-16	Isa 58:5-9a 1 Cor 2:6-13 Mtt 5:13-20
6th Sun. after Epiphany E, L; 6th Sun. Ord. Time RC	Ecclus 15:11-20 1 Cor 3:1-9 Mtt 5:21-24, 27-30, 33-37	Ecclus 15:15-20 1 Cor 2:6-10 Mtt 5:17-37	Deut 30:15-20 1 Cor 2:6-13 Mtt 5:20-37
7th Sun. after Epiphany E, L; 7th Sun. Ord. Time RC	Lev 19:1-2,9-18 1 Cor 3:10-11,16-23 Mtt 5:38-48	Lev 19:1-2,17-18 1 Cor 3:16-23	Lev 19:1-2,17-18 1 Cor 3:10-11,16-23
8th Sun. after Epiphany E, L; 8th Sun. Ord. Time RC	Isa 49:8-18 1 Cor 4:1-5(6-7)8-13 Mtt 6:24-34	Isa 49:14-15 1 Cor 4:1-5	Isa 49:13-18 1 Cor 4:1-13
Last Sun. after Epiphany E, L	Ex 24:12(13-14)15-18 Phlp 3:7-14 Mtt 17:1-9	*	Ex 24:12,15-18 2 Pet 1:16-19(20-21)

*The Roman Catholic lectionary does not use this designation.

Sunday or Feast	Episcopal	Roman Catholic	Lutheran
Ash Wednesday	Joel 2:1-2,12-17 or Isa 58:1-12 2 Cor 5:20b—6:10 Mtt 6:1-6,16-21	Joel 2:12-18 2 Cor 5:20—6:2 Mtt 6:1-6,16-18	Joel 2:12-19 2 Cor 5:20b—6:2 Mtt 6:1-6,16-21
1st Sun. in Lent	Gen 2:4b-9,15-17, 25—3:7 Rom 5:12-19(20-21) Mtt 4:1-11	Gen 2:7-9; 3:1-7 Rom 5:12-19	Gen 2:7-9, 15-17; 3:1-7 Rom 5:12(13-16)17-19
2nd Sun. in Lent	Gen 12:1-8 Rom 4:1-5(6-12)13-17 Jn 3:1-17	Gen 12:1-4 2 Tim 1:8-10 Mtt 17:1-9	Gen 12:1-8 Rom 4:1-5,13-17 Jn 4:5-26(27-30,39-42)
3rd Sun. in Lent	Ex 17:1-7 Rom 5:1-11 Jn 4:5-26(27-38)39-42	Ex 17:3-7 Rom 5:1-2,5-8 Jn 4:5-42	Isa 42:14-21 Eph 5:8-14 Jn 9:1-41 or Jn 9:13-17,34-39
4th Sun. in Lent	1 Sam 16:1-13 Eph 5:(1-7)8-14 Jn 9:1-13(14-27)28-38	1 Sam 16:1,6-7,10-13 Eph 5:8-14 Jn 9:1-41	Hos 5:15—6:2 Rom 8:1-10 Mtt 20:17-28
5th Sun. in Lent	Ezk 37:1-3(4-10)11-14 Rom 6:16-23 Jn 11:(1-17)18-44	Ezk 37:12-14 Rom 8:8-11 Jn 11:1-45	Ezk 37:1-3(4-10)11-14 Rom 8:11-19 Jn 11:1-53 or Jn 11:47-53
Palm Sunday (Liturgy of the Palms)	Mtt 21:1-11	Mtt 21:1-11	*

Palm Sunday (at the
  Eucharist)
	Isa 45:21-25 or
	  Isa 52:13
	  —53:12
	Phlp 2:5-11
	Mtt (26:36-75)
	  27:1-54(55-66)
		Isa 50:4-7
		
		Phlp 2:6-11
		Mtt 26:14-27,66 or
		  Mtt 27:11-54
			Isa 50:4-9a
			
			Phlp 2:5-11
			Mtt 26:1—27:66
			  or Mtt 27:11-54

Easter Vigil **E, RC**	Gen 1:1—2:2 Gen 7:1-5,11-18; 8:6-18;9:8-13 Gen 22:1-18 Ex 14:10—15:1 Isa 4:2-6 Isa 55:1-11 Ezk 36:24-28 Ezk 37:1-14 Zeph 3:12-20 Rom 6:3-11 Mtt 28:1-10	Gen 1:1—2:2 Gen 22:1-18 Ex 14:15—15:1 Isa 54:5-14 Isa 55:1-11 Bar 3:9-15,32—4:4 Ezk 36:16-28 Rom 6:3-11 Mtt 28:1-10	*

*The Lutheran lectionary does not have this service.

Sunday or Feast	Episcopal	Roman Catholic	Lutheran
Easter Day, Principal Service	Acts 10:34-43 or Ex 14:10-14,21-25; 15:20-21	Acts 10:34,37-43	Acts 10:34-43
	Col 3:1-4 or Acts 10:34-43	Col 3:1-4 or 1 Cor 5:6-8	Col 3:1-4
	Jn 20:1-10(11-18) or Mtt 28:1-10	Jn 20:1-9 or Mtt 28:1-10	Jn 20:1-9(10-18) or Mtt 28:1-10
2nd Sun. of Easter	Acts 2:14a,22-32 or Gen 8:6-16;9:8-16	Acts 2:42-47 *	Acts 2:14a,22-32 *
	1 Pet 1:3-9 or Acts 2:14a,22-32	1 Pet 1:3-9	1 Pet 1:3-9
	Jn 20:19-31		
3rd Sun. of Easter	Acts 2:14a,36-47 or Isa 43:1-12	Acts 2:14,22-28	Acts 2:14a,36-47
	1 Pet 1:17-23 or Acts 2:14a,36-47	1 Pet 1:17-21	1 Pet 1:17-21
	Lk 24:13-35		
4th Sun. of Easter	Acts 6:1-9;7:2a,51-60 or Neh 9:6-15	Acts 2:14,36-41	Acts 6:1-9,7:2a,51-60
	1 Pet 2:19-25 or Acts 6:1-9;7:2a,51-60	1 Pet 2:20-25	1 Pet 2:19-25
	Jn 10:1-10		
5th Sun. of Easter	Acts 17:1-15 or Deut 6:20-25	Acts 6:1-7	Acts 17:1-15
	1 Pet 2:1-10 or Acts 17:1-15	1 Pet 2:4-9	1 Pet 2:4-10
	Jn 14:1-14	Jn 14:1-12	Jn 14:1-12
6th Sun. of Easter	Acts 17:22-31 or Isa 41:17-20	Acts 8:5-8,14-17	Acts 17:22-31
	1 Pet 3:8-18 or Acts 17:22-31	1 Pet 3:15-18	1 Pet 3:15-22
	Jn 15:1-8	Jn 14:15-21	Jn 14:15-21
Ascension Day	Acts 1:1-11 or Dan 7:9-14	Acts 1:1-11	Acts 1:1-11
	Eph 1:15-23 or Acts 1:1-11	Eph 1:17-23	Eph 1:16-23
	Lk 24:49-53 or Mk 16:9-15,19-20	Mtt 28:16-20	Lk 24:44-53
7th Sun. of Easter	Acts 1:(1-7)8-14 or Ezk 29:21-29	Acts 1:12-14	Acts 1:(1-7)8-14
	1 Pet 4:12-19 or Acts 1:(1-7)8-14	1 Pet 4:13-16	1 Pet 4:12-17; 5:6-11
	Jn 17:1-11	Jn 17:1-11	Jn 17:1-11

*Roman Catholic and Lutheran lectionaries have no Old Testament lesson during the Easter season.

Sunday or Feast	Episcopal	Roman Catholic	Lutheran
Day of Pentecost	Acts 2:1-11 or Ezk 11:17-20	Acts 2:1-11	Joel 2:28-29
	1 Cor 12:4-13 or Acts 2:1-11	1 Cor 12:3-7,12-13	Acts 2:1-21
	Jn 20:19-23 or Jn 14:8-17	Jn 20:19-23	Jn 20:19-23
Trinity Sunday	Gen 1:1—2:3	Ex 34:4-6,8-9	Gen 1:1—2:3 or Deut 4:32-34,39-40
	2 Cor 13:(5-10)11-14	2 Cor 13:11-13	2 Cor 13:11-14
	Mtt 28:16-20	Jn 3:16-18	Mtt 28:16-20
Proper 4 **E**; 9th Sun. Ord. Time **RC**; 2nd Sun. after Pentecost **L**	Deut 11:18-21,26-28 Rom 3:21-25a,28 Mtt 7:21-27	Rom 3:21-25,28 Mtt 7:21-27	Rom 3:21-25a,27-28 Mtt 7:(15-20)21-29
Proper 5 **E**; 10th Sun. Ord. Time **RC**; 3rd Sun. after Pentecost **L**	Hos 5:15—6:6 Rom 4:13-18 Mtt 9:9-13	Hos 6:3-6 Rom 4:18-25	Hos 5:15—6:6 Rom 4:18-25
Proper 6 **E**; 11th Sun. Ord. Time **RC**; 4th Sun. after Pentecost **L**	Ex 19:2-8a Rom 5:6-11 Mtt 9:35—10:8(9-15)	Ex 19:2-6 Mtt 9:36—10:8	Ex 19:2-8a Mtt 9:35—10:8
Proper 7 **E**; 12th Sun. Ord. Time **RC**; 5th Sun. after Pentecost **L**	Jer 20:7-13 Rom 5:15b-19 Mtt 10:(16-23)24-33	Jer 20:10-13 Rom 5:12-15 Mtt 10:26-33	Jer 20:7-13 Rom 5:12-15 Mtt 10:24-33
Proper 8 **E**; 13th Sun. Ord. Time **RC**; 6th Sun. after Pentecost **L**	Isa 2:10-17 Rom 6:3-11 Mtt 10:34-42	2 K 4:8-11,14-16 Rom 6:3-4,8-11 Mtt 10:37-42	Jer 28:5-9 Rom 6:1b-11 Mtt 10:34-42
Proper 9 **E**; 14th Sun. Ord. Time **RC**; 7th Sun. after Pentecost **L**	Zech 9:9-12 Rom 7:21—8:6 Mtt 11:25-30	Zech 9:9-10 Rom 8:9,11-13	Zech 9:9-12 Rom 7:15-25a
Proper 10 **E**; 15th Sun. Ord. Time **RC**; 8th Sun. after Pentecost **L**	Isa 55:1-5,10-13 Rom 8:9-17 Mtt 13:1-9,18-23	Isa 55:10-11 Rom 8:18-23 Mtt 13:1-23	Isa 55:10-11 Rom 8:18-25 Mtt 13:1-9(18-23)
Proper 11 **E**; 16th Sun. Ord. Time **RC**; 9th Sun. after Pentecost **L**	Wis 12:13,16-19 Rom 8:18-25 Mtt 13:24-30,36-43	Wis 12:13,16-19 Rom 8:26-27 Mtt 13:24-43	Isa 44:6-8 Rom 8:26-27 Mtt 13:24-30(36-43)

Sunday or Feast	Episcopal	Roman Catholic	Lutheran
Proper 12 **E**; 17th Sun. Ord. Time **RC**; 10th Sun. after Pentecost **L**	1 K 3:5-12 Rom 8:26-34 Mtt 13:31-33,44-49a	1 K 3:5,7-12 Rom 8:28-30 Mtt 13:44-52	1 K 3:5-12 Rom 8:28-30 Mtt 13:44-52
Proper 13 **E**; 18th Sun. Ord. Time **RC**; 11th Sun. after Pentecost **L**	Neh 9:16-20 Rom 8:35-39 Mtt 14:13-21	Isa 55:1-3 Rom 8:35,37-39	Isa 55:1-5 Rom 8:35-39
Proper 14 **E**; 19th Sun. Ord. Time **RC**; 12th Sun. after Pentecost **L**	Jonah 2:1-9 Rom 9:1-5 Mtt 14:22-33	1 K 19:9,11-13	1 K 19:9-18
Proper 15 **E**; 20th Sun. Ord. Time **RC**; 13th Sun. after Pentecost **L**	Isa 56:1(2-5)6-7 Rom 11:13-15,29-32 Mtt 15:21-28	Isa 56:1,6-7	Isa 56:1,6-8
Proper 16 **E**; 21st Sun. Ord. Time **RC**; 14th Sun. after Pentecost **L**	Isa 51:1-6 Rom 11:33-36 Mtt 16:13-20	Isa 22:15,19-23	Ex 6:2-8
Proper 17 **E**; 22nd Sun. Ord. Time **RC**; 15th Sun. after Pentecost **L**	Jer 15:15-21 Rom 12:1-8 Mtt 16:21-27	Jer 20:7-9 Rom 12:1-2 Mtt 16:2-27	Jer 15:15-21 Rom 12:1-8 Mtt 16:21-26
Proper 18 **E**; 23rd Sun. Ord. Time **RC**; 16th Sun. after Pentecost **L**	Ezk 33:(1-6)7-11 Rom 12:9-21 Mtt 18:15-20	Ex 33:7-9 Rom 13:8-10	Ezk 33:7-9 Rom 13:1-10
Proper 19 **E**; 24th Sun. Ord. Time **RC**; 17th Sun. after Pentecost **L**	Ecclus 27:30—28:7 Rom 14:5-12 Mtt 18:21-35	Ecclus 27:30—28:7 Rom 14:7-9	Gen 50:15-21 Rom 14:5-9
Proper 20 **E**; 25th Sun. Ord. Time **RC**; 18th Sun. after Pentecost **L**	Jonah 3:10—4:11 Phlp 1:21-27 Mtt 20:1-16	Isa 55:6-9 Phlp 1:20-24,27	Isa 55:6-9 Phlp 1:1-5 (6-11)19-27
Proper 21 **E**; 26th Sun. Ord. Time **RC**; 19th Sun. after Pentecost **L**	Ezk 18:1-4,25-32 Phlp 2:1-13 Mtt 21:28-32	Ezk 18:25-28 Phlp 2:1-11	Ezk 18:1-4,25-32 Phlp 2:1-5(6-11)

Sunday or Feast	Episcopal	Roman Catholic	Lutheran
Proper 22 **E**; 27th Sun. Ord. Time **RC**; 20th Sun. after Pentecost **L**	Isa 5:1-7 Phlp 3:14-21 Mtt 21:33-43	Phlp 4:6-9	Phlp 3:12-21
Proper 23 **E**; 28th Sun. Ord. Time **RC**; 21st Sun. after Pentecost **L**	Isa 25:1-9 Phlp 4:4-13 Mtt 22:1-14	Isa 25:6-10 Phlp 4:12-14,19-20 Mtt 22:1-14	Isa 25:6-9 Phlp 4:4-13 Mtt 22:1-10(11-14)
Proper 24 **E**; 29th Sun. Ord. Time **RC**; 22nd Sun. after Pentecost **L**	Isa 45:1-7 1 Thes 1:1-10 Mtt 22:15-22	Isa 45:1,4-6 1 Thes 1:1-5 Mtt 22:15-21	Isa 45:1-7 1 Thes 1:1-5a Mtt 22:15-21
Proper 25 **E**; 30th Sun. Ord. Time **RC**; 23rd Sun. after Pentecost **L**	Ex 22:21-27 1 Thes 2:1-8 Mtt 22:34-46	Ex 22:20-26 1 Thes 1:5-10 Mtt 22:34-40	Lev 19:1-2,15-18 1 Thes 1:5b-10 Mtt 22:34-40(41-46)
Proper 26 **E**; 31st Sun. Ord. Time **RC**; 24th Sun. after Pentecost **L**	Mic 3:5-12 1 Thes 2:9-13,17-20 Mtt 23:1-12	Mal 1:14—2:2,8-10 1 Thes 2:7-9,13 Mtt 23:1-12	Amos 5:18-24 1 Thes 4:13-14(15-18) Mtt 25:1-13
Proper 27 **E**; 32nd Sun. Ord. Time **RC**; 25th Sun. after Pentecost **L**	Amos 5:18-24 1 Thes 4:13-18 Mtt 25:1-13	Wis 6:12-16 1 Thes 4:13-18 Mtt 25:1-13	Hos 11:1-4,8-9 1 Thes 5:1-11 Mtt 25:14-30

Proper 28 **E**;
33rd Sun. Ord. Time **RC**;
26th Sun. after
    Pentecost **L**
	Zeph 1:7,12-18
	
	1 Thes 5:1-10
	Mtt 25:14-15,19-29
		Prov 31:10-13,19-20,
		    30-31
		1 Thes 5:1-6
		Mtt 25:14-30
			Mal 2:1-2,4-10
			
			1 Thes 2:8-13
			Mtt 23:1-12

27th Sun. after Pentecost **L**	*	*	Jer 26:1-6 1 Thes 3:7-13 Mtt 24:1-14

Proper 29 **E**;
Last Sun. Ord. Time
    (Feast of Christ the
    King) **RC**;
Last Sun. after
    Pentecost (Christ the
    King) **L**
	Ezk 34:11-17
	1 Cor 15:20-28
	Mtt 25:31-46
		Ezk 34:11-12,15-17
		1 Cor 15:20-26,28
			Ezk 34:11-16,23-24
			1 Cor 15:20-28

*Episcopal and Roman Catholic lectionaries do not have this designation.

The Season of Advent

Advent is a time of looking both backward and forward.

We look backward as we prepare to celebrate the historical birth of Jesus of Nazareth at Christmas. Before that birth people longed for the Messiah who would restore Israel to her former power. We identify with that ancient longing for restoration as we await Christ's coming more fully into our lives.

With that longing for restoration in mind, we recognize in Advent a time of preparation and anticipation. What we celebrate as having happened in the past points to what we anticipate is coming again. First, we recognize that Christ is born into *our* lives *each day* as we open ourselves to his grace and love. These moments of discovering birth in Christ are times when we can stand with the shepherds and hear glad tidings proclaimed. Advent is a season that prepares us to discover new birth happening over and over again for us in and through Christ. In Advent we long for new beginnings, a new birth in Christ. We celebrate those birth times at Christmas. Second, we also look forward in Advent to the culmination of Christ's kingdom, when he will return in glory to fulfill the promise of wholeness as all creation responds to his healing presence. In our acclamation during the Prayer of Consecration (Eucharistic Prayer), we identify with this longing when we say "Christ has died, Christ is risen, Christ will come again," or similar words. Through the Holy Spirit, this new age has already begun, and this too we celebrate.

The Old Testament readings of Advent set the mood and theme each week. As we hear those readings, we need to look at our own dreams and expectations. How do we express them? The prophets of the Old Testament used beautiful poetic expressions, such as the lamb lying at peace with the lion, swords being beaten into plowshares, and the great banquet to come that will be presided over by the Lord. What poetic and symbolic expressions would we use to describe the age that is to come when we will know the Lord fully? What does the "day of the Lord" mean for us? Can we identify with the dreams of the prophets? Children's dreams and hopes for fulfillment will of course be limited.

Their hopes for Christmas gifts, the visit of a grandparent, the Christmas vacation may form the stuff of their dreams. But at a deeper level in children as well as in adults there may well be an awareness of a need for healing, for peace within the family, for the freedom to do what they want in life. In presenting Advent, talk about the excitement of anticipation. Our Christian understanding of life means that there is always something more coming; it is a life lived in anticipation. Connect the poetry of the prophet Isaiah with the poetry and dreams of the participants in your learning community. Identify common elements.

But we need to remember that Advent is to some extent a penitential season too. The celebrant wears the garb of penitential purple. We realize our part in turning from God's promises and participating in acts of "darkness." (Images of light and darkness are interwoven throughout the season's readings.) And the feeling of penitence comes as we force ourselves to compare our dreams, our great expectations, with reality. What keeps us from fulfillment in this moment? What hinders us from seeking the freedom that God offers us? Our fear of the unknown and our anxiety about taking risks often keep us enslaved in our old ways and prevent us from reaching out for new ones. Our greed and possessiveness keep us from letting go of what we have so that we can seek the next step in life. God would free us from our enslavement to fear, injustice, poverty, negation, and disease. We dream of liberation. How can we move away from enslavement and towards that liberation?

For additional introductory remarks on Advent, see chapter 6, page 206.

The Old Testament Readings

First Sunday of Advent
All the nations will recognize the power and wisdom of God. The image of the "mountain of the house of the Lord" is used to visualize this dream. All the tools of war will be eliminated. A reign of eternal peace will come.

Second Sunday of Advent
The reading is a beautiful poetic description of the reign of perfect peace that will be ushered in

by a descendant of King David: "There shall come forth a shoot from the stump of Jesse" (Isaiah 11:1). On this descendant the Spirit of God will truly rest.

Third Sunday of Advent
The prophet writes for an exiled people who long to return to their homeland. A new exodus will begin, the prophet promises, even more glorious than the exodus from Egypt under Moses. In this exodus ". . . the eyes of the blind shall be opened, and the ears of the deaf unstopped" (Isaiah 35:5). As Christians looked back at Jesus' mighty acts, they saw him as the "new Moses" bringing about the great exodus that leads us all toward wholeness. As we see signs of healing and wholeness happening around us, we too can know that God is leading us toward wholeness—we too are part of the new exodus.

Fourth Sunday of Advent
God will give a sign of assurance that he is with his people in time of terror as well as in time of hope. When King Ahaz of Judah thought his world and his kingdom were coming to an end, Isaiah reassured him, ". . . the Lord himself will give you a sign. Behold, a young woman shall conceive and bear a son, and shall call his name Immanuel" (Isaiah 7:14). (The name means *God with us.*) In this story, birth became a sign that God was with his people. Jesus' birth (the name Jesus means *Yahweh saves*) was a sign that God had entered directly into his people's lives to usher in a new age and a new relationship with them. We see signs of God's love in birth, in love, in creation, and in gifts that we receive in this season.

The Gospel Readings
The Old Testament writings looked forward to the restoration of Israel. The people were seeking a "son of David" who would lead them back into covenant with Yahweh and concurrently back into power as a nation. They anticipated a reign of peace when all nations would recognize the presence of Yahweh. The New Testament recognizes that the new day began with the birth of Jesus but that it will not be completed until he comes again at the end of time. The time between

birth and final consummation is seen as an interim age in which Christ is working through his Church in a gradual process of bringing in the new kingdom of God. Thus the present age is a time when the kingdom is both here and not yet here. We stand at the door of the kingdom and express our dreams and expectations of a fuller revelation of what lies within. We catch glimpses of where Christ is leading us, but in the next moment the vision fades. Or to state it differently, a seed has been planted and has begun to grow. We are a part of its growth, but we can only begin to discern the nature of the vine that it will become. Both the Old and New Testaments, therefore, look forward to the "new day," even though in Jesus we recognize that the Son of David has already come. With this in mind, we look at the four gospel readings for Advent.

First Sunday of Advent
"Always be ready" is the theme of this reading. "Watch therefore, for you do not know on what day your Lord is coming" (Matthew 24:42). We are called to live as expectant people, helping each other to move into the new life that God makes known to us each day. We are called to be aware of what is going on in the world and in our own lives. We are called to dream about a better day when people can be free. Think about the people of our nation who have had such dreams. Study their writings and actions. Martin Luther King, Jr., is a classic example of a dreamer who took seriously the Advent readings and who moved to seek fulfillment of the Word in his own life and in the lives of his people. If we were to be confronted tomorrow with our response to Jesus' command to be ready always, how would we answer?

Apocalypticism abounds in today's readings. (Refer to the discussion of apocalyptic writings in chapter 2, pages 63 and 69.) Poetry is the vehicle used to express the deep mysteries of life, death, eternity, and Christian hope. Expose participants to the language, the poetry, and the symbols of hope. How do we express our hopes to each other? "Some day I'm going to meet Prince Charming," one may say in speaking of a hoped-for relationship. "Next year we'll be Number One!" shout the team as they walk off the field after losing their last game of the season. "I'm going to live to see a new day when the sun is going to shine all the time," says the person beginning to recover from a serious illness. In this life we may not expect literal fulfillment of those expressed hopes, but we hold them out as our ideals toward which we move.

Look at the poetry and symbols expressed in the Old Testament reading. Share the poetic expressions and symbols from other writings, including children's stories. Then ask participants to share their own expressions that speak of hope. Put together your own expressions of hope and share them in a group. The epistle and gospel for this week warn of judgment and confrontation. The new day that we hope for may come at any moment. If we are not prepared for it, we may not see the dawn when it comes. Worse yet, we may be acting against the very hope we express. The chance to be the number one team may come sooner than we expect, but if we have not prepared for the possibility, we will close the door to that ranking. If we are not working toward God's kingdom, we are working against it by bringing darkness into the world instead of light.

Second and Third Sundays of Advent

Our attention turns these two weeks to John the Baptist, who "prepared the way" for Jesus. He came in judgment and confrontation, calling the people of God to be baptized as a sign of their repentance and recommitment to the covenant. If we are to move toward the kingdom of God, we have to confront the way we live in the present moment. Judgment and confrontation are often necessary for change to take place in my life, for I will not change until I acknowledge in some way the need for change.

A brief study of John the Baptist would be appropriate during Advent. Tell the story of John. How do we "prepare the way" ourselves? Note the tie-in with the Old Testament readings. The Old Testament reading for the third Sunday of Advent describes an exodus to come. The first exodus was marked by passing through the waters of the Sea of Reeds, or the Red Sea. Now John leads the people through the waters of baptism as a sign of *their* exodus, *their* liberation, *their* promise.

Fourth Sunday of Advent

We begin the Christmas story on this Sunday. Joseph and Mary are introduced. Jesus is born. Matthew makes it clear that Jesus is no ordinary child. This reading sets the stage for the parish Christmas celebrations. Note the tie-in with the Old Testament reading: The maiden "shall conceive and bear a son" (Matthew 1:23).

The Epistle Readings

First Sunday of Advent

"Let us then cast off the works of darkness and put on the armor of light" (Romans 13:12). These words would make a good saying for a liturgical banner or a liturgical response to be shared each week in the learning community and in the home. "Besides this you know what hour it is, how it is full time now for you to wake from sleep. For salvation is nearer to us now than when we first believed" (Romans 13:11). The mood for Advent is set: *Wake up. Prepare the way.* Look for signs of the new day. We must live like the people of light, avoiding the things that we feel so ashamed of that we wish to pursue them in darkness.

Second Sunday of Advent

"For whatever was written in former days was written for our instruction, that by steadfastness and by the encouragement of the scriptures we might have hope" (Romans 15:4). The importance of knowing the story of the past is expressed in this passage. I identify my struggle with the struggle of the people of the story. Their hope becomes my hope. Adolescents and adults could study the historical settings out of which our Advent writings come. Those were hopeless times, and yet the faith proclaimed through the prophets, through John the Baptist, and through Jesus of Nazareth gave reason for hope.

Third Sunday of Advent

Patience is an important aspect of the Advent message. We want instant fulfillment, but the epistle reading reminds us of the farmer who patiently plants the seed and waits for the harvest. We are the seed planters. The seed is love (see the epistle reading of the first Sunday of Advent). We prepare the soil, but the Lord brings forth the harvest. So we are cocreators with God. This beautiful idea of working together with God to bring forth the harvest is deeply imbedded in the Old Testament. The farmer and vinekeeper can appreciate this poetry better than most of us in the city, but it is a feeling we all need to recapture.

Fourth Sunday of Advent

As the Old Testament reading and the gospel reading focus this Sunday on the birth of Jesus, the epistle reading helps us appreciate how the early Church proclaimed that birth and how we proclaim it to this day. Paul opens his letter to the Romans with what seems like a credal statement. This Jesus who was born was a descendant of David "according to the flesh" and is "designated Son of God."

The Season of Christmas

At Christmas we celebrate the incarnation of the Word of God. One of the gospel passages for Christmas Day, John 1:1-14, is the key to the Christmas season. "The Word was God. . . . The true light that enlightens every man was coming into the world. . . . And the Word became flesh and dwelt among us . . . ; we have beheld his glory. . . ." The birth narratives of Jesus, as recorded in the Gospels of Matthew and Luke, stir nostalgic feelings of wonder and memory, but the Gospel of John goes to the heart of Christmas.

The concept of God is beyond our comprehension. To speak of God is to speak of the source of all creation, the "ultimate energy" that calls all creation into being. As we realize that creation encompasses stars and galaxies and all the universe, God may become more and more remote to us. And yet the Bible proclaims that this incomprehensible power of creation acts to communicate with us humans. As the Israelites reflected on their story, they could see God acting to call them into the covenant in which they were to be part of God's creative power in the world.

The Bible talks of the word or the wisdom of God. God is known in the wisdom that comes to us so that we can speak his word as the prophets did. Proverbs 9:1-6 refers to wisdom as if it were a person. The writer of the Gospel of John recognizes that indeed this word or wisdom *is* a person. In Jesus, "the Word became flesh" (John 1:14). God communicated directly to the human race, not just through history or wisdom but in the man Jesus. It is as if a teacher said to his or her students at the end of the term "Everything I've talked about all term is a person who is going to walk in the door and meet you face to face." This "personality" of wisdom, moreover, is an eternal presence of God with mankind. As we discover the Jesus of the gospels, we begin to discover "the Word made flesh" in our own daily lives. God comes to us as we discover his Word "in the flesh" of the relationships of love and power we share. Thus we "meet the Word" or "meet Christ" in relationships that move us toward liberation, potential, and peace. We discover it revealed in

the Bible and in the sacraments that grew out of the biblical Word. (The sacraments are ways of experiencing and discovering the Word in "outward and visible" form.)

This is but one way of looking at the concept of Christmas, and it is vastly oversimplified; but we need to think of ways of expressing Christmas that move us from nostalgic remembrance to present reality. Luke and Matthew tell the story. John provides the meaning to that story. As religious educators we must help provide the vehicle to make the story and the meaning come alive for the learning community. Note the use of *light* and *darkness* in the readings. Advent begins in darkness and moves toward light with the lighting of the Advent candles. Christmas proclaims the presence of the light. Epiphany calls us to spread the light.

Christmas is a season of twelve days. Be sure that the Christmas theme is carried on beyond Christmas day. Some parishes have a major celebration for the Feast of Epiphany (or Twelfth Night). This follows a very ancient tradition, for Epiphany was an important feast day of the Christian Church before Christmas was introduced. Chapter 4 also has suggestions for celebrating Twelfth Night in your parish (see pages 103-105).

First Sunday after Christmas   E, L
Sunday in the Octave of Christmas:
Holy Family   RC
Since Christmas is a season of twelve days, ending with the Feast of Epiphany (or Twelfth Night), be sure to carry the Christmas theme throughout this time. If possible, have a major celebration on Epiphany. See chapter 4, pages 103-105, for suggestions about celebrating Twelfth Night.

Christmas is a great storytelling time. We have traditionally told the story in song, drama, and pageantry. Notice, for example, how the familiar carol "The First Noel" tells the story in song. Many such carols or hymns can be adapted for use in pageants, dramas, or readings. Notice that Christmas can teach us to adapt such storytelling techniques to other seasons, Sundays, and festivals of the church year.

(Since so many of the readings of years B and C appear also in Year A, we have grouped all our discussions of *individual* Sundays under Year A. When readings from Years B and C are mentioned below, they will be identified as such.)

The Episcopal Old Testament reading speaks of a new day dawning for Jerusalem. ". . . for Jerusalem's sake I will not rest, until her vindication goes forth as brightness. . ." (Isaiah 62:1). The light theme is also conveyed in the reading from John 1:1-14 discussed above (page 152). Talk about the concept of light today. Prepare children and adults to participate in the Feast of Lights service at Epiphany. This would be a good time to discover in general terms how Jesus brought light into people's lives. What did he do to help people "see the light"?

In the Lutheran readings for this Sunday in Year C, the Old Testament passage is a beautiful poem of hope. The people in exile will be restored to their land:

. . . 'He who scattered Israel will gather him,
   and will keep him as a shepherd keeps his
   flock.'
Then shall the maidens rejoice in the dance,
   and the young men and the old shall be merry.
I will turn their mourning into joy,
   I will comfort them, and give them gladness
   for sorrow.

(Jeremiah 31:10b,13)

This reading expresses the hope we feel at Christmas. In the learning community it offers possibilities for sharing a Christmas-season party, with tambourines and dancing. The words in verse 6, "Arise, and let us go up to Zion, to the Lord our God," could be placed on posters and banners during the time of celebration. Our Epiphany celebration is coming soon, and the words will have meaning for the story of the wise men, too. Tell other stories associated with Jesus' birth. The story of Simeon and Anna as they praised God for the birth of Jesus. (Luke 2:22-38). Jesus in the temple at the age of twelve. (Luke 2:41-50). Talk about the Temple and its customs. Let participants see pictures of what the Temple might have looked like so that they will have a feel for the stories about Jesus that happened there.

For Roman Catholics, the Sunday within the Octave of Christmas is the feast of the Holy Family. The focus of the feast is the ideal Christian family life-style modeled on the words of Scripture. Years A, B, and C each have their own gospel reading about the infancy and childhood of Jesus—passages depicting the life of the Holy Family; the Old Testament passage and the epistle reading are each the same for all three years. The Old Testament reading talks of the importance of honoring and respecting our parents. The epistle reading describes the ideal relationship between husband and wife and between parents and children.

Spend time in the learning community talking about the family today. What traditions bind us closer together as a family? How can we draw closer in Christ's peace? Tell the stories of your family that can help give a sense of rootedness. We recall Jesus' childhood family memories. What are some of ours? Children enjoy hearing the stories that give them a sense of family identity. Share the humorous stories of the family as well as the serious stories that shaped our identity as we grew up.

Feast of the Holy Name—January 1   E
Name of Jesus   L
Octave of Christmas: Solemnity of Mary, Mother of God   RC

The gospel reading recalls the naming of Jesus at his circumcision. Talk about the custom of circumcision and the significance of a name in the Bible. Circumcision is a very ancient custom practiced not only by our people but by many surrounding civilizations as well. The biblical injunction for circumcision is found in Genesis 17:10-14 and Exodus 12:48-49. Health reasons may have been the origin of the practice, but it seems always to have had religious overtones among ancient peoples. It became a mark of the covenant for the Israelites. In the New Testament period, circumcision was a divisive issue as the Church grew among the Gentiles. St. Paul talked of the "circumcision of the heart" which meant a real turning toward Christ and the New Covenant. This would suffice, he insisted. But many others in the Church insisted on physical circumcision as the true mark of the Judeo-Christian.

In any case, Joseph and Mary would follow the custom of circumcising their son on the eighth day after his birth. At this·time he also received his name. Note that the name *Jesus* means *the Lord saves*. It is a Greek version of the Hebrew name *Joshua*. Thus for the Jews of Jesus' time his name alone would indicate his mission. Like Joshua he would be an instrument of the Lord's saving action among his people.

"In biblical thought a name is not a mere label of identification; it is an expression of the essential nature of its bearer. A man's name reveals his character. . . . Hence to know the name of God is to know God as he had revealed himself."*

With this in mind, talk about the names we have given God both in the Bible and in the prayer book. As I mention in chapter 2 (page 53), when God identified himself to Moses at the burning bush, he used the name *I AM WHO I AM*. One way of interpreting that strange name is "I am what's happening" or "I am your history." The name of God implies the nature of God. Now, Jesus called God "Father." What does this say about the nature of God as Jesus understood him? The name given to God in the General Thanksgiving for Morning Prayer *(The Book of Common Prayer)* is "Almighty God, Father of all mercies." The names we give God in our formal and informal prayers express our understanding of God.

Using a Bible dictionary, look up the meaning of some other names we find in the Bible. Notice, for example, how Hosea names his three children (Hosea 1). Notice also how the sons of Jacob (who became the patriarchs of the twelve tribes of Israel) are named in Genesis 29 and 30.

After discussing biblical names, talk about the names of the persons in the learning community. How many people know why they were given their name? See if they can discover the meaning of their names in reference books. How do they feel about their names? The concept of naming is a powerful one. If someone calls out my name, I stop and listen. People can belittle

me or affirm me by the way they use my name. American Indian names express something about the person. Some tribes placed great importance on giving a child a name at puberty that would express the character of that person as he or she reached adulthood. What names might we give each other in a naming ceremony that would express the life we have shared in the group?

(Once during a camping trip, each member of our family took a name for the next day that reflected what we had done or felt on the day that was ending. This suppertime naming event became a very meaningful experience and helped us reflect on our day together.)

January 1 is the feast of Mary, Mother of God, in the Roman Catholic lectionary. The gospel reading is basically the same as that appointed in the Episcopal and Lutheran lectionaries for today's feast. The Old Testament reading in the Roman Catholic and Lutheran lectionaries recalls the ancient blessing of the Israelites. "The Lord bless you and keep you: The Lord make his face to shine upon you, and be gracious to you: The Lord lift up his countenance upon you, and give you peace" (Numbers 6:24-26). The name of the Lord will be a blessing upon the people. The very name of the Lord itself is a blessing to us as we hear it. The Christian blessing is given in the name of the Father, the Son, and the Holy Spirit. As I am blessed, the invoking of God's name is an outward sign of the inward strength that comes to me as a Christian. When I hear the name of my wife or other person I love, the name itself encourages me. The name is an outward sign of the deep relationship between us. In a sense, the name is a blessing to me, and so it is with the name of the Lord.

Second Sunday after Christmas
We continue telling the Christmas story this Sunday. The Episcopal church has three choices for the gospel reading: the story of Joseph taking Mary and Jesus to Egypt to escape Herod's anger; the story of Jesus in the Temple at age twelve; or the coming of the wise men to see Jesus. No matter which reading is used in the liturgy, the learning community can share the stories of Jesus found in the opening passages of Luke and Matthew.

*George Arthur Buttrick, ed., *The Interpreter's Dictionary of the Bible* (Nashville, Tenn.: Abingdon Press, 1962), pp. 500-501.

The Roman Catholic and Lutheran lectionaries appoint John 1:1-18 as the gospel for the second Sunday after Christmas. See the discussion of this passage in the general comments about the Christmas season (page 152) and briefly in connection with the Episcopal lectionary for the first Sunday after Christmas. God's eternal wisdom ("the Word made flesh") has come to live among us, and now God has adopted us as his children through Christ. See also the discussion of wisdom literature in chapter 2, pages 66-68.

The Season of Epiphany

The theme of Epiphany is "spreading the light of Christ." We focus on how the light of Christ spread from the crib of Jesus in Bethlehem to all the nations. The Church has traditionally expressed this theme in candlelight liturgies such as the Feast of Lights service described in chapter 4, pages 103-105. Pageantry is a natural part of the Christmas and Epiphany seasons. Remember that Advent also uses the theme of darkness and light. (The custom of lighting one candle of the Advent wreath the first week, two the second week, and so on, dramatizes the theme of moving from darkness to light.) This theme continues throughout Christmas and Epiphany. Jesus' own mission to "spread the light" was made known as he met John the Baptist and was baptized. He called disciples, and the light was spread farther. We watch this process of spreading the light unfold week after week during Epiphany. Our unique call to be disciples of Christ reveals our own mission of spreading the light. This is the season, then, to focus on the themes of light, discipleship, baptism, and the mission of the Church. In terms of telling the story we talk about the early events of Jesus' life and ministry.

Epiphany is a Greek word meaning *appearance* or *manifestation.* The word was used most often in ancient times to describe the king or ruler "showing himself" before the people of the nation. During Epiphany we see how God "epiphanied" himself through Jesus and therefore how he continues to "epiphany" himself to us through Christ. It is the people of God empowered with the gifts of the Holy Spirit who reveal the risen Christ to the world through acts of creation, love, healing, and liberation. Thus we of the Church are called to be an ever-unfolding epiphany of God's love and power to the dark world seeking desperately for such epiphanies.

This year we concentrate on the Gospel of Matthew.

See chapter 4, pages 102-118, for program ideas that we developed based on the readings appointed during the Epiphany season.

The Epistle Readings

Except for the feast of Epiphany and the first and last Sundays after Epiphany, the epistle readings have no direct tie-in to the gospel and Old Testament readings during the Epiphany season. Anyone who wishes to study these epistle readings should not try to tie them to the theme of the other two readings. We will treat the epistle readings only briefly here.

These weeks after Epiphany cover the first four chapters of the important First Letter to the Corinthians. This letter gives us interesting insights into Paul's struggles with at least one of the churches he helped to establish. Adolescents and adults could examine some of those conflicts and then look at conflicts in the Church today. Sometimes we tend to hold idealistic views about the first-century Church. First and Second Corinthians help us to realize that the Christians of Paul's time were like us. They were not perfect people who always lived up to their calling, but the Holy Spirit could work through their struggle. Today we can benefit from Paul's ideas that came out of the conflict and tensions he encountered with the Corinthians. Could we write a letter from Paul to the Church in our town based on the feelings he expresses in First Corinthians?

Acts 10:34-38 is appointed in place of an epistle for the first Sunday after Epiphany. On this Sunday we recall Jesus' baptism. The reading from Acts helps us see how the Church interpreted the events of Jesus' life after it had reflected on the collective memory of what he had said and done.

The epistle for the last Sunday after Epiphany says that the ultimate goal of life is to follow Christ. ". . .that I may know him and the power of his resurrection. . ." (Philippians 3:10).

The Old Testament and Gospel Readings

The Feast of Epiphany (Twelfth Night)— January 6

Epiphany or Twelfth Night officially closes the Christmas season. The parish would do well to spend the Advent and Christmas seasons preparing—as Trinity Episcopal Parish in Ashland, Oregon, does—for a Twelfth Night celebration with pageantry, drama, singing, festivity, and a banquet of lamb. The people of Trinity Parish and the United Church of Christ walk between the two churches in a procession of lights to proclaim to the community that the Christ light is spreading.

For specific suggestions on celebrating this important and beautiful feast, see chapter 4, pages 103-105.

First Sunday after Epiphany   E, L
Baptism of the Lord   RC

Today we hear the story of the baptism of Jesus. This would be an ideal time to look at the meaning of baptism. The Old Testament reading gives us an idea of what kind of life baptism calls us to. "I, Yahweh, have called you to serve the cause of right" (The Jerusalem Bible, Isaiah 42:6). Baptism calls us to be servants of God. We receive the gift of his Spirit in order to be a part of God's action in the world. "I have given you as a covenant to the people, a light to the nations (Isaiah 42:66). Baptism and discipleship must be seen together. Focusing on the Old Testament as well as the New Testament readings helps us to see the full dimensions of our life in Christ. If there are persons in the parish desiring baptism, this would be an ideal Sunday to offer the sacrament at the main liturgy of the day. These are powerful and beautiful readings. Note the emphasis on serving "the cause of right." We so often focus our attention on the individual's relationship with God that we forget the social implications of our faith—our call to bring justice and to serve the cause of right, to be part of God's own mission of liberating the suffering, the oppressed, and the hungry. We dare not forget the radical nature of our calling.

See also chapter 4, pages 105-107.

Second Sunday after Epiphany   E, L
Second Sunday in Ordinary Time   RC

The Jerusalem Bible entitles the Old Testament reading "The Second Song of the Servant of Yahweh." There are four servant songs in Isaiah. They describe poetically the person (or perhaps the nation) that will bring people to an awareness of God's power, justice, and love. The servant will do this by his whole way of living, but most of all by the way he will bear the suffering brought about by the evil acts of the people. In his suffering, he will justify the people so that they can be restored to God after their separation. The early Church looked back to these servant songs of the Old Testament and began to see how clearly they defined the life and death of Jesus. This Second Song of the Suffering Servant deals more with the "call" of the servant. He was called "from the womb." The "light" theme of Epiphany is picked up in the beautiful line "I will give you as a light of the nations, that my salvation [healing] may reach to the end of the earth" (The Jerusalem Bible, Isaiah 49:6b).

In the gospel reading, Jesus is recognized by John the Baptist, and some of John's disciples begin to follow him. The light of Jesus spreads.

The gospel refers to "the lamb of God." It is important to introduce this concept to participants because it figures so strongly in our eucharistic liturgies. The lamb was an important symbol to the Jews. Exodus 12 directs that an unblemished lamb be slaughtered at the Passover and consumed by the people. Lambs were also offered in sacrifice at other festival days at the Temple. The offering of the innocent lamb at Passover was seen as a way of becoming at-one with God again after the separation that the people had caused by their sinfulness. The sacrifice of the Paschal or Passover Lamb restored the people to God. The Passover was a pilgrim festival; persons came from all over the nation to share this feast in Jerusalem. They would enter the city and then go to the Temple, where they would often buy a lamb from the sellers at the Temple grounds. The lamb was then offered in sacrifice. After the blood was sprinkled on the altar, the people would take the meat to their rented rooms, where it would be cooked and eaten as a part of the Passover meal.

We can now see the significance of Jesus' action at the Last Supper. According to Matthew, Mark, and Luke, the Last Supper was a Passover meal. Jesus took the bread and the cup of wine and spoke of his body and blood being shared among his people. He then offered himself as " a perfect sacrifice for the whole world" (Prayer of Consecration, *The Book of Common Prayer*). The disciples came to realize that Jesus was the true Paschal Lamb that takes away the sins of the people by the forgiving love of God that he showed forth from the cross and at the resurrection. According to the Gospel of John, Jesus died at the time of the slaughter of the Passover lambs. That is why Jesus is identified in today's gospel reading as the "lamb of God."

We cannot appreciate the full significance of Jesus' death on the cross without understanding this title. Nor can we appreciate the words we share at the Eucharist when at the breaking of the bread we say, "[Alleluia.] Christ our Passover is sacrificed for us; therefore let us keep the feast. [Alleluia]" (*The Book of Common Prayer,* page 365). Before the people receive the Sacrament, they sometimes kneel and say "O Lamb of God, that takest away the sins of the world, have mercy on us."

Share these ancient practices with the participants today. Recall them on Maundy Thursday as you celebrate your parish seder and Maundy Thursday Eucharist.

Third Sunday after Epiphany   E, L
Third Sunday in Ordinary Time   RC
In the Old Testament reading the prophet Amos says that he must speak the word of God that he feels coming to him. He has no choice, he says. "The Lord God has spoken; who can but prophesy?" (Amos 3:8b). The words he must speak may be of judgment and disaster, but speak he must. We link this thought to the beginning of Jesus' preaching, mentioned in the gospel reading. John the Baptist has now been arrested; his words have been unpopular. Jesus too must speak out, and he takes his theme from John. "Repent, for the kingdom of heaven is at hand" (Matthew 4:17b). On this Sunday, then, we begin to focus on mission, ministry, and discipleship.

A unit on the apostles and what it means to be an apostle in the Church of today would be appropriate during the Epiphany season. (See chapter 4, pages 107-108.) Jesus is calling his disciples (followers) who became his apostles (ambassadors) after the resurrection. He calls

men and women out to be his followers. In our baptism we too are called by the Lord to point beyond ourselves to God's eternal presence in creation.

The Roman Catholic and Lutheran lectionaries include a reading from Isaiah as the Old Testament lesson for today. It too describes the role of the one who is called by God. A study of the prophets would be helpful at this stage to gain a feeling for the role of the Christian who is called to spread the light and word of the Lord.

The prophets of Israel might be called "theological news commentators." They analyzed the natural and historical occurrences of their day and saw in them the hand of God shaping his people. The Assyrians, for example, were not simply enemies coming to destroy Israel. They were God's instruments who came because the people of Israel had turned from Yahweh. As the Israelites suffered under the hand of the Assyrians, they would be led to return to the ways of Yahweh. The destruction of Israel was coming because of the decadence of the people. Though often speaking in terms of the coming doom, the prophets also held out the vision and hope of a new day coming for the remnant of God's people who remained faithful to the covenant. These are the beautiful poems of hope so often quoted in connection with the coming of Jesus (see the list below). God remains faithful to the covenant. He does not destroy his people but holds out a promise of a new day when "they shall beat their swords into plowshares" (Isaiah 2:4).

Note the strong sense of social justice that lies at the heart of all the prophetic writings. Covenant with Yahweh means justice and integrity and a concern for the orphan, the widow, and the stranger. The Israelites are condemned because in turning from justice and concern for the suffering they turn from God. To acknowledge God is to acknowledge the stranger, the widow, the orphan. In reading these passages we realize that we cannot separate God from our daily lives and relationships in his world. All life and all relationships are sacred and "religious" in the conceptual framework of the Bible upon which our understanding of life is based. Listed below are some well-known passages from the prophets that will give you the flavor of their writings.

Isaiah 1:1-31 These words are directed against a thoughtless people. The sins of the people are causing the destruction of their nation and society.

Isaiah 2:2-5 A beautiful vision of peace is offered. All the nations of the earth will know and respond to Yahweh.

Isaiah 2:6-22 Yahweh is bringing destruction and suffering because of Israel's wickedness.

Isaiah 5:1-30 The parable of the vineyard confronts Judah with its unfaithfulness.

Isaiah 6:1-13 Isaiah has a vision in which he is called to be a prophet of Yahweh. The vision forms our understanding of "call" and ministry in the Lord's name. First there is an intense awareness of the wonder, power, and mystery of God. The beautiful words we hear in the liturgy, "Holy, holy, holy is the Lord of hosts; the whole earth is full of his glory," come from this chapter of Isaiah. The whole created order is called to praise God. We join in that great praise by our daily actions. At the liturgy we join our voices to the great eternal chorus of praise and stand with Isaiah before the throne of God. From our awareness of God's holiness comes an intense sense of unworthiness that must be expressed if we are to serve the Lord in thanksgiving and praise. The Lord purifies us with his love and grace and then sends us forth. "Whom shall I send, who will go for us?" From this intense encounter with God comes our response. "Here I am, send me." Note that this reading describes an ecstatic vision.

Isaiah 9 "The people who walked in darkness have seen a great light. . . ." These are beautiful words of hope about a king who will usher in a new day for Israel. Christians see this passage as describing the reign of Christ.

Isaiah 10:1-4 Isaiah confronts legislators who pass unjust laws.

Isaiah 10:5-19 A prophecy is spoken against Assyria. The Assyrians are boasting of their own power, so the Lord must humble them.

Isaiah 24:1-23 To chastise an unfaithful people, Yahweh will destroy their nation. This is a good example of apocalyptic writing discussed in chapter 2, pages 63 and 69.

Isaiah 26:1-6 This is a psalm of hope and

victory. Yahweh will restore his people after their chastisement.

Isaiah 26:7-19 This is a psalm of hope.

Isaiah 27:2-13 Isaiah describes a day of hope to come. Israel's guilt has been atoned, and a reign of peace will come; Israel's enemies will now be punished.

Isaiah 29:13—30:7 These are words spoken against unfaithful people who make treaties against Yahweh's will.

Isaiah 30:8-18 Isaiah is called to live among a people blind and deaf to Yahweh's will. This passage describes the lonely and painful role of the prophet. He speaks a message that is unpopular with the people. He will be rejected and despised, but he must continue to speak out.

Isaiah 40:1-31 Words of consolation and hope are spoken to Judah by Second Isaiah. A new day of peace is coming.

Isaiah 42:1-7 This is the first of four Songs of the Servant of Yahweh. (See chapter 2, pages 58-59, for a discussion of these songs.)

Isaiah 42:10—44:8 Second Isaiah speaks words of praise, consolation, and hope for a new day coming.

Isaiah 49:1-6 The second song of the servant of Yahweh.

Isaiah 50:4-9 The third song of the servant of Yahweh.

Isaiah 52:13—53:12 The fourth song of the servant of Yahweh.

Isaiah 55:6-11 God's ways are not man's ways. Man must turn and seek God. The word of God is a creative power of God as are the rain and snow that bring the earth to fruition.

Jeremiah 1 Jeremiah's call to be a prophet is described.

Jeremiah 2 The reason for Yahweh's anger at his people is given.

Jeremiah 3:1—5:17 Yahweh will use other nations to chastise Israel. Note how God is seen as acting in history.

Jeremiah 16:1-13 The prophet's life is lived symbolically to express what Yahweh is doing throughout history.

Jeremiah 17:1-13 These are wisdom sayings about trusting in God and not in humans.

Hosea A prophet looks at his own marriage to an unfaithful wife and weaves an allegory as he compares his wife to Israel.

Amos This prophetic book is short enough to read as an "assignment" followed by class dialogue. It offers good insight into the whole prophetic movement and feeling.

Adults and senior high participants might well deal with the prophetic role of the Church in being "a light to the nations" (Isaiah 42:6). Dietrich Bonhoeffer was a prophet of the German Lutheran Church who confronted Hitler and the Nazi regime. Many Christians in Germany, however, did not see the validity of confrontation with the nation. The Church in the United States has a mixed record in "sharing the light." All too often we see ourselves as called to bless whatever our government or society feels is appropriate. At other times, though, Christians have faced imprisonment and death as they cried out against war and oppression.

If the sacrament of baptism was celebrated on the first Sunday after Epiphany, discipleship and "calling" are natural themes to develop as we talk about raising people in the Christian faith in our own parish setting. What might we be called to do in the name of Christ? How can we help the newly baptized person feel the presence of the Christ light as we share that light in the parish family?

Fourth through Eighth
Sundays after Epiphany   E,L
Fourth through Eighth Sundays
in Ordinary Time   RC

The gospel readings from the fourth through the eighth Sundays after Epiphany are all taken from the "Sermon on the Mount." A unit based on that "sermon" would be appropriate in the religious education program during the later Sundays in Epiphany, though not all the ideas expressed will have meaning for younger children. Look over the whole Sermon on the Mount section of Matthew (chapters 5, 6 and 7) and pull out the material that seems suitable for the persons you are working with.

The so-called Sermon on the Mount is actually a loose collection of Jesus' sayings that Matthew gathered together into one section as a way of proclaiming that Jesus came to bring a new law that fulfills the old law of Moses. The sayings give us an idea of the kinds of thoughts that Jesus shared with people. This is what it

means, he might have said, to "share and spread the light" of God in your lives. The Old Testament readings add background to the gospel selections from the Sermon on the Mount.

(In preparing your program, be careful to check the dates of Lent and Easter. An early Easter means fewer Sundays after Epiphany. The later Epiphany readings are then picked up in the Sundays after Pentecost.)

In the *fourth Sunday* Old Testament reading in the Episcopal lectionary, Micah announces that God is calling his people to judgment. The mountains and hills will be the jury. (Help the participants appreciate the beauty and depth of this poetry.) The reading concludes with words suitable for a poster:

. . . what does the Lord require of you
but to do justice, and to love kindness,
and to walk humbly with your God?

(Micah 6:8)

Compare these words with the Beatitudes in the gospel reading.

The reading from Zephaniah in the Roman Catholic lectionary for the fourth Sunday reflects the same kind of call to humble obedience on the part of God's people. For a sense of this humbleness, refer to my discussion of Isaiah 6 in connection with last Sunday's readings. The remnant referred to in the Zephaniah reading is those who have realized that they cannot rely on their own strength. They have suffered in adversity and have seen their nation destroyed by the enemy. Somehow out of this experience has come a sense of the greatness of God rather than a sense of despair. God was working out his purpose in history despite the suffering of the people. Their lack of humbleness before the Lord has brought their downfall, the people have realized. They have been a people of "unclean lips," and the "burning coal" placed upon their lips (to borrow the imagery of Isaiah 6) was the destruction of their nation. Now in humility they stand before the Lord ready to reflect *his* power in their lives rather than their own power. They are merely a remnant because the majority has fallen to despair, to the enemy, to the fate of the cynic.

As you share these beautiful readings in the learning community, see if you can help get persons in touch with those moments of humbleness. After a sickness the business executive feels a whole new appreciation for his or her family and for all of life. The unbeatable baseball team suddenly becomes sensitive to the feelings of the loser as the big game is lost. In such humbling moments our thoughts are lifted from ourselves to the needs and feelings of others.

On the *fifth Sunday* we return to the seasonal theme of Epiphany. Our call as Christ's followers is to show the light and the glory of the Lord in our lives. "You are the salt of the earth. . . . You are the light of the world. . . . Let your light so shine before men, that they may see your good works and give glory to your Father who is in heaven" (Matthew 5:13,14,16).

The gospel reading for the *sixth Sunday* is a perfect example of how Jesus went to the principle or underlying basis of the Old Testament law in setting a higher standard for the New Covenant. At the heart of murder is anger. Jesus would say that to condemn murder is not enough; we must reach into the root cause for murder and set the prohibition there. Anger will not be a problem if we are confronted with the need to make peace as soon as we become angry. This does not mean that Christians should never get angry; Jesus himself got angry at times and showed his anger clearly by his acts and words. The point is that when we feel anger, we need to deal with it creatively and not accept it as a lasting part of the relationship. The anger must lead to dialogue with the "brother" and, if necessary, to mediation or counseling with a third person. The same thesis is followed in the next paragraph in dealing with adultery. The root cause of adultery is looking lustfully at someone, in the sense of desiring sexual relations.

The concern over taking oaths also reflects the higher standard set forth by Jesus. The Christian, by definition, must be honest, so there is no need to take an oath. Christians respond to moral problems with the light of Christ rather than relying on guidelines for merely avoiding sinful behavior. For the Christian it is not so much what I must do to keep out of trouble but what I will do to spread the light of Christ in the world.

On the *seventh Sunday* after Epiphany, the reading from Leviticus says that to respond to God is to respond with justice toward one's neighbors. Response to God and response to one's neighbors dare not be separated. This is a beautiful concept of justice that is found throughout the Old Testament. The gospel reading also points us to a higher standard of behavior than the world demands. The Christian is called to reflect God's love and mercy in the world. The typical response we may be tempted to make in any situation must constantly be confronted in the light of Jesus' words. There is always that extra measure of response. God loves all creation. He is forgiving and loving and "sends rain on the just and on the unjust" (Matthew 5:45). His justice is so far beyond our comprehension that we are tempted to negate Jesus' words as unrealistic, and yet it is God's mysterious wisdom and love, not ours, that we are called to reflect.

In the Episcopal lectionary, the readings for the *eighth Sunday* after Epiphany are also appointed for Thanksgiving Day. It is not what we Christians *have* that leads us to thanksgiving. It is what we feel and experience together with Christ that brings wholeness and the response of thanksgiving. Verse 1 of Psalm 62, the psalm appointed for the day in the Episcopal lectionary, sets the theme: "For God alone my soul waits in silence; from him comes my salvation." The beautiful promises of the reading from Isaiah 49:8-18 are the hopes that lead to thanksgiving in the life that is to come.

Sing for joy, O heavens, and exult, O earth;
   break forth, O mountains, into singing!
For the Lord has comforted his people,
   and will have compassion on his afflicted. . . .
Lift up your eyes round about and see;
   they all gather, they come to you.
As I live, says the Lord,
   you shall put them all on as an ornament,
   you shall bind them on as a bride does.
                 (Isaiah 49:13,18)

The gift of life, the memories of past gifts from God, and visions of the salvation that is coming are the source of the Christian's response in songs of thanksgiving. Today's reading confronts the life-style and the value system of much of our society; it also confronts our own expectations from life. As we devote our hopes and energies to what we can accumulate for ourselves in reputation and possessions, we lose touch with the source of our life and creativity. No wonder it is the poor and the afflicted who are blessed with the awareness of God's power in their lives! During times of crisis, when we suddenly realize that we cannot rely on our own power, we become most aware of the power that lies beyond us. But times of crises and struggle are not the only times when we get in touch with the reality of God's power that so far surpasses our own. When we do "look at the birds of the air" (Matthew 6:26) and concentrate on the simple beauties of God's world, we are humbled and awed at the creation that we are a part of. These words of Jesus are meant to pull us up out of the narrowness of our everyday lives and lift us up to an awareness of the significance of all life.

Last Sunday after Epiphany E
Transfiguration of Our Lord L
(Roman Catholics will hear the transfiguration reading on the second Sunday in Lent, since their lectionary does not include this last Sunday of Epiphany.)

Since the beginning of Advent we have been focusing on the concept of Christ as the light. We started in the darkness and have seen the light spread as Jesus' power and presence became known among people. Now the theme of light is crowned with a blinding revelation of the true nature of Jesus—a revelation made to his closest disciples on the mountain. In a vision they see Jesus standing with Moses and Elijah and "transfigured before them."

The Old Testament reading reminds us that Moses had his mountain-top experience on Mount Sinai. The experience shaped his whole understanding of life and mission until the day he died on the threshold of the Promised Land. The impact of the moment can be felt from the way it is described in the Bible. "Now the appearance of the glory of the Lord was like a devouring fire on the top of the mountain in the sight of the people of Israel" (Exodus 24:17). Compare the description of Moses' mountain-top experience with that of Jesus and the disciples. "And he was transfigured before them, and his face shone like the sun, and his garments became white as light" (Matthew 17:2).

From the Christ candle lit on Christmas, we move to a brilliance like that of the sun. The Kingdom has been revealed in the full presence and brightness of the Word (Jesus) among his people. Talk about those mountain-top moments in each person's life. Participants can make up a "map" of their journey toward the "Promised Land" by pointing to those times in life where they have "seen the light." This concept is one that adolescents can begin to appreciate. Some comic strips use a light bulb to show someone "seeing the light" or understanding some new truth. This kind of analogy may help participants appreciate the symbolism inherent in the transfiguration account. Like Moses, Elijah, and Jesus, it is in those mountain-top, seeing-the-light experiences that we begin to understand what the Lord is calling us to do in our covenant relationship. (See chapter 8, pages 274-275.)

The Season of Lent

Lent originated in the early Church as a season for the preparation of those desiring baptism. "From early times the account of the history of salvation played an important part in the preparation for baptism. Through our baptism we embraced the new and eternal covenant with God brought about by Christ's death and resurrection. But ours is not the only covenant God made with men. The covenants of the Old Testament are a great help in understanding what God has done for us in his definitive one. Consequently, in her preparation for Easter, the Church remembers the covenants of the Old Testament to remind us of the stages of God's plan for our redemption and also to instruct those to be baptized."*

Thus Lent has always been a teaching season, a time to reflect on the mighty acts of God in history, on the covenant realized between God and his people, and on the role of Jesus in the story of salvation. We might call Lent a "primer course in the Christian faith." Obviously, this is an ideal time to tie the readings into the religious education program. To tell the stories of the Lenten readings is to participate in a serial retelling of our covenant story with God.

Ash Wednesday

The story opens as the prophet Joel calls the people of God to declare a time of fasting and penitence so that they will return to God. This sets the focus for our observance of Lent. It is to be a special time to "return to God" by recalling the covenant we have with him and by rededicating ourselves to live in that relationship. Thus we see the importance of reviewing the covenant. We need to center it in our minds by recalling the history of our relationship. In the Episcopal lectionary an alternate reading is offered, Isaiah 58:1-12. This is a beautiful reading that calls the people to fast by outward acts of justice and mercy rather than in ritualistic fashion. The reading reminds us of the kind of life the covenant calls us to. We act out our commitment to God in a life leading toward

*Peter Coughlan and Peter Purdue, *Commentary on the Sunday Lectionary: First Sunday of Advent to Last Sunday of the Year, Cycle A* (Collegeville, Minn.: The Liturgical Press, 1972), p. 70.

justice and liberation for every person. This ties in beautifully with the gospel lesson. In both we practice piety as a means of sharing God's love, not as outward signs of virtue.

We are humbled in the act of kneeling and accepting the imposition of ashes. We can no longer take life for granted or assume that the world was created just for us. The words of Psalm 8:4 may well come to mind:

What is man that thou art mindful of him,
and the son of man that thou dost care
for him?

Only from this humble stance can we move to the next step in the Ash Wednesday liturgy and begin to review the ways we have "strayed from thy ways like lost sheep." The sixth chapter of Isaiah (though not an Ash Wednesday reading) captures the same feelings. "Lifted up" in a vision into the presence of God, Isaiah feels immediately humbled and unworthy. Because of this attitude he is able to receive the assurance of forgiveness and love. Only out of such an experience can come a true calling to discipleship. We become disciples not because we have great gifts to offer or worlds and people to change but because we feel thanksgiving and awe and wonder at God's mercy and creation. The beautiful prayer of General Thanksgiving from Morning Prayer (Rite Two) provides our basis for responding to God in discipleship. ". . . we pray, give us such an awareness of your mercies, that with truly thankful hearts we may show forth your praise, not only with our lips, but in our lives, by giving up our selves to your service, and by walking before you in holiness and righteousness all our days" (*The Book of Common Prayer,* page 101).

Ash Wednesday sends us out into "the wilderness" of Lent with such thoughts. The Israelites were humbled in their forty years of wandering. Jesus confronted his weaknesses and temptations in the wilderness. The prophets often reminded the Israelites that in forgetting the wilderness experience in which they relied on the daily manna provided by Yahweh, they drifted from the way and the covenant of the Lord. Likewise, our quest during Lent as religious educators is a serious one. The wilderness is the place where we deal with the fears and uncertainties of life. It is in hiding from fear and uncertainty that we attempt to make ourselves gods by assuring ourselves that we are powerful and have all the answers to life. Resistance to Lent lies within each one of us. So we must plan carefully, lovingly, and far ahead! Read some of the many books about Lent that outline a broad range of ancient and modern customs. The most ancient practices are often the most powerful if they are understood and interpreted by participants. Know the symbols and signs of the season so that you can use them creatively in telling the story of Lent.

The epistle readings for Lent, unlike those of many other times of the year, do form a unity with the other two readings. So in chapters 5, 6, and 7 we discuss each set of Lenten readings together.

Remember that Lent is a "Christian primer of the faith"—we go through an annual "telling the covenant story." There is continuity in each week's readings. The focus is covenant and our understanding of and response to it.

First Sunday in Lent

We begin the story of God's saving history. The story opens with the ancient Genesis myth that describes the separation of mankind from God. I use the term "myth" as it is defined in the *American Heritage Dictionary of the English Language:* "Any real or fictional story, recurring theme, or character type that appeals to the consciousness of a people by embodying its cultural ideals or by giving expression to deep, commonly felt emotions." (See chapter 1, pages 14-16, of this book for further discussion of myth.) Man and woman are created to participate in God's eternal act of creation. They are to be instruments of his creative power in the world. Instead, we constantly choose separation from God rather than participation with God. We follow our temptation to become gods ourselves (eating of the fruit of the forbidden tree). By that act of separation we bring pain and suffering into our lives. We must realize the truth of this ancient story as it applies to our own lives and to the history of the whole human race.

The epistle harks back to the story we have just heard from the Old Testament. It should be read poetically, not literally: ". . . sin came into the world through one man. . ." (Romans 5:12). The gospel points up the contrast between Adam (representing all men and women) and Jesus. Jesus is tempted in the wilderness, but he does not fall into sin. We need to realize that this account of the temptation of Jesus is symbolic, poetic. Jesus was undoubtedly tempted all his life. The painful reality of that temptation is expressed profoundly in the wilderness scene. But Jesus did not give in to temptation. In this he reversed the story and destiny of Adam and Eve in the garden.

Second Sunday in Lent

The story moves on. We come now to Abram (or Abraham), who lived in the Tigris-Euphrates Valley. Abram had a vision in which God called him to leave his homeland and journey to the land of Canaan. God established a covenant with Abram and his descendants. The epistle refers to Abraham and the faith he showed in following the way of God. It is faith that leads one into a relationship with God. The gospel ties this thought together with the familiar words "For God so loved the world that he gave his only Son, that whoever believes in him should not perish but have eternal life."

This Sunday's readings deal with faith, then. Abram had the faith to move into a strange, alien land. He could face the unknown. With children and adults we can talk about facing the unknown by dealing with their fears and anxieties. What does faith mean to them in their movement into new situations and new life? The Abram story makes a very good launching device for discussing such questions.

The Roman Catholic lectionary presents the transfiguration of our Lord this week rather than on the last Sunday after Epiphany. (See the comments in connection with the Last Sunday of Epiphany, page 162.)

The Lutheran lectionary shares the Old Testament and epistle reading with the Episcopal lectionary for this Sunday, but the Lutheran choice for the gospel reading is the one appointed in the Episcopal lectionary for next Sunday. (See the comments in connection with next Sunday's gospel.)

Third Sunday in Lent

Today the faith of Abram as he moved through unknown lands is contrasted with the lack of faith of the Israelites as they moved through the wilderness on the great exodus from Egypt to the land of Canaan. The people in today's story complained bitterly because they lacked water. Moses discovered water, and the people's faith was temporarily restored. They constantly needed signs of God's presence with them. The epistle reassures people in the midst of their suffering that there is meaning to what they are going through. The gospel returns us to the theme of finding water. Jesus talks with a woman at a well. To know Jesus is to have "living water" continually refreshing us. The writer of the gospel uses imagery of water and refreshment to describe the relationship with God known through Christ.

The author of the Gospel of John often writes in a way that expresses two different levels of reality as Jesus talks with another person. This passage is an example of that style. Jesus is talking about the "living waters" of a life lived in communion with God. The woman thinks about "living waters" as indoor plumbing! Gradually the hearer moves from the literal interpretation of the word to the power of the metaphor. There is humor in this approach. Jesus: ". . . but whoever drinks of the water that I shall give him will never thirst. . . ." Woman: "Sir, give me this water, that I may not thirst, nor come here to draw" (John 4:13, 15).

Today would be a good time to focus on water, refreshment, faith, and the meaning of baptism. In baptism we recognize that water is still a sign of God's power and presence with us. Talk about the signs of God's presence. Can we identify ourselves with the Israelites in their demand for signs? Talk about the Eucharist and the other sacraments as signs of God's presence.

The exciting concept that lies behind all of the Old Testament readings during Lent is the idea of a quest or journey. God is always calling us into a new land and into new adventures. We resist, yet we long to move on. There are tension and tragedy in our response. Focus with participants on our individual journeys through life, and help them to tell their story of where the wilderness and the decisions have come. What have the signs been? Where have we eaten the apple? Where are we moving now? Lent also asks us to face the painful but important questions: What has happened to the quest and to our pilgrimage? Where has the vision gone?

The epistle and gospel readings for Lutherans this Sunday are appointed to be read in the Episcopal church next Sunday, the fourth Sunday of Lent. See comments on the gospel in connection with next week's readings.

The Old Testament lesson appointed in the Lutheran lectionary is Isaiah 42:14-21. Verses 19-20 are connected with the gospel reading appointed for this week in the Lutheran church and for next week in the Episcopal church. The people have been blind and deaf to the Lord's covenant that they were called to live in order to glorify him. In the gospel reading Jesus gives sight to the man born blind. This man now does bring praise to the Lord as he believes in and worships Jesus (John 9:38). This is what we are called to do as Christ heals us of our "blindness" in the waters of our baptism.

Fourth Sunday in Lent

The storytelling of Lent goes on. We move today into a new era of the story of the Israelites. After a generation in the wilderness, they settled in the land of Canaan. After having a loose confederation of tribes (in the period of the Judges), they formed a more central government under their first king, Saul. In the episode appointed for today's liturgy, the prophet Samuel received a vision that sent him to the family of Jesse to find a successor to Saul. He anointed Jesse's youngest son, David. The practice of anointing with oil is an important one for us to understand. The word *christos* in Greek means *anointed one,* as does the Hebrew word *messiah.* The sign that God's spirit rested on the chosen one of God was the anointment of that person with expensive oils. Jesus was the appointed or chosen one of God, and he received the title of "Jesus the Christ" or "Jesus the Anointed One." Oil called chrism is sometimes used when a person is baptized or confirmed. Each Christian is an "anointed one" of God—a chosen person endowed with God's Spirit. Today's reading should lead to a study of the meaning of anointment and of confirmation, for we need to understand the roots of our traditions. Note the mention of the Jesse family. Jesus is the new root from the "tree of Jesse," we are reminded during Advent and Christmas. Hence we talk about the Jesse tree, which includes symbols of the Old Testament stories we relive during this Lenten time. Psalm 23, appointed for this day, contains the words ". . . thou anointest my head with oil." The gospel account deals symbolically with the meaning of baptism. As the man born blind bathes in the pool, his sight is restored. Link this with the concept of baptism. As we "pass through the waters" of our baptism in Christ, our "sight" is restored. We are made whole.

Today the Lutheran lectionary departs completely from the Roman Catholic and Episcopal readings. These Lutheran readings prepare us for Holy Week, which is fast approaching. For the third time Jesus talks to his disciples of his impending death. The mother of James and John then asks Jesus to honor her sons in the kingdom he is to bring about. Jesus confronts here with the reality of God's kingdom: ". . . whoever would be great among you must be your slave. . ." (Matthew 20:27).

The epistle compares life in the flesh with life in the spirit. "To set the mind on the flesh is death, but to set the mind on the Spirit is life and peace" (Romans 8:6).

In the Old Testament reading, Hosea confronts the empty sacrificial practices of the people who though that they could cover over their sins by a couple of days of penitential sacrifice. Reading beyond the appointed verses, we find the beautiful words

For I desire steadfast love and not sacrifice,
　the knowledge of God, rather than burnt
　　offerings.　　　　　　　　　　(Hosea 6:6)

The days of empty sacrifices that the people are accustomed to will soon be replaced by the sacrifice of Jesus, who will rise triumphant on the third day.

Today we look at the two ways of understanding life. Two weeks from now we will be participating in the Palm Sunday drama of Christ's initial triumphant entry into Jerusalem and his subsequent arrest and crucifixion. The actions or "way" of Jesus are incomprehensible as we look at his life and death from the

viewpoint of our usual understanding. His way contradicts everything we value or place faith in. Death suddenly is proclaimed as life, weakness is shown to be power, servanthood is seen as greatness.

Begin to prepare the participants in your learning community for the drama of Holy Week and Easter. What *do* they think of these strange words and acts of Jesus? Tell the gospel story. How do they feel about it? Go on to talk about the drama of Holy Week. Tell the stories of the disciples and early Christians who appeared so weak in the eyes of the world.

How do our goals for life stack up against the strange words of Jesus in today's gospel that were acted out in his own life and in the lives of the apostles? This is not a time for answering questions or resolving doubts. Rather, it is a time to raise questions in the minds of our people. If participants leave this session voicing concern and confusion about what it means to be a Christian, we will have served our role of being true Christian educators. Everyone must find his or her own understanding of what the gospel proclaims, but we can do so only as our own views of life are challenged and confronted.

Fifth Sunday in Lent
Today we complete our "short course" in the faith. After rehearsing briefly the story of God's saving acts and tying those saving acts to our baptism-confirmation, we look this week at the concept of resurrection in Christ. The Old Testament reading is a poem that speaks of God raising up the dry bones of Israel and restoring the people. "And I will put my Spirit within you, and you shall live. . ." (Ezekiel 37:14). The gospel tells the story of the raising of Lazarus. Jesus says "I am the resurrection and the life." The epistle expresses this in its closing words: ". . . the free gift of God is eternal life in Christ Jesus our Lord" (Romans 6:23). In Jesus the understanding of our covenant with God is deepened. As Paul wrote in Romans 8:39: ". . . nor [will anything] be able to separate us from the love of God in Christ Jesus our Lord." Even physical death does not end our growing relationship with the Creator. This covenant is a. far deeper one than was understood by Abram as

he struggled into the land of Canaan. The relationship is eternal.

(The theme of the Roman Catholic and Lutheran epistle readings from Romans 8 is the new life and spirit given by the Lord. This is both gift and confrontation, however. To receive the gift, one must change one's perspective of life and accept a whole new reality.)

The reading from Ezekiel can be dramatized very beautifully. John Westerhoff (Portland Lecture Series, Lewis and Clark College, June, 1978) describes an experience in which several children lay down in the middle of the room and were put in touch with the emotions of feeling dead and "dried out." Then the rest of the group surrounded them, calling out in an ever-increasing chorus "Come from the four winds, O breath, and breathe upon these slain, that they may live" (Ezekiel 37:9). Gradually the children rose up, and the whole group felt a sense of elation. The experience could conclude with the words of the Lord stated in Ezekiel 37:12-13: "Therefore prophesy, and say to them, Thus says the Lord God: Behold, I will open your graves, and raise you from your graves, O my people; and I will bring you home into the land of Israel. And you shall know that I am the Lord, when I open your graves, and raise you from your graves, O my people."

The words came alive for the children as they heard them in the liturgy, for they had experienced the feelings of death and dryness and the new life proclaimed in the prophecy.

The quest for life grows out of our struggle. With this proclamation of covenant renewal, we move into Holy Week, which begins next Sunday with Palm (or Passion) Sunday.

Holy Week

Holy Week is a seven-act drama that begins on Palm Sunday and ends with Easter Eve. During the week we dramatize the last week of Jesus'

life, and in that dramatization we begin to experience Christ leading us through our own darkness, death, and guilt to a new understanding of forgiveness and life in the resurrection. We can identify with Peter this week. He discovered the depth of God's love for him through the love of Jesus. He moved from the sorrow of Good Friday to the joy of Easter morning as he felt this healing, forgiving love drawing him into a new understanding of his relationship with God.

Act One—Palm Sunday

Traditionally, Palm Sunday has been celebrated with drama and pageantry. We reenact the triumphant entry of Jesus into Jerusalem by taking part in the procession as pilgrims ourselves. Form the congregation into a grand procession singing the beautiful hymn "All Glory, Laud, and Honor." Wave palm branches or the branches of trees more native to your area. *The Book of Common Prayer,* pages 270-273, offers directions for this festival. The gospel can be read dramatically, with persons in the congregation taking the parts of the persons named in the narrative. When it comes time for the crowd to shout, "Crucify him!" the entire congregation can join in. As many times as I have taken part in this tradition, I have never failed to feel moved as I find myself caught up in the same sinful separation from God as my ancestors experienced. The story of Jesus' suffering and death becomes *our* story as we dramatize it. The Old Testament readings in the Lutheran and Roman Catholic lectionaries are different from the Episcopal reading, but all of them provide us with a framework from the Old Testament that helps us understand Jesus' role as a servant of the Lord.

Acts Two, Three, and Four—Monday, Tuesday, and Wednesday of Holy Week

Propers provided for each of the days trace the steps that Jesus may have taken during the week that led to his death.

Episcopal Lectionary	Roman Catholic Lectionary	Lutheran Lectionary
—————————————————————————Monday———————————————————————————		
Jesus is anointed by a woman at Bethany (Gospel of Mark or John).	Jesus is anointed by Mary, the sister of Lazarus, at Bethany (Gospel of John).	(See Roman Catholic lectionary.)

Episcopal Lectionary	Roman Catholic Lectionary	Lutheran Lectionary
Tuesday		
Jesus talks about the importance of believing in his words. Many people refuse to believe in Jesus despite the many signs they have witnessed. (An optional reading describes Jesus cleansing the Temple.)	Jesus foretells his betrayal by Judas and predicts Peter's denial.	Greeks come to meet Jesus. He warns them that the hour "for the son of Man to be glorified" is approaching, and he warns them to walk in the light "while you still have it."
Wednesday		
Jesus foretells his betrayal by Judas and Peter's denial of him before the last cock-crow. (The optional selection from Matthew does not include the foretelling of Peter's denial.)	Judas betrays Jesus (Gospel of Matthew).	Jesus foretells the betrayal by Judas.

Act Five—Maundy Thursday

On this day we recall and dramatize the Last Supper. According to Matthew, Mark, and Luke, the Last Supper was the Passover meal Jesus shared with the disciples. The Old Testament reading provides the directions for this ancient meal (seder) which Jewish people share to this day. Some parishes celebrate a Passover seder meal as a prelude to the celebration of the Eucharist. The meal recalls the story of the exodus of the Israelites from Egypt to the land of Canaan and memorializes the "saving history" of God that sets the stage for our understanding of God's action in our lives to this day. We need to study Passover practices and symbols to understand the significance of the events that we recall in Holy Week.

The epistle reading includes the words of Jesus that are repeated in every celebration of the Eucharist.

The gospel reminds us of the humble act of Jesus as he washed his disciples' feet. This is the kind of servanthood to which he calls his disciples. "...I have given you an example, that you also should do as I have done to you. Truly, truly, I say to you, a servant is not greater than his master; nor is he who is sent greater than he who sent him" (John 13:15-16). It is a tradition in many parishes to strip the altar and sanctuary of all the usual hangings and symbols. This custom adds to the impact of the event of Good Friday.

Act Six—Good Friday

We dramatize the death of Jesus. We come to the darkened church and recall the suffering of Jesus on the cross. The passion narrative is again read; we identify with Jesus' suffering so that we can identify with his eternal power on Easter morning. The vigil at the foot of the cross can be shared in various ways, but the congregation should experience it, whether it be in a three-hour vigil or in a briefer liturgy of reading, prayer, meditation, and discussing the feelings of the participants.

Act Seven—Holy Saturday

On this day we recall the burial of Jesus. The church remains darkened, and worshipers are struck by the starkness of the bare altar and sanctuary. The Holy Eucharist is not celebrated during the day on Holy Saturday; the Church feels that it is not appropriate to share in the sacrament today. A quiet liturgy of Morning Prayer can be offered in the morning.

In the early Church those preparing for their Easter baptism would fast and pray from Maundy Thursday until dawn on Easter Sunday.

As the hour of dawn approached, they would rehearse the story of salvation from creation to the coming of Christ. As the light of dawn announced the day of the resurrection, the sacrament of baptism would be celebrated with a feeling of great joy and commitment to the risen Lord. The Holy Eucharist was celebrated and broke the fast of those who had prepared for their baptism with fasting and prayer. This was a day and a commitment that would never be forgotten by the baptized or by the Christian community as a whole.

These ancient first-century customs are again being appreciated in the Church. *The Book of Common Prayer* includes a complete liturgy for the Easter Vigil (pages 285-295). Anyone who has felt the mystery and wonder of the "Midnight Mass" of Christmas can appreciate the significance of a late evening, midnight, or "first light" vigil at Easter. If the vigil is celebrated at dawn, follow the liturgy with a parish breakfast. In many parishes an Easter Watch is kept from Maundy Thursday night until the first light of Easter morning. Ask people to sign up for a one-hour shift of prayer and meditation in the nave of the church. The church is never empty during those final hours of Holy Week. Children need to be included in this tradition. It is in participating in this kind of ancient tradition that they begin to ask "why" questions such as "Why are we doing these things?" It is at such moments that religious education happens in the most effective way. If our children have heard about the early traditions associated with baptism in their learning community, they can feel in touch with their ancestors in the faith as they too participate in an act of faith and commitment.

The Season of Easter

Easter Day and the Season's Readings: An Overview

The liturgies for Easter Day, including the Great Vigil, can be times when the vision of Christ's eternal presence is proclaimed through the active participation of persons who feel themselves a part of the story out of which the resurrection took place. Children may not be able to comprehend the vision nor understand the story, but they can sense the feeling of the people who proclaim it. The words of the story begin to become identified with the feeling, and the children become truly "educated" into the faith. Over the years as the story is interpreted and retold, children begin to "find themselves" in the story. The poetry, symbols, and signs of the story become theirs. At sunrise the shout goes forth: "Alleluia. Christ is risen. The Lord is risen indeed. Alleluia." Times of crisis and of suffering, times of excitement and anticipation, are caught up in that common shout that says yes to life. But the identification of their own story with the resurrection story comes, of course, only as they are "raised up" within the body of the faithful who tell the story and who support them in their pain and struggle.

Easter Sunday is the day of acclamation, of saying yes to life and to the vision of life made known through Jesus Christ. As people arrive at the parish church, have them greet each other with the Easter acclamation. Teach it to even the youngest children. Instead of "Happy Easter" let the greeting be "Alleluia, Christ is risen." Let the response be "The Lord is risen indeed. Alleluia." To prepare for Easter, parishioners can look over the Easter Vigil and other Easter liturgies and talk over the traditions of the Church with the parish priest and others responsible for the liturgy. In religious education groups, brainstorm ways of translating those symbols and traditions to persons of all ages in the parish. (We *all* need to hear again the meaning of some of our accepted customs and traditions. If we lose touch with the roots of the ritual, the symbols and traditions may lose their power for us.) Include the children in as much of the parish Easter celebrations as possible. They need to be part of the solemnity of Good Friday and of the Holy Saturday Vigil, even if for only a brief time. They should experience the sound and feeling of the extended Easter liturgy, even if they spend part of the time coloring, reading, or napping. The feelings and words will enter into their consciousness in ways we may not know for years.

The stories of the resurrection cannot be explained, especially to children. They are a mystery. Children will naturally think of ghosts or ask questions we cannot possibly answer, but that is all right. As I have said elsewhere, we need to be humble. A great theological truth is that we don't know all the answers! Education really takes place when people begin asking questions. The power of the resurrection is that we find ourselves always asking questions about it in our quest for Christ. The mystery of the resurrection constantly calls us into deeper and deeper questioning. Through our questions we move from ghosts into glimpses of eternity. Thus the Easter story needs to be heard, to be experienced, and most of all, to be shared actively by the Christian family gathered in proclamation.

Just as Christmas is not one day but twelve, so Easter is not one day but seven weeks. It is important to help people see the continuity of the season that proclaims resurrection and the effects of Jesus' resurrection on the lives of the faithful. In observing Sunday, we focus one-seventh of each week on the resurrection. Likewise, in celebrating the season of Easter we focus one-seventh of the year on the theme of resurrection.

The readings for Easter Sunday are familiar, but the readings for the weeks of Easter may not be so obvious. As is true with Years B and C, the liturgist and religious education team can choose readings which emphasize themes we want to follow during the Easter season. For the first reading, we can follow the Book of Acts as it gives the story of the postresurrection Church. If we follow this option, we could spend the entire Easter season on a study of the first-century Church as it evolved after the resurrection. It is an adventure story that everyone can appreciate.

A second option is to use Old Testament passages as the first reading and use the same Acts selections in lieu of epistle readings. If we follow the Old Testament option, it will provide background for the gospel reading as it does for the rest of the year. The Old Testament readings not only provide further insights into the gospel selection; they expose us to some of the Old Testament stories that we might not otherwise deal with. Another option is to share a reading from the First Epistle of Peter as the second lesson.

Episcopalians can choose one of the following alternatives for this season:

First reading: The readings from Acts or the Old Testament selections.

Second reading: The readings from Acts or selections from 1 Peter.

Third reading: The gospel selection as appointed.

The Lutheran and Roman Catholic lectionaries do not include the Old Testament options during the Easter season.

In the Roman Catholic lectionary the appointed readings from Acts follow a different order from the Episcopal selections in the second through fifth Sundays of Easter, although the passages are the same.

On the sixth Sunday of Easter the Roman Catholic lectionary includes an anecdote not found in the Episcopal lectionary. Philip goes to the Samaritans and cures many of them, and they accept the gospel with enthusiasm. The apostles then join Philip and lay hands on the Samaritans, at which time they receive the Holy Spirit. Persecution only strengthens the Church. Because the persecutions forced the Christians to leave Jerusalem, the gospel spread even more rapidly into the surrounding areas, including Samaria. We note in this Roman Catholic reading the very ancient practice of the laying on of hands. In the Episcopal, Roman Catholic, and Lutheran churches the minister lays hands on those who are baptized and confirmed. The laying on of hands is a visible way of experiencing the "inward and spiritual" reality of the indwelling of the Holy Spirit. If persons were baptized at Easter or are preparing for their baptism at Pentecost, this would be a good time to talk about the ancient tradition of the laying on of hands.

In the Lutheran lectionary the readings from Acts appointed for the second through the sixth Sundays of Easter vary only slightly from those of the Episcopal lectionary in their arrangement.

The Readings from the Book of Acts

If we choose the readings from the Book of Acts, we have six weeks to devote to telling the story about the growth of the Church. There are many good stories and themes to develop. Here is a week-by-week overview of the story as it develops in Year A.

Second Sunday of Easter

Today's reading is an example of the kind of preaching Peter and the other apostles offered to the people of Jerusalem.

Third Sunday of Easter

As a result of Peter's preaching, many persons were converted to Christ's way and baptized. The account then describes the kind of close communal life the Christians shared. What are the marks of Christian community that you see from this passage? Work with the group to develop some norms for the Christian community of our day. What are the marks of that Christian community, and how does our own community live up to the ideal described in Acts? If you are working with adults, you can spend time brainstorming ideas that will help the parish move closer to that ideal. What are we doing that blocks or enhances the Christian life-style? For example, does our every-member canvass reflect the values of the Book of Acts, or do we ask persons to support the parish in order simply to meet budgetary requirements? How do we deal with crisis and problems in the parish? How vulnerable are we to each other in terms of sharing ourselves and our struggle?

Today's reading is an idealistic description of the early Christian Church; from reading Paul's epistles we know the painful problems and conflicts that tore at the Church. Though we constantly need to stretch for the ultimate commitment in Christ, we would do ourselves a disservice if we allowed ourselves to become defeated because we fall short of what we are called to become. There were no perfect Christians "back then" any more than there are now. Our perfection in Christ lies ahead of us, not behind us in history. Though we must never lose sight of the ideal and must strive for it in every way, we must realize that we are on a pilgrimage of faith. We have not yet arrived.

Fourth Sunday of Easter
The first deacons are appointed. One of the deacons was Stephen, who became the first martyr of the Church. (His feast day is celebrated on December 26.) The reading gives an account of what Stephen might have said before the high priest prior to his execution. Saul (later called Paul) is introduced for the first time in the Book of Acts.

Fifth Sunday of Easter
This week we join Paul on his second great missionary journey. We find ourselves in Thessalonica, where Paul ran into trouble with the Jewish community. This story gives us a glimpse of the kind of problems that Paul encountered on his journeys. As we share this story we need to turn to the First and Second Epistles to the Thessalonians. The epistles of the New Testament were written by Paul and others to the churches that he established on his journeys. Point out the city of Thessalonica on a map so that persons in the learning community can have some feeling for its location. When they hear the epistle read, they might think of the people and the problems that Paul had in that place. The epistle is apt to have far more meaning to the congregation if they have this sense of place and history as the letter is read.

Sixth Sunday of Easter
This well-known passage is an example of the kind of preaching Paul might have done; it shows Paul's missionary methods very well. He talks now not to Jews but to pagans. He refers to Greek customs and ideas to introduce the people of Athens to Christ.

Christianity has often been introduced to persons by using the language and symbols the people are familiar with. The symbols of the people are then gradually translated into the symbols of the Christian faith. For example, we get our festival of Christmas from the northern

European festival of rebirth of the sun god at the time of year when the days begin to get longer. As the Christians came to spread the gospel, they took over this festival and applied it to the story of Christ. "This is the birth of the true *Son,*" they might have said. Thus the Christmas season grew out of a pre-Christian custom and was a way of helping the people move into a new understanding of faith. This is the process we see Paul following in today's reading. We would do well to emulate his example. Easter eggs and Santa Claus do not have to be negated in our celebrations of birth and resurrection. They are symbols of gift-giving and new life that both children and adults understand. As religious educators we need to help make the connection between symbol and faith-story.

Ascension Day, an important holy day of the church year, falls on the Thursday of this week. See chapter 8, pages 275-276, as well as the comments in the next paragraph, for a discussion of Ascension Day.

Seventh Sunday of Easter
(The Ascension of Jesus)
". . . as they were looking on, he was lifted up, and a cloud took him out of their sight" (Acts 1:9). For a time Jesus was seen by his disciples and followers, but he was always preparing them for a new way to experience his presence in the future. Then the time came when they no longer saw him directly but began to experience his presence through the power of the Holy Spirit. The Church marks this new experience with the story of the ascension.

This story may be interpreted either literally as an intense vision shared by the apostles or symbolically as a story told to express the reality that Jesus was lifted up in the sense that his presence was now being felt through the gift of the Holy Spirit rather than through the person of Jesus of Nazareth. As we participate in Christ's "risen" presence, we too are lifted up as we realize the sacredness of our lives that are touched and empowered in his love. Whether this account is seen as a symbolic expression, as a literal experience shared by the apostles, or as a vision the apostles experienced, the significance of the story is the same.

The Old Testament Readings

As an alternative to the readings from Acts during Easter, Episcopalians can follow the practice of the rest of the year and continue with Old Testament readings for the first lesson. If we make this choice, we will continue rehearsing God's mighty saving acts and our covenant relationship as we did in the Lenten Old Testament readings. We can share some of the stories that might not be heard and appreciated as a part of our heritage. Taking this choice, we share the stories discussed in the next section.

Second Sunday of Easter

The Old Testament reading is the conclusion of the story of Noah and the ark. We would need to use the whole narrative in the learning community setting. However, I would use this story carefully with children. This is not a story to be taken literally; it is an ancient folk myth that has common roots in many ancient civilizations. If it is used with children, tell it simply as a story about the rainbow and how it became a sign of our covenant relationship with God. ("Now when we see a rainbow in the sky, we too can think of how much God loves us!") Deemphasize the drowning of the "bad people." Emphasize instead the story about the animals, the building of the ark, and the coming of the rainbow.

For your own interest read 1 Peter 3:20-22 and note the connection made with the Noah story. In a sense, the whole earth was baptized and cleansed from sin so that a new beginning could be made. A second act of creation happens through God's love for his world.

Third Sunday of Easter

"I have called you by name, you are mine" (Isaiah 43:1a) is a beautiful proclamation of God's presence and power among his people. We are witnesses of his power and presence in the world. "For I am the Lord your God." No matter what we go through, God is with us. Connect the "I have called you by name" phrase with being named at baptism. God calls us to make the journey (the quest) with him, just as he called Abram, Isaac, and Jacob.

In the chart (page 174) I outline the calls of various persons in the Bible. Today's reading could launch the group into a telling or discussion of these calls. What happened as a result of the call? How were the calls heard by the persons, and how did they respond? From the biblical story, move to the personal story of the adult or adolescent participants. What brings them into the Christian community? Some may respond that they are there because of a simple need for friendship and community. This may not seem quite like the exciting call of a prophet, but we can see it as a call nevertheless. God reveals his will for us in many ways. The need for community today may lead us into a deeper understanding of "call" another day. The very fact that we are a part of a Christian community that listens for the word of God may make us more sensitive to God's calls. The call of the prophets is usually described in poetic or visionary language. Encourage participants to describe their "calls" in poetic imagery.

Fourth Sunday of Easter

This reading, a hymn of praise to God and a rehearsal of the mighty acts of Israel, makes a good review of the covenant story we have been tracing ever since the beginning of Lent. It is important to note that it was out of this kind of rehearsing that words of praise and thanksgiving came forth from the people. The story became a creed for the faithful. Our creed is a poetic rehearsal of the story of Jesus. We too respond to that story by saying "We believe. . . ."

Fifth Sunday of Easter

A brief recalling of the mighty acts of God is given to the people as a reminder of the necessity to honor the covenant with God. The people are commanded to follow the covenant "for our good always, that he might preserve us alive, as

The Concept of Call expressed in the Seasons of Lent and Easter

Biblical Source	The Person	Manner of Call	Remarks
Genesis 12:1-9	Abraham (Abram)	A vision	
Genesis 28:10-19	Jacob	A dream	
Exodus 3:1-15	Moses	A vision	
Joshua 1:1-5	Joshua	A vision	
Judges 6:11-24	Gideon	A vision	
1 Samuel 3:1—4:1	Samuel the prophet	A vision	
1 Samuel 10:1-8	Saul	Anointing	Samuel anointed Saul as the first king of Israel.
1 Samuel 16:1-13	David	Anointing	David was also anointed with oil by Samuel. His anointing was confirmed by the elders of Israel when they anointed him in public at Saul's death (2 Samuel 5:1-5).
1 Kings 3:4-15	Solomon	A dream	
1 Kings 19:19-21	Elisha	Elijah "cast his mantle upon" Elisha.	Elisha received his prophetic call from Elijah by a direct act of symbolic selection.
Isaiah 6	Isaiah	A vision	This is perhaps the best known call in the Bible. Like that of all the prophets, it was a painful one. Isaiah must talk to a people who will not understand. His life will be filled with pain and tension as a result of his call to speak in the name of the Lord.
Jeremiah 1:4-10	Jeremiah	A vision	God says "I have put my words in your mouth." This is the authority the prophets felt as they went forth among the people.
Ezekiel 2:1—3:3	Ezekiel	A vision	Ezekiel is a book filled with symbolism and visionary language. Notice the beautiful symbols of the call.
Matthew 4:18-22	Simon, Andrew, James, and John	Direct call from Jesus	
Matthew 9:9	Matthew the apostle	Direct call from Jesus	
Acts 9:1-19 and Galatians 1:11-24	Paul (Saul)	A vision	
Acts 1:15-26	Matthias	Prayer and the casting of lots	Matthias was chosen by the disciples to replace Judas as one of the twelve.
Acts 6:1-7	Stephen and the other deacons	Election by the people, and the laying on of hands by the apostles	

at this day. And it will be righteousness for us, if we are careful to do all this commandment before the Lord our God, as he has commanded us" (Deuteronomy 6:24-25).

Sixth Sunday of Easter
The exodus event was a sign to the Israelites of God's action in their history. But he prepares a new exodus for *all* people. The wilderness will be turned into a fertile place. Parched lips will be quenched with water. "I will open rivers on the bare heights" (Isaiah 4:18a). In a sense, this reading summarizes the recalling of the great acts of God we have been sharing ever since the beginning of Lent. By recalling and understanding those mighty acts of God's history-making in the past, we are led to an understanding of how he is leading us into a new exodus in our own time. We can anticipate the greater exodus to come.

Seventh Sunday of Easter
This reading points to God's history-making that will occur in the future as it did in the past. By restoring his people after their exile to Babylonia, God will display his "glory among the nations." God offers a promise of restoration to his people. ". . . I will not hide my face any more from them, when I pour out my Spirit upon the house of Israel. . ." (Ezekiel 39:29).

If these Old Testament readings are chosen, a continuous study of the covenant and the story of God's action in the history of the Israelites can be made from the beginning of Lent till the end of the Easter season. The Old Testament themes can be tied to the New Testament's unfolding of how God acted in Jesus to restore his people and bring wholeness to them through the *new* covenant. These readings can deepen our understanding of Jesus. Both the Old Testament and the New Testament studies lead us to anticipations of acts yet to come. We are reminded that we are to be participants with God in his history-making as it unfolds in our daily lives and in eternity.

The Gospel Readings
On *Easter Sunday* and on the *second* and *third* Sundays of Easter the gospel readings focus on the resurrection appearances of Christ. The account of the risen Christ appearing to two of the disciples on the road to Emmaus (third Sunday) makes a good launching device for discovering how we meet Christ today. Note that before the disciples recognize the risen Christ they have to be exposed to an understanding of how God encountered people in the past. "And beginning with Moses and all the prophets, he interpreted . . . the scripture. . ." (Luke 24:27). Their mood changes from despair to hope as they enter into searching dialogue with the man on the road. In a sense, they have to open themselves personally to experience the Good News. Finally they experience the presence of Christ in the breaking of the bread with the stranger.

Our weekly celebration of the Holy Eucharist follows the pattern of the Emmaus story. First we gather to hear the stories that make us aware of how God is encountering us in our daily lives. Then we gather "with the stranger" for the breaking of bread, and at the altar the risen Lord is revealed in the Sacrament and in our daily lives together. This weekly celebration, in turn, gives us a pattern for our lives as Christians. As the story of our people becomes more a part of our lives, we will become more sensitive to the living presence of the risen Christ. We will see him on many roads and at many passage points. He will be with us whenever we break bread and proclaim his name.

The gospel readings for the *fourth* and *fifth* Sundays refer to Jesus as "the door of the sheep," the "good shepherd," and "the way, and the truth, and the life." The reading for the *sixth* Sunday identifies Jesus as "the true vine." The Roman Catholic and Lutheran lectionaries focus this sixth week on Jesus' promise of the gift of the Holy Spirit. "And I will pray the Father, and he will give you another Counselor, to be with you for ever, even the Spirit of truth. . ." (John 14:16-17).

The gospel reading for the *seventh* Sunday is a portion of the great "priestly prayer of Christ." In this prayer, Jesus asks the Father "Sanctify them in the truth; thy word is truth. As thou didst send me into the world, so I have sent them into the world. And for their sake I consecrate myself, that they also may be consecrated in truth" (John 17:17-19). When we consecrate something we recognize its holiness. It becomes an "outward and visible sign" of God's presence in that person or in that sacramental action. In Jesus' life, suffering, death, and resurrection he is consecrated. He becomes the outward and visible sign of God's presence in him and in us through the Holy Spirit. Jesus prays that his disciples (his Church) will be consecrated so that they too will be outward and visible signs of God's presence in the world.

This thought may add a new dimension to our understanding of our baptism. At each baptism we witness, we are in a sense consecrated. We become sacramental witnesses of God's power and presence in the world. That is, we become "outward and visible signs of inward and spiritual grace" by our lives that reflect God's presence in the world. When the priest takes bread and wine at the Holy Eucharist and consecrates it, the common stuff of life becomes the visible sign of Christ's presence with us. Likewise, Christ takes the common stuff of our lives and consecrates us through the Holy Spirit so that we too become the visible signs of God's healing presence in the world. As mentioned elsewhere in this book (pages 89-90), the prayer of consecration is a recalling of God's mighty acts in history. "Holy and gracious Father: In your infinite love you made us for yourself; and, when we had fallen into sin and become subject to evil and death, you, in your mercy, sent Jesus Christ. . ." (*The Book of Common Prayer,* page 362). We realize the consecration of our lives as we too recall the mighty acts of God in our own individual histories.

A personal "prayer of consecration" could be offered for each participant as a conclusion to this Sunday's shared experience and as a conclusion to the whole Easter season. As the individual history of each of the participants is recalled in summary fashion, the leader could recognize that person's consecration as Christ's apostle by taking that person's hands and saying as a blessing the words of John 17:26: "I made known to them thy name, and I will make it known, that the love with which thou hast loved me may be in them, and I in them." The prayer of consecration for each participant could be phrased in the cadence of the prayer of consecration from the Holy Eucharist. For example, for Sally we might say

Holy and gracious Father, in your infinite love you made Sally for yourself. When Sally was five you sent her to us from another city, and we have shared your love together ever since. When her grandfather died, you revealed your eternal love for Sally by the comfort that came to her at the funeral. Now that she is in the sixth grade, your wisdom is being revealed to her more fully through her teachers and friends. Therefore, we proclaim a mystery of faith with you, Sally. To you, Christ has revealed God's name, and he will continue to reveal it so that God's love may live in you, Sally, and so that Christ may live in you. Go forth this day in the name of Christ.

This personalized prayer may help Sally understand the gift of the Holy Spirit that she will celebrate next Sunday at the feast of Pentecost. The bread and wine at the Eucharist is sanctified by the Holy Spirit "to be for your people the Body and Blood of your Son, the holy food and drink of new and unending life in him." But each Christian is also blessed and sanctified so that *we* may become "outward and visible signs" of Christ's presence in the world. "Sanctify us also that we may faithfully receive this holy Sacrament, and serve you in unity, constancy, and peace; and at the last day bring us with all your saints into the joy of your eternal kingdom" (Prayer of Consecration, *The Book of Common Prayer,* page 363). Now those words that Sally hears week after week at the Eucharist can take on a personal dimension. She, too, is consecrated by the Holy Spirit so that her life can reveal the presence of God in the world. She receives the bread and wine of the Eucharist as the food of that apostleship.

The Easter readings in all three years of the lectionary cycle draw heavily from the beautiful Gospel of John. As we share these readings, we need to appreciate the nature of this gospel, since it is quite different from the other three.

The Gospels according to Matthew, Mark, and Luke contain many passages that are identical or closely related in content and language. For this reason, the first three gospels are called the synoptic gospels (*synoptic* means "presenting an account from the same point of view"). The synoptic gospels developed from the oral tradition handed down by the first-century Christians; the accounts in the gospels were related by word of mouth from person to person. Except for the Passion narrative, the various passages were probably related independently of each other as separate anecdotes or illustrations of what Jesus said and did. When the gospels were written, the accounts were placed within a framework that each compiler felt would convey the "good news" with the most force for the persons reading and hearing it. With this in mind, we can understand why little explanation of background is given for each passage. The synoptic gospels are simply compilations of the things people remembered Jesus saying and doing, placed within a framework deemed most suitable by each of the three compilers.

The Gospel of John is quite different. It was written later than the other three, and its writer provides not only detached accounts of what Jesus said and did but also a highly developed theological understanding of the eternal *significance* of his words and deeds. His gospel is also different in that he avoids the rather dull, abstract language that theology often uses. The author is interested in helping us *experience* the vibrant meaning of what he writes about; to do that he resorts to poetic language far more than the other evangelists do. The first chapter of John is a perfect example of this. Where the Gospel of Luke describes the *event* of Jesus' birth, the Gospel of John describes in poetic language the *meaning* of that event: "In the beginning was the Word . . . the Word was God." His constant use of images of light and darkness is another example of the author's poetic language.

I would describe the Gospel of John, then, as a poetic theological interpretation of the life, death, and resurrection of Jesus the Christ. The writer's method is to introduce an event in Jesus' life and then use it to launch into a theological discourse about the meaning of that event. The entire sixth chapter of John, for example, gives the theological significance of the feeding of the five thousand. Where Matthew, Mark, and Luke report the event, John interprets it theologically. (In this instance the writer of John offers a theology of the Eucharist, as well as providing a theological emphasis that it is in the "daily bread" of living life that we experience Christ in our lives.)

I would suggest that as we share readings from the Gospel of John we need to help our people develop their appreciation for poetry. Encourage participants to talk about some of their favorite poems and to express themselves poetically. The beautiful book *A Celebration of Bees* is an excellent resource.*

With this background of poetry in mind, we can introduce our readings from John with "Here is a beautiful poem about the meaning of Jesus' birth, from the Gospel of John." Then the hearer can appreciate the beauty and wonder of the gospel without being tied down into literalisms and perhaps later getting turned off by confusion of meaning. What I have said here needs, of course, to be applied to the many other portions of the Bible that speak in poetic language to convey the deep truth of the presence of God.

So we need to approach the statements from the Gospel of John with an understanding and appreciation of poetry. Go through the gospel and pull out other poetic expressions that describe the relationship we feel with God as made known through Christ. Listed below are important passages from John that can be studied from this viewpoint:

John 1:1-18   Jesus is the Word of God.
John 1:29   Jesus is "the lamb of God" who takes away the sins of the world.
John 4:1-42   The symbol of living water is used to describe poetically the role Christ plays in bringing life to persons.
John 6:1-15
  and 6:22-59 Jesus is the "bread of life."
John 7:37-39 We hear again the reference to "living water." This time the imagery points to the gift of the Holy Spirit.

*Barbara Juster Esbensen, *A Celebration of Bees: Helping Children Write Poetry* (Minneapolis, Minn.: Winston Press, 1975).

John 8:12	Jesus calls himself "the light of the world."
John 10:1-21	Jesus is the Good Shepherd and the "door of the sheep."
John 11:25	"I am the resurrection and the life."
John 12:46	"I have come as light into the world, that whoever believes in me may not remain in darkness."
John 14:1-7	This is a poem of comfort and strength. Jesus goes to prepare a way for us: "In my Father's house are many rooms." Jesus is now seen as "the way, and the truth, and the life."
John 15:1-17	Jesus is "the true vine." To have life one must be a part of the vine that is the living presence of Christ.

The resurrection of Jesus has shaped our understanding of life and of all creation. To know Jesus, the man from Nazareth, was to know personally the presence of the God of Abraham, Isaac, and Jacob. To know the risen Christ is to experience that same personal relationship with the God of creation, history, and eternity. To know this risen Christ in my daily life is like being given a cool drink of spring water on a hot day. It is like knowing that I am not alone but a part of a "living vine" of God's people. And so John describes our relationship to the resurrection in words of poetry and analogy.

Let Easter be a time of poetry in your learning community. Encourage participants to write their own poetry of creation, love, and power. Celebrate the festival with banners that express each of the "I am" sayings of Jesus listed above. Create additional banners to include the poetic expressions of the participants.

A retreat for the parish council or vestry could focus on how well the life of the parish reflects the feelings of John's poetry. Is Christ's presence as "living water," "good shepherd," and "bread of life" truly reflected in the life we share in the parish? How might we live more fully into the poetry of John? The Book of Acts gives us a model of how the first-century Church attempted to act out discipleship. Is that community a functional model for us?

The Epistle Readings

All epistle readings are taken from 1 Peter (although, as has been pointed out, Episcopalians have the option of using the Book of Acts for either the first or the second reading). This letter of Peter may have been a summary of the Christian faith drawn up for converts and may possibly have been a complete baptismal liturgy for some of the churches of the first century. Claude K. Peifer offers an outline of 1 Peter based on the theory that the letter is a formal baptismal liturgy of the early Church:*

1 Peter 1:3-5 seems to have been a baptismal hymn, which developed the idea that baptism is a regeneration which leads the Christian to an inheritance which he will receive in the last times. 1:13-21 is an outline of a preparatory homily which treats of the exodus as a type of Christian baptism. Some think that the sacrament was conferred after this; 1:22—2:10 would then be a second homily following the baptism.

(1 Peter) 2:11—3:7 represents a series of admonitions to the newly-baptized, applying the Christian ideal to the moral life of various social classes. 3:18—4:6 contains elements of a creed which may have been recited at the baptismal ceremony. 5:5b-9 is probably a fragment of another hymn. Other elements in the epistle may also have had a connection with the baptismal liturgy.

Though not all New Testament scholars would agree with this liturgical theory, it is obvious that the epistle was written for the newly baptized Christian. Thus it is especially appropriate that we share the epistle during the Easter season.

During Lent we carried out the tradition of the early Church in reviewing the meaning of our covenant faith with God in preparation for the baptisms of Easter. Now we follow the tradition of looking at what our new life in Christ

*Claude K. Peifer, "Primitive Liturgy in the Formation of the New Testament," *The Bible Today Reader: Selected Articles from the First Ten Years of "The Bible Today"* (Collegeville, Minn.: The Liturgical Press, 1973), pp. 108-113.

means. On the last Sunday of Easter the participants of the learning community could lead the parish family in a liturgy of baptismal renewal based on the format of 1 Peter outlined above. Have different participants read the admonitions from the second and third chapters. Put the words of the ancient hymns found in chapters 1 and 5 to music and sing them as a part of the liturgy. Have two different participants "preach" the baptismal sermons found in chapters 1 and 2. This will prepare participants to celebrate the baptism of the Holy Spirit that we recognize in the festival of Pentecost next Sunday.

The Feast of Pentecost
As we pointed out in chapter 3 (pages 88-89), our Christian liturgical calendar is based partly on the ancient Jewish calendar. Each year the Jewish people recall the mighty acts of God in their history. As they recall those mighty acts, they see God's power and presence calling them into life and freedom in the present moment. So history for the Jew is a living tradition; the events of the past are a part of the present. The people gather to tell the story of faith year after year in their holy days and festivals, and they feel the power of that story as they realize that they themselves are part of God's history-making.

To understand the Christian Pentecost, we must understand its connection with Easter. These two feasts, in turn, are based on the interconnected Jewish feasts of Passover and Pentecost.

Historically, the Jews celebrated Passover as a way of recalling the great exodus from Egypt. Earlier yet, Passover was a harvest festival when the first-fruits of the new harvest were presented to God as a thank offering. Fifty days after Passover the Jews celebrated the closing of harvest with a thanksgiving festival which also recalled the receiving of the Mosaic Law at Mount Sinai; one of the names of that feast was Pentecost. (*Pentecost* is a Greek word meaning *fiftieth,* signifying that the feast comes fifty days after Passover.) This Pentecost festival became a time when the nation rededicated itself to the covenant.

The early Church found meaning in the ancient Jewish celebration of Passover and Pentecost. Easter is intimately associated with the Passover. The Last Supper may have been the Passover meal that Jesus shared with his disciples. "Christ *our* Passover is sacrificed," we say in the liturgy. Through Christ we recognize God calling us out of slavery into freedom. And according to the Book of Acts it was on Pentecost day that the apostles received the gift of the Holy Spirit, signifying that ever since that day the Christian lives under a new law mediated not through Moses but through the Holy Spirit. (If you read Acts 2 and then read Exodus 19:16-25, you will see some of the same symbols used to represent God's appearance to his people.) Pentecost, then, is a celebration of our covenant relationship with God—a relationship originally made known through the ancient covenant of the Old Testament but now known directly through the abiding power and presence of the Holy Spirit in our lives.

We can help members of the learning community appreciate the significance of the Holy Spirit if we simply look at the way we use the word *spirit* in our daily language. "We've got the spirit," say the cheerleaders. The expression means something about being excited and confident and feeling oneself a part of the body of students. The Church also says "We've got the Holy Spirit." The power of God is with us. We feel excited and "turned on" to life. Thoughts and feelings that give us insight and vision "come to us" (a common expression with some real theological implications!). Look, too, at our words based on the word *spirit.* "I feel *inspired*"; "What an *inspiration* that was!" Pentecost celebrates that inspiration, that "turned-on-ness" to life and wholeness and vision that we proclaim as gospel. Our participation in the ancient covenant is marked by such moments of inspiration and power. Those moments become the signs we see in the wilderness times of our lives.

Plan well ahead so that you can publicize Pentecost and prepare for it properly. Form a Pentecost planning and brainstorming group to work with the priest in celebrating the day. Trace the developing awareness of covenant as it is outlined later in this chapter, pages 182-183. Get books on the Jewish festivals from your parish or city library, and read about their ancient and contemporary celebrations of Pentecost (several are listed in the Bibliography). See if there are ways you can incorporate some of the ancient traditions into your parish celebration. Offer a covenant renewal liturgy incorporating the Decalogue (Ten Commandments) in which you renew your baptismal vows as a sign of your covenant relationship with God. Share the ancient traditions within the learning community so that everyone can appreciate the significance of today's celebration. Trace in a Bible wordbook or concordance the words *spirit* and *wind* and *breath* in both the Old and New Testaments. (The very first verse of the Bible states: ". . . and the Spirit of God was moving over the face of the waters.")

As you think about celebrating the Feast of Pentecost, realize that it is the glorious completion of Easter, which is the central feast in the Christian Church (and traditionally far more important than Christmas, which developed considerably later). If we show our people the significance of Pentecost, the day can be an exciting and deepening occasion for them.

Trinity Sunday
See pages 277-278 for a discussion of the Holy Trinity, celebrated this first Sunday after Pentecost.

The Sundays after Pentecost (Sundays in Ordinary Time)

The following guide is offered with the hope that it might be helpful in quickly determining how you may want to use the readings for the weeks after Pentecost. Where a passage has good storytelling possibilities, I have pointed it out under the "Telling the story" heading. Passages that I feel are important for helping persons discover religious concepts are pointed out by explanations under the "religious concepts" heading. I approach the readings from these two different points of view because I see the religious educator looking at the lessons with varying needs. There will be times when we want to share the story for the sake of the story, as was mentioned earlier in this book. At other times we will want to use the readings to launch a study of a particular concept such as forgiveness or discipleship. In this case the story may become a launching device for involving the participants in a conceptual study.

The readings for the Sundays after Pentecost return to the practice of Epiphany. We read the Gospel of Matthew chapter by chapter as we did during Epiphany. The Old Testament lesson usually adds understanding to the gospel selection, though sometimes it will help to shed light on the epistle reading for the day. The epistle readings will lead us through important segments of 1 Corinthians, Romans, Philippians, and 1 Thessalonians. Since for the most part these readings do not match the theme of the Old Testament and gospel selections, I do not mention them in the following section. Nevertheless, it would be good to have a group that studies these summertime readings. Good study materials are available; see, for example, the William Barclay source in the Bibliography.

Because of the chapter-by-chapter nature of the gospel and epistle readings, there is no overriding theme during these Sundays after Pentecost. However, this is a time of growth in the Holy Spirit as we are exposed to stories from both testaments that help us see the power of the Holy Spirit in the present moment and in the time to come.

In the Episcopal lectionary you can determine the correct readings for the Sunday by finding the Proper number with the date closest to the Sunday in question. (See *The Book of Common Prayer,* page 158, for an explanation.) Propers 1, 2, and 3 have the same readings as those appointed for the sixth, seventh, and eighth Sundays after Epiphany. Whether these lessons will be read during the season of Epiphany or during the Sundays after Pentecost is determined by the date of Easter Sunday. The Roman Catholic lectionary numbers the Sundays after Pentecost as Sundays in Ordinary Time (or Sundays of the Year); the Lutheran lectionary numbers them as Sundays after Pentecost.

Proper 1   E
Sixth Sunday in Ordinary Time   RC
Sixth Sunday after Epiphany   L
See sixth Sunday after Epiphany (pages 112-113) for comments.

Proper 2   E
Seventh Sunday in Ordinary Time   RC
Seventh Sunday after Epiphany   L
See seventh Sunday after Epiphany (pages 114-115) for comments.

Proper 3   E
Eighth Sunday in Ordinary Time   RC
Eighth Sunday after Epiphany   L
See eighth Sunday after Epiphany (pages 115-116) for comments.

Proper 4   E
Ninth Sunday in Ordinary Time   RC
Second Sunday after Pentecost   L
Old Testament: You must follow the word and Commandments of God.

Gospel: These are the concluding words of the Sermon on the Mount. The person who follows Jesus' words is like "a wise man who built his house upon the rock."

Religious concepts: The importance of following God's word is stressed. If we follow his word, we will be whole. If we don't, we will be at "dis-ease." God gives his blessing to the people if they follow the covenant; he threatens a curse if they stray from it. The nation will bring the blessing or curse upon itself. We too bring blessings and curses into our lives as a result of our behavior. A valid response to God's Word is to share his love, compassion, and liberation with others.

Proper 5   E
Tenth Sunday in Ordinary Time   RC
Third Sunday after Pentecost   L

Old Testament: Hosea speaks strong words of sarcasm. The people sin in the sight of God, he points out, and then they offer empty sacrifices, thinking that through those sacrifices the Lord will heal them. "After two days he will revive us; on the third day he will raise us up, that we may live before him" (Hosea 6:2). The Lord speaks through Hosea. "Your love is like a morning cloud, like the dew that goes early away" (Hosea 6:4). What the Lord wants is not empty sacrifice. "For I desire steadfast love and not sacrifice, the knowledge of God, rather than burnt offerings" (Hosea 6:6). Empty ritual dare not replace *doing* the Word in our daily lives (see James 1:22).

Gospel: Today we hear the story of Jesus calling Matthew the tax collector. The Jews hated tax collectors, for they worked for the Romans and made their living by the taxes they collected from their own people. We need to understand this feeling to appreciate the radical nature of Matthew's call as a disciple. Jesus then has dinner with other sinners, and this shocks the Pharisees more. But it is sick people who need the doctor, Jesus reminds the Pharisees. Then he quotes the Hosea passage we heard from the Old Testament reading about God's desire for mercy, not empty sacrifice.

Telling the story: This week and next week we will be focusing on the calling and sending forth of the disciples. In next week's gospel reading, the names of the twelve apostles are listed. In dealing with children, see how many apostles or disciples they can name. Do they know stories about any of them? Some will be able to tell the story about Judas betraying Jesus and about Thomas doubting the resurrection of Christ. Tell the story of the calling of Peter (Luke 5:1-11) and about James and John being with Jesus and Peter at the transfiguration (Matthew 17:1-8). Have older children trace stories of the apostles and disciples, using the index of names in the Good News Bible or in a Bible concordance. You may want to encourage children to memorize the names of the apostles as they are listed in Matthew so that they can be more aware of them as they are named in various readings from the gospels and the Book of Acts during the year.

Religious concepts: Each week as we reflect on the lessons, we need to confront our own reasons for participating in the liturgy. If we are not careful, the sacraments can become mere good-luck omens or empty payments for our sins. What the Lord wants from us is mercy and justice and a true self-offering. The Great Thanksgiving prayer (Eucharistic Prayer or Prayer of Consecration) in the Episcopal liturgy reflects the feelings of today's readings. "And we earnestly desire thy fatherly goodness to accept this our sacrifice of praise and thanksgiving. . . . And here we offer and present unto thee, O Lord, our selves, our souls and bodies. . ." (Rite I, *The Book of Common Prayer,* pages 335-336). "Sanctify us also that we may faithfully receive this holy Sacrament, and serve you in unity, constancy and peace. . ." (Rite II, page 363).

Proper 6   E
Eleventh Sunday in Ordinary Time   RC
Fourth Sunday after Pentecost   L

Old Testament: The Lord promises a covenant to Moses for the people. "Now therefore, if you will obey my voice and keep my covenant, you shall be my own possession among all peoples; for all the earth is mine." The nation will be a "kingdom of priests." The writer looks back at the saving acts of God in rescuing the people from Egypt.

Gospel: Jesus sends out the disciples in his name and with his authority to heal. He gives them instructions for their mission.

Telling the story: Tell the stories of God giving the covenants to his people. The covenant stories are as follows:

1. The covenant with Noah (Genesis 9)
2. The covenant with Abraham (Genesis 15 and 17:1-14)
3. The Mosaic covenant (of which the Ten Commandments are an important part), the heart of the whole Torah (Exodus, chapters 19, 20, and 24)

4. The covenant with Joshua (Joshua 24)
5. The covenant with Jacob (Genesis 28:10-22 and 32:23-32)—Jacob is given the name of Israel after his struggle with the angel.
6. The covenant with David (2 Samuel 7; see also 2 Samuel 23:5)
7. The covenant with King Josiah (2 Kings 23)—The event of making this covenant is established in 2 Kings. The Book of Deuteronomy contains the essential ideas of the reform covenant promulgated by by Josiah. See chapter 2, pages 59-60.
8. The covenant of Ezra (Nehemiah 9 and 10)
9. The prophet Jeremiah foresaw a new covenant that would be written on the hearts of the people (Jeremiah 31:31-34). This is the "new covenant" or "new testament" that the Church proclaims with the coming of the gift of the Holy Spirit in Acts 2. The Holy Spirit dwells within the Christian so that the Christian responds to the word of God through the indwelling presence of God rather than because of an external law.
10. The gift of the Holy Spirit promised by Jesus is the seal of the new covenant (Acts 2). The book of the new covenant, of course, is the New Testament. We understand our new covenant with God through our participation in the story of the New Testament.

Religious concepts: To be a disciple of Christ (a Christian) is to realize our call, as the disciples realized their call. Moreover, to be a disciple of Christ is to accept the New Covenant. We open ourselves to the power of the Holy Spirit and live as servants of the Lord. As we do this, we go forth into the world with a new authority and a new power. Look over the liturgy of baptism in the *Prayer Book* and talk about the kind of commitment that is made in baptism. (The baptismal covenant is found on pages 304-305 in *The Book of Common Prayer.*)

Proper 7 E
Twelfth Sunday in Ordinary Time RC
Fifth Sunday after Pentecost L
Old Testament: Today we hear an anguished cry from the prophet Jeremiah. He feels that the Lord has deceived him. The words

that he feels called to speak to the people bring only derision and ridicule. His life is lived in deep pain and rejection. But then Jeremiah feels strength coming to him as he reflects on his call: "But the Lord is with me as a dread warrior" (Jeremiah 20:11). He is sustained in the pain of speaking out, for he knows the Lord is with him.

Gospel: Jesus warns the disciples that they too must suffer as they speak the words of God. Jeremiah's anguished cry may well have been in their minds as they set out on their mission. But they are not to be afraid, for they know that God is with them. Not a sparrow falls without his knowing it.

Telling the story: Tell the stories of Jeremiah listed in A Guide to Stories of the Bible in chapter 1 (pages 35-37). Then tell the stories of Christian saints and martyrs. Include stories about contemporary martyrs or people who have suffered as a result of witnessing to their faith. Tell about the struggles of the early Christians during the persecutions.

Religious concepts: Today we focus directly on the meaning of discipleship. A disciple or prophet is called to speak and live out the word of God. The disciple may be called to suffer, for the word he or she brings is not always popular with the people.

Proper 8 E
Thirteenth Sunday in Ordinary Time RC
Sixth Sunday after Pentecost L
Old Testament: "For the Lord of hosts has a day / against all that is proud and lofty" (Isaiah 2:12). On the day of the Lord, the proud will be humbled and ". . . the Lord alone will be exalted. . ." (Isaiah 2:17). These are ominous words of warning to those who might look forward to the coming of the Lord to receive their reward.

Gospel: The gospel reading for today is shocking. Jesus has come not to bring peace but division. His words will set son against father. "He who loves father or mother more than me is not worthy of me" (Matthew 10:37). Jesus comes to exalt the Lord and to bring justice and liberation to the poor and the oppressed. His words and acts will inevitably bring conflict.

Telling the story: We are dealing with the same theme of discipleship that we have been focusing on for the past two weeks. Continue the story, telling about those who have spoken God's word and suffered for their witness. St. Francis of Assisi rejected his parents' wealth and power to follow Christ. Martin Luther King, Jr., was controversial as he set about to bring liberation to the Blacks. His words brought divisions within families as people were forced to choose or reject his words and actions.

Religious concepts: Liberation theology focuses on God's liberating action among the oppressed. From this theological perspective, God is always on the side of the oppressed. He led the Israelites out of the oppression of Egypt into the Promised Land. He is acting through the oppressed in Latin America, in Africa, and in our own land. If we are to understand what God is calling us to do and become in our day, we have to understand the liberation movements that rock the complacency of nation and society. The words of Scripture are radical words that confront us this Sunday, and liberation theology calls us to radical obedience. Read the Magnificat or Song of Mary to gain further perspective on this concept (Luke 1:46-53). ". . . he has put down the mighty from their thrones, and exalted those of low degree" (Luke 1:52).

With these thoughts in mind, who are some contemporary persons through whom God may be working in our nation and throughout the world? What is their word, and how is it received by the "proud" and by the "humble"? What is our role as disciples and prophets called to speak out in Jesus' name? What problems in our local community call for our direct participation as Christians? What are the issues before the city council, the school board, or the parish council? Think about these readings in connection with our own Independence Day that we celebrate at this time of year. The Declaration of Independence is a liberation theology document. Tell some of the stories of our American liberation leaders of Revolutionary times. Independence Day is a radical holiday in which we proclaim the justice and liberation that our nation is called to witness to. These readings may help us celebrate our own independence with more than firecrackers and long weekends.

(The theme of discipleship is picked up again in Proper 17.)

The Old Testament reading appointed in the Roman Catholic lectionary helps point up a second major theme in today's gospel. A woman recognizes in Elisha a man of God and invites him to stay in her home. She welcomes him and assists him. This theme is picked up in the second half of today's gospel reading. "He who receives you receives me, and he who receives me receives him who sent me" (Matthew 10:40). The stories of Elijah and Elisha are interesting to share in the learning community. (See A Guide to Stories of the Bible, chapter 1, pages 32-33.) These men were also radical influences on society who confronted the leaders of their day with the word of the Lord and were therefore hated; so the theme of God's liberating action in history is stressed in the lives of these men of God, too.

The Lutheran lectionary assigns Jeremiah 28:5-9 for this Sunday. This is a story of Jeremiah mentioned in A Guide to Stories of the Bible, chapter 1, pages 35-37. Jeremiah was rejected for speaking the word of the Lord. He came speaking of war and defeat, not peace, for the people of Judah.

As the woman received Elisha, so must we be ready to welcome the person who speaks out as prophet in our day, remembering that the words we hear may bring conflict into our lives, too.

Proper 9 E
Fourteenth Sunday in Ordinary Time RC
Seventh Sunday after Pentecost L

Old Testament: This is a familiar reading, for we hear it on Palm Sunday. "Lo, your king comes to you; triumphant and victorious is he, humble and riding on an ass, on a colt the foal of an ass" (Zechariah 9:9).

Gospel: Keep the radical words of the previous Sundays in mind as you share this reading in the learning community and in the liturgy. ". . .thou hast hidden these things from the wise and understanding and revealed them to babes. . ." (Matthew 11:25). It would seem that in the kingdom of God the standards of the world are reversed. The clever and proud are put down, and the lowly and childlike are raised up. The second part of the reading contains the familiar words "Come to me, all who labor and are heavy laden, and I will give you rest"

(Matthew 11:28). The Lord comforts and heals those who come to him in childlike love and humility. He comforts those who experience oppression, sickness, and suffering.

Telling the story: Read the words of the Old Testament passage today and see if participants can identify the connection with Palm Sunday. Then tell the story of Jesus' triumphal entry into Jerusalem. Talk about the disciples Jesus chose. What kind of people were they? Our recent sharing of the stories of the calling of the disciples may be rehearsed to emphasize the humbleness of Jesus' followers. The story of Gideon mentioned in A Guide to Stories of the Bible, chapter 1, page 28, would be another good story to tell this week, for Gideon was the "least in [his] family" (Judges 6:15).

Religious concepts: The radical nature of the gospel is the theme carried over from previous weeks. Notice the sense of justice, healing, and love that Jesus offers to those who do come seeking the wholeness that the Lord offers. The proud and powerful miss that strength as they rely on their own power.

Proper 10   E
Fifteenth Sunday in Ordinary Time   RC
Eighth Sunday after Pentecost   L

Old Testament: The word of God accomplishes the purpose of God. It is like the rain that causes growth.

Gospel: Parable of the sower.

Telling the story: This parable is fun to act out with young children. Take some time this Sunday to plant some seeds. Watch them grow during the balance of the summer; think about the parable as you do so. The beautiful words from Isaiah 55:10-13 could be shared as a closing liturgy for the day.

For as the rain and the snow come down from
     heaven,
   and return not thither but water the earth,
making it bring forth and sprout,
   giving seed to the sower and bread to the eater,
so shall my word be that goes forth from my
     mouth;
   it shall not return to me empty,
but it shall accomplish that which I purpose,

and prosper in the thing for which I sent it.

Religious concepts: The word of God is the concept we deal with here. Tie it in with John 1: "In the beginning was the Word." See chapter 2, pages 66-68, for an understanding of this concept. The word of God is not just something we hear; it is power. It is something we "see" in what is happening all around us. The word is the wisdom that makes sense of creation and puts us in touch with the reality of that sense. The point of today's reading is that nothing can keep the word of God from accomplishing its purpose. No matter how frustrated we may feel with the way our history is seemingly working out, God's word will be accomplished. Though many of the seeds that we attempt to sow soon die, some of them live, and they are enough to accomplish God's will. In the frustrations we feel in the "seeds" that seem to be dying all around us, the parable of the sower can give us the same encouragement as it did to the disciples who saw so many of Jesus' seeds seemingly fall by the wayside. This would be a good Sunday for older participants to focus on happenings of our time. Where and how do we hear God's word being uttered? Where do the seeds of God's word seem to be falling on hard ground and dying?

Proper 11   E
Sixteenth Sunday in Ordinary Time   RC
Ninth Sunday after Pentecost   L

Old Testament: The infinite patience and mercy of God give his people grounds for hope.

Gospel: The parable of the weeds is a parable of patience and judgment. A man sows good seed, but an enemy comes and sows weeds. The servants are anxious to pull up the weeds immediately, but the master urges patience. When the harvest comes, he tells the servants, he will separate the good grain from the weeds.

Telling the story: Last week, today, and next week present several of Jesus' parables. The musical production *Godspell* can be our model in sharing these simple stories of Jesus. The writer of *Godspell* used humor and song in sharing them. Let the children pretend to be the seeds sowed by the farmer. Then tell the story about the enemy coming to sow the weeds, and have additional children literally jump into the skit.

Then have the children grow by doing stretching and reaching exercises. One child can be the landowner and another the servant. Let them discuss the problem and finally root out the weeds at the day of harvest. Talk about Jesus' parables (see A Guide to Stories of the Bible, chapter 1, pages 45-46).

Religious concepts: The gospel reading is a response to our age-old question, Why does God allow evil to exist? The evil in the world seems to grow stronger. But God's time is not our time, we hear today. God's patience encompasses eternity, while we live but a moment. Talk about this concept with adolescents and adults. Share the parable as Jesus shared it. Don't try to explain it. Let the group come to grips with the Word. You might get into the discussion by asking "What do you think prompted Jesus to tell this parable? What kinds of questions do you think the people were asking him? Have you ever wondered about that yourself?"

The Roman Catholic reading for today includes Matthew 13:31-43, the parables of the mustard seed and the leaven. The parable of the leaven is included in next week's reading in the Episcopal lectionary.

The Lutheran Old Testament reading is Isaiah 44:6-8. The prophet calls upon the people to recognize the one and only true God and to reject the idols and false gods of their own devising.

Proper 12   E
Seventeenth Sunday in Ordinary Time   RC
Tenth Sunday after Pentecost   L

Old Testament: We hear the story of Solomon asking God for "an understanding mind to govern thy people, that I may discern between good and evil" (1 Kings 3:9). The Lord is pleased that Solomon asks for wisdom rather than for riches and power.

Gospel: In the Episcopal lectionary we hear the parables of the mustard seed, the treasure and the pearl, and the net. (The Roman Catholic and Lutheran lectionaries do not include the first two parables in this Sunday's reading.)

Telling the story: If you shared the parables last week, turn to the Old Testament this week and share the stories of Solomon. See A

Guide to Stories of the Bible, chapter 1, page 31.

Religious concepts: Contrast the parables in today's gospel with the inability of the rich man to give up what he had to follow Jesus (Mark 10:17-31). When we discover the power of the gospel, we must be ready to completely change our life in order to center it on the Lord. Finding the Lord in one's life is like finding a treasure. The Old Testament reading points up the true treasure that Solomon sought. Unlike the rich man who came to Jesus, Solomon desired wisdom, not riches. So he received the full blessing of the Lord.

Proper 13   E
Eighteenth Sunday in Ordinary Time   RC
Eleventh Sunday after Pentecost   L

Old Testament: The Israelites strayed from God during their wilderness wandering. Because of their fear and lack of faith they worshiped a golden calf and were willing to be led back into slavery. Even then God did not withhold the manna and water from them.

Gospel: Jesus feeds five thousand on the hillside.

Telling the story: Tell the story of the wilderness wandering, the story of the golden calf, and the feeding of the five thousand.

Religious concepts: This would be a good time to focus on the Eucharist. As we offer our possessions in faith, we are fed the manna (bread). Even when we turn from God in doubt and fear, he loves us and brings us back to him as he feeds us with the "bread of life," which becomes for us the sign of his presence.

In the Gospel of John this feeding account is found in chapter 6. A small boy offers a few loaves and fish to be shared with the crowd. The idea of making an offering of our possessions in faith is conveyed in this story. Often we fail to respond to Christ because we feel that what we have to offer cannot make any difference. "I know world hunger is a problem," we say, "but the problem is so big, what difference is my little sacrifice going to make?" In the hands of Jesus, the small and insignificant offering of the boy became enough to feed the crowd. When we offer the risen Christ our time, talent, and commitment, he can *make* it capable of bringing about the Kingdom. This point was made in last week's parable of the mustard seed. The smallest seed grows into a tree large enough for the birds to nest in! Every act, no matter how small, that is done in the name of Christ is "enough" in the hands of the Lord (John Westerhoff, Portland Lecture Series, Lewis and Clark College, June, 1978).

In the Roman Catholic and Lutheran lectionaries, the Old Testament reading is Isaiah 55:1-3(5), an invitation to the hungry and thirsty to "come to the waters; . . . come, buy and eat!" (Isaiah 55:1).

Proper 14   E
Nineteenth Sunday in Ordinary Time   RC
Twelfth Sunday after Pentecost   L

Old Testament: In this reading from the Book of Jonah, we hear the psalm of thanksgiving uttered by the prophet as he was rescued from drowning by being swallowed by a large fish.

Gospel: This is the account of Jesus walking on the water. Peter, in faith, leaves the safety of the boat to walk on the water toward Jesus.

Telling the story: The story of Jonah is a delightful one to tell in the learning community. Read my remarks in connection with this story in A Guide to Stories of the Bible, chapter 1, page 37. Remember that this is an amusing short story, not a literal historical account. Tell it as a short story, and share the love, mercy, and humor reflected in it.

Religious concepts: My remarks in chapter 1, page 18, regarding Jonah's role in Old Testament literature would be helpful here. God's infinite mercy far surpasses our understanding. He loves even our most hated enemy. Both the Book of Jonah and the Book of Ruth can remind us what little understanding and compassion we have for other Christians, let alone for our enemies!

The concept to share as we take the gospel and Old Testament reading together, however, is the faith expressed by Jonah and by Peter as they feel themselves sustained by the Lord. We might well imagine Peter reciting the prayer of Jonah as he found himself saved by Jesus. In faith, we are called to move out into the water toward the

Lord who calls, not faltering at the first sign of storm, but moving with the realization that the Lord is with us. These words bring comfort as they are read in the context of the radical call to speak the Lord's word—a call that we have heard in the past few weeks.

The Roman Catholic and Lutheran lectionaries have 1 Kings 19:9,11-13(18) as the Old Testament reading for this Sunday. Elijah is told to stand at the mouth of the cave. "'Go forth, and stand upon the mount before the Lord.' And behold, the Lord passed by" (1 Kings 19:11). It was in facing the wind and the earthquake that Elijah perceived the presence of the Lord in a "tiny whispering sound." In faith he moved toward the Lord, following the course the Lord called him to take. In faith Peter moved across the water to meet Jesus. His faith faltered, but he was later able to pass through the greater tests of faith and follow the Lord as an apostle.

Proper 15   E
Twentieth Sunday in Ordinary Time   RC
Thirteenth Sunday after Pentecost   L

Old Testament: ". . . my house shall be called a house of prayer for all peoples" (Isaiah 56:7b). This is a universal theme of love for all who come to God.

Gospel: Jesus heals the daughter of a Canaanite woman. See A Guide to Stories of the Bible in chapter 1, pages 43-44, for other healing stories of Jesus you may want to tell today. The point in today's reading is that the healing love made known through Christ is a gift for all God's creation, not just for the Jew or the Christian. All people will come to know this healing power as it happens in history and in eternity. (See also pages 210-211.)

Religious concepts: The love of God for *all* his creation is shown in these readings. My remarks in connection with the Book of Jonah in last week's readings are important to read in connection with this week's theme.

Proper 16   E
Twenty-first Sunday in Ordinary Time   RC
Fourteenth Sunday after Pentecost   L

Old Testament: "Hearken to me, you who pursue deliverance, you who seek the Lord; look to the rock from which you were hewn, and to the quarry from which you were digged" (Isaiah 51:1). This beautiful reading from Isaiah calls the people to look back at the "rock," which is not only God but their history as God's people. They are to look back to their ancestors in the faith. That looking back should be enough to make them realize that the Lord will come again to save his people and bring justice and salvation.

Gospel: Peter recognizes the true nature of Jesus. In response to that recognition, Jesus tells him ". . . you are Peter, and on this rock I will build my church. . ." (Matthew 16:18).

Telling the story: Tell the gospel story today in the learning community. Then turn to the Book of Acts and tell some of the stories about Peter's leadership in the early Christian community. (See A Guide to Stories of the Bible, chapter 1, page 42.)

Religious concepts: A rock is an obvious image of strength and stability. In the Old Testament it sometimes refers to God himself, though in this passage it refers to the traditions of the people. Jesus contrasted the rock with sand in the closing words of the Sermon on the Mount: "Every one then who hears these words of mine and does them will be like a wise man who built his house upon the rock" (Matthew 7:24). This feeling of stability is expressed in Martin Luther's well-known hymn "A Mighty Fortress Is Our God." In today's gospel reading Jesus gives Simon the title of "Rock." (The name Peter means *rock,* so the name Simon Peter given by Jesus means Simon the Rock.) In Roman Catholic and Episcopal tradition the authority given Peter in this reading is seen as being mediated through the apostles and then through the bishops to the people of the Church. The bishop expresses the role of leadership that reaches back through the apostles and Peter to Christ. An adult study could center on the authority that the Church has felt from these words. Children in the learning community could be given rocks to paint and decorate with the phrase *upon this rock* written on them. See how many expressions they can think of that include the word *rock* as a description of stability and strength. (Prudential Insurance, for instance, uses the Rock of Gibraltar as its symbol.) Have the participants come up with their own advertising campaign that uses the rock symbol to describe

the Church "built on" St. Peter.

The Roman Catholic lectionary appoints Isaiah 22:15,19-23, to be read this Sunday. The sense of authority given to the servant Eliakim as he is given the "key of the house of David" (Isaiah 22:22) is reflected in the reading. The reading helps us appreciate the sense of Jesus' words to Peter as he conferred the "keys of the kingdom of heaven" upon him.

The Lutheran lectionary appoints Exodus 6:2-8 for this Sunday. The Lord reveals to Moses his intention to free the Israelites from their slavery in Egypt. Moses is to be the Lord's spokesman and leader in freeing the people. Link this reading to Peter's commission from Jesus.

Proper 17   E
Twenty-second Sunday in Ordinary Time   RC
Fifteenth Sunday after Pentecost   L

Old Testament: Jeremiah cries out to the Lord in anguish for the rejection he feels from the people as he speaks the Lord's word. (See my remarks under Proper 7, page 183.) The Lord responds to Jeremiah. ". . . they will fight against you, but they shall not prevail over you, for I am with you to save you and deliver you, says the Lord" (Jeremiah 15:20).

Gospel: Jesus for the first time predicts his passion and resurrection. Peter is upset with these words of doom and denies them. Jesus confronts Peter. "Get behind me, Satan! . . . you are not on the side of God, but of men" (Matthew 16:23). Then Jesus warns what following him may mean. "If any man would come after me, let him deny himself and take up his cross and follow me" (Matthew 16:24).

Telling the story: See my remarks in connection with Propers 6, 7, 8, pages 182-184.

Religious concepts: We return this week to the concept of discipleship that we dealt with in Propers 6, 7, and 8. We must renounce our own ways and goals in life and accept the will of God. If we attempt to hold on to our lives, we will lose them. As we allow ourselves to be caught up in God's great eternal act of salvation, we will find life at the very moment we think we are losing it. The beautiful prayer appointed for Fridays in the liturgy for Morning Prayer expresses this concept. "Almighty God, whose most dear Son went not up to joy but first he suffered pain, and entered not into glory before he was crucified: Mercifully grant that we, walking in the way of the cross, may find it none other than the way of life and peace; through Jesus Christ your Son our Lord" (*The Book of Common Prayer,* page 56). Share the gospel reading for the day and the prayer. "What does this say to us who are called to be apostles today?" would be a good launching question for an adolescent or adult group.

The Roman Catholic Old Testament reading is basically the one appointed for Proper 7 in the Episcopal lectionary referred to above. But the point of the reading is the same as that of today's Episcopal reading.

Proper 18　E
Twenty-third Sunday in Ordinary Time　RC
Sixteenth Sunday after Pentecost　L

Old Testament: The prophet of God must stand as a sentry, warning the people of approaching danger.

Gospel: "If your brother sins against you, go and tell him his fault..." (Matthew 18:15a).

Religious concepts: We each have a responsibility to confront the evil that we see in ourselves, in one another, and in our society. This week's readings lead naturally into next week's theme. On the other side of confrontation is forgiveness. We do not confront to destroy a person. We confront to lead a person into a deeper relationship with God and with neighbor.

Proper 19　E
Twenty-fourth Sunday in Ordinary Time　RC
Seventeenth Sunday after Pentecost　L

Old Testament: Resentment destroys a person. One must forgive a neighbor.

Gospel: "Lord, how often shall my brother sin against me, and I forgive him?" asks Peter.

Telling the story: The Lutheran Old Testament reading for this Sunday is Genesis 50:15-21, the end of the story of Joseph and his brothers. Tell this story to the children of the learning community today. The Joseph saga is a major story and would need to be told in installments if the entire story were used. Read over the whole story (Genesis 37—50) and tell those portions of the narrative that emphasize today's theme of forgiveness.

Religious concepts: This would be a good time to talk about the confession and absolution in the liturgy. We are forgiven over and over. The liturgy acknowledges that we continually need to seek forgiveness. Each time we come before God and one another with genuine contrition, we receive the healing forgiveness of God made known through the act of Eucharist. The confession and absolution in the liturgy cannot stand on its own, however. It must be preceded or followed by an act of reconciliation to persons hurt by our acts and omissions. Such reconciliation must be our model for Christian life. We, too, need to forgive each other (our neighbor) week after week as genuine "confession" is offered. In the Lord's Prayer we ask to be forgiven only to the extent that we forgive others!

Proper 20　E
Twenty-fifth Sunday in Ordinary Time　RC
Eighteenth Sunday after Pentecost　L

Old Testament: This reading is the conclusion to the Book of Jonah. God's mercy far surpasses Jonah's. See comments in connection with Proper 14.

Gospel: We hear the parable of the laborers in the vineyard. This, too, is a story of mercy with a surprise ending. We expect the laborers who are hired last to be paid less than those who were hired early in the morning. Instead the landowner pays everyone the same. Like Jonah angry at God's generosity, the laborers hired first are angry with the landowner. God's mercy is often incomprehensible to us.

Telling the story: Share the Jonah story this week. Refer to my comments in connection with the Jonah reading under Proper 14 (page 187). This will be the first exposure to the Jonah story for Roman Catholics and Lutherans, since the Jonah reading was not included in the Old Testament lectionary earlier. If the Jonah story was shared earlier, retell it this week, letting the participants fill in the details they remember. Then tell the parable of the laborers in the vineyard and listen for their reactions. What do they think of the surprise ending? The intent of Jesus was not to suggest business ethics but to make a point about God's mercy and acceptance.

Religious concepts: The theme of last week is continued. God's merciful forgiveness is a gift to all who reach out for it. This is God's grace freely offered to all. We cannot earn or deserve God's love. God offers it because he loves us.

The story of Jonah and the parable of the laborers in the vineyard would be good launching devices for a discussion of God's mercy and forgiveness. Participants may find themselves identifying and sympathizing with Jonah and the laborers who were hired first. Let them discuss the story and examine the implications for our own lives. Jesus loves the person who has just been baptized at age ninety just as much as he loves the one who was baptized as an infant, There can be no measuring of the total love of God that is offered to all creation. In the parable of the prodigal son (Luke 15:11-32) the elder son could not understand the love the father offered the younger son who had left home. The elder son could only understand a love built on what the father owed him for all his years of work. The younger son could understand a far deeper love. He knew there was no way that he could possibly earn the love he felt from his father.

The Roman Catholic and Lutheran lectionaries assign Isaiah 55:6-9 for this Sunday:"...let the wicked forsake his way, / and the unrighteous man his thoughts; / let him return to the Lord, that he may have mercy on him, / and to our God, for he will abundantly pardon." We are loved and forgiven by a God whose "ways are not our ways." His infinite love and mercy surpass our understanding.

Proper 21   E
Twenty-sixth Sunday in Ordinary Time   RC
Nineteenth Sunday after Pentecost   L

Old Testament: The prophet Ezekiel denies the assumption that the sins of the past generation are binding on the present generation. "For I have no pleasure in the death of any one, says the Lord God; so turn, and live" (Ezekiel 18:32). God forgives the repentant sinner. We are only responsible for our *own* actions, not for those of our parents. On the other hand, the just person cannot count on past righteous actions to acquit him or her. Whoever sins is open to the Lord's condemnation until he or she repents.

Gospel: Today we hear the parable of the two sons. One promises to work for his father but fails to do so. The other at first refuses to work but then relents and obeys his father. After telling this brief parable, Jesus confronted his hearers. "Truly, I say to you, the tax collectors and the harlots go into the kingdom of God before you," he warned. The sinners and tax collectors repented and turned to the Lord; those who outwardly were holy failed to respond as the Lord commanded.

Telling the story: This parable expresses the actions of Jesus after his triumphal entry into Jerusalem. His first act was to clean out the Temple. He then began to confront the authorities of the Temple with parables that pointed to their unfaithfulness and impending judgement from God. He was there to point to a new kingdom in which repentant sinners—the tax collectors and prostitutes included—would be invited into covenant with God to replace the unfaithful. Tell the story of the triumphal entry (Matthew 21:1-11), the cleansing of the Temple (Matthew 21:12-17), and the parable of the two sons.

Another option is to share portions of the prophet Ezekiel in storytelling fashion:

Ezekiel 12 Ezekiel acted out what it would be like when the people of Judah were hauled off into exile by the enemy.

Ezekiel 33:1-9 The prophet is called to be a watchman for the people. Just as the watchman on the city wall must warn of impending danger, so the prophet must warn the people of the impending danger when they sin. Share the metaphor, and then talk about the role of watchmen in ancient cities. It might be fun to build a walled city with blocks or boxes and play the role of the watchman.

Ezekiel 37:1-14 This is the well-known vision of the valley of dry bones. See my comments in connection with the fifth Sunday in Lent (pages 166-167).

These stories will not all tie in directly with today's theme, but they will give participants a feel for the prophet Ezekiel and for the call for confrontation and repentance that he demanded.

Religious concepts: Our individual responsibility before God is emphasized in today's readings. See my comments under the heading The Individual Within the Community, chapter 2, pages 65-66. The words we hear today may confront us. In the liturgy we outwardly make an offering of ourselves, we pray, we are fed with the Lord's presence, and we go forth "to love and serve the Lord." In self-examination we need to reflect on how much of ourselves we really offer the Lord. Do our prayers for the sick, the lonely, and the suffering lead to *actions* that bring love to those persons? Do we make peace with people after we have confessed our sins against them in the liturgy? If the person down the street who has supposedly denied the Lord is *doing* what we are *saying,* we may find ourselves living in today's parable!

Proper 22 E
Twenty-seventh Sunday in Ordinary Time RC
Twentieth Sunday after Pentecost L

Old Testament: Isaiah's parable of the vineyard.

Gospel: The parable of the vineyard, told by Jesus.

Telling the story: Tell the two stories of the vineyard. Talk about agricultural customs and life in Jesus' time. Could you take a field trip to an orchard, farm, or vineyard this week?

Religious concepts: The concept of stewardship comes out strongly in these readings. We are stewards, not owners, of the Lord's vineyards. We will be called to an accounting of our stewardship. Our responsibility to bring justice, to use our resources wisely, and to be concerned for the environment is a part of our stewardship. Mention could be made this week of stewardship and the Every Member Canvass. We return to God the first-fruits from his vineyard as sign and symbol of our call to be good stewards. The vineyard that we care for is not ours, but God's. What does this say about the way we should take care of our homes, our resources, and one another?

Proper 23 E
Twenty-eighth Sunday in Ordinary Time RC
Twenty-first Sunday after Pentecost L

Old Testament: The messianic banquet described in this reading points to a time of final salvation, when all the faithful will gather at the Lord's table and feast with him. There ". . . the Lord God will wipe away tears from all faces. . . ."

Gospel: The gospel reading is the parable of the wedding banquet. The writer of the Gospel of Matthew has made this parable into an allegory. The Jews who were called and chosen have rejected the Lord's invitation to share in the great banquet. The Lord rejects his chosen and invites those who have been the outcasts of society. These latter accept the invitation gladly. One cannot take one's invitation for granted, however. The guest who showed up unprepared was quickly ushered into the outer darkness. "The Jewish people have not responded to God's invitation, and after punishing them and destroying their city, the king invites men who had no right to an invitation. But if they accept and enter the banquet hall, they must be wearing a wedding garment; that is, they must do God's will. The invitation by itself is not enough to save."*

Telling the story: Tell the parable today in the learning community. Invite the children to a banquet. Let them make wedding garments out of old material scraps and cast-off clothing. Serve them a snack in festive banquet style after they have properly prepared for their feast.

Religious concepts: Our celebration of the Holy Eucharist is a foretaste of the messianic banquet. In a sense, we get a glimpse into the "wedding banquet" that the Lord prepares for us. The Eucharist is a dramatization or a living picture of the banquet described in Isaiah's poem. Notice the words of Jesus at the Last Supper. At the blessing of the cup Jesus said, "I tell you I shall not drink again of this fruit of the vine until that day when I drink it new with you in my Father's kingdom" (Matthew 26:29). Talk about the Holy Eucharist as a foretaste of what Isaiah saw. We are called to live as if the Kingdom were here, and yet we realize that the struggle still goes on. At the Eucharist we share the Word of God, we pray, we care about each other, we offer ourselves totally to God, and we are fed the

*Adrian Nocent, *Sundays Nine to Thirty-four in Ordinary Time,* The Liturgical Year, vol. 4 (Collegeville, Minn.: The Liturgical Press, 1977), p. 156.

"bread of heaven" and the "cup of salvation." This is a vision of the heavenly banquet. As we fall short of the vision in our lives, we are called into confrontation as were the Jews of Jesus' day. This brings us to the continuing theme of these later weeks after Pentecost: a foretaste of Advent, when we prepare for the coming of the Lord with joyful anticipation and yet a touch of fear.

Proper 24   E
Twenty-ninth Sunday in Ordinary Time   RC
Twenty-second Sunday after Pentecost   L

Old Testament: God uses the pagan king Cyrus to accomplish his purpose. God's actions are not restricted to Judah.

Gospel: On paying tribute to Caesar: "Render therefore to Caesar the things that are Caesar's...."

Telling the story: Tell the story from the Books of Ezra and Nehemiah about the return of our people from Babylonian exile. Older participants can appreciate the historical context of the story. Younger children need only be told the story that our people lived in captivity. Our Babylonian captors were defeated in a war by King Cyrus, who allowed us to return to our homeland. Think how excited our people must have been when they found they could return to their homeland. We do not know about the journey back to Judah after exile, but we can imagine how the people felt as they returned, and we can describe these feelings for the children. The following passages from Ezra and Nehemiah will provide you with an outline of the story. (Nehemiah was the builder of the restored community; Ezra was the religious leader of the restoration.) See Ezra 1:1-11; Nehemiah 1:1—2:20; Ezra 3:1—6:22; Nehemiah 3:33—7:3; Nehemiah 8:1-18.

Read chapter 2, pages 66-68, for an overview of the theological understandings of this period.

For the gospel reading, do a brief study of the relationship between the Romans and the Jews in the time of Jesus, and share the story of that period with the participants. Talk about the role of the tax collector, the Jewish Sanhedrin, the office of procurator held by Pontius Pilate, and other details of the time that will make the gospel more relevant to the participants.

Religious concepts: The gospel lesson is a well-known and oft-quoted passage. It does *not* imply that God is only interested in "sacred" matters and leaves matters of state to government. The Old Testament and gospel lessons remind us that God uses all kinds of governments and systems for his purposes. He is concerned about justice and shalom (peace). God used Cyrus the Great, the pagan ruler of the Persian empire, as his instrument to bring justice. So long as the Romans ruled justly, God would not act to overthrow them. Jesus was not interested in leading an uprising or in protesting against Roman rule. (Judas Iscariot may have been a revolutionary zealot who was trying to force Jesus to act against Roman authority.)

Proper 25   E
Thirtieth Sunday in Ordinary Time   RC
Twenty-third Sunday after Pentecost   L

Old Testament: This passage gives the moral imperative of the Israelites: Because they were once enslaved, they dare not enslave others.

Gospel: The greatest commandment is "You shall love the Lord....you shall love your neighbor as yourself."

Telling the story: Use the Exodus passage to tell about the slavery of the Israelites in Egypt.

Religious concepts: Our response to God comes as we respond in justice and love to one another. The one cannot be separated from the other. (See 1 John 4:20-21 for the negative way of stating this.)

The Lutheran Old Testament reading is Leviticus 19:1-2,15-18. We hear in this selection the powerful words "Say to all the congregation of the people of Israel, You shall be holy; for I the Lord your God am holy" (Leviticus 19:1). This saying is at the heart of today's readings. We are called to be holy because God is holy. We must love our neighbor because God does. We must not oppress another person, race, or nation, because God released us from oppression in Egypt. To respond to God is to respond in love to another.

Proper 26 E
Thirty-first Sunday in Ordinary Time RC
Twenty-fourth Sunday after Pentecost L
The Lutheran epistle and gospel lessons heard today are the same as those appointed in the Episcopal lectionary for next week.

Old Testament: The priests and prophets had led the people astray by telling them what they wanted to hear, rather than speaking God's word. Jerusalem will be reduced to rubble because of the nation's perversity.

Gospel: Jesus denounces the Scribes and Pharisees who sit on Moses' seat because they do not practice what they preach.

Religious concepts: The difference between "civil religion" and biblical religion is expressed here. In the former the Church and State are seen as one. The Church blesses all the actions of the State. In the latter the Church must often stand in judgment of State and society. This theme offers good discussion possibilities for adolescents and adults.

The Old Testament reading in the Roman Catholic lectionary is Malachi 1:14—2:2,8-10. The prophet confronts the priests of the time because ". . . you have caused many to stumble by your instruction." The priests have broken covenant with the Lord and led the people astray. To use Ezekiel's metaphor, they have been false shepherds to the people (Ezekiel 37).

Proper 27 E
Thirty-second Sunday in Ordinary Time RC
Twenty-fifth Sunday after Pentecost L
The Lutheran epistle and gospel lessons heard today are the same as those appointed in the Episcopal lectionary for next week.

Old Testament: Amos warns those who look forward to the Day of the Lord, thinking that God will come and reward them in the final age. The day of the Lord will be a day of judgment, Amos warns, for the Lord hates and despises the empty religious practices of his people. The reading concludes with the powerful words ". . . let justice roll down like waters, and righteousness like an ever-flowing stream" (Amos 5:24).

Gospel: The gospel reading is the parable of the ten virgins. Jesus' parable is a warning to

be prepared for the Day of the Lord. Those who are unprepared will be "locked out" of the wedding banquet. Refer to my comments in connection with Proper 23 regarding the metaphor of the banquet (page 191).

Telling the story: Tell the story of the ten virgins simply as a story that Jesus told about being prepared. What might we have to do to prepare for a wedding or for an important visitor in our home?

Religious concepts: Chapters 24 and 25 in the Gospel of Matthew are the apocalyptic sayings and parables of Jesus. Refer to chapter 2, pages 63 and 69, for an understanding of this concept.

The Roman Catholic Old Testament reading is Wisdom 6:12-16. The wise person seeks wisdom. Those who are truly preparing for the Day of the Lord are seeking the wisdom of the Lord. They are the "wise virgins" who are prepared for the bridegroom to come.

The Lutheran lectionary appoints Hosea 11:1-4,8-9 for this Sunday. The Lord reasserts his steadfast love for Israel despite its failings.

Proper 28 E
Thirty-third Sunday in Ordinary Time RC
Twenty-sixth Sunday after Pentecost L
The Lutheran readings appointed this week are Malachi 2:1-10; 1 Thessalonians 2:8-13; Matthew 23:1-12. The epistle and gospel are basically the same as the Episcopal lessons appointed for Proper 26.

Old Testament: The Day of the Lord is coming, but it will be a day of judgment for a people who have fallen to evil.

Gospel: This is the parable of the talents.

Telling the story: Tell the parable of the talents. Let children dramatize it.

Religious concepts: We have the responsibility to use our talents to "image" God's creative action in the world. What we do shows forth the glory of God, no matter how insignificant we think our actions might be. We must face the consequences of our failure to "image" God's creation, whether through fear or rebellion. We face these consequences individually and as a nation and society.

The Roman Catholic Old Testament

reading is Proverbs 31:10-13,19-20,30-31. The reading praises the faithful wife, echoing the faithfulness of the two servants who are praised in the gospel reading.

Proper 29   E
Last Sunday in Ordinary Time:
Feast of Christ the King   RC
Last Sunday after Pentecost:
Feast of Christ the King   L

Old Testament: The prophet Ezekiel writes that in the future the Lord will look after his flock himself. God will be the shepherd of his people.

Gospel: "Truly I say to you, as you did it to one of the least of these my brethren, you did it to me" (Matthew 25:40).

Religious concepts: God is intimately involved in our lives. Through Jesus we know that he is with us personally in the "flesh and blood" of our daily living. As we fail to respond, we turn from Christ. Christ does and will confront us in his living presence in our lives.

The title of this Sunday in the Roman Catholic and Lutheran lectionaries (Christ the King) emphasizes the kingship of the risen Christ. We seek the kingdom of God, where we will feast at the banquet table of the Lord. In the age to come, Christ will reign, and God's will will "be done on earth as it is in heaven."

Chapter 6
A Commentary
on the Eucharistic Lectionary,
Year B

Use the following list to see which Bible passages the commentary is referring to in discussing a given Sunday or feast day. To discover the *calendar* date of a day, consult your own church calendar or liturgy expert.

Despite minor differences and occasional local variations, there is now substantial agreement among Episcopalians, Roman Catholics, and Lutherans (and some other churches as well) on the scriptural readings assigned for Sundays and greater feast days. In the following list, then, assume that the readings are the same for the three churches unless variants are noted. (Notice how minor many variants are—simply a few verses added or omitted.)

Terms for a day or a season may differ. For instance, what Episcopalians and Lutherans call the Sundays after Pentecost are called Sundays in Ordinary Time (or Sundays of the Year) by Roman Catholics; Episcopalians designate the readings and prayers proper to

those Sundays as Proper 1, Proper 2, and so on, indicating in *The Book of Common Prayer* that Proper 11, for instance, is used on the Sunday nearest to July 20. In the following list, terms or observances peculiar to Episcopalians, Roman Catholics, or Lutherans are designated **E, RC,** or **L.**

A sample entry, 1 Cor 10:16-17(18-21), refers to First Corinthians, chapter 10, verses 16-17, with verses 18-21 optional.

Note that the psalms assigned as responses to the readings are not listed here, since this book deals primarily with the readings themselves. Nevertheless, the psalm responses are an important part of the total worship experience, and every effort should be made to familiarize our congregations with them. See Appendix I for comments on psalms that are particularly appropriate for the religious education setting.

A list of the abbreviations used for books of the Bible is found on page 140.

Lectionary Readings for Sundays and Greater Feasts in Year B

Sunday or Feast	Episcopal*	Roman Catholic†	Lutheran‡
1st Sun. of Advent	Isa 64:1-9a 1 Cor 1:1-9 Mk 13:(24-32) 33-37	Isa 63:16-17,19; 64:2-7 1 Cor 1:3-9 Mk 13:33-37	Isa 63:16b-17; 64:1-8 1 Cor 1:3-9 Mk 13:33-37 or Mk 11:1-10
2nd Sun. of Advent	Isa 40:1-11 2 Pet 3:8-15a,18 Mk 1:1-8	Isa 40:1-5,9-11 2 Pet 3:8-14	Isa 40:1-11 2 Pet 3:8-14
3rd Sun. of Advent	Isa 65:17-25 1 Thes 5:(12-15) 16-28 Jn 1:6-8,19-28 or Jn 3:23-30	Isa 61:1-2,10-11 1 Thes 5:16-24 Jn 1:6-8,19-28	Isa 61:1-3,10-11 1 Thes 5:16-24 Jn 1:6-8,19-28
4th Sun. of Advent	2 Sam 7:4,8-16 Rom 16:25-27 Lk 1:26-38	2 Sam 7:1-5,8-11,16	2 Sam 7:(1-7) 8-11,16
Christmas Vigil **RC**	*§	Isa 62:1-5 Acts 13:16-17,22-25 Mtt 1:1-25	*§
Christmas Day I **E**; Mass at Midnight **RC**; Option 1 **L**	Isa 9:2-4,6-7 Titus 2:11-14 Lk 2:1-14(15-20)	Isa 9:1-6 Lk 2:1-14	Isa 9:2-7 Lk 2:1-20
Christmas Day II **E**; Mass at Dawn **RC**; Option 2 **L**	Isa 62:6-7,10-12 Titus 3:4-7 Lk 2:(1-14)15-20	Isa 62:11-12 Titus 3:4-7 Lk 2:15-20	Isa 52:7-10 Heb 1:1-9 Jn 1:1-14
Christmas Day III **E**; Mass during the Day **RC**; Option 3 **L**	Isa 52:7-10 Heb 1:1-12 Jn 1:1-14	Isa 52:7-10 Heb 1:1-6 Jn 1:1-18	Isa 62:10-12 Titus 3:4-7 Lk 2:1-20
1st Sun. after Christmas **E, L**; Sun. in Octave of Christmas (Holy Family) **RC**	Isa 61:10—62:3 Gal 3:23-25;4:4-7 Jn 1:1-18	Ecclus 3:2-6,12-14 Col. 3:12-21 Lk 2:22-40	Isa 45:22-25 Col 3:12-17 Lk 2:25-40

The Book of Common Prayer and Administration of the Sacraments and Other Rites and Ceremonies of the Church (New York: The Church Hymnal Corporation and The Seabury Press, 1979).
†*Lectionary for Mass* (New York: Catholic Book Publishing, 1970).
‡*Lutheran Book of Worship* (Minneapolis, Minn.: Augsburg Publishing, 1978).
*§Episcopal and Lutheran lectionaries do not have this service.

Sunday or Feast	Episcopal	Roman Catholic	Lutheran
Holy Name (Jan.1) **E;** Mary, Mother of God **RC;** Name of Jesus **L**	Ex 34:1-8 Rom 1:1-7 Lk 2:15-21	Num 6:22-27 Gal 4:4-7 Lk 2:16-21	Num 6:22-27 Rom 1:1-7 or Phlp 2:9-13 Lk 2:21
2nd Sun. after Christmas	Jer 31:7-14 Eph 1:3-6,15-19a Mtt 2:13-15,19-23 or Lk 2:41-52 or Mtt 2:1-12	Ecclus 24:1-4,8-12 Eph 1:3-6,15-18 Jn 1:1-18	Isa 61:10—62:3 Eph 1:3-6,15-18 Jn 1:1-18
The Epiphany	Isa 60:1-6,9 Eph 3:1-12 Mtt 2:1-12	Isa 60:1-6 Eph 3:2-3,5-6	Isa 60:1-6 Eph 3:2-12
1st Sun. after Epiphany **E, L** Baptism of the Lord **RC**	Isa 42:1-9 Acts 10:34-38 Mk 1:7-11	Isa 42:1-4,6-7 Mk 1:7-11	Isa 42:1-7 Mk 1:4-11
2nd Sun. after Epiphany **E, L;** 2nd Sun. Ord. Time **RC**	1 Sam 3:1-10 (11-20) 1 Cor 6:11b-20 Jn 1:43-51	1 Sam 3:3-10,19 1 Cor 6:13-15,17-20 Jn 1:35-42	1 Sam 3:1-10 1 Cor 6:12-20 Jn 1:43-51
3rd Sun. after Epiphany **E, L;** 3rd Sun. Ord. Time **RC**	Jer 3:21—4:2 1 Cor 7:17-23 Mk 1:14-20	Jonah 3:1-5,10 1 Cor 7:29-31	Jonah 3:1-5,10 1 Cor 7:29-31
4th Sun. after Epiphany **E, L;** 4th Sun. Ord. Time **RC**	Deut 18:15-20 1 Cor 8:1b-13 Mk 1:21-28	1 Cor 7:32-35	1 Cor 8:1-13
5th Sun. after Epiphany **E, L;** 5th Sun. Ord. Time **RC**	2 K 4:(8-17)18-21 (22-31)32-37 1 Cor 9:16-23 Mk 1:29-39	Job 7:1-4,6-7 1 Cor 9:16-19,22-23	Job 7:1-7 1 Cor 9:16-23
6th Sun. after Epiphany **E, L;** 6th Sun. Ord. Time **RC**	2 K 5:1-15ab 1 Cor 9:24-27 Mk 1:40-45	Lev 13:1-2,44-46 1 Cor 10:31—11:1	2 K 5:1-14 1 Cor 9:24-27
7th Sun. after Epiphany **E, L;** 7th Sun. Ord. Time **RC**	Isa 43:18-25 2 Cor 1:18-22 Mk 2:1-12		

Sunday or Feast	Episcopal	Roman Catholic	Lutheran
8th Sun. after Epiphany **E, L**; 8th Sun. Ord. Time **RC**	Hos 2:14-23 2 Cor 3:(4-11) 17—4:2 Mk 2:18-22	Hos 2:16-17,21-22 2 Cor 3:1-6	Hos 2:14-16(17-18) 19-20 2 Cor 3:1b-6
Last Sun. after Epiphany **E, L**	1 K 19:9-18 2 Pet 1:16-19 (20-21) Mk 9:2-9	*	2 K 2:1-12a 2 Cor 3:12—4:2
Ash Wednesday	Joel 2:1-2,12-17 or Isa 58:1-12 2 Cor 5:20b—6:10 Mtt 6:1-6,16-21	Joel 2:12-18 2 Cor 5:20—6:2 Mtt 6:1-6,16-18	Joel 2:12-19 2 Cor 5:20b—6:2 Mtt 6:1-6,16-21
1st Sun. in Lent	Gen 9:8-17 1 Pet 3:18-22 Mk 1:9-13	Gen 9:8-15 1 Pet 3:18-22 Mk 1:12-15	Gen 22:1-18 Rom 8:31-39 Mk 1:12-15
2nd Sun. in Lent	Gen 22:1-14 Rom 8:31-39 Mk 8:31-38	Gen 22:1-2,9-18 Rom 8:31-34 Mk 9:2-10	Gen 28:10-17(18-22) Rom 5:1-11 Mk 8:31-38
3rd Sun. in Lent	Ex 20:1-17 Rom 7:13-25 Jn 2:13-22	1 Cor 1:22-25 Jn 2:13-25	1 Cor 1:22-25 Jn 2:13-22
4th Sun. in Lent	2 Chr 36:14-23 Eph 2:4-10 Jn 6:4-15	2 Chr 36:14-23 Jn 3:14-21	Num 21:4-9 Jn 3:14-21
5th Sun. in Lent	Jer 31:31-34 Heb 5:(1-4) 5-10 Jn 12:20-33	Heb 5:7-9	Heb 5:7-9
Palm Sunday (Liturgy of the Palms)	Mtt 11:1-11a	Mtt 11:1-10 or Jn 12:12-16	*
Palm Sunday (at the Eucharist)	Isa 45:21-25 or Isa 52:13—53:12 Phlp 2:5-11 Mk (14:32-72) 15:1-39(40-47)	Isa 50:4-7 Phlp 2:6-11 Mk 14:1—15:47 or Mk 15:1-39	Zech 9:9-10 Phlp 2:5-11 Mk 14:1—15:47 or Mk 15:1-39

*The Lutheran lectionary does not have this service.

Sunday or Feast	Episcopal	Roman Catholic	Lutheran
Easter Vigil **E, RC**	Gen 1:1—2:2 Gen 7:1-5,11-18; 8:6-18; 9:8-13 Gen 22:1-18 Ex 14:10—15:1 Isa 4:2-6 Isa 55:1-11 Ezk 36:24-28 Ezk 37:1-14 Zeph 3:12-20 Rom 6:3-11 Mtt 28:1-10	Gen 1:1—2:2 Gen 22:1-18 Ex 14:15—15:1 Isa 54:5-14 Isa 55:1-11 Bar 3:9-15,32—4:4 Ezk 36:16-28 Rom 6:3-11 Mk 16:1-8	*

Easter Day,
  Principal Service
	Acts 10:34-43
	  or Isa 25:6-9
	Col 3:1-4 or
	  Acts 10:34-43
	Mk 16:1-8
		Acts 10:34,37-43
		
		Col 3:1-4 or
		  1 Cor 5:6-8
		Jn 20:1-9 or
		  Mk 16:1-8
			Isa 25:6-9
			
			1 Cor 15:19-28
			
			Mk 16:1-8 or
			  Jn 20:1-9(10-18)

2nd Sun. of Easter	Acts 3:12a,13-15,
	  17-26 or
	  Isa 26:2-9,19
	1 Jn 5:1-6 or
	  Acts 3:12a,13-15,
	  17-26
	Jn 20:19-31
		Acts 4:32-35
		
		**
			Acts 3:13-15,17-26
			
			**

3rd Sun. of Easter	Acts 4:5-12 or
	  Mic 4:1-5
	1 Jn 1:1—2:2 or
	  Acts 4:5-12
	Lk 24:36b-48
		Acts 3:13-15,
		  17-19
		1 Jn 2:1-5
		
		Lk 24:35-48
			Acts 4:8-12
			
			1 Jn 1:1—2:2
			
			Lk 24:36-49

4th Sun. of Easter	Acts 4:(23-31)
	  32-37 or
	  Ezk 34:1-10
	1 Jn 3:1-8 or
	  Acts 4:(23-31)
	  32-37
	Jn 10:11-16
		Acts 4:8-12
		
		1 Jn 3:1-2
		
		Jn 10:11-18
			Acts 4:23-33
			
			1 Jn 3:1-2
			
			Jn 10:11-18

5th Sun. of Easter	Acts 8:26-40 or
	  Deut 4:32-40
	1 Jn 3:(14-17)
	  18-24 or
	  Acts 8:26-40
	Jn 14:15-21
		Acts 9:26-31
		
		1 Jn 3:18-24
		
		Jn 15:1-8
			Acts 8:26-40
			
			1 Jn 3:18-24
			
			Jn 15:1-8

*The Lutheran lectionary does not have this service.

**Roman Catholic and Lutheran lectionaries have no Old Testament lesson during the Easter season.

Sunday or Feast	Episcopal	Roman Catholic	Lutheran
6th Sun. of Easter	Acts 11:19-30 or Isa 45:11-13,18-19 1 Jn 4:7-21 or Acts 11:19-30 Jn 15:9-17	Acts 10:25-26, 34-35,44-48 1 Jn 4:7-10	Acts 11:19-30 1 Jn 4:1-11
Ascension Day	Acts 1:1-11 or Ezk 1:3-5a, 15-22,26-28 Eph 1:15-23 or Acts 1:1-11 Lk 24:49-53 or Mk 16:9-15,19-20	Acts 1:1-11 Eph 1:17-23 Mk 16:15-20	Acts 1:1-11 Eph 1:16-23 Lk 24:44-53
7th Sun. of Easter	Acts 1:15-26 or Ex 28:1-4,9-10, 29-30 1 Jn 5:9-15 or Acts 1:15-26 Jn 17:11b-19	Acts 1:15-17,20-26 1 Jn 4:11-16 Jn 17:11-19	Acts 1:15-26 1 Jn 4:13-21 Jn 17:11b-19
Day of Pentecost	Acts 2:1-11 or Isa 44:1-8 1 Cor 12:4-13 or Acts 2:1-11 Jn 20:19-23 or Jn 14:8-17	Acts 2:1-11 1 Cor 12:3-7, 12-13 Jn 20:19-23	Ezk 37:1-14 Acts 2:1-21 Jn 7:37-39a
Trinity Sunday	Ex 3:1-6 Rom 8:12-17 Jn 3:1-16	Deut 4:32-34, 39-40 Rom 8:14-17 Mtt 28:16-20	Deut 6:4-9 Rom 8:14-17 Jn 3:1-17
Proper 4 E; 9th Sun. Ord. Time RC; 2nd Sun. after Pentecost L	Deut 5:6-21 2 Cor 4:5-12 Mk 2:23-28	Deut 5:12-15 2 Cor 4:6-11 Mk 2:23—3:6	Deut 5:12-15 2 Cor 4:5-12 Mk 2:23-28
Proper 5 E; 10th Sun. Ord. Time RC; 3rd Sun. after Pentecost L	Gen 3:(1-7)8-21 2 Cor 4:13-18 Mk 3:20-35	Gen 3:9-15 2 Cor 4:13—5:1	Gen 3:9-15 2 Cor 4:13-18
Proper 6 E; 11th Sun. Ord. Time RC; 4th Sun. after Pentecost L	Ezk 31:1-6,10-14 2 Cor 5:1-10 Mk 4:26-34	Ezk 17:22-24 2 Cor 5:6-10	Ezk 17:22-24 2 Cor 5:1-10
Proper 7 E; 12th Sun. Ord. Time RC; 5th Sun. after Pentecost L	Job 38:1-11,16-18 2 Cor 5:14-21 Mk 4:35-41; (5:1-20)	Job 38:1,8-11 2 Cor 5:14-17 Mk 4:35-41	Job 38:1-11 2 Cor 5:14-21 Mk 4:35-41

Sunday or Feast	Episcopal	Roman Catholic	Lutheran

Proper 8 **E**;
13th Sun. Ord. Time **RC**;
6th Sun. after
   Pentecost **L**
	Deut 15:7-11
	
	2 Cor 8:1-9,13-15
	Mk 5:22-24,35b-43
		Wis 1:13-15;
		  2:23-24
		2 Cor 8:7,9,13-15
		Mk 5:21-43
			Lam 3:22-23
			
			2 Cor 8:1-9,13-14
			Mk 5:21-24a,35-43 or
			   Mk 5:24b-34

Proper 9 **E**; 14th Sun. Ord. Time **RC**; 7th Sun. after Pentecost **L**	Ezk 2:1-7 2 Cor 12:2-10 Mk 6:1-6	Ezk 2:2-5 2 Cor 12:7-10	Ezk 2:1-5 2 Cor 12:7-10
Proper 10 **E**; 15th Sun. Ord. Time **RC**; 8th Sun. after Pentecost **L**	Amos 7:7-15 Eph 1:1-14 Mk 6:7-13	Amos 7:12-15 Eph 1:3-14	Amos 7:10-15 Eph 1:3-14
Proper 11 **E**; 16th Sun. Ord. Time **RC**; 9th Sun. after Pentecost **L**	Isa 57:14b-21 Eph 2:11-22 Mk 6:30-44	Jer 23:1-6 Eph 2:13-18 Mk 6:30-34	Jer 23:1-6 Eph 2:13-22 Mk 6:30-34
Proper 12 **E**; 17th Sun. Ord. Time **RC**; 10th Sun. after Pentecost **L**	2 K 2:1-15 Eph 4:1-7, 11-16 Mk 6:45-52	2 K 4:42-44 Eph 4:1-6 Jn 6:1-15	Ex 24:3-11 Eph 4:1-7,11-16 Jn 6:1-15
Proper 13 **E**; 18th Sun. Ord. Time **RC**; 11th Sun. after Pentecost **L**	Ex 16:2-4,9-15 Eph 4:17-25 Jn 6:24-35	Ex 16:2-4,12-15 Eph 4:17,20-24	Ex 16:2-15 Eph 4:17-24

Proper 14 **E**;
19th Sun. Ord. Time **RC**;
12th Sun. after
   Pentecost **L**
	Deut 8:1-10
	Eph 4:(25-29)
	   30—5:2
	Jn 6:37-51
		1 K 19:4-8
		Eph 4:30—5:2
		
		Jn 6:41-51
			1 K 19:4-8
			Eph 4:30—5:2
			
			Jn 6:41-51

Proper 15 **E**; 20th Sun. Ord. Time **RC**; 13th Sun. after Pentecost **L**	Prov 9:1-6 Eph 5:15-20 Jn 6:53-59	Jn 6:51-58	Jn 6:51-58

Proper 16 **E**;
21st Sun. Ord. Time **RC**;
14th Sun. after
   Pentecost **L**
	Josh 24:1-2a,
	  14-25
	Eph 5:21-33
	Jn 6:60-69
		Josh 24:1-2,
		  15-18
		Eph 5:21-32
			Josh 24:1-2a,
			  14-18
			Eph 5:21-31

Proper 17 **E**;
22nd Sun. Ord. Time **RC**;
15th Sun. after
   Pentecost **L**
	Deut 4:1-9
	Eph 6:10-20
	
	Mk 7:1-8,14-
	  15,21-23
		Deut 4:1-2,6-8
		Jam 1:17-18,
		  21-22,27
			Deut 4:1-2,6-8
			Eph 6:10-20

Sunday or Feast	Episcopal	Roman Catholic	Lutheran

Proper 18 **E**;
23rd Sun. Ord. Time **RC**;
16th Sun. after
  Pentecost **L**
	Isa 35:4-7a
	Jam 1:17-27
	
	Mk 7:31-37
		Isa 35:4-7
		Jam 2:1-5
			Isa 35:4-7a
			Jam 1:17-22
			  (23-25)26-27

Proper 19 **E**;
24th Sun. Ord. Time **RC**;
17th Sun. after
  Pentecost **L**
	Isa 50:4-9
	Jam 2:1-5,8-10,
	  14-18
	Mk 8:27-38 or
	  Mk 9:14-29
		Isa 50:4-9
		Jam 2:14-18
		
		Mk 8:27-35
			Isa 50:4-10
			Jam 2:1-5,8-10,
			  14-18
			Mk 8:27-35

Proper 20 **E**;
25th Sun. Ord. Time **RC**;
18th Sun. after
  Pentecost **L**
	Wis 1:16—2:1
	  (6-11)12-22
	Jam 3:16—4:6
	Mk 9:30-37
		Wis 2:12,17-20
		
		Jam 3:16—4:3
			Jer 11:18-20
			
			Jam 3:16—4:6

Proper 21 **E**;
26th Sun. Ord. Time **RC**;
19th Sun. after
  Pentecost **L**
	Num 11:4-6,
	  10-16,24-29
	Jam 4:7-12
	  (13—5:6)
	Mk 9:38-43,45,
	  47-48
		Num 11:25-29
		
		Jam 5:1-6
		
		Mk 9:38-43,45,
		  47-48
			Num 11:4-6,
			  10-16,24-29
			Jam 4:7-12
			  (13—5:6)
			Mk 9:38-50

Proper 22 **E**; 27th Sun. Ord. Time **RC**; 20th Sun. after Pentecost **L**	Gen 2:18-24 Heb 2:(1-8)9-18 Mk 10:2-9	Heb 2:9-11 Mk 10:2-16	Heb 2:9-11(12-18) Mk 10:2-16

Proper 23 **E**;
28th Sun. Ord. Time **RC**;
21st Sun. after
  Pentecost **L**
	Amos 5:6-7,10-15
	Heb 3:1-6
	Mk 10:17-27
	  (28-31)
		Wis 7:7-11
		Heb 4:12-13
		Mk 10:17-30
			Amos 5:6-7,10-15
			Heb 3:1-6
			Mk 10:17-27
			  (28-30)

Proper 24 **E**; 29th Sun. Ord. Time **RC**; 22nd Sun. after Pentecost **L**	Isa 53:4-12 Heb 4:12-16 Mk 10:35-45	Isa 53:10-11 Heb 4:14-16	Isa 53:10-12 Heb 4:9-16

Proper 25 **E**;
30th Sun. Ord. Time **RC**;
23rd Sun. after
  Pentecost **L**
	Isa 59:(1-4)9-19
	Heb 5:12—6:1,
	  9-12
	Mk 10:46-52
		Jer 31:7-9
		Heb 5:1-6
			Jer 31:7-9
			Heb 5:1-10

Proper 26 **E**;
31st Sun. Ord. Time **RC**;
24th Sun. after
  Pentecost **L**
	Deut 6:1-9
	Heb 7:23-28
	Mk 12:28-34
		Deut 6:2-6
		
		Mk 12:28-34
			Deut 6:1-9
			
			Mk 12:28-34
			  (35-37)

Proper 27 **E**; 32nd Sun. Ord. Time **RC**; 25th Sun. after Pentecost **L**	1 K 17:8-16 Heb 9:24-28 Mk 12:38-44	1 K 17:10-16 Mk 12:38-44	1 K 17:8-16 Mk 12:41-44

Sunday or Feast	Episcopal	Roman Catholic	Lutheran
Proper 28 **E**; 33rd Sun. Ord. Time **RC**; 26th Sun. after Pentecost **L**	Dan 12:1-4a(5-13) Heb 10:31-39 Mk 13:14-23	Dan 12:1-3 Heb. 10:11-14,18 Mk 13:24-32	Dan 12:1-3 Heb 10:11-18 Mk 13:1-13
27th Sun. after Pentecost **L**	*	*	Dan 7:9-10 Heb 13:20-21 Mk 13:24-31

Proper 29 **E**;
Last Sun. Ord. Time
    (Feast of Christ the
    King) **RC**;
Last Sun. after
    Pentecost
    (Christ the King) **L**
	Dan 7:9-14
	Rev 1:1-8
	Jn 18:33-37
	    or Mk 11:1-11
		Dan 7:13-14
		Rev 1:5-8
		Jn 18:33-37
			Dan 7:13-14
			Rev 1:4b-8
			Jn 18:33-37

*Episcopal and Roman Catholic lectionaries do not have this designation.

The Season of Advent

For more extensive background on Advent, see chapter 5, page 148.

Advent focuses on dreams and expectations. As we read the Old Testament during Advent, we are exposed to the dreams and hopes of the Jewish people who were looking for a new day of the Lord to be ushered in by a son of David. Their dreams of fulfillment are expressed poetically: The lamb will lie down with the lion; swords will be made into plowshares; there will be a great banquet.

But this new day does not come without judgment. When the light is turned on, I see clearly what I have been doing in the dark. A new day always gives me a sense of anxiety as I face the unknown. What will life be like? How will I fit in? Anyone who has ever moved from one city to another knows the feeling well. I can anticipate fulfillment in where I am going, but I am still anxious about the move. As we look at the dreams expressed in the Old Testament, it would be helpful to look also at our own hopes and dreams of fulfillment. What kind of poetic imagery do we find ourselves using? What does the "day of the Lord" mean to us?

The Old Testament Readings

We recall the hopes and dreams expressed by the prophets.

First Sunday of Advent

After the Jewish people returned from Babylonian exile, their nation and even their temple continued to lie desolate. Surely the punishment of the people had gone on long enough. When would God come to restore the fortunes of his chosen people? This passage is a plaintive lament and cry for God to reveal his power and presence among the people and to intervene in the course of human events. This Sunday, trace the historic basis for Isaiah's grief. Identify such times of grief and longing among the participants of your group. Chapter 2, pages 64-65, will be helpful in this review.

Second Sunday of Advent

The prophet Isaiah spoke words of encouragement to his people in exile in Babylonia. "Comfort, comfort my people, says your God." Cyrus of Persia began defeating Babylonian armies in 638 B.C. Now the prophet sees hope (later realized) that under Persian rule the Jewish people may be returned to their homeland. They will build "a highway for our God." In this "highway builder" role they will be preparing the way for their Lord. In the gospel for this Sunday, Mark quotes this passage from Isaiah in introducing John the Baptist.

As Christians we are also called to be highway builders preparing the way for Christ to enter more fully into our lives. We are proclaimers of "glad tidings." Use the story of the Jews at the time of the exile. Talk about the custom of building highways for the conquering kings of that era so that the imagery can be appreciated more fully. Conquered peoples were often put to work building roads for the victors. In the process of road building they would be filling in the valleys and cutting down the high places to make the road smoother. Sometimes roads would be built especially for the victorious ruler to ride in triumph. This would become the "king's way." The Jews in Babylonia dreamed of a day when they could build their own "king's highway" back to their homeland. It would be Yahweh, their king, who would ride triumphantly at the head of their pilgrimage home. Isaiah uses this rich imagery in today's reading. "Every valley shall be lifted up,/and every mountain and hill be made low;/ . . . . And the glory of the Lord shall be revealed." Talk in the learning community today about preparing the way or road of God. How can we prepare the way in our lives? What imagery or metaphors can we use to talk about our preparation for the Lord's coming more fully into our lives?

Third Sunday of Advent

This beautiful reading points toward the new day that the Lord promises his faithful people. "For behold, I create new heavens and a new earth. . . . The wolf and the lamb shall feed together. . ." (Isaiah 65:17,25). See the general remarks in connection with the season of Advent as they apply to this reading.

Fourth Sunday of Advent

The prophet Nathan appeared before David to

announce that God would establish a royal lineage from him. "When your days are fulfilled and you lie down with your fathers, I will raise up your offspring after you, who shall come forth from your body ..." (2 Samuel 7:12). This week needs to be a storytelling time. Tell about David and the house of David.

Talk about the Jesse-tree tradition this Sunday. *The Jesse Tree** and other resource books available at your library would be helpful in this study. This meaningful tradition can be given special emphasis today, since the Old Testament reading refers to the family or house of David. Jesus was a descendant of David through Joseph, and David was the son of Jesse. The prophet Isaiah says "There shall come forth a shoot from the stump of Jesse, / and a branch shall grow out of his roots" (Isaiah 11:1). This is a poetic way of saying that the prophet rejoices at the thought of a descendant of Jesse and David who will take the throne of Judah and rule as a just and righteous king.

As we think about Old Testament readings, we can focus on our own hopes and expectations as well as the anxiety we feel in facing the unknown next moment. We need to look at our lives now and compare them with our dreams. What keeps us from fulfillment right now? What hinders us as nation, society, and individuals from seeking the freedom that God offers us? As we begin to realize our enslavement to fear, injustice, poverty, negation and "dis-ease," we can see the penitential nature of Advent emerging. No wonder the purple of penitence is used in this season! But God would free us from all that enslaves us. How can we move toward that liberation?

The Gospel Readings
See further comments on the gospel readings for year A, pages 149-150.

First Sunday of Advent
"Take heed, watch; for you do not know when the time will come" (Mark 13:33). We are commanded to be aware of what is going on in the world and in our lives. We must be like the watchman at the city gate who warns the city of danger and calls out the glad tidings of messengers of peace. Christians are called out to be the watchmen for an ever-evolving new age in which the word and presence of God can be actualized in the lives of the people.

Think about people of recent history who have acted as such watchmen. Study their writings during Advent. Martin Luther King, Jr., is a classic example of a dreamer who took the Advent readings seriously and moved to seek fulfillment of the word in his own life and in the lives of his people.

Second and Third Sundays of Advent
Our attention turns on these two Sundays to John the Baptist, who prepared the way for Jesus. If we are to move toward the kingdom of God, we have to confront the way we live in the present moment. Judgment and confrontation are the painful seedbeds of change. I will not change my life until I am confronted with the *need* to change. Tell the story of John the Baptist. Reflect on his life and mission in the context of the Old Testament readings for these two Sundays. Can we identify people in our history or in contemporary life who have followed the role of John the Baptist?

The Lutheran lectionary assigns other readings, but the theme is the same as that of the Episcopal and Roman Catholic lectionaries. The Old Testament reading sets forth part of the mission of the one preparing for the way of the Lord: "to bring glad tidings to the afflicted, ... to bind up the broken-hearted." Jesus applied that passage to himself when he began preaching in Nazareth.

Fourth Sunday of Advent
Mary had a vision of such intensity that it was as if an angel (messenger) of God stood before her. She learned that she was to give birth to Jesus. She responded in awe and wonder: "Behold, I am the handmaid of the Lord; let it be to me according to your word" (Luke 1:38). We begin the Christmas story this week. Tell the story of Mary, Joseph, and the birth of Jesus. Talk about Mary's open response to God's word and presence.

*Raymond and Georgene Anderson, *The Jesse Tree* (Philadelphia, Pa.: Fortress Press, 1966).

The Epistle Readings

The epistle reading for the first Sunday in Advent in Year A (last year's reading) includes the beautiful words: "Let us then cast off the works of darkness and put on the armor of light" (Romans 13:12). These words reflect the overall theme of the Advent epistle readings for all three years. They would make a good liturgical response as the Advent candles are lit at the parish liturgy, in the classroom, and in the home. Create a banner for the learning community, using those words.

The epistle readings of Advent focus on life in the interim time between the resurrection and the fulfillment of the reign of Christ. We live in semidarkness until the light of Christ dawns more fully into our lives. But we must live as if the lights will come on in their highest intensity at any moment. "Cast off the works of darkness." Live for the light. On the fourth Sunday we hear that what has been kept hidden throughout the ages is now being revealed. God's presence will be made known to all peoples through Christ.

The Season of Christmas

See chapter 5, page 152, for comments.

The Season of Epiphany

In Advent we began the reading of the Gospel according to Mark. The early chapters of Mark naturally pick up the Epiphany theme. The chapter-by-chapter treatment of Mark begun now is interrupted during Lent and Easter, as we read selected portions of both Mark and John that have special significance during those seasons. But on the Sundays after Pentecost we again pick up the chapter-by-chapter treatment, so that by the end of the liturgical year we will have covered all the major portions of Mark's Gospel, along with segments of the Gospel of John.

See chapter 5, page 156, for a fuller introduction to this season.

The Epistle Readings

Except for the first Sunday after Epiphany, the readings offer a chapter-by-chapter treatment of the middle section of First Corinthians and part of Second Corinthians. Since the epistle readings are not related to the other two readings in this season, we omit commentary on them.

The Old Testament and Gospel Readings

The Feast of the Epiphany
(Twelfth Night)—January 6

This feast celebrates the story of the wise men coming to bring gifts to the Christ child. Matthew sees this as a fulfillment of the prophecy of Isaiah that is read on this day: " . . . nations shall come to your light." From a religious education point of view, the story symbolizes the realization that the nature of Jesus' birth was recognized throughout the world. The "light" spread. Note the emphasis on light rising to end the night that still covers the earth. This symbolic language can be easily shared in pageantry and in classroom experiences.

See extensive comments on Epiphany in chapter 4, pages 103-105, and chapter 5, pages 156-157.

First Sunday after Epiphany   E, L
Baptism of the Lord   RC

See chapter 4, pages 105-107, and chapter 5, page 151.

Second and Third Sundays after Epiphany   E, L
Second and Third Sundays in Ordinary Time   RC

On these two Sundays the readings tell the story of the calling of the first of Jesus' disciples. Use these two Sundays as a time to tell the stories of the disciples and to recognize our call to be disciples of Christ.

The Old Testament reading for the *second Sunday* tells the story of the call of Samuel, a prophet in King Saul's time. This reading ties in with the "calling" theme of the gospel. See page 174 for a list of other stories about persons being called by God to serve. Share some of these stories in the learning community.

The gospel reading for the *third Sunday* helps us appreciate Jesus' words as he goes forth after his baptism. In the gospel reading we will hear: " . . . Jesus came into Galilee, preaching the gospel of God, and saying, 'The time is fulfilled, and the kingdom of God is at hand; repent, and believe in the gospel'" (Mark 1:14-15). The first reading is a similar call to change. The people had strayed from the God of the covenant. They had followed their own ways and their own gods and consequently had suffered. If they return to God they will know his presence and love again.

Notice how discipleship and repentance are tied together in Jesus' mind and in these readings. The baptismal liturgy would be helpful this week in dealing with what it means to be a disciple of Christ. We must make commitment to change and to grow in Christ's way. This means turning away form evil and separation. We *renounce* evil and *accept* Christ. Continue last week's focus on discipleship, but add the dimension of repentance and commitment in the learning community this week.

The Lutheran and Roman Catholic lectionaries appoint Jonah 3:1-5,10 as the Old Testament reading on the third Sunday after Epiphany (third Sunday in Ordinary Time). This story tells how the people of Nineveh, who had been doing evil in the sight of God, repent and

turn to the Lord after Jonah warns them.
Jonah's story would be important to share today.

Fourth through Seventh Sundays after Epiphany   E, L
Fourth through Seventh Sundays in Ordinary Time   RC

Having called his disciples, Jesus goes out to heal
and spread the Word of God. And the Word of
God itself is power, as we see in the readings that
form the last half of the Sundays after Epiphany.
The Word itself destroys evil and brings wholeness
in acts of healing.

Jesus' words and actions confront the
people with the new way of the Lord. They must
turn from their old ways of following evil and
find healing in the light of the Lord. The Old
Testament readings during the latter weeks of
Epiphany follow the same theme as the gospel
readings, recording stories of healings and words
of confrontation and promise. On some of these
Sundays the Lutheran and Roman Catholic Old
Testament selections differ from the Episcopal
readings, but the themes are the same each week.

To help participants appreciate the
important *concept of healing,* I would suggest
putting major emphasis on the subject during the
season of Epiphany. In addition to the healing
stories appointed in the lectionary, I have listed
other important healing stories from the gospels
in the Guide to Stories of the Bible (chapter 1,
pages 43-44). Here are some comments about the
concept of healing and wholeness as it is
expressed in the Bible.

We can lose the significance of the stories
we hear about Jesus' healing if we simply accept
them as narratives about a miracle worker who
lived two thousand years ago. There is a far more
significant level of understanding. *The American
Heritage Dictionary of the English Language*
points out that the words *health, wholeness,* and
holy have a common origin. In terms of theology
this reminds us that to be at one with or in touch
with God is to be whole or holy, while to be
separated or cut off from God is to be in a state
of "dis-ease." We all know how it feels physically
as well as mentally to experience a sense of guilt,
for example.

As you read the passages telling of Jesus
healing people, ask yourself how he was putting
the person in touch with God or helping that
person feel at one with God again. What did he
say that brought wholeness to the person? How
did the person respond? What do you think was
bringing the person "dis-ease," other than the
obvious physical disability? I do not want to
imply that Jesus was simply a good psychiatrist.
He obviously was completely open to the power
of God in bringing health and wholeness. But if
the gospels are to come alive for us, it is
important to see that this power of wholeness
made visible through Jesus is very much a part of
our lives today. We bring wholeness as we
approach one another with the power of Jesus'
love and forgiveness.

From this kind of discussion we can move
to talk about the healing that happens through
medical science. Christ heals through doctors,
nurses, and various scientific means. In *The
Book of Common Prayer* (page 460) we pray
for doctors and nurses: "Sanctify, O Lord,
those whom you have called to the study and
practice of the arts of healing ... strengthen
them by your life-giving Spirit...." The Lord
calls people into the healing ministry as well as
into the teaching and pastoral ministries. We are
all part of the same Body of Christ that brings
wholeness into the world. Adolescents and adults
could spend these Sundays in Epiphany talking
about the healing ministry of the Church. Study
the section of *The Book of Common Prayer*
(pages 453-461) concerned with the ministry to
the sick. Arrange for children to tour the local
hospital; or ask a doctor or nurse who is a
member of the parish to come and talk with the
group. How does this person see his or her
healing ministry?

Another important act to understand is the
anointing of the sick and the laying on of hands.

The Roman Catholic ritual for the
anointing of the sick and the laying on of hands
is similar to that of the Episcopalian tradition.
Services of healing, both as part of the parish
celebration of the Eucharist and at the bedside of
the sick, are an important ministry of the
Church. The priest anoints the person with oil
that has been blessed by the bishop and/or lays
hands on the person who is suffering. This action

becomes the outward and visible symbol of the healing presence of the Holy Spirit in the person's life. "As you are outwardly anointed with this holy oil, so may our heavenly Father grant you the inward anointing of the Holy Spirit" (prayer following the anointing, *The Book of Common Prayer,* page 456). This anointing and/or laying on of hands is not reserved for those at death's door but is available to anyone suffering from physical or emotional illness. If your group studies the rituals and customs of the ministry to the sick, look also at the service of "Ministration at the Time of Death" in *The Book of Common Prayer,* pages 462-467. The Lord heals through death as well as through physical cures, we realize as we study the words of this ancient service. When a person is at the point of death, the priest says "Depart, O Christian soul, out of this world. . . . May your rest be this day in peace, and your dwelling place in the Paradise of God" (*The Book of Common Prayer,* page 464). Our people will encounter the feelings of suffering and death in the weeks to come as we prepare to participate in the Holy Week and Easter drama of the Church. As we focus on healing and the Christian understanding of healing in this life and in the life to come, we will be preparing for our own crises in life as well as for a fuller participation in the life, death, and resurrection of our Lord.

Christ brings us health and wholeness, and we discover his healing presence as we begin to raise such questions among ouselves as, What are our feelings when fear, guilt, or rejection prevent us from feeling whole? Can we recall times when we felt better (more whole or holy) because someone simply showed us love or forgave us or affirmed us as a person?

Now turn to the list of healing stories on pages 43-44 of A Guide to Stories of the Bible. Use the passages to start discussions about wholeness.

It is important to share this concept of healing as these readings are being offered in the liturgy. Too much of our understanding of Christian healing comes from the healers we see on television. We can easily dismiss the whole subject because of our reaction to the showmanship of such programs. But Jesus healed quietly. Look at the nature of his healings.

Realize that the healing power of his love and word is an instrument of healing that we too can share as Christians. As we see our healing mission as disciples, we too spread the light.

The sixth Sunday after Epiphany deals with the cleansing of lepers in both the Old Testament and gospel readings. Tell the story of Elisha cleansing the leper. Leprosy was a particularly foul disease, both because it was physically horrible and because it was considered a sign of sinfulness. Reginald Fuller states: "The fact that leprosy symbolizes sin, like Mark's device of the Messianic secret, compels us to take the first reading. . .and the gospel as a proclamation of the power of the cross to cleanse from sin. It is this cleansing power which is mediated in the sacrament of absolution and experienced in the Eucharist."*

Eighth Sunday after Epiphany   E, L
Eighth Sunday in Ordinary Time   RC
Both Old Testament and gospel readings point to a new life in which God's people are restored. The healings we have talked about since the fourth Sunday were signs of the new age that Jesus proclaimed. Jesus said that this new age is a time of celebration in which we are not enslaved by the past.

Today we recall the stories of the healings we have been focusing on these past few weeks. How do we think the people who were healed understood their new life? Sometimes it is hard to accept the impact of what has happened to us. We slip back into being "lepers" again in our outlook; we attempt to patch the new life onto the old. But Jesus said we must accept the new relationship with God and not be bound by the limitations of the old.

Last Sunday after Epiphany   E
Transfiguration of Our Lord   L
See chapter 5, page 156, and chapter 8, 274-275.

---

* Reginald Fuller, *Preaching the New Lectionary,* p. 322.

The Season of Lent

See chapter 5, page 163, for a general introduction to this season.

Ash Wednesday
See chapter 5, page 163.

First Sunday in Lent
On this first Sunday in Lent, we look back to the ancient covenant between God and Noah. In passing through the waters, Noah became aware of his relationship with God, and the rainbow became the symbol of that covenant relationship. (See pages 20-21 for a further discussion of this story.) The epistle refers to that early understanding of covenant but points beyond it to the greater covenant made known through Jesus. In the gospel reading Jesus passes through the waters at his baptism. Moreover, just as the Israelites entered the wilderness after they had passed through the waters of the Red Sea, after his baptism Jesus enters the wilderness and undergoes a struggle with temptation for forty days. We can talk about the waters we symbolically pass through at our baptism. Water denotes the cleansing and new birth that come through our relationship with God revealed by Jesus.

This would be a good Sunday, then, to reflect on our own baptism. Baptism marks the sign, the covenant, and the saving act. But it also marks the beginning of our struggle with temptation.

The gospel selection in the Roman Catholic and Lutheran lectionaries differs slightly from the Episcopal reading, but the temptation in the wilderness is the important focus in all three lectionaries. In the Episcopal reading we hear of Jesus' baptism and temptation. In the Lutheran and Roman Catholic lectionaries we hear of the temptation and then of Jesus' going forth to proclaim the Good News.

The Old Testament reading in the Lutheran lectionary is the lesson appointed for the second Sunday in Lent in the Episcopal and Roman Catholic churches.

Second Sunday in Lent
Today we focus on the great faith of Abraham, St. Paul, and the disciples. Abraham acted out of faith in offering his own son as a sacrifice. Jesus calls on Peter to exercise faith that out of Jesus' sacrifice will come life. In the epistle, St. Paul talks about our living in the faith that nothing—not even death— can separate us from our loving covenant with God. Jesus calls us into the same kind of faith relationship with him so that we can offer up our *own* lives, in trust that out of risk comes life.

Tell the whole story of Abraham today. (See A Guide to Stories of the Bible, page 21.) Some background needs to be offered to understand the significance of Abraham's actions. Animal sacrifice, as well as human sacrifice, was a fact of life for people of that era. Use the story of Abraham's faith as a "launching device" into our own fears about taking risks that lead us to face the unknown. In an earlier part of the story (Genesis 12:1-9), Abraham was told in a vision to move his family. Can we identify similar times in our lives? This kind of faith, the gospel reading makes clear, forms the basis of discipleship.

The Lutheran Old Testament reading for today tells of God's covenant with Jacob, an important part of our covenant story not found in the Episcopal or Roman Catholic lectionary for Year B. The Jacob stories would be important to share today in all of our churches. (See A Guide to Stories of the Bible, pages 22-23.) When Jacob met with the Lord after returning from his uncle's lands, his name became Israel. He was the forefather of the Israelites and our forefather in the faith through our relationship with Jesus Christ. Be sure to tell the stories of Jacob as you would tell stories about your own ancestors so that participants will feel a relationship with this important figure in our faith history.

Third Sunday in Lent
If we are to understand the significance of our baptism during this baptism-preparation season of Lent, it is essential that we understand the nature of our covenant relationship with God. Thus the readings each week trace the development of the covenant by telling the stories of Noah and Moses. Today we look at the Ten Commandments, which form the basis of our understanding of the entire body of Old Testament law. In the epistle reading Paul speaks

of the struggle of all of us. The harder we try to follow the law of the covenant, the more we realize how much we have fallen short. In the gospel story, Jesus "cleanses" the Temple in Jerusalem as a dramatic sign that Israel has strayed from the covenant. Out of the ashes of the Old Covenant, Jesus will "rise up" to restore a relationship with God in a New Covenant. In his own life and death Jesus is the Law fulfilled in the "flesh and blood" of God's experience among his people. The words of the covenant shift from the stone of Moses' tablets to the flesh of Jesus' life.

Incorporate the Ten Commandments into the liturgy this Sunday. (See *The Book of Common Prayer,* pages 317, 350, and 847). You may want to have the congregation rehearse the Ten Commandments each Sunday during Lent to emphasize the idea of covenant. There is nothing permissive about being a Christian. We are called to proclaim with our lives that the kingdom of God is dawning in all creation. We have a marriage relationship with God that requires us to judge every action on the basis of that relationship. The section of the Catechism dealing with the Ten Commandments (*The Book of Common Prayer,* pages 847-848) will help you translate those ancient words into ideas that even children can understand and appreciate. Encourage children to memorize the Commandments during Lent so that the feeling for their covenant with the Lord is internalized. Explain unfamiliar terms such as *adultery* in light of the Catechism's explanation.

Fourth Sunday in Lent

The Old Testament reading continues the salvation history. Last week we focused on the covenant and renewal of the covenant made known in Jesus Christ. This week the reading from Second Chronicles provides an outline of what happened when the Israelites broke the covenant with God. Their nation fell, and the people were sent into exile in Babylonia. Only later under Cyrus, the king of Persia, were they allowed to return and rebuild their temple in Jerusalem. Likewise, when we stray from the covenant, our society is bound to become decadent, and such a society easily falls prey to the enemy. In reflecting on history we learn how

God is calling us to repent and return to our covenant. Adolescents and adults in the learning community could be provided with an overview of Israel's history and with the theological concept of God working through history to confront and restore his people. Chapter 2 of this book would be helpful for the historical outline.

The gospel reading for today is the story of Jesus feeding the five thousand on the hillside. Though the appointed reading ends at John 6:15, read verses 22 through 59 for your own background study. In the Gospel of John there is no description of sharing bread and wine at the Last Supper, but some scholars feel that the sixth chapter, which talks of Jesus being the "bread of life," is John's poetic way of introducing the concept of the Eucharist.

Lutherans and Roman Catholics will hear John 3:14-21 this Sunday instead of the gospel mentioned above. This reading includes the familiar words "For God so loved the world that he gave his only Son, that whoever believes in him should not perish but have eternal life." The reading goes on to contrast those who live in darkness with those who seek the light. God wants to bring us all into the light, and he sends his Son to bring this about. The reading points to the meaning of our covenant with the Lord. He would show us the way of light and call us to live in that light and proclaim it to the world with our very lives. It is a covenant of good news. (Refer back to the Epiphany theme as the terms *light* and *dark* are heard again this week.)

The Old Testament lesson in the Lutheran lectionary, Numbers 21:4-9, is a background reading for the gospel reference to Moses' lifting up the serpent in the desert. While in the wilderness the people had again sinned by losing faith in the Lord. Yahweh sent serpents into their camp to punish them. Those who looked at a bronze serpent that Moses held up were saved from their punishing death. In the Gospel of John this story becomes a metaphor of salvation: All of us sinners who look at the Son of Man "lifted up" on the cross will be saved from the judgment of God. Share the story of the bronze serpent from today's readings, and then offer the poem from the gospel reading. While sharing the story of the serpents in the wilderness from the Book of Numbers, you may want to expose participants to the amusing story of Balaam found in Numbers 22. See A Guide to Stories of the Bible, page 27, for background.

Fifth Sunday in Lent
The covenant story has been told week by week during Lent. We have looked at Abraham, Isaac, Jacob, and Moses. We have looked at the signs of the covenant: the rainbow, the Temple, manna or bread, the stone tablets of the Ten Commandments, the "tent of the meeting," and other signs. We need to fill in the story a bit for the parish. The people broke covenant; they lost faith, the nation fell, and the Israelites went into exile in a strange land. In today's reading, the prophet Jeremiah foresees a "new covenant." "I will put my law within them, and I will write it upon their hearts; and I will be their God, and they shall be my people" (Jeremiah 31:33).

The New Testament readings form a story of covenant-making, too. They tell the story of the understanding of that new covenant referred to by Jeremiah as it became known in the life, death, and resurrection of Jesus Christ. From Jesus' baptism the readings have moved week by week to reflect on the meaning of his life and death. Old Testament words and symbols take on a new significance with Christ.

Today's readings conclude our "primer" for baptism and prepare us for the epic story of Jesus' passion that will be heard next week.

Holy Week
See chapter 5, pages 167-168.

The Season of Easter

See chapter 5, pages 173-180, for the readings for the seven weeks of the Easter season.

Episcopalians can choose one of the following alternatives for this season:

First reading: The readings from Acts or the Old Testament selections.

Second reading: The readings from Acts or selections from John.

Third reading: The gospel selections as appointed.

The Lutheran and Roman Catholic lectionaries do not include the Old Testament options during the Easter season.

See chapter 4, pages 119-122, for program ideas based on the season of Easter.

The Readings from the Book of Acts

If we choose the Acts selections for either the first or second reading, the story will flow as follows:

Second Sunday of Easter
Acts 3:12a,13-15,17-26: This is an example of Peter's preaching to the people of Jerusalem.

Third Sunday of Easter
Acts 4:5-12: Peter and John defend the apostles' actions before the Sanhedrin.

Fourth Sunday of Easter
Acts 4:23-37: Last week's story is continued. After their trial the apostles return to the community of the faithful. The reading offers insight into the communal life of the Christians.

Fifth Sunday of Easter
Acts 8:26-40: The gospel spreads beyond the Jewish people. Philip baptizes a eunuch from Ethiopia after interpreting the meaning of the Old Testament passage that the man is reading.

Sixth Sunday of Easter
Acts 11:19-30: We are introduced to St. Paul, the great missionary of the first-century Church.

Thursday is Ascension Day. See chapter 8, pages 275-276, for background.

Seventh Sunday of Easter
Acts 1:15-26: Matthias is chosen to replace Judas as one of the twelve apostles.

The Roman Catholic lessons for the second through the sixth Sundays of Easter are different from the Episcopal lessons mentioned above, but the overall impact of telling the story of the Book of Acts week by week is the same. Look over the whole Book of Acts and choose those stories you want to emphasize in the learning community, whether or not they are read as a part of the lectionary selections. A Guide to Stories of the Bible, chapter 1, pages 47-48, will help you in this selection process.

The Old Testament and Gospel Readings

Second and Third Sundays of Easter
The gospel readings for the second and third Sundays of Easter, as well as that of Easter Sunday, focus on the resurrection appearances of Christ. The concept of the resurrection is difficult to deal with. We must be careful not to make the appearances sound like ghost stories. With this in mind we may be tempted to avoid mentioning the resurrection. Though it is difficult to talk about something we may feel awkward or unsure about ourselves, it is important to talk with our people about what they will be hearing in the liturgy these Sundays. The resurrection is the central proclamation of our faith, after all.

Hope for the Flowers is a beautiful book about caterpillars and butterflies that will help children appreciate the concept of dying to become fully alive.* C. S. Lewis' *Last Battle,* the final volume of the *Chronicles of Narnia,* would be helpful for children nine years old and older (see Bibliography). Conceptually, the resurrection will be over the heads of most children, but it is still important to tell the story and let it enter their consciousness. Seeds and flowers, caterpillars and butterflies are ways of expressing the idea of the resurrection for adults as well as for children.

The Old Testament reading for the *second Sunday* of Easter is a prophecy of hope based on

*Trina Paulus, *Hope for the Flowers* (Paramus, N.J.: Paulist Press, 1972).

faith that God can be trusted forever. The day will come when the proud will be humbled and those who have kept faith will know God's presence. The reading closes with the promise finally recognized in the risen Christ: "Thy dead shall live, their bodies shall rise. / O dwellers in the dust, awake and sing for joy!" (Isaiah 26:19).

On the *third Sunday* of Easter we read from the prophet Micah, who foresaw a day when God's people would be restored. He described poetically what that restoration would be like: "...they shall beat their swords into plowshares, and their spears into pruning hooks" (Micah 4:3). Those who experienced the resurrection looked back to the prophecy and felt that the predicted new age was beginning to dawn in Christ.

Fourth, Fifth, and Sixth Sundays of Easter

The gospel readings for the fourth, fifth, and sixth Sundays of Easter express the meaning of the resurrection for today. The lessons, taken from the Gospel of John, express in poetic form what it means for a Christian to have a relationship with the risen Lord. Christ is our Good Shepherd. Or, in a different figure, he is the vine and we are the branches.

The *fourth Sunday* of Easter is Good Shepherd Sunday in all three years of the lectionary. The optional Old Testament reading from Ezekiel helps us appreciate the background of this poem. We have a relationship with God that is as close and personal as that between a shepherd and his sheep. The Lord lays down his life for us so that we may live. The curriculum *Sheep and Shepherds* is designed to help seven- and eight-year-old children understand the concept of the Good Shepherd.*

In the Old Testament reading of the *fifth Sunday* of Easter, the writer recalls Israel's history and points out the close relationship that must exist between God and his people if the nation is to survive. The gospel reading appointed for the day picks up this theme. Christ's people must follow the covenant of love he has revealed. They must reflect on that love and respond to it.

*Ronald J. Goldman, ed., *Sheep and Shepherds,* Readiness for Religion Series (Wilton, Conn.: Morehouse-Barlow, 1970).

As they do so, Christ will be revealed to them.

The Lutheran and Roman Catholic gospel reading is the poem of the vine and the branches mentioned in connection with next Sunday's reading.

On the *sixth Sunday* of Easter the prophet speaks words of promise. Because God is creator, he will fulfill his promise to those he has created. The gospel reading continues the theme from last week. The followers of Jesus are to love one another as he has loved them; this is the new commandment. Note Christ's statement that he has chosen his followers and that they must therefore bear fruit. This refers to an earlier portion of John 15, where Jesus is called the true vine. Jesus as the true vine is a concept that can be expressed simply and graphically in the spring season. A branch cut away from the vine soon dies. But the branches are expected to bear fruit. We bear fruit when we "live on in" love the way Christ does.

The gospel for the *seventh Sunday* of Easter is a portion of the great prayer of Jesus for the Church. (See chapter 5, pages 175-176, for additional background on this section of the Gospel of John.) This week the focus in the learning community is the role of the Church in the world today. We are the Body of Christ—the "hands and feet" of Christ—, called to bring healing into the world in that place where the Lord has put us. "As thou didst send me into the world, so I have sent them into the world" (John 17:18). Jesus commissioned his apostles, and they commission us through the Church to be God's representatives in the world. The Old Testament lesson is the story of the appointment of the first priests to serve God in the wilderness. They are to represent the people before God and to express God's presence before the people. This is our role as baptized Christians as we go out into the world, filled with the gifts of the Holy Spirit. These readings prepare us for the Feast of Pentecost next week, when we recognize the gifts of the Holy Spirit as they came to the apostles and as they come to us.

The Epistle Readings

The first letter of John is read each Sunday if the epistle option is chosen. This letter emphasizes the direct connection between loving God and loving our neighbor. Read this epistle yourself and then expose participants to it in every possible way. Its ideas can be adapted to fit all age groups. Though some children may not understand certain poetic images for years, the images are so beautiful and so profound that all children need to be exposed to them early in order to grow up with them. The epistle and gospel readings for the sixth Sunday are complementary, for both speak of the power of God's love revealed through Jesus Christ.

The Easter season readings help us to understand the impact of the resurrection on the followers of Jesus, the formation of the early Church, and the early Church's understanding of these events.

The Feast of Pentecost
See chapter 5, pages 179-180, for comments.

The Sundays after Pentecost
(Sundays in Ordinary Time)

See chapter 5, page 181, for introductory comments.

The Epistles used this year are
2 Corinthians, Ephesians, James, and Hebrews.
The Gospel is that of Mark.

Trinity Sunday
See chapter 8, pages 277-278, for a discussion of Trinity Sunday.

Proper 1   E
Sixth Sunday in Ordinary Time   RC
Sixth Sunday after Epiphany   L
See sixth Sunday after Epiphany, pages 210-211.

Proper 2   E
Seventh Sunday in Ordinary Time   RC
Seventh Sunday after Epiphany   L
See seventh Sunday after Epiphany, pages 210-211.

Proper 3   E
Eighth Sunday in Ordinary Time   RC
Eighth Sunday after Epiphany   L
See eighth Sunday after Epiphany, page 211.

Proper 4   E
Ninth Sunday in Ordinary Time   RC
Second Sunday after Pentecost   L
Old Testament: The Ten Commandments are given, with emphasis on keeping the Sabbath.
Gospel: Jesus speaks about the Sabbath.
Telling the story: Tell the story about the Israelites in the wilderness and Moses receiving the covenant. We need to help the learning community appreciate the nature of Jesus' encounters with God. If we take the narrative literally, it sounds as if Moses met God face to face and talked with him "man to man." This literalism will not lead people to a deeper understanding of God's action in their lives. We sometimes say that inspirations "come to us." In describing these inspirations we might well say "God spoke to me and said...." Let your telling convey the reality that God speaks to us in our time as truly as he did to Moses.
Religious concepts: Talk about the concept of the Sabbath. The biblical injunction to rest

stems from the first story of creation in Genesis 1, where God is said to have rested on the seventh day. The weekly observance of the Sabbath is to be a constant reminder to the Jew of God's continuing presence in creation and in history. In addition, there is a beautiful feeling that when we set aside one day of the week and consider it holy, the entire week is sanctified and declared holy. The Sabbath is a vivid dramatization of the reality that all of our life is holy and filled with wonder and meaning in the sight of God. The strict practices of the Sabbath were meant to ensure that every Jew treat the day as special. The routine of life had to be broken. The people of God are required to celebrate within the family the abiding presence of God with them. Although that purpose was often lost in a barrage of intricate regulations concerning what could and could not be done on the day, the intent of the Sabbath is beautiful and powerful.

We can talk about the Sunday observances of the first-century Church this week. See Acts 20:7, Matthew 28:1, John 20:1, and 1 Corinthians 16:2 for the few biblical glimpses of Christian practices for observing the Lord's Day. The Matthew and John passages establish the proclamation of the resurrection as occurring "after the sabbath, toward the dawn of the first day of the week." This would be our Sunday, since the Jews figured a day from sundown to sundown. Their Sabbath, or seventh day, started Friday evening and ended with sundown on Saturday evening. Christians, however, marked the day of the resurrection as their day of celebration. The high point of their celebration was the "breaking of bread," a technical term for the Eucharist and the fellowship meal that was a part of the eucharistic celebration. Because many of the people were slaves or Gentiles, they did not observe the Sabbath laws. However, some of the Jewish-Christians attended the Sabbath ritual at the synagogue and then joined their Christian brethren for the Eucharist on the first of the week.

We see the results of this practice in our present eucharistic liturgy. The first half of our liturgy, the Liturgy of the Word, is basically the synagogue service of Scripture, praise, prayer, and interpretation of Scripture. At the offertory we leave the synagogue service to join our Lord at the altar, as our ancestors did "on the first day of the week." This is the liturgy of the Holy Communion, or the Liturgy of the Bread.

Proper 5   E
Tenth Sunday in Ordinary Time   RC
Third Sunday after Pentecost   L

Old Testament: We hear the story of Adam and Eve's temptation and fall.

Gospel: The good news is proclaimed, giving us hope in the face of the first reading. Jesus comes to conquer the power of Satan. Satan cannot endure, and every sin will be forgiven. Everyone who does the will of God is a member of Jesus' family.

Telling the story: In telling the story of Adam and Eve use my comments in A Guide to Stories of the Bible, chapter 1, page 16.

Religious concepts: The concept of the fall is also discussed on page 20.

Proper 6   E
Eleventh Sunday in Ordinary Time   RC
Fourth Sunday after Pentecost   L

Old Testament: Ezekiel compares Pharaoh and the mighty nation of Egypt to a giant cypress tree. With great pride and arrogance the tree had risen far above everything else in the world. But God has humbled the tree. It lies flat upon the face of the earth with its broken boughs strewn across the ravines. The Lutheran and Roman Catholic lesson is from the 17th chapter of Ezekiel. Here the allegory of the great cedar tree is used as a hopeful sign that in the future God will build up Judah again.

Gospel: We hear the parable of the seed today. Once a seed is planted, it grows by itself. Once the kingdom of God has been planted, its growth also is inevitable. The two readings taken together remind us that is is God's creative power, not ours, that brings life to fruition.

Religious concepts: God plants his kingdom in us and in creation. This can be a beautiful time to talk of the wonder of growth in ourselves and in the world around us. Sometimes growth comes so slowly that it is imperceptible.

We become discouraged, but God's kingdom is happening nevertheless.

Proper 7   E
Twelfth Sunday in Ordinary Time   RC
Fifth Sunday after Pentecost   L

Old Testament: The appointed reading is God's response to Job's constant questions about the reason for his suffering. Life is a mystery, the reading makes clear. God's ongoing act of creation is so far beyond our comprehension that we cannot understand everything. God is the creator and master of all things, including the mighty seas.

Gospel: Jesus calms the sea. The disciples raise a Job-like question: "Teacher, do you not care if we perish?" Jesus admonishes them for their lack of faith. The disciples say to one another "Who then is this, that even wind and sea obey him?" Jesus represents the same awesome mystery to the disciples as the Lord speaking out of the storm did to Job.

Religious concepts: This would be a good week to discuss the book of Job with adults and adolescents. We must not offer pat answers to the questions of life as Job's "friends" attempted to do. Portions of Job could be offered as a dramatic reading. Allow time for dialogue and discussion following the reading.

Another way of approaching this theme that would be more appropriate for younger participants would be to let the group play the role of Job and the disciples. After telling the story of Job and the disciples, let the participants raise their questions to the Lord. What are the questions that bother and anger us? Write them on newsprint. Close the session with a portion of today's readings. Life is incomprehensible, and sometimes it just doesn't seem fair. So it is well to encourage persons to raise questions and to realize that they are following the biblical tradition in doing so! In telling the story of Job, you will need to tell only the high points. Let it be known that Job raised anguished questions and that his "comforters" attempted to answer the questions with simplistic thoughts that Job resented. This is an important book that our people need to have a feeling for.

Proper 8 E
Thirteenth Sunday in Ordinary Time RC
Sixth Sunday after Pentecost L

Old Testament: To live in covenant with God means caring about each other as God cares for us. We cannot ignore the needs of our kinsmen nor be selfish about helping. The Lutheran selection is from Lamentations. It talks of God's favor and love for those who seek him. The Roman Catholic lesson proclaims God's desire for life rather than death. "God did not make death, and he does not delight in the death of the living" (Wisdom 1:13).

Gospel: Jesus heals the daughter of Jairus, an official of the synagogue. The Lutheran lectionary offers an optional gospel reading that tells the story of the healing of the woman with a hemorrhage.

Telling the story: Share the gospel stories in the learning community so that participants can respond in a more personal way to what they hear. See A Guide to Stories of the Bible, chapter 1, pages 43-44, for other healing stories.

Religious concepts: See chapter 6, pages 210-211, for a discussion of the concept of healing.

Proper 9 E
Fourteenth Sunday in Ordinary Time RC
Seventh Sunday after Pentecost L

Old Testament: Ezekiel is called to be a prophet and has the painful responsibility of speaking out in God's name. The people are unable to hear and respond. They vent their animosity against God's spokesman.

Gospel: Jesus is not accepted as a prophet by his own neighbors.

Telling the story: Stories of the Old Testament prophets are interesting to tell, and children will begin to appreciate the role of the prophet as they hear them. The Guide to Stories of the Bible, found in chapter 1, will be helpful for this Sunday. See also the discussions of the prophets in chapter 5, pages 158-159.

Religious concepts: Talk about the role of the prophets in the Old Testament and about Jesus' role as prophet. How do we respond to the prophets of our own age?

Jesus confronted persons in somewhat the same way as the prophets did. We often use the term *the teachings of Jesus,* but most of the words Jesus said were not spoken in the context of a sermon or lecture but arose out of a particular situation in which Jesus found himself. His words or teachings, like this parable, confronted his hearers with a new reality and a new way of looking at life that contradicted their current perceptions. Like the prophets of the Old Testament, Jesus angered people because his words, parables, and actions were so confrontational. They gave persons a new understanding of how God was working in their history and of the radical response that it called for.

Jesus, unlike Confucius, Buddha, and others, did not set down absolute maxims or truths for generations of persons to follow. What he did was to confront persons with the presence and love of God in the life that he lived with them. What Jesus said grew out of that life. For that reason it is important to see Jesus' words as dynamic, living encounters with the reality of God's presence and power rather than as static maxims to be memorized and codified. We read the words of Jesus in the gospels to see what he might be saying to us "in the flesh" of our human experience. The gospel readings are offered as a way of moving us to discover how Christ is encountering us personally in our daily lives.

It is imperative that we help each other move beyond the introduction to Christ that we receive from the gospels into our own living relationship with him. That relationship should be based on our understanding of Jesus from the gospels but should move out dynamically into an ever-changing and ever-evolving encounter with "the true light that enlightens every man..." (John 1:9).

Note the method Jesus used in his dialogue with persons. He did not answer questions; he raised them. He led persons in their own quest for God's truth rather than nailing down truth for them.

As we explore these passages, it is important to raise these questions for discussion.
• What do you think may have been the situation that led Jesus to say what he did? (You may be able to provide a brief background from your own study of the passage. The Bible commentaries listed in the Bibliography would

also be helpful.)

• What might he say to them (or us), and how might they (or we) respond? How did the persons who heard Jesus respond to him? Why?

As we raise such questions as these, it is important that we move from the biblical situation to our own. Do not allow the discussion to remain safely "back there," but gradually shift the focus to the group. The goal of Bible study is to help us become aware of Christ in our daily lives and in our world as he confronts us, heals us, and brings us alive in God's love.

Proper 10   E
Fifteenth Sunday in Ordinary Time   RC
Eighth Sunday after Pentecost   L

Old Testament: God calls Amos to be a prophet.

Gospel: Jesus calls his disciples and sends them out.

Telling the story: Today's Old Testament reading and last week's discussion about the role of the prophet will help set the stage for this week's focus on the disciples of Jesus. God called Amos out and sent him on a mission that brought struggle into Amos' life as he spoke the word of God to a people who often did not want to accept confrontation with that word. Jesus called his disciples into a life of power but also into a life of struggle and confrontation with the established order and world view.

Tell the stories of the call of the disciples as described in A Guide to Stories of the Bible, page 38.

Religious concepts: Last week's study can be continued. The nature of discipleship is the concept to focus on here. Part of the disciple's role is to follow Christ's example and speak the prophetic word. The covenant we make at our baptism states the prophetic role of our discipleship in terms that can lead to discussion. As a part of our covenant with Christ we accept our call: "... proclaim by word and example the Good News of God in Christ ... seek and serve Christ in all persons ... strive for justice and peace among all people, and respect the dignity of every human being" (*The Book of Common Prayer,* page 305). If you are working with adolescents or adults, think of situations where we as Christians might be called to confront

injustice or to proclaim the good news where it might not be accepted. Let participants role play or discuss how they would exercise their prophetic call to be followers of Christ.

It is important to communicate to people that they too are disciples of Christ. Notice the many words of Jesus (outlined in last week's discussion) that deal with the meaning of discipleship. We need to move our concept of discipleship from thinking about the twelve apostles to understanding that what Jesus said and did with them affects our own personal discipleship.

Propers 11-15   E
Sixteenth through Twentieth Sundays
   in Ordinary Time   RC
Ninth through Thirteenth Sundays
   after Pentecost   L

Religious concepts: This series of Sundays deals with the same overall theme. It begins (in Proper 11) with Mark's account of the feeding of the five thousand. (In the Lutheran and Roman Catholic lectionaries, this same story is told next week by the writer of the Gospel of John.) Then we shift from Mark's narration of the feeding to look at the theological concept of the feeding in the Gospel of John. Jesus is the bread of life. To feed on that bread of life is to have eternal life. The bread our ancestors ate in the wilderness was only a foretaste of the true bread from heaven, Jesus. The Old Testament readings give us a background for these theological statements from the Gospel of John.

Since the Gospel of John does not include an account of the Last Supper, some scholars feel that John 6 is a theological explanation of the Holy Eucharist. The bread that we receive at the Eucharist is the bread of heaven. (These are the words the priest in the Episcopal Church may say while offering the communicant the bread of the Eucharist.) To eat of this bread is to receive Christ and the eternal life he offers.

As we celebrate the Holy Eucharist week after week, we dramatize the truth that we hear in the Gospel of John. The bread, wine, and money that we offer at the Eucharist symbolize the offering of ourselves to the Lord to use us as he wills for the salvation (healing) of his creation. Our simple life is not going to heal this world, we realize as we present ourselves at the Eucharist. (The boy on the hillside may have had the same thoughts as he made a gift to the Lord of his few loaves and fishes.) But in the hands of the Lord, what we offer becomes the living presence of Christ. The simple gift of bread becomes the Body of Christ. The simple gift of ourselves in his service becomes an act of salvation and wholeness in the world. We offer ourselves in the faith that what we do is significant and that through Christ the feeding will happen. This can become an attitude of life so that we can live as expectant, hopeful people rather than as defeated cynical people withdrawing from problems because we feel helpless in dealing with them.

With younger children we may use the analogy of a birthday cake to help express the mystery of the readings we hear during these midsummer weeks. I come to the party bearing my gifts, and I offer them as a sign of my friendship. Then the cake is brought out, and my friend divides the cake and give me a piece. As I eat the cake I become a part of the celebration of my friend's birthday. It becomes a sign that we are a part of each other's life.

This analogy, though it hardly touches the mystery of the Sacrament in which we proclaim the presence of the risen Lord, may nevertheless help the child to appreciate our relationship with Christ that is expressed as we participate in the Sacrament.

The curriculum *It's All About Eucharist* will give you helpful ideas about sharing some of the concepts of the Holy Eucharist during this five-week period.* Take advantage of this midsummer focus on the Eucharist to explore the meaning of our sacramental life together. Be sure to keep in mind the irregular attendance of these midsummer Sundays as you plan for this five-week focus, however. Each week must be a complete unit, since you may be dealing with a whole new group the next week!

Telling the story in the Episcopal Church during the "Feeding" Sundays:

Proper 11 The story of the feeding of the five thousand is heard today in the gospel. The

It's All About Eucharist (Minneapolis, Minn.: Winston Press, 1977).

Old Testament reading is a poem of comfort and strength from the prophet Isaiah.

Proper 12 Today we hear the story of Jesus walking on the water. At first glance this story may not seem to tie in with the theme of feeding and Eucharist. The disciples are afraid as they see Jesus and are confounded by the event. The reading closes with the words "And they were utterly astounded, for they did not understand about the loaves, but their hearts were hardened" (Mark 6:52). To accept the reality of Christ's presence in the bread of the Sacrament is to be open to a whole new dimension of life. It is the Lord who is the source of our life and strength. It is he who quiets the waters and the winds around us if we have the faith to perceive his presence. Our eyes become open to the events that happen around us as we see the Lord feeding us in the Sacrament.

The Old Testament reading today relates the story of Elijah's death and Elisha's succeeding him as the great prophet of Israel. Both these stories speak of God's unspeakable power as it has been related from generation to generation by his people. In telling the Elijah story, refer to my comments about sharing miracle stories and legends, chapter 1, pages 13 and 16. Tell the stories of Elijah and Elisha that deal with feeding, mentioned below (Propers 13 and 14) in connection with the Lutheran and Roman Catholic lectionaries and in A Guide to Stories of the Bible, chapter 1.

Proper 13 We begin the poem from the Gospel of John about the bread of life. We hear the great proclamation "I am the bread of life." Display the words on posters or banners. Talk about bread and the importance of this staple of life. We hear the story of the manna and quails today in the Old Testament reading. A more extensive story about the quails is found in Numbers 11. You may want to tell the story of Moses getting water from the rock (Exodus 17:1-7) as a part of the stories about the Lord feeding and caring for his people.

Proper 14 We continue to hear the great poem on the bread of life in the gospel. The Old Testament reading is a strong warning to the Israelites: When they enter the Promised Land they are not to forget that it was the Lord who provided for them in the wilderness and who will continue to provide for them in their own land. As life gets easier, they may forget the Lord. This is the warning that turns to judgment in the words of the prophets. The people *did* forget their struggle in the wilderness and turned from the Lord.

Proper 15 John's great discourse on the bread of life is concluded today in the gospel reading. The saying from this reading "The man who feeds on me will have life because of me" would be good material for a poster or banner project today. The Old Testament reading is from the Book of Proverbs; it adds further theological insight into the poem we have been hearing from John. To know the wisdom of the Lord is like being invited to a feast at a table. "Come, eat of my bread / and drink of the wine I have mixed." Christ *is* the wisdom of God who has come to us in the flesh of human life. To know Christ is to know God's wisdom. To know that wisdom is like being fed at a banquet table. (See my comments about the wisdom literature of the Old Testament, chapter 2, pages 66-68.)

Telling the story in Roman Catholic and Lutheran churches where readings vary from the Episcopal lectionary:

Sixteenth Sunday in Ordinary Time **RC;** *Ninth Sunday after Pentecost* **L:** Lutherans and Roman Catholics will hear Jeremiah's poem promising that the Lord will sheperd his sheep and "raise up for David a righteous branch, and he shall reign as king and deal wisely." Jesus expressed the feeling of this reading as he thought of the people gathered on the hillside as being like "sheep without a shepherd. . . . "

Seventeenth Sunday in Ordinary Time **RC;** *Tenth Sunday after Pentecost* **L:** Elisha is able to feed a hundred men from twenty barley loaves, we hear in today's story from the Old Testament. I would suggest that you tell the story of Elijah's providing flour and oil for the widow and her son (1 Kings 17:7-16) at some time during this five-week focus, too. Lutherans hear the story of Moses and the Israelites ratifying the covenant at Mount Sinai.

Nineteenth Sunday in Ordinary Time **RC;** *Twelfth Sunday after Pentecost* **L:** Roman

Catholics and Lutherans will hear the story of the Lord providing food for the prophet Elijah as he fled into the wilderness from Queen Jezebel. These stories of feeding could be shared in the learning community of the Episcopal Church during the weeks when the Old Testament reading does not include a story.

Proper 16   E
Twenty-first Sunday in Ordinary Time   RC
Fourteenth Sunday after Pentecost   L

Old Testament: This week we are faced with the necessity of making a choice for the Lord. Joshua gathered the tribes of Israel at Shechem and reminded them of the mighty acts of God in their history. He called them to make a choice: Will they follow the Lord, or the gods of the Canaanites? He called the twelve tribes of Israel to enter into a covenant with the God of their ancestors and commit themselves to follow him. We may have here a remnant of an annual covenant renewal ritual.

Gospel: Jesus called the people into covenant with him. Like Joshua, he called them to make a choice. He too had recited the mighty acts of God and had tied his feeding them with bread and fish on the hillside with the feeding of the Israelites in the wilderness. (See the readings for previous weeks.)

Telling the story: Tell the story of Joshua that leads up to today's reading. Joshua's call to enter the covenant with God is a dramatic one as we read it in the context of Joshua's life with the people. (See especially Exodus 31:7-9,23 and Joshua 1:1-10.)

Religious concepts: God is a God of history. We make our choice to follow God as we recall his mighty acts in our history. Joshua and Jesus recited that history before the people. On the basis of that recalling, the people are called to covenant with God to be his people. We are a part of that great story, but we also have our own individual stories that we need to reflect on. How do we see God acting in our lives? In a sense, the weekly Eucharist is a covenant renewal ceremony in line with Joshua's challenge to the people. We gather to recall the mighty acts of God: in the readings of the Bible, in the sermon, and in the Eucharistic Prayer. We then make an affirmation to choose and follow the Lord. The

Creed and the offertory are our ways of responding. The receiving of the Sacrament is our feeding that strengthens us in following Christ.

Proper 17   E
Twenty-second Sunday in Ordinary Time   RC
Fifteenth Sunday after Pentecost   L

Old Testament: These are words of warning regarding the observance of the Old Testament covenant. In addition to the Old Testament reading specified for this Sunday, read the following passages to gain a greater perspective on the meaning of covenant:

Exodus 19—20 This passage expresses the idea of covenant. The people of God were related to Yahweh by an absolute legal bond. This covenant established their relationship not only with God but with one another as well. They related to God in community, not simply as individuals. The covenant was based on absolute commitment. The Ten Commandments are only a very small portion of the covenant, but they stand as a symbol for the whole. Four of the commandments deal with our relationship with God, and six with our relationships within the covenant community. We relate to our neighbor, to one another, and to the person in need not simply out of desire but out of a commitment to do so arising out of the covenant. Christians understand the same kind of covenant relationship with one another and with God based on a New Covenant (New Testament) realized through Christ.

Exodus 32—34 The Israelites turn from Yahweh to a golden calf. Yahweh renews the covenant with the people with a second set of stone tablets.

Deuteronomy 5:1-22 The Ten Commandments are restated. Compare this version with that of Exodus 20.

Deuteronomy 5:32—6:13 To love Yahweh is the essence of the Law: " . . . you shall love the Lord your God with all your heart, and with all your soul. . . . "

Deuteronomy 6:14—9:6 A warning to the Israelites while they were still in the wilderness: Do not be tempted to stray from God once you are in the Promised Land.

Deuteronomy 10:12-22 The meaning of the commandment is summarized—the *Judeo-*

Christian concern for social justice is set forth.

Deuteronomy 11 Yahweh's blessing and curse are given—the people will be blessed if they follow his way; they will suffer if they do not. *This passage explains the Old Testament understanding of history.*

A simulation experience would be helpful this week. Tell the participants that they are to be part of a special group, learning survival skills. They will be sent off into a wilderness area for six weeks with only basic food and clothing. To receive the coveted certificate in the survival school, they must prove that they can act resourcefully during this time. Before leaving on their venture, the group decides to make a pact or covenant among themselves that they can live by during the six weeks. Have the participants discuss what ten points they would include in that survival covenant. The most obvious points will include conservation of food and sharing of work responsibilities, but the group will also need to deal with rules for handling conflicts, rules for taking care of each other, and so forth. After the group or several small groups have drawn up their list, narrow the points down to ten and read those points in a very formal way. Invite the participants to share in a covenant-making ceremony, perhaps modeled on the Old Testament readings. If this covenant is not followed to the letter, they will bring suffering upon themselves and will not survive. This is the idea behind the covenant of the Old Testament. The covenant sets forth the minimum requirements for justice and fairness. When it is broken, some people will be oppressed, and oppression will lead to conflict and a breakdown of the social order. Close the session with a formal reading of the Decalogue or Ten Commandments as found in *The Book of Common Prayer,* page 350.

Gospel: Jesus confronted religious leaders of his day because they had added a heavy overlay of ritualistic practices that kept them from dealing with the meaning behind the covenant.

Telling the story: We hear of Jesus' encounters with religious leaders that led to his death on the cross.

Religious concepts: The Old Testament law was sacred to the Jewish people, for it was a constant reminder that they were God's people and that he was with them in their struggle. The law consisted of statutes to assure justice and equity and of ritualistic codes. Properly applied, the law was not a burden, but Jesus confronted the decadent practices that brought about injustice and suffering in direct contradiction to God's will.

Proper 18 E
Twenty-third Sunday in Ordinary Time RC
Sixteenth Sunday after Pentecost L

Old Testament: Isaiah's beautiful poem tells of God's coming to heal and save the people.

Gospel: Jesus heals the deaf man.

Religious concepts: See the fourth through seventh Sundays after Epiphany, pages 210-211, for remarks concerning the important concept of healing.

Proper 19 E
Twenty-fourth Sunday in Ordinary Time RC
Seventeenth Sunday after Pentecost L

Old Testament: The Third Song of the Servant of Yahweh speaks of the reality of suffering for the servant of God. See the discussion of this concept in chapter 2, pages 64-65.

Gospel: Peter is the first to acknowledge that Jesus is the Messiah, the one whom the Jews have been waiting for to bring in the kingdom of God. But Peter soon learns that the kind of Messiah that Jesus talks of resembles more the suffering servant described by Isaiah than the victorious warrior king expected by the Jews. Moreover, if one is to become a follower of Christ, " ... let him deny himself and take up his cross and follow me" (Mark 8:34b).

An optional gospel reading in the Episcopal lectionary is Mark 9:14-29, the story of Jesus healing the boy possessed by a demon. The disciples lacked the faith to heal the child. Jesus in his frustration says "O faithless generation, how long am I to be with you? How long am I to bear with you?" (Mark 9:19). The child's father implies a lack of faith too as he prefaces his request for healing with "If you can."

I am always struck that this story of Jesus' frustration comes immediately after the story of the transfiguration. After a moment of intense vision comes a moment of utter frustration

accompanied by a lack of faith on the part of his disciples. We may be able to identify times in our own lives when we have moved from the mountain top to a low place in our pilgrimage with the Lord.

If this story is to be heard as the gospel reading, tell it in connection with the prediction of Jesus' suffering. With the suffering servant in mind, we can talk about how the servant of the Lord identifies with the suffering of the sick and possessed. In identifying with their suffering and in being open to bear their pain, the servant is able to bring wholeness through complete faith in God.

Telling the story: Tell the story from today's gospel; then tell some of the stories of Paul found in the book of Acts. (See A Guide to Stories of the Bible, chapter 1, page 48.) Paul followed in the footsteps of Christ and told of bearing the suffering of Christ in his own body. As we suffer for truth and participate in the suffering of God's people, we too are suffering servants of the Lord. Any of the stories of Christian saints or heroes of faith who suffered for the gospel would be appropriate today. Tell stories of persons who participate in the suffering of others to bring healing into their lives. Stories of doctors, nurses, researchers in medical science who risked their lives, social workers in the ghettos, political leaders and others who have attempted to enter the struggle of the suffering would be appropriate.

Religious concepts: See chapter 2, pages 64-65, for a background of the Suffering Servant concept.

Proper 20 E
Twenty-fifth Sunday in Ordinary Time RC
Eighteenth Sunday after Pentecost L

Old Testament: One who acts and speaks the word of God is often despised. Those around such a person wish to "test him with insult and torture" (Wisdom 2:19).

The Lutheran lectionary appoints a reading from Jeremiah. The prophet feels he is "like a gentle lamb led to the slaughter" (Jeremiah 11:19). Jeremiah sees the inevitable consequences of his actions done in the name of God.

Gospel: Jesus again talks of the suffering

he knows is coming. He talks of discipleship. "If any one would be first, he must be . . . servant of all" (Mark 9:35).

Telling the story: Tell the stories of those who suffered and were rejected because they spoke the word of God. Focus on the prophets, Jesus, and the saints of the Church. Whom would we consider to be prophets in our nation's history? Some of those who spoke out for liberty and justice at the time of our nation's struggle for independence were Christians who had a deep sense of the prophetic tradition of the Bible. The framers of the Declaration of Independence saw the need for creative tension if the government was to be just. Our system of checks and balances insures this creative tension among the branches of government. Martin Luther King, Jr., certainly spoke from the prophetic tradition. His speeches were filled with biblical references coming out of his pastoral background. Some of those who disturbed us so deeply during the trying days of the Sixties saw themselves speaking from the prophet's viewpoint.

Religious concepts: Last week's Suffering Servant focus can be continued. Pick up the theme of discipleship we shared earlier in the year (pages 209 and 221) and talk about the servant role of the disciple.

Proper 21   E
Twenty-sixth Sunday in Ordinary Time   RC
Nineteenth Sunday after Pentecost   L

Old Testament: Poor old Moses cries out to the Lord. He is sick and tired of having to bear the responsibility for a bickering, complaining people. As a matter of fact, he would rather die than put up with them for another day. Now they want meat, he tells the Lord. How in the world am I going to provide that? The Lord's response is twofold. Prepare the people, the Lord tells Moses, for tomorrow they will have their meat. Assemble seventy of the elders, the Lord continues, so that some of the spirit that has rested on you may be distributed to them and they can share the burdens of leadership. The spirit does come to the seventy, but it also falls on two men who were not with the others when the spirit was received. This is reported to Moses as a possible problem, but Moses shows joy that the spirit cannot be

contained within the seventy who were assembled. "Are you jealous for my sake? Would that all the Lord's people were prophets" (Numbers 11:29), he says.

I suggested telling this story in connection with Proper 4. Even if you told this story earlier, I would repeat it today. Ask participants to join you in telling the story if they are familiar with it. This is an important narrative to share, for it gives us a sense of our own understanding of ministry. The spirit of God is a gift that the Lord offers for the leadership of the people. (This reading is appointed to be read at the ordination of priests in the Episcopal church.) Tell also the story found in Luke 10:1-19, in which Jesus sends the seventy-two followers to spread the good news among the people of the surrounding towns. "He who hears you hears me, and he who rejects you rejects me, and he who rejects me rejects him who sent me," Jesus tells them.

But there is a second important point in today's Old Testament story. The spirit of the Lord is unpredictable. Even though Eldad and Medad were not in the tent at the time of the "ordination," they could receive God's spirit. Likewise, the Holy Spirit is not restricted to the ordained priest nor to the baptized Christian. We may see the Holy Spirit's activity in places where we least expect it. Our response as Christians in the institutional church may be like that of the young man who wanted Moses to stop Eldad and Medad from prophesying because they lacked the necessary credentials of ordination! Notice the humor in verses 10 through 15. Picture yourself on a long trip with a carload of children crying out for rest stops and hamburger breaks! Then tell the story with those feelings in mind.

Gospel: The gospel story reflects the Old Testament story. John complains to Jesus as the young man in the Old Testament story complained. "Teacher, we saw a man casting out demons in your name, and we forbade him, because he was not following us" (Mark 9:38). Jesus' response is a simple one: " . . . he that is not against us is for us" (Mark 9:40). The gospel reading goes on to include sayings of Jesus that warn of the consequences of leading innocent followers of Jesus astray.

Telling the story: Tell the Old Testament

story today, along with a brief account of Jesus' sending out the seventy-two and the story of John's concern over outsiders expelling demons in Jesus' name.

Religious concepts: You will have to make a choice about the direction you want to take today in the learning community. Check with the preacher to see the approach he or she will follow in the sermon. One focus is for adolescents and adults to talk about ordination and baptism/confirmation. The laying on of hands at ordination and baptism/confirmation is the "outward and visible sign" of the gift of the Holy Spirit. The ordained ministry reflects the Old Testament reading. The Lord calls forth leaders as shepherds to the people and as leaders of his Church. The Lord also calls forth *all* Christians at their baptism to be his servants in the world. As baptized Christians we are filled with the Holy Spirit. We "belong to Christ," and "He who hears you hears me" (Mark 9:41 and Luke 10:16). We go forth as Christ's apostles or ambassadors.

But the stories we hear today also confront the Church. The Holy Spirit also rests on those outside the Church who are called by God. The Holy Spirit is present wherever healing is happening, peace is proclaimed, justice is fought for, or suffering is lifted up in love. Many times the institutional Church has blocked the action of the Holy Spirit and acted as oppressor rather than liberator. So this is a second major focus that adolescents and adults could look at today. What are the movements in history and in our own time that reflect the Spirit's presence outside the Church? How is the Holy Spirit confronting the Church in these movements? What guidelines can we use to judge where and how the Spirit is calling us?

Proper 22   E
Twenty-seventh Sunday in Ordinary Time   RC
Twentieth Sunday after Pentecost   L

Old Testament: The second creation story from Genesis establishes the origin of the marriage relationships that Jesus refers to in the gospel reading. We need to keep in mind the poetic nature of this passage as we share it in the learning community.

Gospel: Jesus' words regarding marriage and divorce are read in the context of the Old Testament reading.

Religious concepts: The Christian family and marriage are the natural focuses for this week. The Church does not take Jesus' words literally insofar as divorce is recognized in certain cases where reconciliation is impossible. It would be meaningful to have a renewal of marriage vows for persons in the parish who are celebrating their anniversaries during the summer. Use portions of the marriage liturgy as part of the liturgy of the Word this week. Encourage persons to plan the liturgy and to have a party or reception after the service. Talk about the symbols used in the liturgy, and listen for the Bible readings appointed for today as they are expressed in the marriage rite itself.

Proper 23   E
Twenty-eighth Sunday in Ordinary Time   RC
Twenty-first Sunday after Pentecost   L

Old Testament: The prophet Amos accuses the rich people of the nation. Their riches have come at the expense of the poor and at the expense of justice and integrity, he claims. Amos 5:23-27 is an indication of what God does want from his people. "But let justice roll down like waters, and righteousness like an ever-flowing stream."

The Old Testament reading in the Roman Catholic lectionary helps us understand Jesus' concern over the rich man. In his yearning for wealth, the man missed the true riches of life, which is to know the wisdom and love of the Lord; the Old Testament reading depicts a person who knows the supreme importance of wisdom. Refer to my remarks in chapter 2, pages 66-68, about the wisdom writings of the Old Testament.

Gospel: Jesus tells a rich man that he must give up all his possessions to be a follower of Jesus.

Religious concepts: To know God and to act with justice is the greatest wealth that one can possess. As we seek riches, we often do so at the expense of others. Focus this week on Christian *values* in regard to possessions and life goals. Use the Bible readings as a way of introducing a discussion about the values we see in our society. What might the prophet Amos say to us? Have the group write its own adaptation of Amos.

Proper 24   E
Twenty-ninth Sunday in Ordinary Time   RC
Twenty-second Sunday after Pentecost   L

See Propers 19 and 20, pages 225-226, for comments about today's readings.

Proper 25   E
Thirtieth Sunday in Ordinary Time   RC
Twenty-third Sunday after Pentecost   L

Old Testament: The reading from Isaiah uses blindness as an analogy of how the people of God act when they disregard the covenant and offend the Lord.

The Lutheran and Roman Catholic lectionaries appoint a joyful reading from Jeremiah this Sunday. The people in exile will return in joy to their homeland. The Lord will "gather them from the farthest parts of the earth, / among them the blind and the lame. . ." (Jeremiah 31:8). As we hear this reading we realize that the healing of the blind Bartimaeus had a deeper significance for the Jews who witnessed it than we might realize. For the followers of Jesus this was a sign of the new age that the Lord had promised through the prophets. The blind were being gathered, the lame were being healed. We need to read all of Jesus' healings in the light of this understanding.

Gospel: This important passage serves as a transition from Jesus' "roadside ministry" to his entry into Jerusalem. The blind Bartimaeus recognizes Jesus as the true Son of David, a messianic title.

Telling the story: The story of Bartimaeus could be told this Sunday along with other healing stories from the Bible. See A Guide to Stories of the Bible, chapter 1, pages 43-44, for a listing of some of the gospel accounts. In Acts 3:1-10, the disciples found that they were able to bring wholeness to persons just as Jesus did. The prophets Elijah and Elisha are remembered for healing. (See 1 Kings 17 and 2 Kings 4.) Both of these healing accounts would seem to be miracles. Introduce the stories with the preface suggested previously: "These are stories that our people have told for many years. How they have happened I cannot tell you. I share them with you in just the way they were told to me."

Religious concepts: This healing narrative carries a symbolic overlay. The Old Testament speaks of blindness. Bartimaeus sees Jesus by faith even before he sees him literally. We often use the term *blind* to refer to someone who cannot accept or comprehend the truth. When a new reality comes into our lives, we may find ourselves saying "I see it clearly now. I must have been blind all these years!" We *have* been blind in terms of that reality; our world view did not include the new truth we have discovered. But now we are sensitive to nuances we were never aware of before. Life as we perceive it and life as someone else perceives it may be entirely different. Both of us may be certain about what we perceive to be truth; until we can view the world from each other's perspective, we will be blind to that understanding of life. This is an exciting concept to share. As we discover new realities it's almost as if we sail with Columbus and discover a new world. Life is opened up to us, and we come alive in all kinds of ways through Christ.

We can show an interesting contrast between today's gospel passage and last week's. In their request for power in Christ's kingdom (Mark 10:35-45), the disciples James and John were "blind" to the true meaning of discipleship. It is Bartimaeus, sitting blind by the roadside, who can see the true power that Jesus brings into his life.

Proper 26   E
Twenty-first Sunday in Ordinary Time   RC
Twenty fourth Sunday after Pentecost   L

Old Testament: The greatest commandment is "You shall love the Lord your God. . . ." (Deuteronomy 6:4). As the notation in the New American Bible points out (page 174), "This passage contains the basic principle of the whole Mosaic law, the keynote of the Book of Deuteronomy...." This is the Shema, the statement of faith for the jew that was literally worn on the wrist and forehead.

Gospel: Jesus quotes the Shema in responding to the Scribe's question about the first of all the commandments. The Scribe's response reflects an understanding of the covenant and of the prophets. To act in love is to offer the true sacrifice to God. (See Amos 5:22,24: "Even though you offer me your burnt offerings, ... I will not accept them.... But let justice roll down like waters, / and righteousness like an ever-flowing stream.")

Religious concepts: The nature of the covenant can be seen in today's readings. Notice the strong ethical dimension of the Ten Commandments: To respond to God is to respond in love to all his creation.

We cannot love God without loving our neighbor. The First Epistle of John (4:7-21) expresses the Judeo-Christian understanding of the covenant in our actions in the community. Are the adults of our parish modeling this understanding of covenant for our children? In the light of the words we hear today, what kind of offering are we making to the Lord individually and as a parish family? Advent is approaching, with its theme of being prepared for the Lord's coming and judgment. As adolescents and adults look at the parish church through the eyes of Christ, we may be led to a deeper awareness of our need to truly prepare for the Lord's coming.

Encourage children to memorize the Shema from Deuteronomy 6. The entire Shema is found in Deuteronomy 6:4-9, Deuteronomy 11:13-21, and Numbers 15:37-41. Study the Jewish practice of literally wearing the words on the wrist and forehead. Refer to Deuteronomy 11:20, where the Israelites are enjoined to place the words on their doorposts. Each time the faithful Jew entered the house, as a sign of his faith he touched the *mezuzah* containing the Shema. Make a *mezuzah* and place it on the door of the learning community room. Directions for this project are given in *The Jewish Catalog* (Siegel, Strassfeld, and Strassfeld). Additional ones could be made to take home and place on the doorposts of participants' houses. The practice of touching the *mezuzah* on entering the house is not unlike that of Roman Catholics and some Episcopalians dipping their fingers in holy water as they enter the church. The water is the sign of the baptismal covenant we have with the Lord as Christians in much the same way that the *mezuzah* is the sign of the Mosaic covenant of which the Shema is the heart. For the next several weeks, have the children follow the custom of touching the *mezuzah* and saying the Shema at the beginning of the learning community as a way of reinforcing this concept. In churches that do not use holy water, suggest that on this Sunday the priest bless water, using the form for blessing the baptismal waters. Place the water at the entrance of the nave, and have parishioners dip their fingers in the water and make the sign of the cross. During the liturgy, remind participants of our baptismal covenant that commands us to seek justice and peace and to "love our neighbors as ourselves." The water we touch is a sign of our New Covenant just as the *mezuzah* is a sign of the Old Covenant. Make phylacteries for them to wear into the liturgical celebration. (We hear a portion of the Shema read as a part of the liturgy when Rite One of the Holy Eucharist is used in the Episcopal church.)

Proper 27   E
Thirty-second Sunday in Ordinary Time   RC
Twenty-fifth Sunday after Pentecost   L

Old Testament: The prophet Elijah provides for the poor widow who was willing to share her meager food with him.

Gospel: Jesus speaks of the widow's faith as she shares her "mite" in the Temple.

Telling the story: The prophet Elijah is an important figure. The New Testament frequently refers to him. A chair is kept for his return at the Jewish Passover meal. Tell the Elijah stories from 1 Kings 17—19, 21, and from 2 Kings 2. Miraculous powers are a part of Israel's memory of Elijah. Tell the stories as adventure stories of faith.

This would be a good week to deal with "faith response" to God's action in our lives. Use the two widow stories as a launching device to look at the way we respond to life. Are there times when we have been able to make such a faith response? Tithing and stewardship are related concepts that might lead toward the parish every-member canvass.

Proper 28   E
Thirty-third Sunday in Ordinary Time   RC
Twenty-sixth Sunday after Pentecost   L

Old Testament: A poem of apocalyptic hope points to a time of restoration for God's people ushered in by "Michael, the great prince." This is an important passage, for it is the first clear statement in the Old Testament of the hope of the resurrection. See chapter 2, pages 69-70, for a discussion of this concept.

Gospel: The gospel reading focuses on the apocalyptic words of Jesus as expressed in the Gospel of Mark. See chapter 2, page 69, for a discussion of apocalypticism. Though the Lutheran gospel reading differs from the Episcopal and Roman Catholic reading, the theme is the same.

Religious concepts: This week we deal with the concept of the future coming of Christ, or apocalypticism. Be sure to read the background discussion in chapter 2, noted above. These readings help us to enter the season of Advent, a time to prepare for the Lord's coming in power at the end of the age as well as for his coming in grace and power in the present age.

Proper 29   E
Feast of Christ the King   RC
Last Sunday after Pentecost: Christ the King   L

Old Testament: This reading from Daniel expresses in poetic terms that the Lord will be victorious. Though evil seems to be such a powerful force in the world of the writer (and in ours as well), God's kingdom will come! The figure of the "son of man" was taken by the early Church to refer to Christ. This title is often applied to Jesus in the gospels. The point of the reading is the promise that the Lord will reign. "His dominion is an everlasting dominion, which shall not pass away, / and his kingdom one that shall not be destroyed" (Daniel 7:14b). Christians see these words as applying to Christ because it is through Christ that we have come to see how God's reign is coming in our lives.

Gospel: In the reading from the Gospel of John we hear Jesus' words to Pilate. He speaks of a kind of kingship that Pilate cannot comprehend. Jesus' kingship relates directly to the reason for his being sent into the world: ". . . for this I have come into the world, to bear witness to the truth" (John 18:37). The Episcopal lectionary offers an optional gospel reading from Mark that describes Jesus' triumphal entry into Jerusalem. He comes into Jerusalem and is hailed as the new king. His first actions in Jerusalem sound like that of a king. He "looked round at everything" before returning to Bethany for the night. The next day he entered the Temple and cleansed it of the money changers and sellers who were abusing their privilege there.

Jesus' actions were symbolic or parabolic. He entered the city as a victorious king in order to claim it as the Lord. This action symbolized the new age that had been announced by the prophets of old. Zechariah had talked of the day when the people's king would come "triumphant and victorious, . . . humble and riding on an ass, on a colt the foal of an ass" (Zechariah 9:9). The same prophet closed his writings with the statement that on the triumphant day of the Lord's final victory ". . . there shall no longer be a trader in the house of the Lord of hosts. . ." (Zechariah 14:21). From this Old Testament background we see that Jesus was dramatizing the words of the prophets. These symbolic dramatizations were not lost on the people. They recognized the radical proclamation of his true kingship in the Lord's name. Jesus' triumphal entry was the Lord's triumphant entry into his city to be at last a shepherd to his people.

This reading from Mark relates to the passage from John discussed above. In both readings the new kingdom that Jesus speaks of exists far and above the limited kingship that Pontius Pilate represented. It was the kingship of the Lord himself coming in the final times to herald the defeat of evil in a world that had been created by God for good. The words from the Gospel of John should not be interpreted as meaning that Jesus had nothing to do with this world and was concerned only with the spiritual world. The two men who faced each other that day at the praetorium represented two different kingdoms. That of Pontius Pilate was a human kingship, existing only by the grace of God for a moment in time. That of Jesus was the kingship of God, existing beyond time and space to all eternity; a kingship that will have no end and that will triumph over evil and chaos. Jesus' coming was the beginning of that kingship that is being worked out even now in our own time.

These are the hopeful and powerful words that lead us into the first Sunday of Advent, a New Year's Day in the church year. Next Sunday we prepare for the fullness of that kingdom to appear. The day has dawned, but the sun is not yet full in the sky. How shall we dwell in the full brightness of that sun? How can we prepare ourselves to stand in the full revelation of that light?

For further ideas on today's theme, see my comments for Year C, chapter 7, page 268.

Chapter 7
A Commentary
on the Eucharistic Lectionary,
Year C

Use the following list to see which Bible passages the commentary is referring to in discussing a given Sunday or feast day. To discover the *calendar* date of a day, consult your own church calendar or liturgy expert.

Despite minor differences and occasional local variations, there is now substantial agreement among Episcopalians, Roman Catholics, and Lutherans (and some other churches as well) on the scriptural readings assigned for Sundays and greater feast days. In the following list, then, assume that the readings are the same for the three churches unless variants are noted. (Notice how minor many variants are—simply a few verses added or omitted.)

Terms for a day or a season may differ. For instance, what Episcopalians and Lutherans call the Sundays after Pentecost are called Sundays in Ordinary Time (or Sundays of the Year) by Roman Catholics; Episcopalians designate the readings and prayers proper to those Sundays as Proper 1, Proper 2, and so on, indicating in *The Book of Common Prayer* that Proper 11, for instance, is used on the Sunday nearest to July 20. In the following list, terms or observances peculiar to Episcopalians, Roman Catholics, or Lutherans are designated **E, RC,** or **L.**

A sample entry, 1 Cor 10:16-17(18-21), refers to First Corinthians, chapter 10, verses 16-17, with verses 18-21 optional.

Note that the psalms assigned as responses to the readings are not listed here, since this book deals primarily with the readings themselves. Nevertheless, the psalm responses are an important part of the total worship experience, and every effort should be made to familiarize our congregations with them. See Appendix I for comments on psalms that are particularly appropriate for the religious education setting.

A list of the abbreviations used for books of the Bible is found on page 140.

Lectionary Readings for Sundays and Greater Feasts in Year C

Sunday or Feast	Episcopal*	Roman Catholic†	Lutheran‡
1st Sun. of Advent	Zech 14:4-9 1 Thes 3:9-13 Lk 21:25-31	Jer 33:14-16 1 Thes 3:12—4:2 Lk 21:25-28,34-36	Jer 33:14-16 1 Thes 3:9-13 Lk 21:25-36 or Lk 19:28-40
2nd Sun. of Advent	Bar 5:1-9 Phlp 1:1-11 Lk 3:1-6	Bar 5:1-9 Phlp 1:4-6,8-11	Mal 3:1-4 Phlp 1:3-11
3rd Sun. of Advent	Zeph 3:14-20 Phlp 4:4-7(8-9) Lk 3:7-18	Zeph 3:14-18 Phlp 4:4-7 Lk 3:10-18	Zeph 3:14-18a Phlp 4:4-7(8-9) Lk 3:7-18
4th Sun. of Advent	Mic 5:2-4 Heb 10:5-10 Lk 1:39-49(50-56)	Mic 5:1-4 Lk 1:39-45	Mic 5:2-4 Lk 1:39-45(46-55)
Christmas Vigil **RC**	*§	Isa 62:1-5 Acts 13:16-17,22-25 Mtt 1:1-25	*§
Christmas Day I **E**; Mass at Midnight **RC**; Option 1 **L**	Isa 9:2-4,6-7 Titus 2:11-14 Lk 2:1-14(15-20)	Isa 9:1-6 Lk 2:1-14	Isa 9:2-7 Lk 2:1-20
Christmas Day II **E**; Mass at Dawn **RC**; Option 2 **L**	Isa 62:6-7,10-12 Titus 3:4-7 Lk 2:(1-14)15-20	Isa 62:11-12 Titus 3:4-7 Lk 2:15-20	Isa 52:7-10 Heb 1:1-9 Jn 1:1-14
Christmas Day III **E**; Mass during the Day **RC**; Option 3 **L**	Isa 52:7-10 Heb 1:1-12 Jn 1:1-14	Isa 52:7-10 Heb 1:1-6 Jn 1:1-18	Isa 62:10-12 Titus 3:4-7 Lk 2:1-20

1st Sun. after
  Christmas **E, L**;
Sun. in Octave of
  Christmas (Holy
  Family) **RC**
	Isa 61:10—62:3
	Gal 3:23-25;4:4-7
	Jn 1:1-18
		Ecclus 3:2-6,12-14
		Col 3:12-21
		Lk 2:41-52
			Jer 31:10-13
			Heb 2:10-18
			Lk 2:41-52

The Book of Common Prayer and Administration of the Sacraments and Other Rites and Ceremonies of the Church (New York: The Church Hymnal Corporation and The Seabury Press, 1979).
†*Lectionary for Mass* (New York: Catholic Book Publishing, 1970).
‡*Lutheran Book of Worship* (Minneapolis, Minn.: Augsburg Publishing, 1978).
*§Episcopal and Lutheran lectionaries do not have this service.

Sunday or Feast	Episcopal	Roman Catholic	Lutheran
Holy Name (Jan.1) **E**; Mary, Mother of God **RC**; Name of Jesus **L**	Ex 34:1-8 Rom 1:1-7 Lk 2:15-21	Num 6:22-27 Gal 4:4-7 Lk 2:16-21	Num 6:22-27 Rom 1:1-7 or Phlp 2:9-13 Lk 2:21
2nd Sun. after Christmas	Jer 31:7-14 Eph 1:3-6,15-19a Mtt 2:13-15,19-23 or Lk 2:41-52 or Mtt 2:1-12	Ecclus 24:1-4,8-12 Eph 1:3-6,15-18 Jn 1:1-18	Isa 61:10—62:3 Eph 1:3-6,15-18 Jn 1:1-18
The Epiphany	Isa 60:1-6,9 Eph 3:1-12 Mtt 2:1-12	Isa 60:1-6 Eph 3:2-3,5-6	Isa 60:1-6 Eph 3:2-12
1st Sun. after Epiphany **E, L**; Baptism of the Lord **RC**	Isa 42:1-9 Acts 10:34-38 Lk 3:15-16,21-22	Isa 42:1-4,6-7	Isa 42:1-7
2nd Sun. after Epiphany **E, L**; 2nd Sun. Ord. Time **RC**	Isa 62:1-5 1 Cor 12:1-11 Jn 2:1-11	1 Cor 12:4-11 Jn 2:1-12	1 Cor 12:1-11 Jn 2:1-11
3rd Sun. after Epiphany **E, L**; 3rd Sun. Ord. Time **RC**	Neh 8:2-10 1 Cor 12:12-27 Lk 4:14-21	Neh 8:2-10 1 Cor 12:12-30 Lk 1:1-4;4:14-21	Isa 61:1-6 1 Cor 12:12-21,26-27 Lk 4:14-21
4th Sun. after Epiphany **E, L**; 4th Sun. Ord. Time **RC**	Jer 1:4-10 1 Cor 14:12b-20 Lk 4:21-32	Jer 1:4-5,17-19 1 Cor 12:31—13:13 Lk 4:21-30	Jer 1:4-10 1 Cor 12:27—13:13 Lk 4:21-32
5th Sun. after Epiphany **E, L**; 5th Sun. Ord. Time **RC**	Judges 6:11-24a 1 Cor 15:1-11 Lk 5:1-11	Isa 6:1-8 1 Cor 15:1-11	Isa 6:1-8(9-13) 1 Cor 14:12b-20
6th Sun. after Epiphany **E, L**; 6th Sun. Ord. Time **RC**	Jer 17:5-10 1 Cor 15:12-20 Lk 6:17-26	Jer 17:5-8 1 Cor 15:12,16-20 Lk 6:17,20-26	Jer 17:5-8 1 Cor 15:12,16-20 Lk 6:17-26
7th Sun. after Epiphany **E, L**; 7th Sun. Ord. Time **RC**	Gen 45:3-11,21-28 1 Cor 15:35-38,42-50 Lk 6:27-38	1 Sam 26:2,7-9,12-13, 22-23 1 Cor 15:45-49	Gen 45:3-8a 1 Cor 15:35-38a,42-50
8th Sun. after Epiphany **E, L** 8th Sun. Ord. Time **RC**	Jer 7:1-7(8-15) 1 Cor 15:50-58 Lk 6:39-49	Ecclus 27:4-7 1 Cor 15:54-58 Lk 6:39-45	Jer 7:1-7(8-15) 1 Cor 15:51-58 Lk 6:39-49
Last Sun. after Epiphany **E, L**	Ex 34:29-35 1 Cor 12:27—13:13 Lk 9:28-36	*	Deut 34:1-12 2 Cor 4:3-6

*The Roman Catholic lectionary does not use this designation.

Sunday or Feast	Episcopal	Roman Catholic	Lutheran
Ash Wednesday	Joel 2:1-2,12-17 or Isa 58:1-12 2 Cor 5:20b—6:10 Mtt 6:1-6,16-21	Joel 2:12-18 2 Cor 5:20—6:2 Mtt 6:1-6,16-18	Joel 2:12-19 2 Cor 5:20b—6:2 Mtt 6:1-6,16-21
1st Sun. in Lent	Deut 26:(1-4)5-11 Rom 10:(5-8a)8b-13 Lk 4:1-13	Deut 26:4-10 Rom 10:8-13	Deut 26:5-10 Rom 10:8b-13
2nd Sun. in Lent	Gen 15:1-12,17-18 Phlp 3:17—4:1 Lk 13:(22-30)31-35	Gen 15:5-12,17-18 Lk 9:28-36	Jer 26:8-15 Lk 13:31-35
3rd Sun. in Lent	Ex 3:1-15 1 Cor 10:1-13 Lk 13:1-9	Ex 3:1-8,13-15 1 Cor 10:1-6,10-12	Ex 3:1-8b,10-15 1 Cor 10:1-13
4th Sun. in Lent	Josh (4:19-24);5:9-12 2 Cor 5:17-21 Lk 15:11-32	Josh 5:9-12 2 Cor 5:17-21 Lk 15:1-3,11-32	Isa 12:1-6 1 Cor 1:18-31 or 1 Cor 1:18,22-25 Lk 15:1-3,11-32
5th Sun. in Lent	Isa 43:16-21 Phlp 3:8-14 Lk 20:9-19	Jn 8:1-11	Lk 20:9-19
Palm Sunday (Liturgy of the Palms)	Lk 19:29-40	Lk 19:28-40	*

Palm Sunday (at the
Eucharist)
	Isa 45:21-25
	  or Isa 52:13—53:12
	Phlp 2:5-11
	Lk (22:39-71)
	  23:1-49(50-56)
		Isa 50:4-7
		
		Phlp 2:6-11
		Lk 22:14—23:56
			Deut 32:36-39
			
			Phlp 2:5-11
			Lk 22:1—23:56
			  or Lk 23:1-49

Easter Vigil **E, RC**	Gen 1:1—2:2 Gen 7:1-5,11-18; 8:6-18;9:8-13 Gen 22:1-18 Ex 14:10—15:1 Isa 4:2-6 Isa 55:1-11 Ezk 36:24-28 Ezk 37:1-14 Zeph 3:12-20 Rom 6:3-11 Mtt 28:1-10	Gen 1:1—2:2 Gen 22:1-18 Ex 14:15—15:1 Isa 54:5-14 Isa 55:1-11 Bar 3:9-15,32—4:4 Ezk 36:16-28 Rom 6:3-11 Lk 24:1-12	*

*The Lutheran lectionary does not have this service.

Sunday or Feast	Episcopal	Roman Catholic	Lutheran
Easter Day, Principal Service	Acts 10:34-43 or Isa 51:9-11 Col 3:1-4 or Acts 10:34-43 Lk 24:1-10	Acts 10:34,37-43 Col 3:1-4 or 1 Cor 5:6-8 Jn 20:1-9 or Lk 24:1-12	Ex 15:1-11 or Ps 118:14-24 1 Cor 15:1-11 Lk 24:1-11 or Jn 20:1-9(10-18)
2nd Sun. of Easter	Acts 5:12a,17-22, 25-29 or Job 42:1-6 Rev 1:(1-8)9-19 or Acts 5:12a, 17-22,25-29 Jn 20:19-31	Acts 5:12-16 ** Rev 1:9-13,17-19	Acts 5:12,17-32 ** Rev 1:4-18
3rd Sun. of Easter	Acts 9:1-19a or Jer 32:36-41 Rev 5:6-14 or Acts 9:1-19a Jn 21:1-14	Acts 5:27-32,40-41 Rev 5:11-14 Jn 21:1-19	Acts 9:1-20 Rev 5:11-14 Jn 21:1- 14
4th Sun. of Easter	Acts 13:15-16, 26-33(34-39) or Num 27:12-23 Rev 7:9-17 or Acts 13:15-16, 26-33(34-39) Jn 10:22-30	Acts 13:14,43-52 Rev 7:9,14-17 Jn 10:27-30	Acts 13:15-16a,26-33 Rev 7:9-17 Jn 10:22-30
5th Sun. of Easter	Acts 13:44-52 or Lev 19:1-2,9-18 Rev 19:1,4-9 or Acts 13:44-52 Jn 13:31-35	Acts 14:21-27 Rev 21:1-5	Acts 13:44-52 Rev 21:1-5
6th Sun. of Easter	Acts 14:8-18 or Joel 2:21-27 Rev 21:22—22:5 or Acts 14:8-18 Jn 14:23-29	Acts 15:1-2,22-29 Rev 21:10-14,22-23	Acts 14:8-18 Rev 21:10-14,22-23
Ascension Day	Acts 1:1-11 or 2 K 2:1-15 Eph 1:15-23 or Acts 1:1-11 Lk 24:49-53 or Mk 16:9-15,19-20	Acts 1:1-11 Eph 1:17-23 Lk 24:46-53	Acts 1:1-11 Eph 1:16-23 Lk 24:44-53

**Roman Catholic and Lutheran lectionaries have no Old Testament lesson during the Easter season.

Sunday or Feast	Episcopal	Roman Catholic	Lutheran

7th Sun. of Easter	Acts 16:16-34 or
	  1 Sam 12:19-24
	Rev 22:12-14,
	  16-17,20 or
	  Acts 16:16-34
	Jn 17:20-26
		Acts 7:55-60
		
		Rev 22:12-14,16-17,20
			Acts 16:6-10
			
			Rev 22:12-17,20

Day of Pentecost	Acts 2:1-11 or
	  Joel 2:28-32
	1 Cor 12:4-13 or
	  Acts 2:1-11
	Jn 20:19-23 or
	  Jn 14:8-17
		Acts 2:1-11
		
		1 Cor 12:3-7,12-13
		
		Jn 20:19-23
			Gen 11:1-9
			
			Acts 2:1-21
			
			Jn 15:26-27;16:4b-11

Trinity Sunday	Isa 6:1-8 Rev 4:1-11 Jn 16:(5-11)12-15	Prov 8:22-31 Rom 5:1-5 Jn 16:12-15	Prov 8:22-31 Rom 5:1-5 Jn 16:12-15

Proper 4 **E**;
9th Sun. Ord. Time **RC**;
2nd Sun. after
  Pentecost **L**
	1 K 8:22-23,27-30,
	  41-43
	Gal 1:1-10
	Lk 7:1-10
		1 K 8:41-43
		
		Gal 1:1-2,6-10
			1 K 8:(22-23,27-30)
			  41-43
			Gal 1:1-10

Proper 5 **E**; 10th Sun. Ord. Time **RC**; 3rd Sun. after Pentecost **L**	1 K 17:17-24 Gal 1:11-24 Lk 7:11-17	Gal 1:11-19	Gal 1:11-24

Proper 6 **E**;
11th Sun. Ord. Time **RC**;
4th Sun. after
  Pentecost **L**
	2 Sam 11:26—12:10,
	  13-15
	Gal 2:11-21
	Lk 7:36-50
		2 Sam 12:7-10,13
		
		Gal 2:16,19-21
		Lk 7:36—8:3
			2 Sam 11:26—12:10,
			  13-15
			Gal 2:11-21
			Lk 7:36-50

Proper 7 **E**; 12th Sun. Ord. Time **RC**; 5th Sun. after Pentecost **L**	Zech 12:8-10;13:1 Gal 3:23-29 Lk 9:18-24	Zech 12:10-11 Gal 3:26-29	Zech 12:7-11 Gal 3:23-29
Proper 8 **E**; 13th Sun. Ord. Time **RC**; 6th Sun. after Pentecost **L**	1 K 19:15-16,19-21 Gal 5:1,13-25 Lk 9:51-62	1 K 19:16,19-21 Gal 5:1,13-18	1 K 19:14-21 Gal 5:1,13-25
Proper 9 **E**; 14th Sun. Ord. Time **RC**; 7th Sun. after Pentecost **L**	Isa 66:10-16 Gal 6:(1-10)14-18 Lk 10:1-12,16-20	Isa 66:10-14 Gal 6:14-18 Lk 10:1-12,17-20	Isa 66:1-11,14-18 Gal 6:1-10,14-16 Lk 10:1-12,16(17-20)
Proper 10 **E**; 15th Sun. Ord. Time **RC**; 8th Sun. after Pentecost **L**	Deut 30:9-14 Col 1:1-14 Lk 10:25-37	Deut 30:10-14 Col 1:15-20	Deut 30:9-14 Col 1:1-14

Sunday or Feast	Episcopal	Roman Catholic	Lutheran
Proper 11 E; 16th Sun. Ord. Time **RC**; 9th Sun. after Pentecost **L**	Gen 18:1-10a(10b-14) Col 1:21-29 Lk 10:38-42	Gen 18:1-10 Col 1:24-28	Gen 18:1-10a(10b-14) Col 1:21-28
Proper 12 E; 17th Sun. Ord. Time **RC**; 10th Sun. after Pentecost **L**	Gen 18:20-33 Col 2:6-15 Lk 11:1-13	Gen 18:20-32 Col 2:12-14	Gen 18:20-32 Col 2:6-15

Proper 13 E;
18th Sun. Ord. Time **RC**;
11th Sun. after
  Pentecost **L**
	Eccles 1:12-14;
	  2:(1-7,11)18-23
	Col 3:(5-11)12-17
	Lk 12:13-21
		Eccles 1:2;2:21-23
		
		Col 3:1-5,9-11
			Eccles 1:2;2:18-26
			
			Col 3:1-11

Proper 14 E; 19th Sun. Ord. Time **RC**; 12th Sun. after Pentecost **L**	Gen 15:1-6 Heb 11:1-3(4-7)8-16 Lk 12:32-40	Wis 18:6-9 Heb 11:1-2,8-19 Lk 12:32-48	Gen 15:1-6 Heb 11:1-3,8-16 Lk 12:32-40
Proper 15 E; 20th Sun. Ord. Time **RC**; 13th Sun. after Pentecost **L**	Jer 23:23-29 Heb 12:1-7(8-10)11-14 Lk 12:49-56	Jer 38:4-6,8-10 Heb 12:1-4 Lk 12:49-53	Jer 23:23-29 Heb 12:1-13 Lk 12:49-53
Proper 16E; 21st Sun. Ord. Time **RC**; 14th Sun. after Pentecost **L**	Isa 28:14-22 Heb 12:18-19,22-29 Lk 13:22-30	Isa 66:18-21 Heb 12:5-7,11-13	Isa 66:18-23 Heb 12:18-24
Proper 17 E; 22nd Sun. Ord. Time 15th Sun. after Pentecost **L**	Ecclus 10:(7-11)12-18 Heb 13:1-8 Lk 14:1,7-14	Ecclus 3:17-18,20,28-29 Heb 12:18-19,22-24	Prov 25:6-7 Heb 13:1-8
Proper 18 E; 23rd Sun. Ord. Time **RC**; 16th Sun. after Pentecost **L**	Deut 30:15-20 Phm 1-20 Lk 14:25-33	Wis 9:13-18 Phm 9-10,12-17	Prov 9:8-12 Phm 1(2-9)10-21
Proper 19 E; 24th Sun. Ord. Time **RC**; 17th Sun. after Pentecost **L**	Ex 32:1,7-14 1 Tim 1:12-17 Lk 15:1-10	Ex 32:7-11,13-14 Lk 15:1-32	Ex 32:7-14 Lk 15:1-10
Proper 20 E; 25th Sun. Ord. Time 18th Sun. after Pentecost **L**	Amos 8:4-7(8-12) 1 Tim 2:1-8 Lk 16:1-13	Amos 8:4-7	Amos 8:4-7
Proper 21 E; 26th Sun. Ord. Time **RC**; 19th Sun. after Pentecost **L**	Amos 6:1-7 1 Tim 6:11-19 Lk 16:19-31	Amos 6:1,4-7 1 Tim 6:11-16	Amos 6:1-7 1 Tim 6:6-16

Sunday or Feast	Episcopal	Roman Catholic	Lutheran

Proper 22 **E**;
27th Sun. Ord. Time **RC**;
20th Sun. after
  Pentecost **L**
	Hab 1:1-6(7-11)
	  12-13;2:1-4
	2 Tim 1:(1-5)6-14
	Lk 17:5-10
		Hab 1:2-3;2:2-4
		
		2 Tim 1:6-8,13-14
		Lk 17:5-10
			Hab 1:1-3;2:1-4
			
			2 Tim 1:3-14
			Lk 17:1-10

Proper 23 **E**; 28th Sun. Ord. Time **RC**; 21st Sun. after Pentecost **L**	Ruth 1:(1-7)8-19a 2 Tim 2:(3-7)8-15 Lk 17:11-19	2 K 5:14-17 2 Tim 2:8-13	Ruth 1:1-19a 2 Tim 2:8-13
Proper 24 **E**; 29th Sun. Ord. Time **RC**; 22nd Sun. after Pentecost **L**	Gen 32:3-8,22-30 2 Tim 3:14—4:5 Lk 18:1-8a	Ex 17:8-13 2 Tim 3:14—4:2	Gen 32:22-30 2 Tim 3:14—4:5
Proper 25 **E**; 30th Sun. Ord. Time **RC**; 23rd Sun. after Pentecost **L**	Jer 14:(1-6)7-10,19-22 2 Tim 4:6-8,16-18 Lk 18:9-14	Ecclus 35:12-14,16-18	Deut 10:12-22

Proper 26 **E**;
31st Sun. Ord. Time **RC**;
24th Sun. after
  Pentecost **L**
	Isa 1:10-20
	2 Thes 1:1-5
	  (6-10)11-12
	Lk 19:1-10
		Wis 11:22—12:1
		2 Thes 1:11—2:2
			Ex 34:5-9
			2 Thes 1:1-5,11-12

Proper 27 **E**; 32nd Sun. Ord. Time **RC**; 25th Sun. after Pentecost **L**	Job 19:23-27a 2 Thes 2:13—3:5 Lk 20:27(28-33)34-38	2 Mac 7:1-2,9-14 2 Thes 2:16—3:5 Lk 20:27-38	1 Chr 29:10-13 2 Thes 2:13—3:5 Lk 20:27-38
Proper 28 **E**; 33rd Sun. Ord. Time **RC**; 26th Sun. after Pentecost **L**	Mal 3:13—4:2a,5-6 2 Thes 3:6-13 Lk 21:5-19	Mal 3:19-20 2 Thes 3:7-12	Mal 4:1-2a 2 Thes 3:6-13
27th Sun. after Pentecost **L**	*	*	Isa 52:1-6 1 Cor 15:54-58 Lk 19:11-27

Proper 29 **E**;
Last Sun. Ord. Time
  (Feast of Christ the
  King) **RC**;
Last Sun. after
  Pentecost (Christ
  the King) **L**
	Jer 23:1-6
	Col 1:11-20
	Lk 23:35-42 or
	  Lk 19:29-38
		2 Sam 5:1-3
		Col 1:12-20
		Lk 23:35-43
			Jer 23:2-6
			Col 1:13-20
			Lk 23:35-43

*Episcopal and Roman Catholic lectionaries do not have this designation.

The Season of Advent

See the comments on Advent in chapters 5 and 6, pages 148 and 206, for background on this season.

The Gospel of Luke makes the point that through the Holy Spirit, Christ's second coming has already begun.

The Old Testament Readings

First Sunday of Advent

On the "day of the Lord," Israel will be restored after a time of suffering. The writer uses the beautiful language of poetry to describe a day of perfection and complete oneness with God. "And the Lord will become king over all the earth; on that day the Lord will be one and his name one" (Zechariah 14:9). (Notice the theme of the Lord as king. Chapter 7, page 268, will be helpful on this theme.)

In the Roman Catholic and Lutheran lectionaries the Old Testament reading says that the Lord will "cause a righteous Branch to spring forth for David; and he shall execute justice and righteousness in the land" (Jeremiah 33:15). This reading reminds us that Jesus was a descendant of King David, who was a son of Jesse. The Jesse-tree tradition is important to share during Advent. It represents Jesus' family tree, but instead of showing the names of his ancestors, the tree is decorated with the symbols of the stories of his heritage. As the tree is decorated during the course of the season, we display Jacob's ladder, Noah's ark, the apple of Adam, and other Old Testament symbols. Today's reading could be used to introduce the Jesse-tree tradition. (See chapter 6, page 207.)

Second Sunday of Advent

The reading from the Book of Baruch is similar to last week's reading from Zechariah. All the valleys will be raised and the mountains lowered "so that Israel may walk safely in the glory of God" (Baruch 5:7). This is powerful poetry that provides us with images of the perfect day of the Lord. The Lord will provide his people with a smooth highway leading them back to their own land from the Babylonian captivity. How would the participants in our learning community describe a "perfect day of the Lord"? It might be a day when all the ball games are won or a day when everyone acts with love. Let children also share their ideas about that "perfect day." Record the ideas as they are shared, and then make up your own poetic prophecy of hope. This poetry could be shared as a part of the Liturgy of the Word at the Eucharist.

The Lutheran Old Testament reading says "Behold, I send my messenger to prepare the way before me" (Malachi 3:1a). This reading prepares us to hear the story of John the Baptist in today's gospel reading.

Third Sunday of Advent

The theme of the first two weeks is carried on with this week's selection from Zephaniah. "On that day" the people of God will be restored. "The Lord, your God, is in your midst" (Zephaniah 3:17a).

Fourth Sunday of Advent

The words of hope focus on one who is to be born in Bethlehem and who will bring in the day of peace when all nations will look to Jerusalem.

The Gospel Readings

First Sunday of Advent

The season of Advent is launched in Year C with the apocalyptic writings from Luke. (See chapter 2, pages 63 and 69, on apocalypticism.) These are times of expectant waiting, Luke reminds his readers. We must not grow tired or lazy but be ready and alert, able to read the signs of the times. Everything that happens, including suffering and trauma, has significance in understanding God's presence and activity in creation. The parable of the fig tree is a part of the reading. As we see trees begin to leaf, we know that summer is coming. And so it is with the coming of Christ: We see signs in history and creation that God is acting to bring creation to fruition. As usual in apocalyptic writings, we deal here with the language of poetic truth, not literal truth. Hence it is futile to tie symbols to actual historical events in attempting to predict, for example, the exact date of Christ's second coming.

The Lutheran lectionary offers an alternative gospel reading: the account of Jesus' messianic entry into Jerusalem that we hear also on Palm Sunday. Though the reading may seem strangely out of place at the beginning of Advent, it was traditionally used in the Episcopal church because in Advent we look ahead to that final time when Jesus will enter triumphantly into his world to redeem all creation.

Second Sunday of Advent
John the Baptist is a key symbol of Advent preparation. The prophet Isaiah is quoted to show how John is preparing the people for Christ's coming. When the Jews were held captive in Babylonia, they built roads for their captors. A day would come, Isaiah wrote, when they would build a highway for their God to prepare the way for his coming. Valleys would be filled in, and hills would be lowered for the "king's highway." In similar fashion, the Church says today, John the Baptist is calling on us to prepare a road so that Christ can come. Since we are a road-building nation, this makes good imagery for the religious education setting. Begin to tell the story of John the Baptist today in the learning community.

Third Sunday of Advent
The story of John the Baptist is continued from last week. John gives directions to those who come to him and tells them that he is not the Messiah. He points beyond himself to Jesus, who is to come.

Fourth Sunday of Advent
On the Sunday before Christmas we prepare to celebrate the birth of Jesus by noting the coming birth of his forerunner. In this prebirth story, Mary visits Elizabeth, the mother-to-be of John the Baptist. The reading contains the beautiful Magnificat that we may know from the Morning and Evening Prayer liturgy. Note the radical words: "He has scattered the proud in the imagination of their hearts, / he has put down the mighty from their thrones, / and exalted those of low degree" (Luke 1:51-52). These words, though referring generally to God's actions in history, accurately describe the life of Jesus.

We need to look this week at the humbleness of Jesus' birth and realize again how radical his life was. This passage contains words that threaten the social order and the accepted values of society. Jesus called into question the social order and the accepted values in almost everything he said and did. What does that say to us in our day? The words of the Christmas story are so familiar and so filled with nostalgic memories that we can easily forget their power to call our lives into question. Christ calls for radical change in our individual lives and in society. His call is a part of the Christmas proclamation and is the reason for the penitential tone of Advent.

The Epistle Readings

First Sunday of Advent
The epistle selections for the first two Sundays were written for a people who were waiting for Christ to return. Paul prayed for the people of Thessalonica that ". . . the Lord make you increase and abound in love to one another and to all men . . . so that he may establish your hearts unblamable in holiness before our God and Father, at the coming of our Lord Jesus with all his saints" (1 Thessalonians 3:12-13).

Second Sunday of Advent
Paul writes to the people of Philippi with the same concern that we heard expressed in last week's epistle reading. The people must always be ready for "the Day of Christ" which can come at any time. This concern lies at the heart of Advent. If we are to be true to the Advent season we must emphasize the Second Coming of Christ before we move to the first coming in Bethlehem. As background for this reading, you may want to share the story of Paul's life in Philippi found in the 16th chapter of Acts.

Third Sunday of Advent
We move from the beginning to the ending of the letter to the Philippians. Paul concludes his letter with instructions for the people living in expectation of Christ's coming. "Rejoice in the Lord always. . . ." Familiar words will be heard in this reading, as they are often said in a blessing: ". . . the peace of God, which passes all

understanding, will keep your hearts and your minds in Christ Jesus."

Fourth Sunday of Advent

The sacrifices by the priest in the Temple did not restore the people and bring them into oneness with God. Rather, it is the perfect offering of Christ that restores us. Jesus came to do the will of God perfectly. In that perfect obedience and in his suffering and death, he overcame the power of evil that separates us from God. Though we still fall into evil, we now have in Christ a bridge back to God. This is a complicated theological concept for youth to grasp. The important point to make for participants of all ages is that God's love is far more powerful than any evil, as Romans 8:38-39 makes clear: "For I am sure that neither death, nor life, nor angels, nor principalities, nor things present, nor things to come, nor powers, nor height, nor depth, nor anything else in all creation, will be able to separate us from the love of God in Christ Jesus our Lord." This reading from Romans sets the framework for understanding the celebration of Christmas this week. We celebrate far more than the birth of a baby in the manger. We celebrate the birth of the realization that nothing "will be able to separate us from the love of God."

The Season of Christmas

See chapter 5, page 152.

The Season of Epiphany

The remarks about the season in connection with Year A, page 156, apply to Year C as well. The Feast of the Epiphany is January 6. The Feast of Lights service mentioned in chapter 4, pages 103-105, is a beautiful tradition that will help convey the concept of Christ being the "light of the world." It will also reinforce the idea that we are called to spread that light in the world.

First Sunday after Epiphany   E, L
Baptism of the Lord   RC
This Sunday recalls the baptism of Jesus. The Old Testament reading is the first of the four so-called suffering servant songs from Isaiah. It describes the true servant of the Lord. "I have taken you by the hand and kept you; / I have given you as a covenant to the people, / a light to the nations, / to open the eyes that are blind, / to bring out the prisoners from the dungeon, / from the prison those who sit in darkness" (Isaiah 42:6b-7). The second reading describes the ministry of Jesus. Good news was proclaimed. Jesus was anointed by the Holy Spirit with power so that healing occurred. People were released from the oppression of evil. The reading from Luke describes the baptism of Jesus. With the readings for a background, we have a firm basis for discussing the meaning of baptism. Baptism is commitment to be "a light to the nations." We are called to be a part of the healing, liberating mission of God. We are empowered by the Holy Spirit to act. There is strong emphasis on liberation in these readings. We are enslaved. God calls us to be free and to bring freedom to others. See chapter 4, pages 105-107, for suggestions about sharing the baptism theme in the church school. This Sunday would be an appropriate time to celebrate baptisms in the parish.

Second Sunday after Epiphany   E, L
Second Sunday in Ordinary Time   RC
We need to keep the Epiphany theme in mind as we focus on this Sunday's readings. Christ begins

to reveal or manifest (or "epiphany") his power in the early chapters of the gospels. After his baptism, he goes forth, calls disciples, and begins to speak and heal. He "shows himself" to people. They are touched by his words and acts. The Gospel of John, as has been mentioned, is the poetic interpretation of these acts. In today's readings Jesus' power is shown in a miracle: Water is changed into wine at a wedding feast. The story symbolizes that Jesus turned the common struggles of life into celebrations and joy. It also expresses the sacredness of marriage in the eyes of God. Jesus was at a wedding, and his living presence in all relationships of love is expressed in this act. The Old Testament reading reminds us that the Bible frequently uses the analogy of marriage to express the relationship between God and his people. The Church is the bride of Christ.

Talk about marriage today in the learning community. Study the wedding customs of Jesus' time to better appreciate the significance of the parables and of the Old Testament references to weddings and marriage. Talk about the Church's wedding liturgy. Note the reference to the marriage feast at Cana in the introduction to the wedding liturgy (*The Book of Common Prayer,* page 423).

The epistle readings for Epiphany come from 1 Corinthians. Today's lesson talks about the various gifts we receive as Christians. "Now there are varieties of gifts, but the same Spirit; and there are varieties of service, but the same Lord; and there are varieties of working, but it is the same God who inspires them all in every one" (1 Corinthians 12:4-6). We recognize and affirm these diverse gifts of ministry that we *all* are given at baptism.

Third Sunday after Epiphany   E, L
Third Sunday in Ordinary Time   RC
We return to the Gospel of Luke today. Jesus goes into a synagogue, reads from the prophet Isaiah, and announces: "Today this scripture has been fulfilled in your hearing." (The Lutheran Old Testament selection is the Isaiah passage that Jesus reads.) The Old Testament reading from Nehemiah describes a covenant renewal ceremony after the Jews had returned from exile in

Babylonia. The scribe Ezra reads the law to the people. "And Ezra opened the book in the sight of all the people, . . . and when he opened it all the people stood. And Ezra blessed the Lord, the great God; and all the people answered, 'Amen, Amen,' lifting up their hands; and they bowed their heads and worshiped the Lord with their faces to the ground" (Nehemiah 8:5-6).

Both Jesus and Nehemiah saw their own actions in the light of Scripture. Jesus saw himself as fulfilling an Old Testament prophecy; Nehemiah brought the people back into living contact with the word of Scripture and made it operative in their lives by calling on the people to renew the covenant their ancestors had made with God—a covenant recorded in Scripture.

Today, then, would be a good time to focus on how important the Bible is, pointing out how God has worked in our history, and to emphasize that he continues to be present and active in our lives today. Like Jesus, we are called to fulfill God's prophecies of a new age; like Nehemiah and the Jewish people, we are continually called upon to renew our covenant with God, to live out our own story recorded in the Scriptures.

No small part of our heritage consists of the rich biblical traditions that are a part of our liturgy. Much of our ritual that we might think of as medieval in origin actually comes out of our ancient biblical heritage. Today's reading from Nehemiah is a good example of this. When the gospel is read, our liturgical tradition calls on us to stand as a mark of awe and devotion to the Word of God. Also, when the gospel is announced in the Episcopal church, we acclaim "Glory to you, Lord Christ," and at the conclusion of the reading we acclaim "Praise to you, Lord Christ." Look again at the Nehemiah reading and you will see the origins of this ritual: The people stand respectfully to hear the Scripture read, and they respond with an acclamation, "Amen, Amen." Our gospel ritual puts us in touch, then, with our people who for hundreds of years have acclaimed the Lord's presence in the Word. Moreover, our words and actions not only *proclaim* our faith and awe and love of God's word; they *reinforce* that faith and awe and love. Ritual, as always, telescopes our faith story and affirms us in our story.

Fourth Sunday after Epiphany   E, L
Fourth Sunday in Ordinary Time   RC
Last week's gospel reading and theme continue. Jesus is rejected by those in the synagogue because they cannot believe that "Joseph's son" can be a great prophet and healer. Though they speak well of his ability to interpret Scripture, they are not open to the possibility of his authority or power. Quoting Scripture, he reminds them that a prophet is not accepted by his own people and therefore must go to strangers. This infuriates his townsmen, and they try to kill him.

Tell the story of Jesus' rejection. Talk about the call of the prophets reflected in the Old Testament reading. Compare Jeremiah's call as a prophet, which we hear today, to Isaiah's call in Isaiah 6. The prophet's call was usually expressed in symbolic or poetic terms. Rejection and suffering were a part of a prophet's life; focus on the words of the prophets and of Jesus to discover why. See the comments in chapter 2, pages 57-59, for background information on the prophets. See A Guide to Stories of the Bible, chapter 1, pages 35-37, and chapter 5, page 159, for some of the stories about Jeremiah that could be shared today in the learning community to give participants a deeper appreciation of the painful role of prophet. See chapter 5, pages 158-159, for a discussion of the call of the prophets and others to speak the word of God. (Next week's reading will continue to focus on the calling of God's prophets, leaders, and disciples.)

Fifth Sunday after Epiphany   E, L
Fifth Sunday in Ordinary Time   RC
This Sunday we turn to the calling of the disciples. The Old Testament reading gives the account of Gideon's call to lead the Israelites against the Midianites. The account reads as if Gideon were having a face-to-face conversation with God. To help our people appreciate that God also speaks and calls us as disciples, I would suggest using phrasing such as "In his mind, Gideon heard the Lord say. . . ." The story of Gideon is fun to tell, for it shows how God used an insignificant man with a small army to outwit the mighty army of the Midianites. God's wisdom, rather than the power of weapons, won

the day. Read the whole story of Gideon and tell it in your own words. Tie it to the gospel reading in which Jesus calls his disciples to be fishers of men. He, too, chose the humble and the struggling as his disciples. This may give us some encouragement when we find ourselves wondering how we can possibly be a part of God's plan for salvation. It is not our power that we proclaim as Christians; it is the power of God working through his people that brings life and wholeness.

The Lutheran and Roman Catholic lectionaries appoint Isaiah 6:1-8 for today. This is the call of Isaiah mentioned in connection with last week's readings. See chapter 5, page 160, for further comments about this passage, and chapter 5, pages 173-174, for a list of other passages in which persons feel God's call to speak his word.

Sixth Sunday after Epiphany   E, L
Sixth Sunday in Ordinary Time   RC

Luke's "Sermon on the Plain" is a much shorter collection of sayings than Matthew's "Sermon on the Mount" but contains some of the same material. (See references to the Matthew readings under Year A, fourth through eighth Sunday after Epiphany, pages 159-162.) The poor and struggling will be blessed with the presence of God made known in Christ. The rich and powerful will lose their sense of power. These strong words need to be read in the context of today's Old Testament reading and of last week's readings. Powerful people tend to trust in their own resources and forget their call to share God's love in covenant. The more possessions we have, the more we are apt to be caught up in protecting them. Jesus had deep concern for the wealthy, for he could see them turning from a life of love and grace to one in which they were condemned to endlessly protect what they felt would bring them life. If the rich man was to have everlasting life, Jesus said, he must sell all he had and give to the poor. "How hard it is for those who have riches to enter the kingdom of God! For it is easier for a camel to go through the eye of a needle than for a rich man to enter the kingdom of God" (Luke 18:24-25).

The reading from Jeremiah helps us appreciate the source of Jesus' concern. "Cursed is the man who trusts in man and makes flesh his arm. . . " (Jeremiah 17:5). Our own affluent society is a case in point. Among the wealthy in the suburbs of our major cities, suicide, divorce, and alcoholism are prevalent—a sign of emptiness and despair.

Adolescents and adults in the learning community need to spend time this week looking at their own values and the values reflected in our affluent way of life. What would the prophets of the Old Testament say to us? What kind of life-style is the Lord calling us to?

Notice how the light of Christ spreads during this Epiphany season. The Christ light was announced at Christmas and recognized by the wise men on Twelfth Night. The light spreads as Jesus begins to speak and heal. Now the light spreads farther as he calls disciples and prepares to send them forth. You might recall the Feast of Lights service of Twelfth Night (pages 103-105 and 156-157), in which the congregation were given candles to carry out into the world. We, too, are disciples called to "spread the light." On these fourth, fifth, and sixth Sundays, Jesus offers words that spread the light of God's wisdom.

Seventh Sunday after Epiphany   E, L
Seventh Sunday in Ordinary Time   RC

The radical words of Jesus from the Sermon on the Plain are heard today. "Love your enemies," Jesus says. The words are so powerful that if people listen to them, they will be compelled to talk about them in the learning community. How can we love our enemies? What do these words lead us to proclaim to our world? Tell the beautiful story in the Old Testament reading today. (See the remarks in connection with the story of Jonah, chapter 1, page 18, and chapter 1, page 37.)

The Old Testament reading assigned in the Roman Catholic lectionary is 1 Samuel 26:2,7-9,12-13,22-23, the story of David's flight from King Saul. David has two opportunities to kill Saul. (See 1 Samuel 24 for the first story of David's mercy.) Because Saul is the Lord's anointed, David considers him sacred and will not kill him even though Saul is pursuing David to kill him. There is a deep sense of the reverence for life in these stories, a mercy that is hard for us to comprehend. This is the kind of understanding, mercy, and forgiveness that Jesus calls us to as his disciples. I would suggest sharing the David or Jonah stories in the adolescent and adult groups as a way of launching a discussion about love of enemies, the concept we focus on this week.

Eighth Sunday after Epiphany   E, L
Eighth Sunday in Ordinary Time   RC

The Sermon on the Plain continues into the third week. We are not to judge nor be hypocritical. The familiar words are read: "Why do you see the speck that is in your brother's eye, but do not notice the log that is in your own eye?" (Luke 6:41). We share a common shortcoming as we think about these words. It is hard not to be judgmental. What happens when we judge people? Talk about the prejudice and the hatred that have existed for generations in some places. What makes us judge one another? Social scientists point out that we tend to project our self-hatred onto others. What we dislike in ourselves we see and reject in others. We ourselves will be judged by the fruits of what we do rather than by our pious words. Think back to our Feast of Lights celebration at the beginning of this Epiphany season. We must not hide the Christ light or lead others astray into deeper darkness, for we will be judged on how much light we have shared. Jesus and Jeremiah condemn the Temple leaders who not only have not shared the light but have brought deeper darkness.

The Roman Catholic Old Testament reading from the Book of Sirach (Ecclesiasticus) says "Do not praise a man before you hear him reason" (Sirach 27:7). Those words will reveal the true nature of the person just as the fruit of a tree shows the kind of care it has had.

The Old Testament reading is a rejection of the empty Temple rituals and of the people's false reliance on the Temple to protect them from harm. So long as they acted unjustly, Jeremiah warned the people, the Temple would not protect them. "Behold, you trust in deceptive words to no avail. Will you steal, murder, commit adultery, swear falsely, burn incense to Baal, and go after other gods that you have not known, and then come and stand before me in this house, which is called by my name and say, 'We are delivered!' . . .?" (Jeremiah 7:8-10). The Lord demands: ". . . truly execute justice with one another, . . . do not oppress the alien, the fatherless or the widow. . ." (Jeremiah 7:5-6). Tie in this reading with the demands of love mentioned in the gospel. We cannot attend church filled with hate and expect to find the strength and presence we seek.

The true test of our discipleship will be how we lead our lives. As we prepare for the confession in the liturgy today, help persons reflect back over their week. Are those around us able to perceive the light of Christ coming through our words and actions, or are we part of the darkness in what we said and did?

Last Sunday after Epiphany   E, L
Last Sunday in Ordinary Time   RC

The transfiguration of Jesus is described. (See comments on pages 116-118, 162, and 274-275. The transfiguration story is shared on the second Sunday of Lent in the Roman Catholic lectionary.)

The Season of Lent

The comments under Years A and B for the season of Lent (pages 163 and 212) also apply to this year's Lenten readings. We have a period of preparation for baptism. The readings offer a short course in the faith, with special emphasis on the covenant and the history of salvation (God's healing). "The covenants of the Old Testament are a great help in understanding what God has done for us in his definitive one. Consequently, in her preparation for Easter, the Church remembers the covenants of the Old Testament to remind us of the stages of God's plan for our redemption, as well as to instruct those to be baptized. The Old Testament readings in Year C recall the ancient creed of Israel, and the covenants with Abraham and Moses. We also hear of the first Passover in the promised land, and the promise of the new act of God to renew his people."* The epistle readings tie in with the Old Testament and gospel readings. The gospel readings point up the constant need to stand against evil and to repent. Thus the Old Testament readings review salvation history, and the gospel readings are demands upon the convert and the Christian to live up to that history and call to covenant.

Ash Wednesday
See comments for Year A, pages 163-164.

First Sunday in Lent
The Old Testament reading recalls the ancient creed of Israel. "A wandering Aramean was my father; and he went down into Egypt and sojourned there. . ." (Deuteronomy 6:5). Note that the creed is a rehearsal or recalling of how God has acted for his people. In the learning community we need to emphasize that the statement of belief for the Jew and Christian comes as we recall God's mighty acts. Our belief comes from our story, our history. I believe as a Christian because through that recalling I have become sensitive to how God has acted and is

acting in my story and my people's story. In other words my belief in God comes out of rehearsing the story of God's saving acts. This belief leads to the credal statement "I believe." From such a statement comes in turn the willingness to make covenant with this God who is active in my history. "I will be your instrument of history-making in your world. I will judge my actions by my belief that you are a just and loving God who calls all creation into wholeness and oneness with you." Such a covenant statement leads to my values and actions in God's name. Finally, out of this story-creed-covenant-action-awareness comes my response of celebration. The final command to the Israelites in this section of Deuteronomy orders God's people to ". . . rejoice in all the good which the Lord your God has given to you" (Deuteronomy 26:11). We celebrate the story, the creed, the covenant, and the actions we take in the Lord's name. Our celebration, the Eucharist, has little meaning without the background of story, creed, covenant, and action. That is why we all must see the Eucharist in its proper context. It cannot be an isolated event that is stuck into one's weekly schedule. Rather it must be an outgrowth of a people's sharing their story and faith together. The religious education team plays an important role in helping this to happen by sharing the story that leads to the creed, covenant, and action.

Suppose that a young couple, formerly strangers to each other, have now met. After a few dates they begin to have a story to share— the story of their relationship and of their backgrounds. Out of this story comes the conviction that they believe in each other and want to be married. This leads to their "making covenant" before friends and pastor. This covenant has a radical effect on their lives. Their values and world view change as they focus on what they together want rather than on what they each wanted in their own way. And their actions change; for example, it is no longer appropriate for them to date other persons.

Our Christian creeds are telescoped forms of the story of Jesus Christ. Look at the words of the Apostles' Creed and the Nicene Creed, and you see the story told in poetic form. "He came down from heaven" and "he ascended into heaven" are poetic statements that God's

*Peter Coughlan and Peter Purdue, *Commentary on the Sunday Lectionary: First Sunday of Advent to Last Sunday of the Year, Year C* (Cleveland, Ohio: Corpus Books, 1970), p. 82.

presence was made known in Jesus. Write a group creed based on how members of the learning community have perceived God acting in their lives. For example, "We believe in one God who gave us life, who. . . ."

See Year A, page 164, for remarks on the gospel.

Second Sunday in Lent
In all three years we tell the story of Abraham today. (See chapter 1, page 21, and comments in connection with Years A and B, pages 164 and 212.)

In the gospel reading we are reminded of the covenant. God made covenant with Abraham, but many of Abraham's people forgot that covenant. Simply being sons and daughters of Abraham does not automatically make one a child of the covenant, Jesus would say. "Then you will begin to say, 'We ate and drank in your presence, and you taught in our streets.' But he will say, 'I tell you, I do not know where you come from; depart from me, all you workers of iniquity!'" (Luke 13:26-27). The children of Abraham's covenant have heard the word but have not responded. When they have broken that covenant trust, the Lord will say "I tell you, I do not know where you come from; depart from me, all you workers of iniquity!"

Luke 13:31-34 moves to a direct confrontation with the city of Jerusalem itself. The Jews considered the city and the Temple sacred and indestructible because they saw Jerusalem as God's city. The Temple was a witness to the world of the presence of the Lord. Both Jeremiah and Jesus denied the impregnable nature of the city. It *will* fall, they foresaw. Because the people had abandoned the covenant, the Lord would abandon his people and his city. Jesus and the prophets spoke the wisdom of the Lord, but it was a wisdom rejected by the people as they sought their own evil understanding of life. These words were unthinkable to the people. To understand their anger we must put ourselves in their place. If someone came to us saying that the city of Washington would be "desolate, without inhabitant" (Jeremiah 26:9), how would we respond? From this warning not to take one's covenant relationship with God for granted, Jesus makes a promise to the people of the new

covenant, or new testament. "And men will come from east and west, and from north and south, and sit at table in the kingdom of God. And behold, some are last who will be first, and some are first who will be last" (Luke 13:29-30). Those who will cry out in confidence "Blessed is he who comes in the name of the Lord!" (Luke 13:35b) will be the seal of the covenant.

Abraham's faith in God's promise is what made him righteous in the eyes of God. (See today's Old Testament reading and Paul's reference to it in Romans 4:1-25 and Galatians 3:6-9.) It is this kind of faith that Jesus calls people to as he foresees the crumbling of the old order and the making of a new covenant. The new covenant will be written on their hearts (Jeremiah 31:31-34) and will become a reality through Jesus' death and resurrection and the gift of the Holy Spirit.

The Lenten covenant "primer" continues this Sunday as we look at the foundation of God's covenant with Abraham and Jesus. This would be a good Sunday to tell stories of persons who lived out their faith. Abraham believed in God's promise in a time when Abraham's life was changing—when he was called out of his own land to enter a strange land. Jesus talked of the new covenant to people at a time when their world was being shattered by conquest and destruction. Go to sources outside the Bible and tell the stories of contemporary Christians such as Dietrich Bonhoeffer, who lived and died by the covenant in time of change and destruction. The stories of people of faith told this Sunday will help participants sense the depth of what covenant faith means to the Jew and to the Christian and will reinforce the kind of response Christ calls for in his Church.

Roman Catholics will hear the transfiguration story as the gospel reading. (See my comments in connection with this reading on page 274.) The Old Testament story from Abraham is shared with Episcopalians this week. Lutherans will hear Jeremiah 26:8-15 rather than the Abraham story. This is a painful reading that matches the gospel lesson for today. The prophet must speak the words that the Lord places on his lips. The Jeremiah reading will help participants understand the feelings of Jesus' day. Jesus' words echoed the words of the prophets and brought out the same rejection and anger that had been evidenced in that earlier time. Share today the stories of Jeremiah listed in A Guide to Stories of the Bible, chapter 1, pages 35-36. Tell the stories of Jesus in his final days in Jerusalem. This storytelling will prepare participants to appreciate the power of the Holy Week drama that is coming soon. Adolescents and adults could focus on the words of confrontation from the prophets. How would they feel if their own city were named in the prophecy and their own ways confronted?

Third Sunday in Lent
The salvation story continues. The Old Testament reading is crucial to understanding God's action in history. Moses is commissioned by "the God of your father, . . . the God of Abraham, the God of Isaac, and the God of Jacob" as he appears to Moses in the vision of the burning bush. This God identified himself as I AM WHO I AM. One understanding of this strange name is to see it as meaning that this God who calls Moses is the God of history: "I am what's happening to you." The God who covenants with Moses to lead his people from slavery to freedom will be known in the saving history of his people. This is an important understanding to share in the religious education setting. As we reflect on our own individual, personal history (our story), we can begin to see how God is also calling and forming us as his people. The epistle reading today mentions the wilderness struggle of the Israelites, so it ties into the story of Moses and the people. The gospel reading is a mid-Lenten call for repentance that provides a continuing balance to the Old Testament stories of covenant-making between God and the people. God called Moses and the Israelites. He demanded that the people of the covenant live a life of repentance and turn back to the Lord lest they suffer the pain of separation from God. The people of the covenant are expected to bear fruit. Our relationship with God cannot be taken for granted any more than our marriage relationship can. Husband and wife must constantly make decisions of love for each other. Priorities have to be set in which the marriage relationship comes first; otherwise the marriage falters, dries up, and often dies. The covenant must be renewed day after day after day with decisions for the covenant of marriage. This is the kind of constant decision-making that is essential if we are to live into the call that Moses received at the burning bush.

Fourth Sunday in Lent
We add another chapter to the story of the Israelites today. Moses has died; Joshua is the new leader. The people have crossed the Jordan River on dry land and are now about to take the city of Jericho. Symbolically, Joshua sets up a monument of twelve stones to recall the crossing of the Jordan for future generations. The people celebrate the first Passover in the new land. These Old Testament Lenten readings allow for a natural week-by-week telling of the exodus story.

The gospel reading is the parable of the prodigal son. If we have heard the gospel readings of the past two weeks, we need to hear today's parable. On the other side of Jesus' stern and harsh words of confrontation is this beautiful parable of the loving mercy and grace that God offers his people even before they ask for it. As we stumble up the road with words of confession on our lips ("Father, I have sinned against heaven and before you; I am no longer worthy to be called your son"—Luke 15:18-19), God is waiting by the side of the road to welcome us back into the household of faith and to celebrate our rebirth. As we honestly examine our lives, we realize that the covenant known through Jesus is one of grace and mercy. This we know through Jesus' death and his words of mercy from the cross. This we know from his gift of the Holy Spirit to Peter and the apostles who had left Jesus at the Garden of Gethsemane but turned back in penitance after the crucifixion. Peter, too, was the prodigal son on Good Friday who was welcomed home on Easter morning and fed bread and fish at the lakeside in celebration. To understand the new covenant, we need to be in touch not only with the faith demands expressed in the earlier weeks of Lent but also with the forgiveness expressed in today's readings.

The story of Joshua makes good telling, as does the parable of the prodigal son. Talk about times when participants have felt like the prodigal son. It's All About Eucharist has a unit on penance.* (This six-session course is designed to help young children and their families explore the concepts of the Eucharist.) The story offered in the penance unit and the discussion questions following the story would be helpful as an application of this week's gospel reading. Be aware that the parable of the prodigal son is a sophisticated story. Most adults find themselves identifying with the elder brother who stayed behind to work on the father's land! God's mercy really is incomprehensible for most of us.

The Lutheran lectionary appoints Isaiah 12:1-6 for the first reading. This poem of thanksgiving for God's mercy offers a good introduction to the parable of the prodigal son.

Fifth Sunday in Lent
This week the story of the exodus from Egypt into the land of Canaan is replaced with a forward look at a new exodus that God promises through the prophet Isaiah. This new exodus will be far more wonderful than the first. ". . . for I give water in the wilderness, rivers in the desert. . ." (Isaiah 43:20). God promises to restore his people after they have suffered in exile.

The gospel reading is a pointed parable told by Jesus to remind his hearers that they had been chosen to tend the vineyard of the Lord but had not done so. The owner of the vineyard will "come and destroy those tenants, and give the vineyard to others" (Luke 20:16). This parable can be used as a good launching device to help participants understand the nature of covenant. Jesus saw the Jews as failing to uphold the covenant with God just as the tenants broke their covenant with the landlord. The educator needs to move from history to personal identification. Our world, our communities, and our lives are

*It's All About Eucharist (Minneapolis, Minn.: Winston Press, 1971, 1977).

also the vineyards. We are but the tenants; God is the landlord. We, too, must give an accounting.

This is also a good parable to use in talking about stewardship. We return to God "some of the fruit of the vineyard" as an act of thanksgiving and as an appropriate "rent" to God. That offering is used to spread the Kingdom of God today. (See also the "vineyard song" in Isaiah 5 to get the feel of this parable.)

Roman Catholics will hear John 8:1-11 this Sunday. God's infinite mercy proclaimed through Jesus is offered to the woman taken in adultery. A woman is about to be stoned by the men of the town because she has committed adultery. Jesus confronts those men with the quiet words "Let him who is without sin among you be the first to throw a stone at her" (John 8:7). In one stroke Jesus proclaims the forgiving love of God and confronts the sinfulness of the accusers. *All* of us have sinned. All of us must turn to the Lord in grateful thanksgiving for his mercy rather than lashing out at others in self-righteous anger.

Begin to prepare the people for the drama of Palm Sunday and Holy Week that begins next Sunday. If we have told the stories of Lent, participants will have a better grasp of that drama. Jesus' words of wisdom are rejected. Like the prophets before him, he will suffer for the sins of the people who turn against God's word. After recalling the Lenten stories, tell the story of Christ's passion that will be shared in the liturgy next week. In many parishes the passion drama is read or dramatized. Have participants in the learning community act out the drama this Sunday and talk about it. The impact of what they share next week will be heightened. Be sure to explain the tradition of the palms. Encourage participants to make palm crosses to be blessed and handed out next week at the liturgy.

Palm Sunday and Holy Week
See the remarks for Year A, pages 167-169.

The Season of Easter

See Year A, pages 170-171, for a discussion of the Easter-season readings and the options available for the liturgist and educator. It is important that people from both fields work together so that liturgical and educational events are tied together in one common experience. The Old Testament selections, as usual, offer background for the gospel readings.

The Lutheran and Roman Catholic lectionaries do not include an Old Testament option as the first reading. The selections from Acts, appointed for the first reading in the Roman Catholic lectionary, differs from the Episcopal selections shown below. This difference, however, does not affect the overall sharing of the stories from the Book of Acts that you may want to offer during this Easter season.

The Readings from the Book of Acts

Second Sunday of Easter
The apostles begin to minister to people in the same way that Jesus had done. They find that they are empowered by the Holy Spirit to bring wholeness (health) to people in the name of Jesus. Jewish authorities have them arrested, but the apostles miraculously escape. Nothing can stop the spread of the gospel.

Third Sunday of Easter
This passage tells of the conversion of Saul (Paul) on the road to Damascus and of his subsequent baptism.

Fourth Sunday of Easter
This is an example of the kind of preaching that Paul might have done after his conversion. Note the description of a typical synagogue service. Discuss synagogue worship in the time of the apostles. Our Christian liturgy comes directly from the synagogue service, which was later combined with the celebration of the Eucharist to form our Sunday liturgy.

Fifth Sunday of Easter
Paul begins to realize that the Jews are not going to accept the Word, so he turns more and more to the Gentiles. The Jews stir up the citizens of Antioch against him.

Sixth Sunday of Easter
Paul heals a crippled man in Lystra. The people of the town, thinking that Paul and Barnabas are gods, want to make sacrifices to them. Paul and Barnabas plead with them and explain that they are not gods, but that they speak and act for the one God. God "did not leave himself without witness, for he did good and gave you from heaven rains and fruitful seasons, satisfying your hearts with food and gladness" (Acts 14:17). This is a good passage for introducing the concept of stewardship, thanksgiving, and the awareness of God's presence and action in creation and history.

Seventh Sunday of Easter
Paul exorcises a slave girl who has brought her master money by telling fortunes. Her owner is furious, and the people of Philippi rise up against Paul and Silas. Again they are thrown into jail, but again the jail cannot hold them. This time an earthquake opens the door. The jailer is converted when he discovers that they have not tried to escape.

The Readings from the Revelation to John

If the Revelation option is chosen for liturgy and education, it will be important for resource persons in the learning community to understand the nature of apocalyptic literature. Be sure to study some background material pertaining to it. The New American Bible has an excellent introduction, as does The Jerusalem Bible. The New American Bible warns, "Symbolic descriptions are not to be taken as literal descriptions, nor is the symbolism capable of being pictured realistically."* As apocalyptic literature, Revelation needs to be appreciated for its poetry and underlying message; it is not an exact prophecy of the endtime. Unfortunately, the book is often used in the latter way. Those who interpret the Bible literally find in Revelation evidence for various theories about the second

*The New American Bible (Nashville, Tenn.: Thomas Nelson, 1971), p. 1379.

coming of Christ and the end of the present age. The remarks in chapter 2, pages 63, 69, and 74, may be helpful here.

The message of Revelation is a beautiful one. The power of God will overcome the powers of evil and separation. The pain and struggle that we face now *does* have meaning. Out of struggle and out of our commitment to the gospel come an ultimate healing and oneness with God. "He will dwell with them, and they shall be his people, and God himself will be with them; he will wipe away every tear from their eyes, and death shall be no more, neither shall there be mourning nor crying nor pain any more, for the former things have passed away" (Revelation 21:3-4). If Revelation is used in the liturgy, focus on the poetic concept of the reading. Encourage the participants to express the poetry with posters and banners. High school students and adults would benefit from a study of apocalyptic literature in general.

I list below those portions of the Revelations readings which might be appropriate for conceptual study with younger members.

Second Sunday of Easter
" 'I am the Alpha and the Omega,' says the Lord God, who is and who was and who is to come, the Almighty!" (Revelation 1:8). This is a familiar passage. The Greek letters Alpha and Omega are the first and last letters of the Greek alphabet and are often found among Christian symbols because they remind us that God is the beginning and the end for all creatures.

Fourth Sunday of Easter
A poetic vision of eternal life is described. "They shall hunger no more, neither thirst any more. . ." (Revelation 8:16). How might participants describe a perfect life of wholeness with God?

Fifth Sunday of Easter
Words of praise from Revelation 19:5 would make a good poster for this Sunday's learning community. "Praise our God, all you his servants, you who fear him, small and great." A "collage" of people could be created around the theme. In this way the words of the liturgy could become part of the experience of the participants.

Sixth Sunday of Easter
The vivid imagery of Revelation unfolds new visions of hope for us this 6th Week of Easter. A new and perfect city of Jerusalem descends from the heavens. There will be no need for a Temple in the new Jerusalem since Jesus' death on the Cross has replaced all need for further sacrifice. It is a city of perfect light and peace to which all peoples shall come. Next, our imagery shifts to an image of further perfection. The picture is of Eden re-visited. Compare the opening verses of chapter 22 with Genesis 2:8-10. *And out of the ground the Lord God made to grow every tree that is pleasant to the sight and good for food, the tree of life also in the midst of the garden, and the tree of the knowledge of good and evil. A river flowed out of Eden to water the garden, and there it divided and became four rivers.* What God intended at the beginning has now happened. This is a new creation. Perfection expressed in the new Jersualem and in the new Eden is the promise of the new life of Resurrection proclaimed all during the Easter season.

Seventh Sunday of Easter
The theme of Christ as the Alpha and Omega is picked up again this final week of Easter. To those who persevere in the faith, Christ promises that he will return soon. "'Surely I am coming soon.' Amen. Come, Lord Jesus!" (Revelation 22:20).

The concept that Christ is the beginning and the end and that he will come again at the end of time is difficult for children, but since it is so important in the Christian faith, we should try to find ways of expressing its many facets in simple language. Whatever children grasp of it will be all to the good. Here are some ideas to work on; use your good judgment as to which ones can be made understandable to your particular group.

Our lives are not aimless; God's purpose somehow is being acted out in history through the struggles of his people. Even in the darkest hours of our story we must proclaim this with faith. (With older people we can discuss how history is not cyclical, not meaningless repetition, but full of direction and purpose.) Again, God does not cause the evil we suffer; our sinfulness causes much of the pain and destruction (it will be easy to illustrate this from current events—world hunger, war, poverty caused by selfishness). We can point out, on the positive side, that there is wonderful creation going on around us all the time—growth in nature, growth in the lives of people who become more unselfish, more heroic, more understanding as they observe life and pray and serve others. The Book of Revelation was written during a period of painful upheaval and persecution, but its author saw hope even in those times—hope that a new day was dawning in which God would intervene with power and great glory.

Our liturgy is filled with acclamations of hope. Every time we gather to celebrate the Eucharist together, we dramatize our faith in God's saving acts in history. The Book of Revelation contains many liturgical phrases, including the powerful words in today's reading, that were probably used by early Christians. Have participants pull out the words from Revelation that have a liturgical ring to them. Create your own celebration of hope, using those words and acclamations. You might even set some of the words to music or dance. Offer the celebration as a part of the Liturgy of the Word at the Eucharist. Match the words with slides, film presentation, or other visual art forms.

The Old Testament and Gospel Readings

The Old Testament readings are chosen to add dimension to the gospel reading so that there will be a carryover between the two readings if you choose to use the Old Testament rather than the Book of Acts as the first reading during Easter.

Second Sunday of Easter

Job's response to God at the end of the Book of Job is "I have uttered what I did not understand, things too wonderful for me, which I did not know. I had heard of thee by the hearing of the ear, but now my eye sees thee; therefore I despise myself, and repent in dust and ashes" (Job 42:3,5-6). The Book of Job is important to share with older adolescents and adults. It should not be treated as history but as wisdom literature. In reading the book, we are exposed to the truth that many problems, including the reason for

suffering, are beyond our understanding. God's response to Job's endless questions is merely a rhetorical question that tells Job to submit humbly to God: "Where were you when I laid the foundation of the earth?" (Job 38:4a).

The gospel reading is a resurrection appearance of Jesus—the apostles receive the Holy Spirit as they experience Jesus' presence among them. Thomas, who is not with the apostles at the time, doubts the appearance until Jesus appears to him a week later. Both Job and Thomas were questioners. Questioning leads to faith and discovery, but the point of questions is to lead to further search and partial new discoveries, not necessarily to final answers.

Third Sunday of Easter

The Old Testament reading is a promise that God will restore his people after their exile: "I will make with them an everlasting covenant, that I will not turn away from doing good to them; and I will put the fear of me in their hearts, that they may not turn from me" (Jeremiah 32:40).

Today's gospel reading tells of another resurrection appearance. This time Jesus appears to Peter and the disciples at the Sea of Tiberias. The day promised in Jeremiah (Old Testament reading) has come with Christ.

Fourth Sunday of Easter
(Good Shepherd Sunday)

Moses, at the point of death, is led by God into the Abarim Mountains, where he can view the Promised Land that he will never enter. Moses asks God to appoint a new leader so that the people will not be like "sheep which have no shepherd." This reading introduces the theme of the Good Shepherd that is developed in the gospel lesson.

The theme for the Fourth Sunday of Easter is the same in all four years: Jesus as the good shepherd. This beautiful metaphor is familiar from several Old Testament passages including the 23rd Psalm. The image is not one that speaks clearly to those living in an urban setting. See if you can find someone in the congregation who can talk first hand about life on a farm and what it meant to care for animals. Do a little research about the life of shepherds and share stories of shepherding with your group. Then read the passage from John and tell the story of Moses on the mountain.

Fifth Sunday of Easter
In the Old Testament reading, commandments of the Lord are spoken to the people. This reading helps to show the justice demanded in our relationship with God. "You shall be holy; for I the Lord your God am holy" (Leviticus 19:2). The reading concludes with the beautiful words quoted by Jesus, ". . . you shall love your neighbor as yourself" (Leviticus 19:18). This is the kind of love demanded by Jesus as he gives his followers a new commandment in the gospel reading: ". . . love one another even as I have loved you. . ." (John 13:34). These selections begin to point us toward Pentecost, where we celebrate the gift of the Holy Spirit and our covenant with God. We are called and chosen to love as Christ has loved us. This is his special commandment; this is our covenant. At Pentecost we celebrate our receiving the gift of the Holy Spirit, but we also celebrate our commissioning by the Holy Spirit to be Christ's Body in the world. Covenant and commandments come down to us through the Holy Spirit much as they came down to the people through Moses on Mount Sinai.

The commandment of Jesus to his disciples is given in today's gospel: "A new commandment I give to you, that you love one another" (John 13:34). Refer to the comments given in the Old Testament reading. The law of the Old Testament demanded love and justice among the people of God; the covenant between God and the Israelites was based on this love and justice. During Easter we look at the new covenant (new testament) we have with God through Jesus Christ. It too is based on love and justice, but now the kind of love that God calls forth from us is made clear through Jesus' love for us. These readings prepare us to celebrate our new covenant at the Feast of Pentecost.

Sixth Sunday of Easter
God's people will live in peace and plenty, the Old Testament reading tells us. They will know the abiding presence of God after he restores them. This reading complements the gospel reading, in which Jesus promises his followers the gift of the Holy Spirit. "Peace I leave with you; my peace I give to you" (John 14:27).

Further preparation for the Feast of Pentecost comes this week. Jesus promises the gift of the Paraclete, the Holy Spirit, to anyone who covenants to "keep my word." Jesus promises his peace to those who follow him. The idea of shalom or peace is a very important one in the Bible. In the context of this idea, talk about "passing the peace" (giving the greeting of peace) during the liturgy. Our covenant with God is a covenant of peace. This peace that Jesus promises is a gift, then, to those who hear and respond to his word. Those who do not or cannot hear the Word will not know the gift of this peace. The Holy Spirit will come as the bearer of the gift in the sense that the Spirit will help the faithful remember the Word and understand it. In other words, the Holy Spirit will sensitize God's people to the Word as it is being revealed in the present moment. Their awareness stems from their remembering the story of how God has acted in the lives of his people in the past. We must be reminded of all that Jesus has told us through Scripture if we are to be instructed in the ways of God now.

The importance of our biblical and liturgical heritage can be stressed this week as we prepare for the major festival of Pentecost. Through our liturgical remembering, the Holy Spirit brings the past into the present. The liturgy is therefore one of the instruments of the Holy Spirit. That is why in the Eucharist we "do this in remembrance of (Jesus)" week after week. This remembering brings awareness in the present moment.

The word *peace* or *shalom* is a very important one. "'Peace' (*shalom*) was and is the common Jewish formula of greeting and farewell. The word had a much deeper significance, however, as an expression of the harmony and communion with God that was the seal of the covenant (cf. Numbers 6:26). Hence it came to have an eschatological and messianic meaning (cf. Isaiah 9:6), virtually the same as 'salvation'" (*The Jerome Biblical Commentary*, page 454). The concept of shalom would make a study in itself.

According to the *Dictionary of the Bible* the concept of peace, or shalom, in the Old Testament "signifies such things as to finish, to complete, to pay (i.e., to complete a transaction by paying a debt); thus the word may be said to signify in general completeness, perfection—perhaps most precisely, a condition in which nothing is lacking . . . The Israelite conceived peace as a gift of Yahweh, and as such it becomes a theological concept. . .when one possesses peace, one is in perfect and assured communion with Yahweh."*

This, then, is the kind of peace that Jesus promises to those who are open to the Word and the indwelling of the Holy Spirit. This is the kind of peace we wish for each other as we "pass the peace" in the liturgy.

The story of the Bible from Genesis through Revelation is the story of a people seeking after this peace, or shalom. God offers shalom, but our story includes instance after instance where we have turned from that offer and found "dis-ease" and pain instead of wholeness. Let participants study various passages from the Old Testament and talk about what has blocked the persons in the story from experiencing the shalom of God. Then talk about how God has attempted in each case to reestablish the peace that has been broken. Study groups could report on the ways in which people of the story have broken peace and the ways in which God has attempted to establish and reestablish it. List the reports on newsprint, and then see if participants can personally identify similar times of separation and times of reconciliation in their own lives. This will help persons get in touch with the concept of shalom and enable them to identify with the biblical story. That story still goes on in our lives. We too are the people of the Story.

Ascension Day
See chapter 8, page 275, for a discussion of Ascension Day, which comes on Thursday of this week.

*John L. McKenzie, ed., *Dictionary of the Bible* (New York: Macmillan, 1965), p. 651.

Seventh Sunday of Easter
In the Old Testament reading the people realize their sinfulness in asking Samuel to anoint a king for them. Samuel assures them that God will not abandon his nation. The reading concludes with "Only fear the Lord, and serve him faithfully with all your heart; for consider what great things he has done for you" (1 Samuel 12:24). The people of God are called to proclaim God's presence and action in their history. Samuel saw the anointing of Saul as a dangerous transition point for the people. As they focused their attention on the king and his authority, they could easily forget the great things that the Lord had done for them in the past. They could see themselves as the king's people rather than God's people. An awareness of God's saving help in the past is essential if the generations to come are to remain faithful to the Lord and see themselves as his people.

The gospel reading centers on Jesus' prayer for his followers. As Jesus prepares for his death, he prays that his disciples will "see (his) glory" in the days to come. Earlier in the chapter Jesus says that his words and actions have made the Father's name known. The disciples are now entrusted with carrying the Father's name to the world.

Thus we see in both the Old and the New Testament readings that we must remember our history as we move through times of transition. These are important words for the educator! In the learning community we must reflect on God's actions as they have been revealed in the past, so that we may see and proclaim his glory in times of transition today and tomorrow. Part of the covenant we seek through the Holy Spirit next Sunday (Pentecost) is to reveal the glory of Christ so that "the world may believe. . . ." And the world will believe to the extent that Christ's people tell the story in their lives.

The Feast of Pentecost
See the remarks in chapter 5, pages 179-180.

Trinity Sunday
See the remarks in chapter 8, page 277.

The Sundays after Pentecost (Sundays in Ordinary Time)

This year the Sundays after Epiphany and after Pentecost offer a continuous reading of Luke. Old Testament readings add dimension to the gospel reading, as usual; but in these seasons the epistle is typically not meant to form a unified theme with the other two readings. This year the epistle readings provide exposure to 1 Corinthians, Galatians, Colossians, Hebrews, Philemon, 1 Timothy, 2 Timothy, and 2 Thessalonians.

Below, I discuss those Old Testament and/or gospel readings that seem to have particular significance in "telling the story" or in sharing a religious concept. I begin with Proper 4, since the first three propers listed under the Season after Pentecost are also appointed for the sixth, seventh, and eighth Sundays after Epiphany. The varying date of Easter determines whether these readings are used after Epiphany or after Pentecost. I have placed them after Epiphany, on pages 246-247.

Proper 4   E
Ninth Sunday in Ordinary Time   RC
Second Sunday after Epiphany   L

Old Testament: At the dedication of the Temple in Jerusalem King Solomon prays that even foreigners will sense the power of God's presence as they approach the Temple: ". . . that all the peoples of the earth may know thy name and fear thee, as do thy people Israel. . ." (1 Kings 8:43).

Gospel: Jesus heals the Roman centurion's servant.

Religious concepts: God's power was made known to Jew and Gentile alike as the Jewish people proclaimed his presence. The Temple was the symbol of that power and presence. Jesus, rather than the Temple, now becomes the living reality of God's presence. Solomon's prayer takes on a new significance with Jesus: The Roman centurion does see the glory of God just as Solomon had prayed would happen. This week stress the importance of Christian witness. The church building and the liturgy of the Church are a constant proclamation to the community at large of God's presence among all people. We may know of someone who has never considered himself or herself a Christian but who goes to church in time of crisis and finds a sense of comfort and strength. The greatest witnesses of God's power, however, are the people who make up the Church as they proclaim that power in daily words and acts of love and healing. People are drawn to Christ as they, like the centurion, seek the healing strength evidenced in his Body, the Church.

Proper 5   E
Tenth Sunday in Ordinary Time   RC
Third Sunday after Pentecost   L

Old Testament: During a drought, Elijah the prophet goes to live with a widow and her son. The son dies. The mother, in anguish, cries out to Elijah in anger, "You have come to me to bring my sin to remembrance, and to cause the death of my son!" (1 Kings 17:18). Elijah restores the son to life and health, and the widow recognizes Elijah as a true man of God.

Gospel: With the Old Testament story fresh in our minds, we hear the gospel story of Jesus restoring a widow's dead son to life. This miraculous healing brings faith to the people.

Telling the story: Our people need to have an appreciation for Elijah the great prophet. Tell the stories of the prophet found in 1 Kings 17—19. No wonder people thought Elijah had returned as they saw Jesus healing people in his time! See my remarks in chapter 1, pages 13-14 and 43-44, and chapter 6, pages 210-211, regarding the telling of miracle and healing stories.

Religious concepts: God is the source of our life. We take our lives for granted until some crisis comes to shake our confidence. Then we face the frightening reality that our world is not secure, that we are not really in control of our own destiny. Such moments are humbling as well as frightening; we can either fall into despair or recognize the power of God that exists beyond time and beyond the limits of life that we know. The stories we hear today symbolize the truth that life is a gift from God. It is God who has the power to raise us to life at our birth, at moments of healing, and at the final moment of resurrection.

Encourage participants to talk about their times of crisis. Their own awareness of God's giving them life and healing may not sound quite as dramatic to them as the Old Testament and gospel account, but the miracle is no less powerful as we reflect on the meaning of those moments.

Proper 6   E
Eleventh Sunday in Ordinary Time   RC
Fourth Sunday after Pentecost   L

Old Testament: The story of David and Bathsheba is told. The prophet Nathan confronts David with his sin.

Gospel: Jesus speaks words of love and forgiveness to a woman known as a sinner. Her acts of love toward him far outweigh his host's acts of courtesy. Jesus tells a parable to reinforce the point that the person most aware of sin is most responsive to the forgiving love of God.

Telling the story: The story of David and Bathsheba is a powerful one. David's ability to acknowledge his sin is a key point. One cannot really be forgiven until one has acknowledged the sinful act. This would be a good time to tell other stories of David. He was a great king and religious leader, but he also had weaknesses. His story is a vivid reminder that the people of the Bible share the struggle for wholeness that we can identify with. They were not perfect people. They were people on a pilgrimage, a journey of faith.

Religious concepts: The concept of forgiveness can be dealt with this week in the powerful story of David amplified with the gospel reading. To be forgiven, sin must first be acknowledged. Then we must still live with the results of what we have done. Grace and forgiveness are powerful, but they do not come cheaply. The parable of the prodigal son (Luke 15:11-32) would be a good tie-in for today's gospel. The person who is aware of sin can appreciate God's love in ways the elder brother cannot.

Proper 7   E
Twelfth Sunday in Ordinary Time   RC
Fifth Sunday after Pentecost   L

Old Testament: Zechariah speaks of a time when the people will mourn for one whose death they feel responsible for.

Gospel: As Peter recognizes that Jesus is the Messiah, the disciples are led to understand what that will mean for Jesus and for themselves. The Messiah must suffer, Jesus warns them. He will be rejected and scorned by the people. Moreover, if the disciples are to have life they must follow the way of the cross themselves.

Telling the story: The suffering of Jeremiah will help participants understand what it means to be a spokesman for God as prophet or as Messiah. See the Jeremiah stories in *A Guide to Stories of the Bible,* pages 35-36. The suffering of the martyrs and saints would be good stories to share this week. Check your library for stories of persons who have suffered in proclaiming the truth. Tell stories of people like Becket, Thomas More, Joan of Arc, Dietrich Bonhoeffer, or Martin Luther King, Jr.

Religious concepts: See my comments in chapter 2, pages 64-65, on the suffering servant of the Lord.

Proper 8   E
Thirteenth Sunday in Ordinary Time   RC
Sixth Sunday after Pentecost   L

Old Testament: The story of Elisha's call as a prophet is heard today.

Gospel: Jesus talks about the demands of following him. One who is called cannot look back but must move with Christ and follow the will of the Lord.

Telling the story: Tell the stories of Elijah and Elisah today in the learning community. See *A Guide to Stories of the Bible,* pages 32-33.

Religious concepts: The Lord comes to transform our lives. If we are to accept new life, we must be prepared to move with the Lord and leave the security of where we have been. There can be no looking back. A creative teacher challenges students by offering them ever-evolving concepts to discover. The teacher cannot allow students to rest or look back if they are to move into their potential as students. We look today at the nature of conversion. Those of us who are raised in the Christian faith often take our relationship with Christ for granted. We fail to realize the radical nature of our call. We need to be in dialogue with those who have felt a conversion or call to Christ. Their story of struggle, confrontation, and acceptance may help us get in touch with how the Lord has called us. It may encourage us to seek a deeper relationship or to experience conversion ourselves. The Alcoholics Anonymous program offers a good analogy for the Church. The alcoholic is "converted" through the witness of other alcoholics, leaves his or her former life-style without looking back, and accepts the new life of a converted alcoholic. Another analogy to use is that of marriage. Once I accept my call to marriage, I leave behind the values and life-style of my single life to move into a whole new reality of life with my spouse.

Proper 9   E
Fourteenth Sunday in Ordinary Time   RC
Seventh Sunday after Pentecost   L

Old Testament: Isaiah speaks words of hope to the people of Judah returning from exile in Babylonia: "I will extend prosperity to her like a river" (Isaiah 66:12).

Gospel: Jesus sends seventy-two followers to the cities he intends to visit. They are called to take "the peace" of God to the people.

Religious concepts: The Christian is "sent out" like the people in today's gospel story to bring peace (shalom) into the world. Tie in the major theme and concept of shalom discussed in connection with the gospel and Old Testament reading for the sixth Sunday of Easter (pages 255-256). How can we, individually and as the Body of Christ, be a part of the "shalom mission" of Christ?

Proper 10   E
Fifteenth Sunday in Ordinary Time   RC
Eighth Sunday after Pentecost   L

Old Testament: This beautiful reading from Deuteronomy places the Word of God "very near you; it is in your mouth and in your heart, so that you can do it" (Deuteronomy 30:14).

Gospel: The parable of the good Samaritan is heard today.

Telling the story: The parable is a well-known story that is easily dramatized.

Religious concepts: God's words are to be acted on. The commandment "Love your neighbor" calls forth a response from the heart. To respond to God is to respond to the neighbor. The Old Testament reading confronts us with the nature of God's Word. The Word of God is not something we simply listen to externally and nod agreement to. The Word is within us, empowering us to *act* in union with what the Word proclaims. God's people are to put hands and feet to the words they proclaim. The Samaritan acts in concert with the commandment of the Lord, "You shall love . . . your neighbor as yourself."

Proper 11   E
Sixteenth Sunday in Ordinary Time   RC
Ninth Sunday after Pentecost   L

Old Testament: This is the delightful story in which Abraham and Sarah discover that they are to become the parents of Isaac. Sarah laughs at the thought that she can give birth at her age, but in Genesis 21:1-8 we find that the promise was indeed fulfilled. (Tell the story of Abraham in the way it was told around the campfires of our people many generations ago. Refer to A Guide to Stories of the Bible, page 21, for other parts of the Abraham and Sarah story. They are the ancestors of our faith, and it is important for our people to have a feeling for them.) We will be hearing more about Abraham and Sarah next week and again in Proper 14. Plan your storytelling time accordingly.

Gospel: The story of Mary and Martha is heard today.

Religious concepts: In the Old Testament reading the Lord comes in the guise of three men. Today, too, the Lord visits us, and we are called to respond in faith. As we hear the Bible stories, we can respond with our own stories of faith. Encourage people to share their "visits" from the Lord—times when he has touched and guided them.

Proper 12   E
Seventeenth Sunday in Ordinary Time   RC
Tenth Sunday after Pentecost   L

Old Testament: Abraham asks God to spare Sodom if there are righteous people in the city.

Gospel: Jesus talks to his disciples about prayer and offers the Lord's Prayer as a model.

Telling the story: The point of the Old Testament story is Abraham's persistence in praying for the people of Sodom and Gomorrah. God, in the guise of a stranger, is about to destroy the decadent cities, but Abram (Abraham) begs him to spare them if there are just a few good people living there. (The cities are later destroyed, but Lot's family is saved.) Tell the story simply, and avoid telling it as if it were literal history. "I want to tell you a story about our forefather Abraham. It is a story that our people have told in this way for hundreds of years."

The story expresses our need to pray for ourselves and for others, as Abraham did. It also shows that prayers are heard. If God appears as a harsh figure in this story, remember that the story is reflecting a primitive understanding of God.

Religious concepts: We deal directly with the important concept of prayer today. Note the simplicity of the Lord's Prayer. We pray for his will to be done. Note also the Jewish concept of prayer: I cannot ask for what I am not ready to do myself. Thus I ask forgiveness to the same extent that I am willing to offer it. (I ask for peace to the same extent that I am ready to bring peace.) Our petitions to God need to be patterned on the example of the Lord's Prayer. Proper 24 also centers on the concept of the Christian prayer. Refer to my remarks regarding prayer under that proper, pages 265-266.

Proper 13 E
Eighteenth Sunday in Ordinary Time   RC
Eleventh Sunday after Pentecost   L

Old Testament: The writer of the Book of Ecclesiastes sees the accumulation of riches as meaningless. When we die, we simply pass on to someone else what we earned.

Gospel: The parable of the rich fool is told.

Telling the story: The parable is a good story to tell. Concordia Publishing House has included this parable in the *Arch Books* series.*

Religious concepts: Value formation is at the heart of today's readings. Possessions are not inherently evil. We lose our sense of wholeness with God, however, when we begin to think that

---

*Janice Kramer, *The Rich Fool,* Arch Book Series (St. Louis, Mo.: Concordia, 1964).

we can control our destiny through what we have.

Proper 14 E
Nineteenth Sunday in Ordinary Time   RC
Twelfth Sunday after Pentecost   L

Old Testament: Abraham's faith in God's promises makes him righteous. Abraham's descendants will be as many as the stars in the heavens, God promises.

Gospel: A continuation of last week's reading: "For where your treasure is, there will your heart be also" (Luke 12:34). We need to live in constant expectation that Christ will come to confront us with his kingdom.

Telling the story: See Proper 12.

Religious concepts: The Old Testament reading today in the Episcopal and Lutheran lectionaries (Genesis 15:1-6) is tied to the epistle reading that talks of our ancestors who had faith in the Lord. The gospel focus is on being prepared for the Lord's coming. We have an early taste of Advent in this reading. Living a life of expectation means that we are filled with hope and faith in what is to come. In practice, we live for the kingdom to come and attempt to live as if it had already arrived. To many, Christians may appear foolish, but our standards and values must differ from those of people who have no greater expectations of life. The gift of faith leads us into greater responsibilities. "Every one to whom much is given, of him much will be required" (Luke 12:48a).

The Roman Catholic Old Testament reading is Wisdom 18:6-9. The reading refers to the Israelites' anticipation as they waited in Egypt for the Passover and for their liberation. Their faith gave them courage even as they continued to struggle as slaves.

Proper 15 E
Twentieth Sunday in Ordinary Time   RC
Thirteenth Sunday after Pentecost   L

Old Testament: Words of confrontation from the prophet Jeremiah: "Can a man hide himself in secret places so that I cannot see him?" (Jeremiah 23:23). When we speak and take actions, we are responsible for them. We will be confronted for the evil in which we participate. God's word is like fire as it confronts us in our alienation.

The Old Testament lesson in the Roman Catholic lectionary is Jeremiah 38:4-6,8-10. In this passage we hear of Jeremiah's suffering that results from his speaking the word of God.

Gospel: Jesus speaks words of grim warning. He has come to bring division, not peace, for people will find themselves separated from family and friend as they respond to him.

Religious concepts: Today's gospel makes rather shocking reading. These are bitter and biting words from "gentle" Jesus. But we need to hear and internalize this reading. As Christians we must be ready to take stands for the gospel. Talk about the German Christian resistance movement under Dietrich Bonhoeffer in Germany during the Nazi regime, when families and friends were divided over the gospel. Then look at other Christians, including our contemporaries, who have taken stands for the gospel. How do we feel about the Berrigan brothers? We may not agree with their feelings, but the writings of Daniel Berrigan would be interesting to read in light of today's gospel lesson. What stands have we taken or may we find ourselves taking?

Proper 16   E
Twenty-first Sunday in Ordinary Time   RC
Fourteenth Sunday after Pentecost   L

Old Testament: The prophet Isaiah warns the people that they are to suffer because they have rejected the covenant with God and made a covenant with death instead.

The context of this reading is that Judah had chosen a false alliance with Egypt to save itself rather than relying on God's power. Because the people have so little faith in him, the Lord will rise up and judge them accordingly.

The Roman Catholic and Lutheran lectionaries' reading, Isaiah 66:18-21(23), is a prophecy of hope. A time will come when people of every nation will see and recognize the glory of the Lord. They will travel to Jerusalem, where they will offer sacrifices to the Lord. The conversion of the nations is a sign of the final times, when God's kingdom will come. This sign of conversion is what Jesus refers to in the gospel reading.

Gospel: Jesus warns that traveling the way of faith is like passing through a narrow door. Many will claim entrance to the Master's house, but they will not be admitted, for the Master has not known them. They may have eaten and drunk in his company, but they have sought no deeper relationship. Then Jesus points to the great day when persons will come from all over the world to take their place at the banquet table of the Lord.

With these words Jesus warns the people that they dare not count on mere outward religious practices to bring them into relationship with God; they must constantly strive for righteousness and faith in the Lord. Those who will enter through the narrow door to the great banquet of the Lord in the kingdom of God are those who have constantly prepared themselves by their actions as well as by their words to come before the Lord. Those who assume they will be admitted to the kingdom (those who were called first) may be the very ones left outside because they took their relationship for granted. Those who entered last (the peoples from "east and west, and from north and south") may find themselves entering into the kingdom first because they have prepared themselves.

Telling the story: Tell the story of Isaiah and King Hezekiah in Isaiah 36:1—38:8 as background for today's Old Testament reading and as an appreciation for the role the prophet played in our people's history. The Assyrians come to destroy Jerusalem, and they taunt the residents and their leaders. "Nothing can stop us," they say derisively to the leaders and people of Jerusalem. King Hezekiah falls into despair, but Isaiah informs him that the Lord will save the city. Isaiah calls for faith in Yahweh even against what appear to be impossible odds.

Religious concepts: We could paraphrase today's gospel reading to apply it to our present situation. Have Jesus address his words of confrontation and derision to us who are the Church of Christ. *We* may be the last to enter if we take our relationship with God for granted with our weekly participation in the Eucharist ("We ate and drank in your presence"). Share the paraphrase, and encourage participants to respond to Jesus' words as they apply to us.

Proper 17 E
Twenty-second Sunday in Ordinary Time   RC
Fifteenth Sunday after Pentecost L

Old Testament: The Lord overturns the thrones of princes and enthrones the gentle in their place. A confrontation of the proud takes place; they will be humbled. Fear (awe) of the Lord is the only thing we can boast of!

The Old Testament lesson in the Roman Catholic lectionary is Sirach (Ecclesiasticus) 3:17-18,20,28-29. The Lutheran selection is Proverbs 25:6-7. Both are writings from the wisdom tradition, appealing to the people for humbleness in their dealings with one another and in understanding their relationship with God.

Gospel: Jesus confronts the proud. Be humble, he says. Take the lowest seat at the banquet table. Invite the poor, not the rich, to the banquet, for the rich will simply turn around and repay your hospitality.

Religious concepts: The Christian is called to be humble and to live in awe of God's presence. The words of Ephesians 3:20-21 have meaning in this context. "Now to him who by the power at work within us is able to do far more abundantly than all that we ask or think, to him be glory. . . ." All we can boast of is the awareness of God's power that we sometimes feel is at work within us. The Christian may well celebrate the gifts that God has given to each person. Pride interferes with our faith when we forget that our lives and talents are gifts, not possessions. (See chapter 5, pages 159-162, for further discussion of this concept.)

Proper 18 E
Twenty-third Sunday in Ordinary time   RC
Sixteenth Sunday after Pentecost L

Old Testament: If the people of God follow his ways, they will find life and be blessed. If they do not conform to God's ways, they will be separated from his love.

The Lutheran lectionary appoints Proverbs 9:8-12 as the first reading. "The fear of the Lord is the beginning of wisdom, and the knowledge of the Holy One is insight" (Proverbs 9:10). The word *fear* includes the feeling of awe and wonder. In the gospel, Jesus talks about the cost of discipleship. It is only by the power of the

Holy Spirit that we are enabled to be disciples, we realize as we hear those demands.

The Roman Catholic lectionary appoints Wisdom 9:13-18 for this week. The will of God is inconceivable. It is only because God has "given wisdom and sent (his) holy Spirit from on high" that we can search out the things of heaven. In the gospel, Jesus warns his would-be followers that they had better be ready to count the cost of following him. They will be moving into a whole new realm of reality, and to do so they must renounce what holds them in their limited worldly sphere. ". . . for a perishable body weighs down the soul, and this earthly tent burdens the thoughtful mind" (Wisdom 9:15).

Gospel: To follow Christ is to make a definite choice. It means conforming to his way and Word, even at the cost of being separated from one's family and bearing one's own cross.

Telling the story: Tell the story of Hannah and Samuel (1 Samuel 1:1—2:11) in the learning community today. Hannah desperately wants a child, and her fervent prayer is finally answered. In her prayer she offers to dedicate the child to the Lord's service. Then tell the story of Samuel's call in 1 Samuel 3. This story will help to reinforce the idea of what it means to offer oneself to the Lord's service.

Religious concepts: The Old Testament and gospel readings confront us with the need to make a choice in following Christ. Conversion to Christ means witnessing to a way that often contradicts the ways of society. We are blessed as we follow the way of the Lord, but life is closed off to us as we turn away from the Lord. The choice is often costly and painful, and yet we are called to choose life (Deuteronomy 30:19). Talk about the meaning and cost of conversion and discipleship today.

Proper 19 E
Twenty-fourth Sunday in Ordinary Time   RC
Seventeenth Sunday after Pentecost L

Old Testament: We hear today the story of Moses interceding with God at Mount Sinai after the people worshiped the golden calf. Moses begs forgiveness, and God spares the people.

Gospel: Jesus comes to bring God's forgiveness to sinners and outcasts. He tells the parables of the lost sheep and lost coin as illustrations of his mission.

Telling the story: Tell the story of the Israelites in the wilderness and at Mount Sinai and of Moses interceding with God to forgive his people. The Israelites wanted a god they could see and control, not an unseen god acting in their history. (Recall the story of Abraham interceding with God that we heard in Proper 12.)

Religious concepts: God constantly reaches out to bring us back into oneness with him. Our prideful actions (discussed in previous weeks) separate us from God, from ourselves, our neighbors, and all of creation. Reconciliation seems impossible, though we may make attempts to bridge the gap. But Jesus' death on the cross, with God's words of forgiveness on his lips, was the great act of atonement ("at-one-ment"). It stands as an eternal proclamation that God has already acted to bring us back into relationship with him. The cross, then, is the sign of our "at-one-ment" with God. There is nothing we ourselves can do to bridge the gap except to acknowledge God's love and accept it. This is one way of understanding the common evangelical expression "Accept Jesus Christ as Lord and Savior and be saved." We accept the reality of Jesus' death on the cross as the eternal sign that God reaches out to us in forgiveness. As we internalize that truth, the weight of our separation is lifted. We feel "at-one" again and are saved or made whole.

Atonement is an important theological concept. The parable of the prodigal son follows the assigned verses in Luke 15. This parable expresses the concept simply and dramatically. If we look honestly at any human relationship, we realize that we cannot *earn* the love of the other person, whether it be spouse, friend, or relative. But we begin to appreciate just how strong and beautiful the relationship is when we realize that someone loves us not because we have been lovable but because that person accepts us in our weakness as well as in our strength. Atonement is the basis for family and friendship relationships as well as for our relationship with God. Until we have experienced and accepted this reality, we live within the shadow of our doubts and our guilt. (See the fourth Sunday in Lent, pages 250-251, for further discussion of the parable of the prodigal son.)

Proper 20   E
Twenty-fifth Sunday in Ordinary Time   RC
Eighteenth Sunday after Pentecost   L

Old Testament: The prophet Amos denounces the people for their greed and injustice to the poor. They can hardly wait for the Sabbath to be over so they can start selling again. They cheat and steal from the poor in their constant grasping for wealth.

Gospel: Jesus tells a parable that may sound strange to us. A steward is about to be fired. He goes to those who owe his master money and reduces their debt. Yet he is praised for this act. Jesus' point is not without humor. The people of God should have at least as much ability to prepare for their judgment as does a dishonest person! The rest of the gospel reading is a series of loosely connected sayings that speak of our need to be prepared for the Lord's judgment by the way we handle whatever wealth the Lord gives us. We had better use it in a way that will bring us friends, not condemnation. We cannot possibly serve God if we are self-indulgent and untrustworthy in handling the world's goods.

Telling the story: Tell the story of Naboth's vineyard today (1 Kings 21). King Ahab and his wife Jezebel gain the vineyard of their neighbor dishonestly; the prophet Elijah confronts them with their sin.

Religious concepts: Social justice is an important theme today. Do a quick survey of the writings of Amos; then read the day's newspaper with his words in mind. Where do we see social injustice in our community? More important, how do we see *ourselves* involved in that injustice? We may find that even our parish or national church is taking advantage of the poor, discriminating, or misusing the public trust. Next week's readings will continue this theme.

Proper 21   E
Twenty-sixth Sunday in Ordinary Time   RC
Nineteenth Sunday after Pentecost   L

Old Testament: Strong words from the prophet Amos condemn the idle rich. They will be the first to go into exile.

Gospel: The parable of the rich man and Lazarus.

Telling the story: The parable of the rich man and Lazarus is a powerful one to share, though we need to be careful not to literalize the concepts of heaven and hell, especially in the minds of children. Jesus was using the language of metaphor in the story, not providing us with literal descriptions of a place where we go after death. In telling the story, include "as if" in your descriptions at appropriate places. "When the rich man died, it was *as if* he was in a place separated. . . ." The purpose in sharing the story is not to discuss heaven and hell but the injustice to the poor man that resulted from the rich man's total indifference to the needs of those about him. When you finish sharing the story, ask questions that will help participants identify with the poor man and experience the injustice that comes out of indifference. Have they ever been hungry? How long have they gone without eating? How would they feel if they saw someone throw half a hamburger away right in front of them while they obviously were suffering from hunger?

Religious concepts: Social justice and the Christian responsibility to respond to suffering and injustice is the theme and concept for this week. Study Amos; talk about the injustices he felt. The rich withdrew into their summer homes and ignored the needs of people and nation. In so doing, they also withdrew from their covenant with God. The covenant demands a concern for the widow, the orphan, the stranger, the oppressed. Jesus aims a pointed barb at the same class of people in today's parable. Talk about our lives in our own country today. What are the people of the inner city saying to the people of the suburbs? What is happening to our cities? Study the writing of the other prophets. This is a time to raise our social consciousness.

Proper 22   E
Twenty-seventh Sunday in Ordinary Time   RC
Twentieth Sunday after Pentecost L

Old Testament: This reading from Habakkuk contains the beautiful words "Behold, he whose soul is not upright in him shall fail, / but the righteous shall live by his faith" (Habakkuk 2:4). People have come to the prophet asking the questions we all ask: "Why dost thou make me see wrongs and look upon trouble?" Habakkuk raises these questions to the Lord, realizing that he must stand as a watchman ". . . and look forth to see what he will say to me. . . ." The Lord's response is that we must live by our faith.

Gospel: Jesus, too, calls his followers to have faith. If they even had faith the size of a tiny mustard seed they could cause a sycamore tree to be transplanted into the sea. The point of the second portion of the reading is that we can't expect special treatment for doing only what is expected of us. Of course we are involved in the struggle for social justice in our community. We can't expect applause from the Lord for that. ". . . we have only done what was our duty."

Telling the story: Tell the stories of Daniel listed in A Guide to Stories of the Bible, page 37. These are folk stories that our people have told to show the power of faith; they are not literal events.

Religious concepts: Paul's letter to the Romans deals with our justification by faith, and Martin Luther was influenced by this epistle. The words of both men echo the beautiful Old Testament reading appointed for today. This is an extremely important concept in our Christian understanding of life in Christ.

Proper 23   E
Twenty-eighth Sunday in Ordinary Time   RC
Twenty-first Sunday after Pentecost L

Old Testament: We hear the beautiful story of Ruth today.

The Roman Catholic lesson is the conclusion of the story of the cure of Naaman, commander of the King of Aram's army. He contracted leprosy and could not find a cure. An Israelite girl in the service of Naaman's wife urged him to go to Elijah the prophet for his cure. In today's lesson we hear Naaman's words of praise and thanksgiving. He takes back earth from Israel so that he can worship Yahweh on Israel's soil.

Gospel: Jesus cleanses ten lepers. Only one, a Samaritan, returns to give thanks.

Telling the story: The story of Ruth is a beautiful one to share with persons of all ages. We get a good insight into the folkways of Old

Testament people from this book.

The story of Naaman could be shared today in Roman Catholic parishes. God brings healing not only to the Israelites but to others as well. In a sense, the stories of Ruth and of Naaman are healing stories that deal with God's love for both foreigner and Israelite. Ruth's grief and alienation are healed through the love she shares in Naomi's family. Naaman's leprosy is healed by Yahweh's prophet. Both foreigners appreciate the healing they have felt in Yahweh's presence.

Religious concepts: Today's readings are an argument against feelings of religious or ethnic superiority. King David was the descendant of Ruth, a foreigner, we learn in the closing verses of the Book of Ruth. Jesus notes the appreciation of the Samaritan, who was a foreigner and an outcast. He contrasted the Samaritan's appreciation and responsiveness to God with the arrogance and decadence of his own people.

Proper 24   E
Twenty-ninth Sunday in Ordinary Time   RC
Twenty-second Sunday after Pentecost L

Old Testament: In this portion of the Jacob-Esau narrative, Jacob wrestles with an angel and prevails.

The Roman Catholic lesson for today is Exodus 17:8-13. Moses intercedes constantly for his people as they engage Amalek in battle. The raising of Moses' hands was a sign of his intercessions for the people. This is a symbol of the kind of intercessions we are called to offer.

Gospel: Jesus tells a parable to emphasize the need for perseverance in prayer.

Telling the story: The Jacob-Esau tales from the Book of Genesis are good for storytelling. (See A Guide to Stories of the Bible, chapter 1, page 22.)

These are folk tales that need to be shared as part of our ancient "lore." Tell the stories as you would tell a story around a campfire.

Religious concepts: We return this week to the important concept of Christian prayer that we last dealt with in the readings of Proper 12. Jacob strove with God and finally received a blessing. Jesus told an amusing parable about a widow whose nagging drove an unjust judge to

his wits' end until he finally gave in from sheer desperation. If this crooked judge would respond to the widow's petition, surely our loving Father will respond to our needs stated in prayer.

This encouragement to pray needs to be balanced with the point made in connection with Proper 12, however. God hears us, but we must also listen to God in our prayers so that we may understand his will as it applies to our petitions. The section in *The Book of Common Prayer* entitled Prayers and Thanksgivings (pages 809-841) would make a good study for older participants this Sunday. These, in a sense, are model prayers that express concern and petition about a wide variety of subjects. Give each participant several of the prayers to study briefly. What concerns are expressed? How are the petitions to God phrased in the formal prayers of the gathered church? What name or title of God is used in the prayer? What might God be saying to us this moment if we were to listen after offering this prayer?

On this Sunday we could study liturgical prayer form. Notice that each prayer contains common elements. First there is an invocation of God. Each prayer will name God in a title and/or describe God's saving action in the world. For example, "O Lord Jesus Christ, you became poor for our sake, that we might be made rich through your poverty. . . ."

Second, there is the petition itself. The same prayer says "Guide and sanctify, we pray, those whom you call to follow you under the vows of poverty, chastity, and obedience, that by their prayer and service they may enrich your church, and by their life and worship may glorify your Name. . . ." Finally, there is an offering of the prayer in Jesus' name or a doxology of praise. For example, "For you reign with the Father and the Holy Spirit, one God, now and forever. Amen."

A quick study of the prayers could be done by having participants take several prayers and record the titles of God, the petitions, and the closing words of doxology or of petition in Jesus' name. Make a newsprint synopsis of the names, the petitions, and the closing words; at the completion of the feedback session, talk about the diversity of titles and concerns expressed. Such a study will show participants how the Church has traditionally understood God's saving action in the world and will teach them our theology of prayer and praise.

A similar study could be done with the weekly Collects assigned as part of the proper for each Sunday. These are found in *The Book of Common Prayer,* pages 211-261. Talk about the role of the Collect in the propers. The word *collect* comes from the Latin word *collecta,* meaning *assembly.* Traditionally it is the prayer said before the assembled faithful and is followed by the reading of the Bible.* A proper is assigned to each week of the church year and to all the special holy days and festivals. A brief study of the Collects would help persons appreciate the beauty of these ancient prayers that have been used by generations of worshiping Christians. These are our models for prayers that we offer God in our own words.

Let this be "prayer week" in the parish. Tell the story of Jacob and Esau, and take time to talk about prayer. If there are prayer groups active in the parish, publicize their activities and encourage persons in their life of prayer. In the Episcopal Church, Morning and Evening Prayer are provided in the *Prayer Book* as a way of framing each day in Bible readings, prayer, and thanksgivings. A daily lectionary is provided to be used with these "daily offices" (from the Latin word meaning *daily obligation*) so that persons are led through the Bible in a two-year cycle of readings.

Proper 25   E
Thirtieth Sunday in Ordinary Time   RC
Twenty-third Sunday after Pentecost   L

Old Testament: The prophet Jeremiah acknowledges Judah's sins.

Lutherans will hear Deuteronomy 10:12-22 this Sunday. The reading is a strong call for justice. We must keep the commandments of the Lord. "Love the sojourner therefore; for you were sojourners in the land of Egypt" (Deuteronomy 10:19). The words are humbling, for in hearing them we become aware of the great

*Howard Harper, *The Episcopalian's Dictionary* (New York: Seabury Press, 1974), pp. 45-46.

gulf between our call to covenant and our response as sinful people.

The Roman Catholic reading appointed for today is Sirach (Ecclesiasticus) 35:12-14,16-18, the prayer of a lowly person. "The prayer of the humble pierces the clouds; and he will not be consoled until it reaches the Lord. . ." (Sirach 35:17).

Gospel: The parable of the Pharisee and the tax collector is heard today. The Pharisee is proud. The tax collector humbly acknowledges his sin. The conclusion is, ". . . every one who exalts himself will be humbled, but he who humbles himself will be exalted."

Telling the story: Some of Jeremiah's adventures would make good storytelling today. Jeremiah 26: Jeremiah's life is threatened because of the unpopular words he speaks. Jeremiah 36: King Jehoiakim hears the words of Jeremiah and burns the scroll containing Jeremiah's prophecies. Jeremiah 37—38: Jeremiah suffers in prison because of his continuing words of doom for Judah. Jeremiah 39—42: When the Babylonians do invade the land, they free Jeremiah and treat him well. Jeremiah's suffering at the hands of his people comes because he confronts them with their sinfulness.

Tell the story of the Pharisee and the tax collector.

Religious concepts: The Christian must approach God in humility. As we acknowledge our sin and separation, we are open to forgiveness and reconciliation with God and each other. Go through the Sunday liturgy and note the places where we acknowledge our humbleness and separation.

Proper 26   E
Thirty-first Sunday in Ordinary Time   RC
Twenty-fourth Sunday after Pentecost L

Old Testament: In this reading we hear Isaiah's strong condemnation of the empty, meaningless sacrifices the people offer in the Temple. These sacrifices will not replace the covenant's call of justice, he warns.

The Roman Catholic lectionary's reading from Wisdom 11:23—12:1 describes the Lord's love for all people. The Lord does not hate the sinner: ". . . thou lovest all things that exist, / and hast loathing for none of the things which thou hast made. . ." (Wisdom 11:24). Because of this deep love, the Lord patiently leads the sinner to repentance and a renewed relationship.

The Lutheran lectionary appoints Exodus 34:5-9 as the first lesson. Yahweh forgives his people after they worship the golden calf.

Gospel: This is the familiar story of Jesus and Zacchaeus.

Telling the story: The gospel story of Zacchaeus is delightfully human.

Religious concepts: God loves and seeks out the sinner. (The Old Testament lesson appointed in the Roman Catholic lectionary is a beautiful expression of this love.) Zacchaeus was considered a sinner and an outcast because of his hated occupation. In the eyes of the Lord, though, he was loved and forgiven. In seeking the Lord that day, Zacchaeus found forgiveness and peace with Jesus. Isaiah's angry words might well be directed against his unforgiving neighbors. We can compare their empty sacrifices in the Temple with Zacchaeus' true offering of himself to the Lord.

The words ". . . thou lovest all things that exist, and hast loathing for none of the things which thou hast made" (Wisdom 11:24) are important. We often hate ourselves because of how we perceive our actions, thoughts, and feelings. But God loves us and forgives us as we reach out for his love as Zacchaeus did.

Proper 27 E
Thirty-second Sunday in Ordinary Time RC
Twenty-fifth Sunday after Pentecost L

Old Testament: Episcopal lectionary—Job's words of hope are heard today. He knows, even in his agonizing suffering, that his vindicator *does* live and that ". . . at last he will stand upon the earth; . . . whom I shall see on my side, and my eyes shall behold, and not another" (Job 19:25,27).

Lutheran lectionary—This reading is David's fervent prayer of thanksgiving. David recognizes that the Lord is responsible for everything. ". . . for all that is in the heavens and in the earth is thine; thine is the kingdom, O

Lord, and thou art exalted as head above all" (1 Chronicles 29:11).

Roman Catholic lectionary—This story includes words that speak of the promise of the resurrection.

Gospel: Jesus talks about the resurrection in response to questions from the Sadducees.

Telling the story: Today I would tell the story of the man born blind (John 9). This is not a story of resurrection, but it tells about a man who experienced a new life in Christ. As he went at Jesus' command and washed in the pool, he could see for the first time in his life. He was able to experience life as he had never been able to before. ". . . one thing I know, that though I was blind, now I see." The Jewish authorities could not understand the healing nor accept the validity of what was happening. Share the story to help participants experience a taste of the new life that the Lord brings us. Those who do not have faith in that new life cannot comprehend the promise of life offered by Christ.

Religious concepts: See the discussion of the resurrection in chapter 2, pages 69-72.

Proper 28 E
Thirty-third Sunday in Ordinary Time RC
Twenty-sixth Sunday after Pentecost L

Old Testament: The reading is a grim warning of the coming day of wrath when the faithful will be saved and the unrelenting will perish at the hand of the Lord.

Gospel: Jesus warns that the day of judgment is at hand. This is the apocalyptic section of the Gospel of Luke.

Telling the story: The story of David and Bathsheba (2 Samuel 11:1—12:25) would help participants in the learning community feel a sense of judgment that comes when we break covenant with the Lord. See the remarks about this story in A Guide to Stories of the Bible, chapter 1, page 30. There is no need to go into the details about the nature of David's sin. With younger children we can simply say that David wanted to marry another man's wife and arranged to have her husband killed.

Religious concepts: Read the remarks about apocalyptic literature in chapter 2, pages 63 and 69.

Proper 29   E
Last Sunday in Ordinary Time:
Feast of Christ the King   RC
Last Sunday after Pentecost:
Christ the King   L

Old Testament: Jeremiah looks forward to the day when the Lord will "gather the remnant of (his) flock" and raise up from the house of David a righteous leader.

Roman Catholics will hear 2 Samuel 5:1-3 today. This reading describes the anointing of David as King of Israel. As mentioned elsewhere in this book (page 29), it was the practice of our people to pour oil on the heads of those who became king. *Messiah* means *anointed one* in the Hebrew language. *Christos* is the Greek word for *the anointed one.* This reading helps us appreciate the nature of Christ's kingship. The anointed one of the Lord speaks the word of the Lord and is the "outward and visible sign" of the Lord's presence with his people. Jesus is the anointed one of the Lord. His words are the Father's. To know Jesus is to know the Father. Christ the King points to the eternal presence of God the Father.

Gospel: Two choices of readings are given: 1) the crucifixion account, in which Jesus responds to the repentant criminal by saying ". . . today you will be with me in Paradise"

(Luke 23:43) and 2) Jesus' entry into Jerusalem (the Palm Sunday reading).

The Lutheran and Roman Catholic lectionaries do not include the latter reading (Luke 19:29-38) as an option.

Religious concepts: This is the final week of the church year. In Roman Catholic tradition, this day is the Feast of Christ the King. The Collect and the readings reflect that theme and concept. The epistle is a beautiful hymn that expresses the meaning of this feast day. "He is before all things, and in him all things hold together. He is the head of the body, the church, he is the beginning, the first-born from the dead, that in everything he might be pre-eminent" (Colossians 1:17-18). In the age to come, Christ will reign fully over all creation. The separation from Christ that we experience because of our sinfulness will be erased. Jesus promised this kind of total kingship to the criminal on the cross. Christ as King forgives the repentant sinner at the moment of death. The alternate reading for the gospel expresses the thought that a new king of Israel enters the Holy City to consecrate it anew.

This final reading points toward Advent and the beginning of a new church year which looks forward to Christ's return when he will establish his kingdom in its fullness.

Chapter 8
A Commentary on the Saints' Days and Other Holy Days

Celebrating Saints' Days

The saints' days form an important part of our liturgical calendar, and yet they are sometimes overlooked.

Saints are the heroes of the Christian faith. We know very little about some of them, and some of what we do know is merely legendary. Though time may have dimmed the details of their lives, our celebrations of their struggle nevertheless put us in touch with our roots and with our sense of calling as Christian people. And in celebrating the witness of those people, we point to our own potential as Christian witnesses.

Moreover, it's fun to tell and listen to adventure stories. In the learning community, share the adventure stories of the various saints as their festival days approach. The legends should be told as legends. Even if they are not literally true, they reveal the people's feelings about their heroes.

The ancient custom of having a patron saint for each parish and mission is a beautiful one that is carried on in some of our Christian traditions. The patron saint of the parish is its protector or benefactor and has a special relationship with the people of that parish. But the idea of patron saints extends beyond parishes

and missions. For instance, St. George is considered the patron saint of England, and St. Nicholas has traditionally been the patron saint of sailors and children. With this special and eternal relationship in mind, nations, parishes, and many other special groups have traditionally celebrated patronal feast days to remember and honor their saints.

In the parish these festivals can be a time of drama, song, carnival, feasting, pageantry, and partying. Set up a brainstorming group to talk about ideas for a celebration. Check out books and resource material on your special saint. If you are dealing with a national patron saint such as St. George, find out the customs associated with that country's celebration of its saint. Tell the stories and legends, and help to make the memory of that saint come alive in your parish or mission family. *The Book of Common Prayer* contains propers (prayers and Bible readings) for the major saints' days. *Lesser Feasts and Fasts* contains the calendar, prayers and lessons for less-known saints, as well as biographical sketches.* The saints' days are not usually celebrated on Sundays, so their feast days often pass by unnoticed in our parish

---

Lesser Feasts and Fasts, rev. ed. (New York: Church Hymnal Corporation, 1973).

life. The festival of the saint for which the parish is named may be celebrated on the Sunday closest to the appointed day. Form a "saints' day celebration group" composed of priest, musicians, lay readers, religious educators, and other interested persons. Choose some of the saints you want to focus on this year. Make sure their story is told in the religious education setting. Mention and celebrate their lives and witness in the Sunday liturgy. Plan a parish festival, picnic, play, pageant, film, or other event to mark the memory and emphasize the vision of sainthood that Christ pointed out for all his people.

The suggestions that follow are for observing *some* of the more important feast days celebrated by many churches.

"Festivals of Revelation"

In addition to the typical saints' days we celebrate what I call "festivals of revelation." They celebrate six special times when God very clearly revealed his presence and his will to certain people who were closely associated with Jesus. These festivals are:

The Confession of St. Peter
(January 18)

Peter was the first of the disciples to realize and acknowledge that Jesus was more than a prophet or good teacher: He was the Christ, "the Son of the living God." Peter's acknowledgment or "confession" led Jesus to say ". . .you are Peter, and on this rock I will build my church."

Since the feast day of St. Peter and St. Paul comes during the summer (June 29) when many of our people may be gone on vacation, this "festival of revelation" might be a more appropriate time to celebrate Peter's special role in the church. Explore the Gospels and the Book of Acts for all the facts about St. Peter. Let children play detective and see how much they can find out about him. Make up a profile or resume sheet on him. If you were interviewing him for the position of bishop of the diocese, would you accept him? Why do you think Jesus chose him

as "the rock" upon which he founded the Church?

The Conversion of St. Paul
(January 25)

Paul was an early persecutor of the Christians and was a witness to the stoning of the first Christian martyr, St. Stephen. While on the road to Damascus to persecute the Christians, Paul had an intense vision in which he felt the call to become an apostle. So God's will was revealed to him in a very dramatic way.

On the day or the Sunday closest to this feast day, ask several persons in the parish to tell the story of how they feel God's will has been revealed for them. Why are they involved in the Church? What has led them into the kind of work they do? How have their ideas and feelings of faith been formed? What events and people have shaped their lives into the kind of Christian people they are now? We may not find ourselves lying in the road blinded by a flash of God's revelation, but if we begin to look at our lives in the context of St. Paul's struggle, we may begin to see how God is uniquely calling us and sending us into his world.

Children need to hear this story of Paul (see Acts 9 and 26). When the children have grasped how God called Paul and changed his life, help them to see how God does the same in their lives. Have they moved from one city to another? from one school to another? Has a parent or brother or sister been called to a new job? Have they or their families gained new insights and embarked on new projects? These can be true "conversion experiences," though not as dramatic as St. Paul's.

The Presentation
(February 2)

Mosaic Law demanded that the firstborn male of the family must be consecrated to the Lord on the eighth day after his birth. (The prescription and supposed origin of this custom is found in Exodus 13:2-16.) This ancient tradition may have come out of the Canaanite practice of sacrificing the firstborn male to the local deity. When the Israelites inherited the custom, they replaced the human sacrifice with a symbolic sacrifice in which the male was first offered to God to acknowledge that the child truly belonged to the Lord. Then the child was "redeemed" or returned to the family by the offering of five shekels (Numbers 3:47). According to the ancient custom, too, the mother had to be ritually purified after giving birth (see Leviticus 12:1-8). The loss of blood was considered a sign of sinfulness, since blood was seen as the expression of life itself. So the menstrual cycle and childbirth both rendered a woman unclean. To be restored to communion with God and with the community of the faithful, the woman had to purify herself ritually by offering a lamb, or in the case of the poor, two turtledoves or pigeons. We need to understand these customs if we are to appreciate the significance of the festival for ourselves.

When we celebrate the presentation of Jesus, we recognize that he was born and raised under the Law of the Old Covenant. The epistle appointed for this day explains why. If Jesus was to bring wholeness to men and women, he must fully share their life and follow their ways, even to being tempted as they are. "Therefore he had to be made like his brethren in every respect, so that he might become a merciful and faithful high priest in the service of God, to make expiation for the sins of the people. For because he himself has suffered and been tempted, he is able to help those who are tempted" (Hebrews 2:17-18).

In taking part in those ancient rituals of the Old Law, however, Jesus brought a new significance to the practice of his people. He was truly presented to God, and so God's people were purified and their relationship fully restored by Jesus' presence among them. The Temple was the visible reminder to the people that they met God in their daily life in his world. Similarly, when Jesus was brought into the Temple, Simeon and Anna recognized that his body would become the new Temple, the new meeting place between God and his people (Luke 2:22-38). The faithful would know the living presence of God in their midst in a new and deeper way as they met the person Jesus and as they experienced his risen presence in the Body of Christ, his Church.

The beautiful sense of offering all of our sons and daughters to God can be experienced in the ancient practice of the Episcopal Church expressed in the liturgy for A Thanksgiving for

the Birth or Adoption of a Child (*The Book of Common Prayer,* pages 439-455). Though the emphasis in the *Prayer Book* is on thanksgiving, the sense of dedicating the child to God is felt in such prayers as ". . . give them (the parents) calm strength and patient wisdom as they seek to bring this child to love all that is true and noble, just and pure, lovable and gracious, excellent and admirable, following the example of our Lord and Savior, Jesus Christ." The parents and the assembled faithful recognize their commitment to raise the child to know God's presence, and they dedicate the child to God's love and service.

This concept of dedication is a beautiful one to share. We begin to see the added significance of each one of our lives as we realize that we, like Jesus, are dedicated to the Lord's service. Our lives "reveal God's glory in the world," as another liturgical prayer says.

When a couple announces that they are expecting a baby, we can begin to prepare the congregation to celebrate the Feast of the Presentation. Talk in the religious education setting about the significance of the child's life in the eyes of God. Share the custom of Jesus' time of offering the firstborn male to God. Let the parish celebrate the event by a formal presentation of the infant during the main liturgy of the day. Remind the people that just as God's presence was revealed to Simeon and Anna when Jesus was presented in the Temple, so God's presence is revealed to us in the love and creation we celebrate as we offer our child to God in grateful thanksgiving. Let the children make symbolic gifts to offer to the infant and its parents. This presentation may not come on February 2, the date of the church's festival, but when that day is celebrated in the church it will certainly have more meaning to those who gather to proclaim the significance of Jesus' presentation in their lives.

The Annunciation
(March 25)

This moment of revelation celebrates the announcement or annunciation to Mary that she was to give birth to Jesus. What is revealed in this festival is not only the miraculous nature of the birth of Jesus but the complete obedience and trust expressed by Mary as the announcement was made to her. "I am the handmaid of the Lord; let it be to me according to your word" (Luke 1:38).

Nine months from this date the parish will celebrate Christmas. We should realize the sense of trust that any woman must have as she carries her unborn child in her womb. As with the feast of the Presentation, this holy day needs to be linked with the actual experience of pregnancy and expectation that happens in the everyday life of the parish. Pregnancy really does represent the unknown. Will it be a boy, or a girl? Will the baby be all right? What does life hold in store for this child? What kind of parents and friends of the child will we be? What kind of response may we be called upon to make in the years ahead for the sake of this child? What might God be calling us into with this birth? Expectant mothers are not limited to human mothers. Let children talk about their pets and about the excitement they feel when a pet animal is going to have young ones. Parents often remind their children that the birth of kittens is going to mean some extra responsibilities around the house!

After discussing the significance of pregnancy and the feelings connected with it, we can shift our attention to Mary and Joseph. In an intense vision Mary learns that she will give birth to a child who will change the course of history and the significance of human life. What must have run through her mind as the words of the vision came to her? Compare Mary's vision to Abraham's vision in Genesis. "Now the Lord said to Abram, 'Go from your country and your kindred and your father's house to the land that I will show you'. . . . So Abram went, as the Lord had told him" (Genesis 12:1,4). God's will was revealed to Abraham and to Mary in strange, powerful visions. The responses were faith responses. But God also reveals his will for us as *we* conceive and give birth and as *we* face other times of change and transition in our lives. Moments of revelation come to *us* in moments of birth and promised birth, whether that birth be physical or whether it be a birth into a new phase of our life. Who have been the "messengers" or angels that have spoken to us and announced these promises? How have we responded? What "announcements" can we foresee in the months

ahead, and how do we feel about the possibilities they may open up to us?

As Christmas comes, recall the parish celebration of the Annunciation. As you now celebrate the birth date of Jesus, celebrate all those "birth dates" you have experienced within the parish between March and December.

The Transfiguration of Christ (August 6)

The account of the transfiguration of Jesus on the mountain is also heard and celebrated each year on the Last Sunday after Epiphany in Episcopal and Lutheran churches and on the Second Sunday of Lent in Roman Catholic churches. Jesus went up the mountain with Peter, John, and James. "And as he was praying, the appearance of his countenance was altered, and his raiment became dazzling white. And behold, two men talked with him, Moses and Elijah, who appeared in glory. . ." (Luke 9:29-30). The Old Testament reading appointed in the Episcopal Church for this day (Exodus 34:29-35) is the obvious reference point for the gospel account; when the covenant between God and his people was revealed to Moses, the experience was so intense that the face of Moses shone as he came down the mountain.

As I mentioned in discussing this account in the context of the Last Sunday after Epiphany (page 162), we can get the sense of the shining face if we think about how we use the phrase *seeing the light* to describe a new realization or revelation. Moses and the people "saw the light." They were God's people linked to him in covenant. Peter, John, and James "saw the light." Jesus represented a New Covenant between God and the faithful. It was a covenant sealed with the forgiving love expressed on the cross. Now everything that Jesus had said and would say took on a new significance for the disciples. This intense experience of "seeing the light" was a turning point for them and for the Church.

A "mountain-top experience" is also a common idiom today. The celebration of the Transfiguration celebrates those mountain-top and seeing-the-light experiences that we share—experiences in which God's presence is revealed to us. This feast would be a very good time to reflect with adults and children on the mountaintop experiences of their lives. What has been revealed to them in those experiences? How would they describe the revelation poetically? For example, a mountain-top experience for a child may be the visit of a grandparent. What makes it a mountain-top experience? The revelation in "My grandparents took me to all kinds of exciting places during their visit, and I felt like a very special person" is that the child *is* a very special person in the eyes of the grandparents and in the eyes of God. That was the revelation to the disciples on the mountain top too. Because Jesus was a special person, they also were special because of their relationship with him. List on newsprint the mountain-top experiences of the group.

Then shift the idiom to seeing-the-light experiences in order to gain a sense of how our lives are transfigured in the light of Christ's presence with us. Then see if you can move from a story description of the event to a poetic expression that helps the group share the *feeling* of that experience with the person. For example, "When my grandparents visit, I feel as if I've been named to the Baseball Hall of Fame" or "When I read that book, the sun came out from behind dark clouds and made me want to dance in the grass." Combine the beautiful poetry of the New Testament with the poetry expressed by the participants in a closing liturgy that celebrates our common and unique mountain-top experiences.

Notice that Peter wanted to stay on the mountain top. This is a common feeling that we can express too; we want to keep the beautiful feeling that we have in a moment of revelation. But we are always called to move on and face the world as it is, realizing that we are part of God's continuing transfiguration of creation. When Jesus came down from the mountain, he had to face the failure of his disciples in curing an epileptic boy. In frustration he said ". . . how long am I to be with you and bear with you?" (Luke 9:41). He moved from the high experience to the low experience. We too cannot always expect to live on the mountain and plateau. We too must "come down from the mountain" and confront disillusionment and frustration, and we must see this as a part of our pilgrimage.

The Ascension
(Thursday after the Sixth Sunday of Easter)

The revelation we celebrate today is that the direct experience of God revealed to men and women in Jesus of Nazareth *continues* to be experienced when the Body of Christ, the Church, gathers in witness, love, and mission. Jesus brought power and hope to people. As he talked, healed, and loved them, they felt the direct presence of God. To be in the company of Jesus was to be in the company of God. Jesus appeared to his disciples after his resurrection. Those appearances were more than their seeing a vision or acknowledging that death could not destroy the Lord. In his appearances Jesus told his disciples that the faithful would continue to experience his presence even though they could no longer see him. The Holy Spirit would make them aware and sensitive to that presence, and they would know him "in the flesh" of their life together in the Church. They would feel the same healing power freeing them from their enslavement to sin and guilt. Their vision of life would be enlarged as they felt a covenant relationship with God through the love expressed by Jesus.

To say "My life has significance because I am a child of God called to carry out his will in my life" is to make a statement that opens one's life to new power and possibilities. Experiencing Jesus the Christ, in other words, was not to cease with the death of Jesus nor with the last of his resurrection appearances. The experience would continue among the faithful.

We express this truth poetically when we say in the Nicene Creed, ". . . he ascended into heaven and is seated at the right hand of the Father." In sharing the feast of the Ascension in the religious education setting, we need to keep in mind the poetic nature of the statement of the Creed and of the Acts account. The power and presence of Christ are *eternal* experiences, not limited to time and space. The presence of Christ is as much our experience as it was the experience of the disciples. Christ "reigns" eternally with God, the creative power that calls us into being.

A second important point needs to be made as the story of the ascension is told. For a time, the followers of Jesus saw distinct visions of his presence. These are the resurrection appearances described in the New Testament. But after a time his presence was marked by a feeling more than by vision. He ascended in the sense that he was no longer seen.

We need to look at what Jesus did with people that made them aware that being in his presence was being in the living presence of God. He healed persons. He told stories that opened people to new reality and power. He confronted people and turned them back into the way of the covenant. Jesus released people from the slavery of guilt and let them know that as they acknowledged their separation from God and from one another, they were forgiven and accepted as God's people. He often ate with them and sometimes fed them. Finally, he died in such a way that those who knew him realized the kind of total love that God had for them. This love empowered them to move beyond the boundaries defined for them under the Old Covenant and opened to them a whole new kind of life under the New Covenant of love.

As Ascension Day draws near, talk with participants in the learning community about those times during the past year when they experienced acts of healing, caring, forgiving. Have them share their stories of these events. Then talk about how the ascended Christ *is* feeding and healing us in our own day through those experiences. From this sharing you can develop your own gospel that expresses the good news of how Christ is touching the participants today. Close the session by tying the good news stories of the group with the good news stories recorded in Matthew, Mark, Luke, and John. Point out how our stories continue the gospel narrative. These personal experiences shared by the group can become our own "ascension stories." They are stories that show how the reign of Christ continues even in our own time. If the good news accounts from parishioners were recorded prior to the feast of the Ascension, then the good news as proclaimed by the learning community can be shared as a part of the sermon. The connection for younger participants will be tenuous, but reciting contemporary ascension experiences will at least provide a more concrete understanding of the ascension than the poetic gospel narrative does.

"Concept" Festivals

Most of the holy days and seasons of the church year center on the story of Jesus' life, death, resurrection, ascension, and sending of the Holy Spirit. But the festivals of Trinity, Rogation, All Saints' Day and the Commemoration of All Faithful Departed express religious truths or concepts rather than points in the Jesus story. In other words, the vast majority of our festivals, fasts, and seasons are dramatizations of The Story, whereas the ones just mentioned are intellectual understandings that have arisen as a *result* of The Story. As we celebrate these festivals, we proclaim eternal truths that help us better understand how God's story continues to be told and experienced in our lives.

Rogation

The word *rogation* comes from a Latin word meaning *to ask*. Traditionally, the Monday, Tuesday, and Wednesday preceding Ascension Day (the week following the Sixth Sunday of Easter) have been set aside as special days to ask the Lord's blessing for the growing crops that have recently been planted. English custom called for the folk of the parish to "beat the bounds" of the parish. This meant that the faithful walked through the fields of the parish and blessed the growing crops. The truth expressed in this beautiful ancient tradition is that all life is blessed by God. The growing seeds become signs of his creative presence in our midst. The tradition of "beating the bounds" meant an extensive procession through the fields of the parish. The physical movement through the fields in solemn procession and with song and chanted psalm could not fail to proclaim the truth to all participants that "All things come of thee, O Lord."

Celebrate Rogation in the parish by blessing growing things on the grounds of the parish church. If you feel more adventuresome, follow the ancient tradition more closely by going out to a nearby parishioner's farm and blessing the fields in procession. Gather afterwards in the yard and share a potluck picnic. Trinity Episcopal Parish in Ashland, Oregon, shares an annual procession in the city park. The entire congregation joins the procession through the park in a colorful witness to God's presence in the midst of the city. When possible, a baptism is celebrated, using the waters of the stream that runs through the park. In our parish we combine the blessing of the animals with the blessing of the seeds and growing things. During the prayer of Intercession we offer the Rogation prayers found in *The Book of Common Prayer*. After the celebration of the Eucharist, the people leave the nave of the church and go to their cars to retrieve their pets left there during the liturgy. Coming back into the church yard, they stand in a circle with their pets. Each animal is named. Then, placing my hand on the animal's head, I say: "Father, we thank you for the life of __(name)__. May __(name)__ grow in the love and life that you offer all your creatures. Amen."Not only does this blessing recognize the significance and importance of our pets, but it reminds us that we are stewards of God's gifts. The animals of the world are also signs of God's love for us and for all creation.

As a part of our celebration we also bless packets of seeds and offer them to the children of the parish to plant in their home yards, and we give crosses that can be placed in the garden as an all-summer reminder of the significance of the life growing there.

A simple celebration that the entire parish can appreciate together is a spring picnic or an afternoon of games and fellowship as a natural followup of the liturgy.

Trinity Sunday

The doctrine of the Trinity describes the unique ways that we experience God's presence in our lives. It is a confusing doctrine, even for adults, because it seems to imply three gods who are yet one God. The Collect for Trinity expresses the difficulty. "Almighty and everlasting God, you have given to us your servants grace, by the confession of a true faith, to acknowledge the glory of the eternal Trinity, and in the power of your divine Majesty to worship the Unity. . ." *(The Book of Common Prayer,* page 228). When we speak of the mystery of creator and creation, we can only apprehend that mystery by analogy, poetry, and symbolic language. What we describe with the doctrine of the Trinity is an *experience* of God.

First, we know God through his creation and through our own creative acts. Rogation, mentioned above, celebrates God in creation. When my wife sculptures with wood, she feels fulfilled and at peace with herself. Speaking theologically, I would say that she feels fulfilled because she is in touch with God in an act of creation by which she herself shapes something into a figure or form. The intense fulfillment of childbirth is another example of a creative time. When we are creative, we feel whole and fulfilled. God is creating through us, and we have a sense of being an instrument for the divine. We call this way of experiencing God "Father," since the Hebrews felt that the father of the family was the source of life in the conception of a child.

Secondly, we know God in the sense expressed in the First Epistle of John: "God is love, and he who abides in love abides in God, and God abides in him" (1 John 4:16). God is as close to us as the healing love that is shared among his people. It was Jesus who proclaimed this reality by the power of love he showed in his life, death, and resurrection. Using the metaphors of biblical language, we could say that we "meet Christ" in the acts of love and healing. We know God through the "flesh and blood" of his presence in our lives and through the power of love that leads us into deeper life. We call this way of experiencing and knowing God "Son," since Jesus was called the Son of God.

Finally, we feel the spirit and are "turned on" to God's power. We know God through the *inspiration* that comes to us. Our secular use of the word *spirit* describes very well the experiences of God we feel through spiritedness and inspiration. When I say that certain words "came to me" in a moment of crisis, I feel I am describing the experience of receiving inspiration. As Christians we simply add the word *holy* to the everyday word *spirit* to define the spirited way of knowing God in our lives. Thus we can say that we know God as Father, Son, and Holy Spirit or as Creator-Love-Spiritedness; or we can say we know him in moments of creativeness, in moments of loving and caring, and in moments of inspiration.

This brief explanation hardly does justice to the ancient doctrine, but it may provide some handles to help participants talk about the "trinity experiences" of God in their lives. The festival of Trinity can be a joyful celebration in the parish, for it can express our own daily experience of God as we are touched by Father, Son, and Holy Spirit.

Furthermore, the doctrine of the Trinity comes out of the story of God meeting us throughout time. First God was known in acts of history. He was the God who acted for and with his people. From that experience came the deeper realization that God was as close to his people as the love they shared together, and out of that realization came the understanding that God's spirit or breath is within each of us.

All Saints' Day and the Commemoration of All Faithful Departed

All Saints' Day has traditionally been a holy day that celebrated the lives of all martyrs who were not otherwise recognized in the liturgical calendar. We might compare this feast to the tomb of the unknown soldier, since it was a day to recognize the witness of *all* the martyrs, known and unknown. The day is celebrated on November 1. The following day is set aside in the Episcopal church as a "lesser feast" and is called the Commemoration of All Faithful Departed. On this day we recall with love all those who have died in the faith, and we pray that they may have "continual growth in the love and service" (Prayer for the departed, Rite One, *The Book of Common Prayer,* page 330). Though the tradition of the Church makes a distinction between the martyrs whose lives are celebrated on All Saints' Day and the rest of the faithful departed whose lives are celebrated the following day, the New Testament calls all Christians "saints" or "holy ones." With this in mind we now celebrate All Saints' Day as a feast on which we proclaim a continuing and ever-growing relationship through Christ with all those martyrs and saints who have gone before us into the closer presence of God. The Collect for All Saints' Day is a beautiful expression of this truth. "Almighty God, you have knit together your

elect in one communion and fellowship in the mystical body of your Son Christ our Lord: Give us grace so to follow your blessed saints in all virtuous and godly living, that we may come to those ineffable joys that you have prepared for those who truly love you. . ." (*The Book of Common Prayer*). The *Prayer Book* allows us to celebrate All Saints' Day on the Sunday following November 1 so that we can give a major emphasis to this eternal truth in our parish life.

A tradition our parish follows at All Saints' time is to pray for all the departed of the parish during the prayer of Intercession. The list of persons is extensive and includes deceased parents and grandparents of the families active in the parish, along with members of the parish whose deaths our parishioners still remember. This extensive prayer puts us in touch with our personal parish and family saints. We remember them in love and feel their presence as we receive the Eucharist. The love of Christ that binds the living together at Communion time also ties us to those who have died. Christ's love made visible in the sacrament of the Lord's Supper is our personal meeting place with the *whole* of his Church. The week before our celebration of All Saints' Day we talk about our personal and parish saints in the learning community. Children are encouraged to talk about the people they know who have died. They hear the names of the people the next Sunday during the prayer of Intercession.

As we talk about "our saints" we realize that saints are contemporary people as well as long-ago-and-far-away heroes of faith. The whole concept of sainthood can be enriched if we can help persons proclaim and celebrate the saints of our own individual and community histories. The liturgical calendar published in the *Prayer Book* can be the jumping-off place to begin a more localized parish (or even family) liturgical calendar. Who are the saints of America, of your state and city, of the parish itself, and of the individual families of the parish? What makes those persons saints in the eyes of the faith community? What date on our calendar should we choose to celebrate their witness to Christ's kingdom? How can we make that celebration come alive for our parish family?

The children and adolescents of the learning community would be the natural compilers of this liturgical calendar. Take a Sunday to talk to them about saints in general. Let them come up with their definition of sainthood. Then begin to think with them about the people you would want to include in your parish liturgical calendar. You will have to do a bit of research on each person in order to issue your parish booklet of "Lesser Feasts and Fasts." How can the parish at large be drawn into recognition and celebration of your chosen saints? You might even design a weekend or day-long retreat centered around creating your calendar and saints' day celebration booklet. Drama, skits, puppet shows, radio shows produced on tape recorders, slide presentations, 8mm film productions, poetry and prayers, songs, and other artistic offerings can grow from a time of study, dialogue, and other preparation. Share the results with the parish at large during the education time or as part of the liturgy.

The preceding idea came from Gabe Huck and Virginia Sloyan's excellent book *Children's Liturgies*. The book goes on to suggest, "Anniversaries associated with particular heroes or groups of people should be considered in the building of such a calendar. Local events and people must play a part, too. Almost every realm of man's world should be included: science, poetry, writing, exploring, raising a family, helping others, teaching, pioneering, reforming social and legal and political systems, etc. Only those ways of life which would seem inconsistent with the gospel would be omitted" (page 193). The Liturgical Conference has published two other very helpful idea books: *Signs, Songs and Stories* and *Parishes and Families* (see the Bibliography).

Find out who the founders of your community were. Trace their stories in the library. Talk to some of the older persons of the parish and find out about the early leaders of the parish or mission. What were their dreams for the parish and the community? Can anyone remember some things they said? Piece together their story and witness. Are there anecdotes that form a part of the community's memory of them? Tell those stories in the learning community and link them with the stories shared about the biblical and other saints of the church. Perhaps some legends have grown up around the memory of your local people that can be shared too. ("Ole man Hawkins could cut down twenty fir trees before lunch.")

Have fun with your calendar. You may not plan any major parish festivals, but just publishing a calendar and booklet that families can follow at home can be a satisfying learning experience.

All Saints' Day is a time to talk about death and life and to realize that God's creation is present as much in death and dying as in birth and growth. Spend a Sunday or two prior to All Saints' Day exploring the subject of death in the learning community. Talk with adults about the importance of the funeral as a "rite of passage" and a powerful act of faith, prayer, and sacrament for the faithful.

In our parish we study the liturgy of the Burial of the Dead and discuss the decisions that need to be made at the time of death. Keep in mind the context of All Saints' Day as the ideal time to expose children and adults to this very important subject. If death is seen as a part of life in a natural yearly cycle of proclaimed truth, the reality of death will not be so forbidding when it comes into every person's life. We cannot be fully alive until we have faced the reality of our aging and death. All Saints' Day is one of the most important celebrations of the church year.

Summary

The saints' days and other feast days of the Church will often be celebrated on week days rather than on Sundays. The weekday nature of some of the feasts need not discourage us, however. Potlucks and parish family times can be set up on a weekday evening. Children and adults can make Saturday pilgrimages to various points or conference centers, or they can spend a day around the parish church experiencing the feeling of a particular feast day. Coordination with the pastor and with those responsible for the parish liturgy is obviously very important. In some cases feast days can replace or be added to the usual Sunday observance. (See *The Book of Common Prayer*, pages 16-18, for specific directives.)

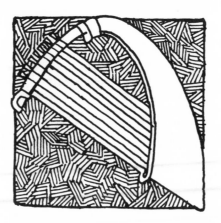

Chapter 9
Telling the Whole Story

Putting the salvation story together is the focus of this chapter. Week by week we hear portions of scripture read as prescribed in the lectionary. Week by week we hear the whole sweep of the salvation story rehearsed in creed and in eucharistic prayer, but if the details of that salvation story are not firmly established in our minds, the place of each individual story is lost to us. If, on the other hand, we know something about the Babylonian exile, then we can more fully appreciate the significance of the literature that was produced by our biblical ancestors during the Exile. If we know something of the expectations that the Jews had for a second King David, then our reading of the gospel of Matthew read in Year A of the eucharistic lectionary cycle takes on a new dimension of meaning. An understanding of the cycle of pilgrimage festivals celebrated in the time of Jesus will give us a clearer picture of the gospel of John. To understand Mark is to appreciate the role of the suffering servant as expressed in the writing of Second Isaiah.

This is not to say that a text lacks any meaning or power if read out of context. The Word may often speak to one who has no knowledge of the Bible whatsoever. However, being able to see the larger frame into which the text under consideration fits enhances one's appreciation of the passage. And, if we are to

be drawn into the salvation story and find our identity as Christians in accepting that story as Truth, then a basic knowledge of what Michael Goldberg calls the "master story" is essential. ". . . for all future generations, Israel's story—the Jewish master story—will provide the matrix for legitimizing and making sense of her tradition . . . If that tradition ever loses sight of the master story which is its point of reference, it will also likely lose its significance and warrant in a mire of obscure legalisms. Hence, if traditional rites are not to degenerate into mere rituals, those who would claim to be the bearers of tradition must make sure that they are more fundamentally the bearers of the story. For what is tradition in the end but a community's way of telling its story over time? . . . tradition requires us to act out our larger master story in each of our own individual life stories such that in the process, we become transformed. For then we no longer simply study or recite the story; instead, we become the story" (Michael Goldberg, *Jews and Christians Getting Our Story Straight: The Exodus and the Passion-Resurrection,* Nashville: Abingdon Press, 1985, p. 99).

For many Christians, the "master story" is never clearly established. One of the complaints leveled against using the lectionary as the basis for Christian education is that children and adults don't get to hear the whole story. Though the gospel readings follow the life and ministry of Jesus from birth, to crucifixion and to resurrection, the Old Testament is never read in sequential order because readings are always chosen to be in thematic harmony with the gospel text. Thus we read the Old Testament by season and topic rather than with any sense of sequential development.

The early Church recognized the need to tell the whole story in order for conversion and renewal to happen among the people year after year. As people were prepared for baptism, the first concern of the Church was to share the salvation story with the catechumens. The preparation period for adult baptism took some three years; a humbling confrontation to all of us who tend to crank up the inquirer's class five or six weeks before the bishop arrives for the annual visitation! A major concern during that three year period of preparation, called the Catechumenate, was the sharing of the basic story of salvation along with a doctrinal interpretation of the story and a reflection on how the story was unfolding in the lives of the people.

We see a remnant of that story sharing process in the great Easter Vigil (The *Book of Common Prayer,* pp. 285-295). The congregation gathers with those preparing for their baptism (parents and godparents of infants as well as adult candidates for baptism), and the salvation story is rehearsed through the reading of nine selections from the Old Testament. The assigned readings give us an insight into what the Church considers to be the essential chapters in the Old Testament story. At the conclusion of each reading the congregation joins in singing or saying a psalm that reflects the impact of the reading. The readings in the *Book of Common Prayer* are preceded with this solemn statement: "Let us hear the record of God's saving deeds in history, how he saved his people in ages past; and let us pray that our God will bring each of us to the fullness of redemption" (*The Book of Common Prayer,* p. 288).

"Chapter" 1: The story of Creation; Genesis 1:1-2:2, (Psalm 33:1-11 or Psalm 36:5-10).

"Chapter" 2: The Flood; Genesis 7:1-5, 11-18, 8:6-18, 9:8-13, (Psalm 46).

"Chapter" 3: Abraham's sacrifice of Isaac; Genesis 22:1-18, (Psalm 33:12-22 or Psalm 16).

"Chapter" 4: Israel's deliverance at the Red Sea, Exodus 14:10-15:1, (Response is portions of the "Song of Moses", Exodus 15:1-6, 11-13, 17-18).

"Chapter" 5: God's Presence in a renewed Israel; Isaiah 4:2-6 (Psalm 122).

"Chapter" 6: Salvation offered freely to all; Isaiah 55:1-11 (Psalm 42:1-7 or Isaiah 12:2-6).

"Chapter" 7: A new heart and a new spirit, Ezekiel 36:24-28, (Psalm 42:1-7 or Isaiah 12:2-6).

"Chapter" 8: The valley of the dry bones; Ezekiel 37:1-14 (Psalm 30 or Psalm 143).

"Chapter" 9: The gathering of God's people; Zephaniah 3:12-20 (Psalm 98 or Psalm 126).

At the Eucharist that follows the baptisms, the congregation hears Romans 6:3-11 (Paul's explanation about the significance of baptism) and Matthew 28:1-10 (the empty tomb).

As mentioned in chapter 5, the season of Lent and Holy week are designed to be primers in the Christian faith. Along about the middle of January, many of us search about for the right lenten program. We look through catalogs and nervously ask our neighbors in ministry what they are planning to do this year. But there is really only one agenda for the Church during Lent; that is to prepare people for baptism and for the renewal of their baptismal vows. The Church provides us with a model for this preparation and renewal. It is the annual re-telling of the whole sweep of the salvation story. But the story is not just told. It is proclaimed as a way to call people into covenant with the God who first whispered the possibility of the story into the minds of Abraham and Sarah. The hearing of the story leads to the creedal statement, "I believe in God, the Father almighty, creator of heaven and earth. I believe in Jesus Christ, his only Son, our Lord."

This chapter explores a way to share the whole salvation story within the normal course of the lectionary and in special periods of intensive study.

Getting the story in mind.

One cannot share a story they don't know and feel a part of. The Daily Office lectionary available in the Episcopal *Book of Common Prayer,* the *Lutheran Book of Worship,* and in the *Book of Alternative Services of the Anglican Church of Canada* provides us with a convenient way to read through the historic narrative of the Old Testament, for the lectionary leaves out portions of the text that are of no immediate concern to the Christian. The historic narrative selected for reading in the daily lectionary is listed below. A beginning point for any teacher of the Bible is familiarity with the core story. Nothing can replace the experience of reading the story from the Bible itself. For convenience, the narrative portions of the lectionary are shown below.

In the Book of Genesis:
1:1-4:26
6:1-22
7:1-23
8:6-9:29
11:1-9
11:27-14:24
15:1-11,17,21
16:1-19:29
21:1-21
22:1-18
23:1-20
24:1-38,49-51
24:50-67
25:19-26:6,12-33
27:1-28:4,10-22
29:1-31:24
31:25-50
32:3-33:17
35:1-20
37:1-36
39:1-46:1-7,28-34
47:1-50:26

In the Book of Exodus:
1:6-6:1
7:8-8:19
9:13-35
10:21-11:8
12:1-20:21
24:1-25:22
28:1-4,30-38
32:1-34:35
40:18-38

In the Book of Leviticus
8:1-13,30-36
16:1-34
19:1-18
19:26-37
23:1-44
25:1-17
25:35-26:20
26:27-42

In the Book of Numbers
3:1-13
6:22-27
9:15-23
10:29-12:16
13:1-3
13:21-14:45
16:1-17:11
20:1-21:9
21:21-22:38
22:41-24:25
27:12-23
32:1-6,16-27
35:1-3,9-15,30-34

In the Book of Deuteronomy
1:1-18
3:18-4:40
5:1-6:25
7:6-8:20
9:4-10:5
10:12-22
11:18-28
12:1-12
13:1-11
16:18-20
17:14-20
26:1-11
29:2-31:13
31:24-32:14
34:1-12

In the Book of Joshua
1:1-4:7
4:19-5:1
5:10-7:13
8:1-22
8:30-10:15
23:1-24:33

In the Book of Judges
2:1-5
2:11-23
3:12-8:12
8:22-9:16

9:19-25
9:50-57
11:1-11
11:29-18:31

The entire Book of Ruth

In the Book of First Samuel
1:1-6:16
7:2-12:6
12:16-14:45
15:1-3
15:7-17:11
17:17-18:16
18:27-19:18
20:1-22:23
23:7-18
24:1-25:44
28:3-20
31:1-13

In the Book of Second Samuel:
1:1-2:11
3:6-5:12
5:22-7:29
9:1-13
11:1-19:43
23:1-7
23:13-17
24:1-2
24:10-25

In the Book of First Kings and Second Chronicles
1:5-31
1:38-2:4
3:1-28
5:1-6:7
7:51-8:40
2 Chronicles 6:32-7:7
8:65-9:9
9:24-10:13
11:1-13
11:26-13:10
16:23-19:21
21:1-22:45

In the Book of Second Kings and Second Chronicles
1:2-2:18
4:8-37
5:1-6:23
9:1-37
11:1-20a
17:1-18
17:24-41
2 Chronicles 19:1-3; 30:1-27

18:9-21:18
22:1-23:25
23:36-24:17

In the Book of Jeremiah, Second Kings, Lamentations
Jer 35:1-38:28
2 Kings 25:8-12,22-26
Jer 29:1,4-14
Jer 44:1-14
Lam 1:1-12
Lam 2:8-15

In the Book of Ezra and Nehemiah
Ezra 1:1-11
Ezra 3:1-13
Ezra 4:7,11-6:22
Neh 1:1-2:20
Neh 4:1-6:19
Neh 12:27-31a
Neh 12:42b-47
Neh 13:4-22
Ezra 7:1-28
Ezra 8:21-10:17
Neh 9:1-38
Neh 7:73b-8:3
Neh 8:5-18

The next step in teacher preparation is to read through the gospel appointed for the liturgical year; the gospel according to Matthew in Year A, Mark in Year B, Luke in Year C. The "Acts of the Apostles" and "The Letter of Paul to the Romans" are essential reading for they help us understand how the Church responded to the gospel.

The Common Lectionary: one way of getting the Old Testament story across to the congregation.

The Consultation on Common Texts is an ecumenical committee called together to achieve closer unity in the liturgical texts that are shared in common. It was originally formed in the mid-sixties with the idea of agreeing on commonly accepted texts for the Lord's Prayer, the creeds, canticles and some of the prayers for the eucharistic liturgy. But in March of 1978, the Consultation began to look at the lectionary texts used by the participating denominations.

A review of the principles of the lectionary developed by the Roman Catholic Church and adapted with some modifications by Episcopalians and Lutherans will help to understand the direction taken by the

Consultation. The three year lectionary cycle came out of the Second Vatican Council held in the early sixties. Though the Roman Catholic lectionary has served as the basis for all three lectionaries, each denomination has made adaptations to the pattern. A quick glance at the lectionary guide printed at the beginning of chapters 5, 6, and 7 of this book shows the extent of the variations. The gospel readings are almost always the same in the three lectionaries. There is general uniformity with the second readings, though in many cases the lections in the Episcopal and Lutheran lectionaries are longer than the ones prescribed in the Roman Catholic lectionary. The greatest variation between the three lectionaries comes with the Old Testament readings, but in all the lectionaries the principle of selection for the first reading is the same. The Old Testament readings are chosen to be in thematic harmony with the gospel reading.

During the major seasons of the church year, Advent through Pentecost Sunday, Old Testament, responsory psalm, epistle and gospel may sometimes all be read in thematic harmony. Those preparing for the liturgy and the education that supports the liturgy can usually find that theme with little problem. Moreover, the theme of each individual week fits in with the overall theme of the entire season.

During the other half of the church year, however, (what the Roman Catholics call "Ordinary Time" and the rest of us call "Sundays after Pentecost") we follow the principle of semi-continuous reading of the gospel and epistles. What has not been read in the gospel during the major seasons is now read sequentially, chapter by chapter. Epistles that were not read between Advent and Pentecost Sunday are read sequentially from beginning to end during "Ordinary Time." The Old Testament readings, however, are always selected in thematic harmony with the gospel lection.

"Typology" is an important term to keep in mind as we talk about the relationship between the Old Testament and gospel lections. "Typology sees a correspondence between people and events of the past and of the future

(or present). . . . typology does not ignore the historical meaning of a text, but rather takes that as its starting point. Typological exegesis then is based on the conviction that certain events in the past history of Israel, as recorded in earlier scriptures, thereby revealed God's ways and purposes with men and did so in a typical manner. In particular, certain high moments of revelation in the history of salvation, especially events of the beginning, whether of the world (creation and paradise) or of Israel (exodus, wilderness), and events from the high period of Israel's national life (kingdom of David), manifest a pattern of God's acts and so prefigure the future time when God's purpose will be revealed in its fullness in the age to come." (James D. G. Dunn, *Unity and Diversity in the New Testament: An Inquiry Into the Character of Earliest Christianity*, Philadelphia: The Westminster Press, 1977, page 86). A typical example of typology is found in the Episcopal lectionary for the Last Sunday after the Epiphany, Year C. Moses' encounter with God at Mt. Sinai is read as preparation for hearing the story of the transfiguration of Jesus on the mountain (". . . the people of Israel saw the face of Moses, that the skin of Moses' face shone" Exodus 34:35. "And as he was praying, the appearance of his countenance was altered, and his raiment became dazzling white" Luke 9:29). Typology is certainly not the only principle of thematic harmony, but it tends to influence the way we approach the Old Testament.

A major complaint raised about the present lectionary is that the Old Testament never stands on its own. We get the sweep of the gospel story. We get the overall impact of the epistles over a course of weekly readings, but the Old Testament is heard in bits and pieces to fit the gospel lection.

With this and other concerns for a unified lectionary in mind, the 1978 meeting of the Consultation on Common Texts established the North American Committee on Calendar and Lectionary and published what is now called "the Common Lectionary" in 1983. This lectionary was adapted by the Anglican Church of Canada and printed in its *Book of Alternative Services*. It was accepted for optional use by the United Presbyterian Church, the United Methodist Church, the United Church of Christ, the United Church of Canada and the Disciples of Christ. The Common Lectionary is being used as the basis of new curriculums being published by the United Presbyterians and United Methodists. In the fall of 1992, the experience with the Common Lectionary will be evaluated by all the participating denominations, and changes will be made growing out of the extensive experimental use. After initial study, the Roman Catholic, Episcopal and Lutheran churches decided to remain in the consultation but chose not to adapt the Common Lectionary as it presently stands.

The "Common Lectionary" breaks away from the thematic harmony principle during the long season after Pentecost (Ordinary Time). Instead, three major segments of the Old Testament are read in sequence. In Year A, the Common Lectionary follows a semi-continuous reading of portions of Genesis and Exodus. In Year B, the story of King David is read from 1st and 2nd Samuel, and in Year C we hear the Elijah-Elisha stories from 1st and 2nd Kings along with selections from the prophets. Though there is not a Sunday by Sunday correlation between the Old Testament and gospel readings, ". . . it was the judgment of the revision committee that to read the pentateuchal material along with Matthew was to respect the gospel's own preoccupation, as also is the case with the pairing of David and Mark, and the prophets with Luke. Where individual wisdom or prophetic lessons were chosen which were not particularly sequential week-after-week, then 'harmony' with the gospel was a criterion of selection" (*Common Lectionary: The Lectionary Proposed by the Consultation on Common Texts,* New York: Church Hymnal Corporation, p. 22).

For the teacher and preacher who wants to share the power of the Old Testament story in serial fashion the idea of the Common Lectionary is a boon, and there are many Sundays when the Roman Catholic, Lutheran and Episcopal lectionaries do not include a narrative text that can be picked up by the storyteller. For example, in mid-summer of Year B, we spend four weeks in the sixth

chapter of John with a poetic theological exposition on the meaning of the feeding of the 5,000. On two of those Sundays, the Old Testament reading is a speech by Moses and a reading from Proverbs. "What do we do on these Sundays?" asks the storyteller and the narrative preacher. The Common Lectionary responds with a full range of sequential stories from the Old Testament.

As noted above, the Roman Catholic, Episcopal and Lutheran churches, though committed to the consultation, have chosen not to use the Common Lectionary. Several concerns have been raised. First, having the Old Testament lections follow their own sequence means that any sense of thematic focus is lost since all three readings are unrelated. Secondly, it is pointed out, the liturgy is not meant to be an educational experience. As important as it is for the people to know their salvation history, we should not burden the worship experience with all the teaching needs of the Church. Thirdly, the principle of typology is one that has framed the reading of the gospels for generations. To lose the thematic harmony between the Old Testament and the gospels is to lose some of the impact of the proclamation of the Good News.

As appropriate as these objections are, there is something to be said for recognizing the reality of contemporary life in the Church today. The hour or so set aside for worship on Sunday morning will be the only exposure to scripture that many of our people will have on a regular basis. Moreover, the Easter Vigil reminds us that there is historic precedent for letting the Old Testament stand as its own witness in the liturgical context. And, Aidan Kavanagh points out that descriptions of baptismal instruction found in the Apostolic Tradition of Hippolytus ". . . suggests that instruction did not take place in a classroom setting, pursuing exclusively intellectual matters in an abstract manner. Rather, it seems to have taken place at least within a prayer context: it may have assumed a more pronounced liturgical or quasi-liturgical setting, perhaps that of an actual service of the Word. This may even have been the origin of such a service—involving reverent reading of biblical lessons, an expounding of their meaning by a teacher in homiletic fashion, formal petitionary prayer, concluding with a laying of hands by the teacher and dismissal" (Aidan Kavanagh, *The Shape of Baptism: The Rite of Christian Initiation,* New York: Pueblo Publishing Company, 1978, pp. 56-57). He points out that the formal instruction of the catechumens was not the same experience as the Liturgy of the Word experienced by the baptized, but the two were certainly similar. Those preparing for their baptism heard salvation history in a liturgical setting. The story was shared and interpreted, and the people responded to the Word received in praise and prayer.

The production of the Common Lectionary is one way of combining the need for sharing the story with the need to gather as a faith community for the hearing of the Word and the sharing of the Eucharist. Whether or not we agree with the concept expressed in the production of the Common Lectionary, it does provide us with an opportunity to open up the Old Testament as a part of our weekly worship and communal experience. Those of us in the Roman Catholic, Lutheran and Episcopal traditions can look to the Common Lectionary Old Testament texts as opportunities for summer Bible storytelling outside the formal liturgical experience, and the texts provide us with a handy curriculum for storytelling and Bible teaching programs at any time of the year.

Outlined below is a storyteller's commentary on the selected readings from the Old Testament for the Sundays after Pentecost (Ordinary Time). This brief commentary is offered as a way of putting the lections into their historic context. Additional stories are suggested for those who want to expand on the lectionary texts and use them as focal points in a more detailed sharing of the salvation story from the Old Testament.

The Common Lectionary Old Testament Readings Sundays after Pentecost (Ordinary Time) Year A

In this year we read the major portions of the Torah (first five books of the Old Testament) beginning with the call of Abraham and Sarah to the death of Moses. This course of readings runs from Proper 4 through Proper 26. During the last three Sundays of the Church year, the old Testament readings are the same as those appointed in the present Episcopal lections already noted in chapter 5.

Proper 4: Genesis 12:1-9. The call of Abram and Sarai.

We begin our sequential reading with the calling of our biblical foreparents, Abraham and Sarah. They are called out from among their people to "make a great nation." We do not begin with the creation accounts, and the early stories of Genesis. Rather we begin with the story that gives us our first sense of identity as a chosen people. When God was identified to Moses at the burning bush, Moses was told, "I am the God of your fathers, the God of Abraham, the God of Isaac, and the God of Jacob" (Exodus 3:6). The summer storytelling begins with our ancient biblical ancestors.

The following stories about Abram and Sarai (later named Abraham and Sarah) could be told to fill out the picture of these important figures.

Genesis 15:1-21: God makes a covenant with Abram. God's promise of a great blessing makes no sense to Abram, for children were seen as essential in any promise of reward and the couple was childless in their old age. Abram was 75 years old and Sarai was 66 when they were called to leave Haran. Nevertheless, Abram believed the promise and God "reckoned it to him as righteousness" (Genesis 15:6). Paul quotes that statement in the fourth chapter of Romans as a part of this argument that faith and not works are what leads to righteousness. Abram evidenced faith even in the midst of an unexplainable mystery.

An ancient custom of contract making is evidenced in this story. The parties to the contract walked between the halves of animal and bird carcasses. In this case, one party to the contract was God who moved between the animal pieces as a burning firebrand.

Genesis 17:1-27: A covenant of circumcision is made with Abram and his descendants.

Sarah, it is reported, is 90 years old and Abraham is 99. No wonder Abram is a little anxious about being blessed with offspring! In this story, he is again promised a son and the very thought causes him to fall to the ground in laughter. Notice the name change in this story. Abram is henceforth to be called Abraham. Sarai is to be called Sarah. (At baptism, we are named as God's. In a sense we take on a new name.) Part of this story deals with the demand for circumcision. It is important for people to know that God's people were set apart in a distinct way from the beginning of the Covenant relationship. Christians today are marked with the sign of the cross at baptism. Sally/John "you are sealed by the Holy Spirit in Baptism and marked as Christ's own forever" (Book of Common Prayer, page 308, Baptism). God's people have been set aside by a mark of the Covenant since Abraham and Sarah's call.

Genesis 18:1-14: The promise of the birth of Isaac. This is a wonderful story of hospitality and promise. Three strangers approach Abraham and Sarah's tent "by the oaks of Mamre." After sharing a meal with Abraham, one of them promises that Sarah will give birth to a child. Now it is Sarah's turn to laugh! In the previous story, we learned that the child is to be named Isaac. It would seem that God has a sense of humor. The name comes from the verb meaning "he laughs."

Genesis 21:1-7: The birth of Isaac. A brief account of Isaac's birth leads to next week's lectionary text.

Proper 5: Genesis 22:1-18. Abraham's sacrifice.

This is a painful story that you may feel hesitant to share with children, but it forms an important part of our heritage and our people need to know it. (See Chapter Two, "An Overview of the Historical, Literary, and Theological Development of the Bible," for a discussion about the evolving understanding of God evidenced in the Bible.) Abraham understood that God would demand the ultimate sacrifice of his firstborn son; a practice common among some ancient tribal peoples. He was prepared to make that sacrifice as a sign of his total commitment to the God who had called him into Covenant.

This story is appointed in the lectionary during Lent (Year B) as a vivid reminder that baptism means a total giving of one's life to God. It has been understood by Christians as typology for the crucifixion of Jesus. God the father offered his own son up in sacrifice and Jesus was the obedient son carrying the wood of the fire on his back in the form of the cross.

An additional story to tell: *Genesis 24:1-67.* This passage offers an interesting account of Isaac's marriage to Rebekah. Though this is certainly not an essential part of the tradition, it gives us some insights about life in biblical times and helps to add dimension to the characters.

Proper 6: Genesis 25:19-34. The birth of Esau and Jacob to Isaac and Rebekah.

This was one of the key stories told by our biblical ancestors to explain the struggles that existed between nations. As we hear these stories about the ancient families of the patriarchs, we are hearing the explanations given for the historic situation facing Israel during the time of the Kingdom of Israel and Judah. Esau was seen as the forefather of the Edomites. Edom was conquered by David and remained under Israel's control until the reign of King Joram (died 842 BC). The stories of the patriarchs also tended to ridicule the alien nations by pointing up the wisdom of Israel's ancestors. In this case, the ancestor of the Edomites did not even have sense enough to hold on to his birthright!

Another point made by the ancient storytellers was the power of God's election. Esau was the first born and rightful heir to Isaac's blessing and property. But God does not always follow the established pattern. In this case the elder shall serve the younger. We see this pattern repeated frequently throughout the Bible.

The two week focus on our biblical forefather Jacob provides a setting in which to offer other important stories about Jacob, Leah and Rachel. Appropriate stories are listed on pages 22 and 23.

Proper 7: Genesis 28:10-17. Jacob's dream.

The covenant with Abraham is now

extended to Jacob. (Compare this passage with Genesis 15:1-21.) In a dream, Jacob discovers a new understanding of his life and the lives of his descendants. God enters into the affairs of history, the vision of the ladder between heaven and earth reminds us. The response to the vivid dream is a commitment by Jacob to the "God of Abraham and Isaac" expressed in his act of cultic worship and in the offering of tithes. As is true with all of the Genesis stories, there are ancient roots of ritual and territorial imperative expressed here. Bethel was an important place of worship for the northern tribes until the fall of Israel to Assyria in 721 B.C. A storytelling of the dream of Jacob that took place at Bethel added legitimacy to this sacred place of worship.

The United Presbyterian curriculum published in 1971 (*Christian Faith and Action* series) suggested that teacher and students dress in appropriate costume to hear the biblical stories. The stories of the Exodus, for example, were to be told sitting outside a tent set up in the classroom. If you are sharing the Genesis stories with children, spend some time having participants build a stone altar with rocks. Tell the story and offer worship in your own sacred place of memory. Talk about monuments we erect today, including church buildings, that remind us of our sacred memories as a people. Another idea that is often used when telling the stories of the Exodus is to have participants construct an Ark of the Covenant; a rectangular box with poles that was carried by the people as they wandered through the wilderness. During Solomon's reign, the Ark of the Covenant was placed in the Temple at Jerusalem. A description of the Ark is found in Exodus, Chapter 25.

Proper 8: Genesis 32:22-32. Jacob wrestles with God.

As preacher or storyteller you may want to share at least the outline of Jacob's adventure with his uncle Laban in preparation for today's reading found in Genesis 29:1 through 32:2. Comments about these stories are found in "Guide to the Stories of the Bible," page 22.

The importance of the story assigned to

this Sunday comes partly in the giving of a new name for Jacob. He is now to be called "Israel," the forefather of God's covenant people. A footnote in the Jerusalem Bible explains that the name Israel could mean either "May God show his strength!" or "He has been strong against God." In either case, the name implies a struggle with God. To be God's covenant people brings a mixed blessing, we see from this story, for God's election means that we enter into the struggle of being God's people in the arena of history. We are called, as was Jacob, to struggle with God and with the people of the world in order to understand our call and our response.

Another important point to raise this week is that Israel (Jacob) and his wives Leah and Rachel were the ancestors of the twelve tribes of Israel. Twelve sons were born between the two wives and their slave women and each son became the patriarch of one of the tribes of Israel.

Proper 9: Exodus 1:6-14, 22-2:10. The oppression of the Hebrews in Egypt and the birth of Moses.

We begin a whole new chapter of salvation history in this first week of July. The great stories of Joseph are passed over in this lectionary. You may want to make at least a reference to Joseph's enforced journey to Egypt as you open this week's account. Another option for church teachers is to take this week and focus on Joseph since you will have several weeks to talk about Moses. The Joseph saga extends from 37:2 through 50:26, but the heart of the narrative is found in the following passages:

Genesis 37:1-36
Genesis 39:1-46:7
Genesis 46:28-34
Genesis 47:1-7
Genesis 47:27-31

With this Sunday's text, we shift from the ancient stories that gave Israel a sense of identity as a nation to the historic account of God's call to Moses and the liberation of our biblical ancestors from slavery in Egypt. In the Book of Exodus we hear of an oppressed people whose needs became known to a saving God. "I have seen the affliction of my people who are in Egypt, and have heard their cry because of their taskmasters; I know their sufferings and I have come down to deliver them out of the hand of the Egyptians, and to bring them up out of that land to a good and broad land, a land flowing with milk and honey . . . And now, behold, the cry of the people of Israel has come to me, and I have seen the oppression with which the Egyptians oppress them" (Exodus 3:7-9). Despite Pharaoh's best efforts to kill all the male babies born to Hebrew women, Moses had survived. Indeed he had been raised in Pharaoh's very household! A common biblical theme; nothing can hinder God's purpose. Those who opposed God's will find themselves as unwilling instruments in God's plans. God's people are always stronger, smarter, quicker than the people of other nations. Thus the Egyptian midwives became accomplices of God and refused to kill the male babies born to Hebrew women. They reported to Pharaoh that they were unable to follow his orders. "Because the Hebrew women are not like the Egyptian women; for they are vigorous and are delivered before the midwife comes to them" (Exodus 1:19).

Proper 10: Exodus 2:11-22. Moses leaves Egypt and goes to the Sinai peninsula to dwell with the Midianites.

Even though Moses was raised in Pharaoh's court, his identity and feelings rested with his own people. In this week's text we hear of Moses' flight and his marriage to Zipporah, daughter of a priest of Midian. The Midianites were a nomadic people.

Proper 11: Exodus 3:1-12. The call of Moses.

On this mid-summer Sunday we hear one of the key stories of the Bible. To appreciate the significance of this story, see the discussion of "Wilderness Religion," pages 53-54.

As you tell the wilderness stories, set up a tent in the parish hall and gather participants together at the front of the tent. Keep the tent set up during the weeks you will be in the wilderness. Make an "Exodus mural" for the room you are meeting in that depicts the wilderness story of our biblical ancestors.

Proper 12: Exodus 3:13-20. God's name and relationship revealed to Moses. The mission is described.

Today's text is a continuation of the story we heard last week. The divine name is revealed; "I am who I am." The mission seems impossible, and Moses is quick to point out the difficulties to the God of the burning bush. (See page 53 for a discussion about this strange name.)

This week in sermon or in the learning center tell some of the stories of Moses that happened after his call and that lead up to the event that will be heard next week.

Exodus 4:10-23: Moses resists God's call to set his people free, but finally leaves with his wife and son for Egypt where he will meet with Pharaoh and with the Hebrews.

Exodus 4:27-31: Moses meets his brother Aaron and together they tell the Hebrew slaves the good news of God's saving action on their behalf.

Exodus 5: Moses' message to Pharaoh is not received with enthusiasm! Pharaoh gives orders that the Hebrew slaves are to be worked harder, and they begin to complain loudly to Moses. They were better off before they ever met Moses or listened to his hopeful words of liberation, they tell him.

Exodus 7:14-11:10. The Ten Plagues. Read the section on "Wilderness Religion." (pages 53-54) as you prepare to share these stories. The events narrated in this section are all natural phenomena, but they became events that were larger than life when seen in the light of God's acting for the Hebrew slaves. The plagues are still remembered with pain by Jews as they celebrate the Passover. One of the traditions associated with the Passover meal is the spilling of wine from the second cup prescribed for the meal. "When the plagues of Egypt are mentioned, it is customary to spill some wine from the second cup. The reason for this being that although the plagues killed the oppressors, sadness should still be felt at human suffering. The joy cannot be complete; the wine cup will not be full" (Mordel Klein, editor, *Passover,* Jerusalem: Keter Books, 1973, p. 76).

Proper 13: Exodus 12:1-14. The Passover.

For a fuller description of the Passover liturgy read Chapter 12 and Chapter 13:3-10. Notice the importance of "remembering." As the faithful people gather year after year to remember the mighty acts of God, those acts become a present reality for them. The Passover is not an act of nostalgia, but an act of identity and empowerment for the people living in every generation. "And you shall tell your son on that day, 'It is because of what the Lord did for me when I came out of Egypt' " (Exodus 13:9). In the eucharist, Christians do this in remembrance of me. As we remember the mighty acts of Jesus of Nazareth they become present realities for us. We too are called. We too are healed and brought into the family of God. The past becomes present in mighty acts of remembrance.

Proper 14: Exodus 14:19-31. The crossing of the Sea of Reeds (Red Sea).

The reading of Exodus 13:17-14:14 will help to put the crossing of the Sea in context. It is important to realize that we really have at least two distinct accounts of the Crossing of the Red Sea woven together in the text appointed for this Sunday. The earlier of the two accounts gives us a clear picture of the event as it was remembered. The later account helps us see the importance of that event as it was shared over many generations. Read the section, Miracles, in chapter 1, page 13 as background for sharing this great story. Then read the two accounts to yourself separately so that you can appreciate the way tradition added to the details of the narrative.

The earliest story: Exodus 14:5-7, 10-14, 19-20, 21b, 24-25, 27b, 30-31. (An "a" or "b" after a verse number denotes the first or second half of the verse).

The later account: Exodus 14:1-4, 8-9, 15-18, 21a, 22-23, 26-27a, 28-29. (Ellis, Peter, F., *The Men and the Message of the Old Testament,* Collegeville, MN: The Liturgical Press, pp. 66-67).

The Sea of Reeds is a more accurate name for the body of water that the Hebrews crossed than the name Red Sea. The Hebrew term translated Red Sea ". . . must then refer in this account, not to the body of water properly known as the Red Sea, but to the marshy area North of the Gulf of Suez . . ." (The Interpreter's Dictionary of the Bible, Volume 4, Nashville: Abingdon Press, 1962). The Hebrew word for "sea" is also used to describe a lake.

Picturing the Hebrews crossing a dry marsh rather than walking through walls of raging sea water makes the event one that we can imagine out of our own experience. On the other hand, if we picture the crossing as a mighty miracle that happened only once in history we are apt to miss the events of our own day where God is acting to bring life out of death.

The event we hear today is the key story in the life of our biblical ancestors. The prayer that the bishop or priest in the Episcopal church says over the water as it is blessed at baptism refers back to the saving event at the Sea of Reeds. "We thank you, Almighty God, for the gift of water. Over it the Holy Spirit moved in the beginning of creation. Through it you led the children of Israel out of their bondage in Egypt into the land of promise. In it your Son Jesus received the baptism of John and was anointed by the Holy Spirit as the Messiah, the Christ, to lead us, through his death and resurrection, from the bondage of sin into everlasting life" (Book of Common Prayer, page 306). Just as the walking through the waters of the Sea of Reeds expressed God's salvation to the children of Israel, so the "walking" through the waters of our baptism is the sign to us of God's salvation in our lives. We cannot fully appreciate our baptism without being rooted in the Sea of Reeds tradition.

Proper 15: Exodus 16:2-15. The manna and the quail.

(In the Episcopal, Lutheran and Roman Catholic lectionaries, this lesson is appointed for Proper 13, in Year B). As noted in A Guide to Stories of the Bible, chapter 1, the feeding of the Hebrews with manna and quail is a natural phenomena. "A substance like the manna described in the Bible is still found in Sinai . . . Quails flying over the desert become exhausted and can easily be caught for food" (p. 25).

Traditionally, Christians have seen this story as pointing to the significance of the eucharist. (Another example of "typology" discussed earlier in this chapter.) In our wilderness wandering, God feeds us with the manna that is the sacrament. Read John 6:31-35 for an example of the kind of teaching that was done in connection with the manna in the early Church. ("Our fathers ate the manna in the wilderness . . . I am the bread of life; he who comes to me shall not hunger, and he who believes in me shall never thirst.") When telling stories from Old Testament, however, it is important to respect the integrity of the original story and not add Christian interpretations to the ancient narrative. Leave the Christian interpretation to those times when you are talking about the eucharist.

Proper 16: Exodus 17:1-7. The water from the rock.

This week we encounter another story told to show how God provided for the Hebrews during their wilderness wandering. This is an important story, for later on we learn that God punished Moses for his lack of faith shown at Meribah. Numbers 20:2-13 provides a second account of this experience in which Moses and Aaron are punished for their lack of faith. What Moses did to anger God is not clear from either account of the event. (The rest of the people were doomed to die in the wilderness after their rebellion against Moses and Aaron; an event described in Numbers 13 and 14.)

Proper 17: Exodus 19:1-9. Preparation for the Covenant.

Moses had been hearing every case of judgment and complaint brought by the people. His father-in-law, Jethro, urged the appointment of judges who could make decisions for groups assigned to their care leaving Moses to judge only the most important questions.

When telling the story of Covenant making, refer to the remarks in A Guide to Stories of the Bible, page 25.

Proper 18: Exodus 19:16-24. The meeting between God and Moses on Mt. Sinai.

Smoke, earthquake, fire and thunder surround Mt. Sinai as God appears to Moses in an intense vision. The Temple ritual would replicate this great theophany in later years. Great clouds of incense filled the sacred space, and people felt the presence of God in their midst as they too experienced the theophany of God. We hear an awesome scene described this week. Moses and the people are prepared for the key event that will affect their lives and the lives of all God's people for generations to come.

Proper 19: Exodus 20:1-20. The Ten Commandments or Decalogue.

The remarks in A Guide to Stories of the Bible are important to keep in mind as you plan for this week (see page 25). The Law of the Torah is actually composed of some 613 commandments. The Ten Commandments that we are familiar with give us an outline of the intention of the Law of Torah. Some commandments in Torah deal with the Jew's relationship with God including many detailed ritual prescriptions. But many of the commandments deal directly with the relationship between people. Justice is to be at the heart of the Covenant with God. To relate to God is to relate justly with one's neighbor, spouse, family, and servant. The Law demands compassion for the widow, the orphan and the poor. For example, the Torah directs landowners to leave grain in the fields after the harvest so that the poor can glean some of the grain. The demands of the Torah are not ethereal religious laws. Jesus summarized the Law well when he quoted from the Torah in response to the Pharisees' question about the greatest commandment. "You shall love the Lord your God with all your heart, and with all your soul, and with all your mind . . . You shall love your neighbor as yourself." He was quoting directly from the Torah in his response (Deut. 6:5 and Leviticus 19:18).

Adults and older children could get a flavor of the commandments of Torah with a brief survey of Exodus 21:1-23:19. Assign a portion of the text to each participant and simply ask them to list the topics of the commandments assigned to them. Talk about impressions the group has as they reflect on their survey.

Refer to the suggestions for the Third Sunday in Lent in Year B (page 212) for other ways to share today's reading in the learning community and liturgy.

Proper 20: Exodus 32:1-14. The Golden Calf.

Exodus 24 would be an important story to add to your repertoire as you prepare people to hear today's lectionary text. God spoke into the mind of Moses and commanded that he build an altar at the foot of the mountain consisting of twelve standing stones, representing the twelve tribes of Israel. Bullocks were sacrificed and half of their blood was poured on the people and half was poured on the altar. "Then he (Moses) took the book of the covenant, and read it in the hearing of the people; and they said 'All that the Lord has spoken we will do, and we will be obedient.' And Moses took the blood and threw it upon the people, and said, 'Behold the blood of the covenant which the Lord has made with you in accordance with all these words.' Then Moses and Aaron, Nadab and Abihu, and seventy of the elders of Israel went up, and they saw the God of Israel; and there was under his feet as it were a pavement of sapphire stone, like the very heaven for clearness. And he did not lay his hand on the chief men of the people of Israel; they beheld God, and ate and drank" (Exodus 24:7-11).

Do not add Christian interpretation as you share these wonderful stories from the Old Testament, but keep this vivid scene in mind as you talk at other times about the Holy Eucharist. The Covenant with the Hebrews was sealed with the blood of bullocks. The Covenant revealed through Jesus was sealed by his blood shed on the cross; the blood we share as the "cup of salvation." To understand the New Testament, we must know and appreciate the Old Testament.

After the covenant was ratified, Moses went up into the mountain for forty days. This story sets the stage for today's lectionary text. No sooner was Moses out of sight than the people cried out to Aaron his brother for another god whom they could see and control. While still on the mountain, Moses learned from God about the apostasy happening down below. Notice the bargaining that Moses does with God in the appointed text (Exodus 32:7-10). Moses argues that God will look foolish in front of the Egyptians if the Hebrews are saved from oppression only to be destroyed by God in the wilderness!

The appointed text ends with 32:14, but the story goes on and is important to share. Moses was furious with the people. Aaron offers a wonderful excuse for his role in this disastrous action in verse 24. "And I said to them, 'Let any who have gold take it off; so they gave it to me, and I threw it into the fire, and there came out this calf." This refusal to accept responsibility harks back to Adam's excuse before God in the garden. "The woman whom thou gavest to be with me, she gave me fruit of the tree and I ate" (Genesis 3:12).

Proper 21: Exodus 33:12-23. The prayer of Moses.

After the high drama of the last few weeks, this Sunday we find a note of calm. Moses goes into the Tent of the Meeting and prays for guidance. He asks who God will send with the people to guide them. God's response is simply, "My presence will go with you, and I will give you rest . . . for you have found favor in my sight and I know you by name" (Exodus 33:14, 17). God would always walk with the people. The Collect for Guidance (BCP, p. 100) reflects this understanding of God's constant presence. "Heavenly Father, in you we live and move and have our being: We humbly pray you so to guide and govern us by your Holy Spirit, that in all the cares and occupations of our life we may not forget you, but may remember that we are ever walking in your sight; through Jesus Christ our Lord."

Proper 22: Numbers 27:12-23. Joshua appointed to succeed Moses.

We take a long jump through the Torah between last week and this week's text. Most of the intervening material are detailed legal codes and ritual commandments, but there are a few pieces of the narrative that are important to fill in.

Exodus, chapter 34 describes the renewal of the Covenant. A second set of tablets is cut and God appears again before Moses. The description of God in this passage is a key one in understanding the attributes of God. "The Lord, the Lord, a God merciful and gracious, slow to anger, and abounding in steadfast love and faithfulness, keeping steadfast love for thousands, forgiving iniquity and transgression and sin, but who will by no means clear the guilty, visiting the iniquity of the fathers upon the children and the children's children, to the third and fourth generation" (Exodus 34:6-7). This is the passage that Jonah refers to in anger when he tells God that he did not want to go on a mission to Ninevah to warn the citizens to repent. ". . . for I knew that thou art a gracious God and merciful, slow to anger, and abounding in steadfast love, and repentest of evil" (Jonah 4:2).

Other intervening stories that are important to share are listed in the Guide to Stories of the Bible, pages 26-27. (Numbers 11:4-35; Numbers 13:1-14:38; Numbers 22:1-24:15.)

In the passage appointed for today we find Moses begging God for a successor so that the people ". . . may not be as sheep which have no shepherd." Moses will not enter the promised land as punishment for what happened at the Waters of Meribah (see Proper 16 above). In the present passage, we hear the results of God's punishment. Moses realizes that a new leader must take the people into the Promised Land. Note that the passing on of authority happens with the laying on of hands. At baptism, confirmation, and ordination, the laying on of hands becomes the mark of ministry and leadership. The origins of this symbol reach back to old Moses and Joshua standing before the people on the mountain of the Abarim range. The mention of the "judgement of Urim" (v. 21) is a reference to the dice-like objects sometimes consulted to discern the will of God.

Proper 23: Deuteronomy 34:1-12. The death of Moses.

We've lived with Moses now for fifteen weeks. Today we witness his death. He gets one glimpse of the Promised Land from the top of Mount Nebo, and then lies down and dies. The closing words of the Torah pay tribute to

Moses. "And there has not arisen a prophet since in Israel like Moses, whom the Lord knew face to face, none like him for all the signs and wonders which the Lord sent him to do in the land of Egypt, to Pharaoh and to all his servants and to all his land, and for all the mighty power and all the great and terrible deeds which Moses wrought in the sight of all Israel" (Deut. 34:10-12).

In following the lectionary texts appointed in the Common Lectionary these summer Sundays, we have been witnesses to the mighty works of God manifested in our biblical forefather Moses. If you have been sitting outside your tribal tent during this time, you can take it down at the end of this session. We leave the wilderness for a more settled situation next week.

Propers 24, 25 and 26: Ruth 1:1-19a; Ruth 2:1-13; Ruth 4:7-17.

To understand the purpose behind the delightful story of Ruth, read Ezra 10:1-5 and Nehemiah 13:23-27. These passages contain strong promulgations against intermarriage between Jews and Gentiles. Both Nehemiah and Ezra were concerned to keep Judah pure following the people's return from exile in Babylonia. Jews who had intermarried were forced to divorce their spouses.

Into this painful situation, the Book of Ruth was written and circulated. Ruth was a reminder that King David's great grandmother was a foreign woman from Moab! So much for religious purity, the writer of Ruth gently pointed out. The story had circulated as a part of the nation's oral tradition for generations, but it was written down and circulated again in the difficult period following the exile. The major point of the story is the willingness of the Jewish people to take Ruth in as a daughter of Israel. Ruth's faithfulness to her mother-in-law, Naomi, of course, is another mark of the book. (". . . for where you go I will go, and where you lodge I will lodge . . ." Ruth 1:16).

Tell, or read, the entire story. There are some delightful details in the narrative that help us appreciate the customs of the day. A marriage contract was negotiated at the town gate. As noted in connection with Proper 19, Year A, above, the poor were allowed to glean for grain on the lands that had been harvested. Chapter 3 describes Ruth's formal introduction to Boaz, her kinsman by marriage. Naomi directed Ruth to go to the threshing floor after Boaz had his fill of food and drink and lie at his "feet." Though some commentators accept this rather risque behavior as a normal part of the nuptial and harvest customs of the time, the storyteller can be assured of an attentive audience as the story is shared!

Propers 27, 28 and 29:
During these last three Sundays of the church year, the Common Lectionary is in harmony with the Old Testament readings set forth on page 147 of this book. For comments about these three Sundays, see pages 193-194.

The Common Lectionary Old Testament Readings Year B

King David is the focus of the Common Lectionary for the first fourteen weeks of the Sundays after Pentecost (Ordinary Time). For the remaining Sundays after Pentecost, the Common Lectionary turns for four weeks to selections from Wisdom literature and then for the last eight weeks to texts that are in thematic harmony with the gospel reading. The discussion that follows will concentrate first on the David story and then on the texts that are unique to the Common Lectionary during the last eight weeks of the liturgical year.

Proper 4: 1 Samuel 16:1-13. The anointing of David.
See A Guide to the Stories of the Bible, pages 29-30 for remarks about the important stories that lie behind this first appointed text.
The focus on David during the sequential reading of the Old Testament in Year B emphasizes his crucial role in Israel's history. In years to come when Judah dreamed of a coming Messiah who would save the people, it

was David who served as an inspiration for their dream.
Our series of story opens with a visit from the prophet Samuel who comes to the home of Jesse to anoint a new king for Israel. Saul, the present king, had lost favor with God and with Samuel and must be replaced. The more obvious choices for king are not God's choices, Samuel discovers as he meets the sons of Jesse. This theme of the "last or least shall be first" is found throughout the biblical narrative. Jacob, the second child of Isaac and Rebekah, became the first child in the eyes of God, for example. Emphasize the anointing ceremony that marked God's call to be king. The Hebrew word for *anointed one* is transliterated *Messiah*. The Greek word for *anointed one* is transliterated *Christos*. Jesus the Christ is *Jesus the anointed one*. The origins and significance of that title go back to Samuel's anointing of Saul and David.
The ancient symbol of anointing is expressed today at the time of baptism in many of our churches. Moments after a person is baptized in the Episcopal church, ". . . the Bishop or Priest places a hand on the person's head, marking on the forehead the sign of the cross (using Chrism if desired) and saying to each one, 'You are sealed by the Holy Spirit in baptism and marked as Christ's own forever' " (*The Book of Common Prayer,* p. 308). We too become Christ—that is, an anointed one—at the moment of our baptism. We too are set apart, marked, filled with God's spirit, for the ministry in Christ's name that we are called to live out.

Proper 5: 1 Samuel 16:14-23. David enters the service of King Saul.
Though David is anointed, the world does not know it yet. His introduction to Saul is by a referral from Saul's servants. The king needs help with depression, and the servants know just the music therapist who can help! In this innocent way, Saul's replacement as Israel's king enters into the court scene.
The more familiar account of David's introduction to Saul is found in 1 Samuel 17:1-18:5; the story of David and Goliath. These two entirely different accounts circulated independently for several generations, but both

were included in the final written text
of the present book of 1 Samuel.

Proper 6: 2 Samuel 1:1,17-27. David's grief at Saul's death.

We take a huge leap in time between last
week's reading and this Sunday's text. Read 1
Samuel 18:6-16 and 19:1-24:22 for important
stories about David's struggle with Saul. (See
pages 30, A Guide to Stories of the Bible.) As
we pick up the story in the Sunday readings,
Saul has died. Despite the terrible pain that
Saul imposed on David, the new king still
mourns for God's anointed king. Part of the
reading is a beautiful elegy attributed to David
at his time of grief.

Proper 7: 2 Samuel 5:1-12. David anointed king and the capture of Jerusalem.

Read the intervening chapters as you
prepare for this Sunday's storytelling and/or
preaching. David was from the southern tribe
of Judah and was first declared king in the
south, but he had to maneuver his way into
power among the northern tribes where the
people felt a strong loyalty to Saul's memory
since the former king came from the tribe of
Benjamin.

When David was finally anointed king
over the northern tribes at Hebron, his first act
was to capture the city of Jerusalem as a
symbol of his authority over all the people of
the land. Since it had never before been
captured by the Hebrews, it was not identified
with either the northern or southern tribes.
Thus it could become a symbol of David's reign
and provide a new sense of national pride
and power. Jerusalem's geography gave it
credibility; a city set on a high hill between the
northern and southern tribal areas.

There is a strange reference to the blind
and lame in the passage appointed for this
Sunday. "And David said on that day,
'Whoever would smite the Jebusites, let him
get up the water shaft to attack the lame and
the blind, who are hated by David's soul.' " The
Jebusites had taunted David claiming that he
could never take their city. "You will not come
in here, but the blind and the lame will ward
you off." The biting words attributed to David

were probably his sarcastic response to the
taunts of the defenders.

Proper 8: 2 Samuel 6:1-15. David brings the Ark of the Covenant into Jerusalem.

The new king knows the power of
symbolic actions. The Ark of the Covenant that
accompanied the Hebrews in their forty years of
wilderness wandering is now to be brought into
the City of David. This action would tie David
to the powerful memories of the people. He
would march with Moses in their minds.

Pointers for the biblical storyteller:

• The Ark was held in awe by the
people. 1 Samuel chapters 6 and 7 provide some
background for this feeling. Numbers 4:15
states ominously, ". . . but they must not touch
the holy things, lest they die." Thus when
Uzzah reaches out his hand to steady the Ark
and dies, his death is seen as an immediate sign
of God's displeasure. David must wait for a
time before continuing with his joyful
procession into the city of Jerusalem.

• David dressed in the priestly garb of a
linen loincloth or ephod. He sacrificed sheep
and later blessed his household. These are the
duties of a priest. In this scene we see David
acting as both priest and king.

• To tell the whole story of this triumphant
scene, you will need to read beyond the
appointed text to the end of the chapter.
David's wife Michal was Saul's daughter. As
she observes her husband dancing before the
Ark dressed only in a loin cloth she is
disgusted. The scene between David and Michal
at the end of the day contains all the familiar
elements of prideful exuberance confronted by a
spouse's all too accurate accusations of self-
glory. David's humanity is portrayed realistically
in these stories. The biblical writers did not try
to protect him. We are offered scenes of
David's weakness as well as his power.

Proper 9: 2 Samuel 7:1-17. Nathan's prophecy about David's royal lineage.

This is an important text. Nathan the
prophet refuses to authorize the building of a
Temple in David's time, though he does
promise that David's heirs shall reign forever.
"When your days are fulfilled and you lie down

with your fathers, I will raise up your offspring after you, who shall come forth from your body, and I will establish his kingdom . . . And your house and your kingdom shall be made sure for ever before me; your throne shall be established for ever" (2 Sam 7:12-13, 16). Though David cannot build a "house" for God, God shall build a "house" for David!

When Judah was forced to live in Babylonian exile, the promise that David's household would live forever became a dream for the future. A new Son of David, the Messiah, would reign as David's heir. For some, this meant a restored political reign. For others it meant a reign existing beyond history and yet breaking into history. The writers of the gospel, especially Matthew, pointed out that Jesus was a descendant of David. Matthew began his gospel with the genealogy of Jesus that harks back to Abraham and David. Jesus had the qualifications, Matthew pointed out, to be the long expected Messiah who would at last establish the reign of God in time and beyond time.

Proper 10: 2 Samuel 7:18-29. David's prayer.

David's response to the promise announced by Nathan last week is heard this week in a prayer of praise and gratitude to God. The prayer expresses the reason David was held in such high esteem. Much of David's story is sordid at best, but here we see attributed to the king the best motives for rule as God's servant.

Proper 11: 2 Samuel 11:1-15.

From a prayer of perfect service to God read last week, we turn to face David's sinfulness this week. The assigned text is the beginning of the story of David's affair with Bathesheba, the wife of one of the king's officers fighting on the front. The opening lines of the story announce the power of what follows. "In the spring of the year, the time when kings go forth to battle, David sent Joab, and his servants with him, and all Israel; and they ravaged the Ammonites, and besieged Rabbah. But David remained at Jerusalem" (2 Sam 11:1). We have a king, bored from life lived temporarily on the sidelines of history.

The men of the city are gone. Their wives are left behind. The stage is set for tragedy and it begins to unfold in the very next verse. If possible share the entire chapter this week. The details of the story are captivating and the stage will be set for hearing God's response to David's sin told in next week's text.

Proper 12 and 13: 2 Samuel 12:1-14; 2 Samuel 12:15b-24. David confronted by the prophet Nathan.

God's angry response to David spoken through the prophet Nathan is shared over a two week period. After David orders Bathsheba's husband killed in battle in order to save face in the light of her pregnancy, the prophet Nathan approached David to ask him to judge a simple case of injustice. It seems that a wealthy man had taken a poor man's one ewe lamb and offered it to his guest. The injustice of the situation was immediately apparent to David. He could recognize injustice from a distance even if he could not recognize it in his own actions! He quickly prescribed a four fold restitution of the lamb, and was infuriated at the very thought of the crime. Nathan deftly turns David's righteous indignation at the unjust act of another to recognize the sin in himself. Nathan's words to David were devastating. *"You are the man."* David's repentance was accepted by Nathan, but notice that the effects of David's sin remain. What David has put into motion can't be undone. A life will be lost. David's house will be in turmoil. Forgiveness can be offered, but nothing can reverse David's actions that destroyed trust and broke the bonds of justice.

Proper 14: 2 Samuel 18:1-5, 9-15, and Proper 15: 2 Samuel 18:24-33.

Read Chapters 13 through 17 of 2 Samuel so that you feel the power of the texts assigned for these two weeks. Remember Nathan's warning. David's house will always be in turmoil. Absalom, one of David's sons, rebels against his own father, driving him out of Jerusalem. In the narrative assigned in this mid-August time, we learn of Absalom's death and David's grief. Absalom had been the eldest living son at the time he seized power. With

Absalom's death, the stage is set for Solomon's ascension to power, though not without further struggle as is revealed in the First Book of Kings, Chapter 1.

Proper 16: 2 Samuel 23:1-7. David's dying words.

A short psalm of praise associated with David's death is read this week. The psalm refers to David being a singer of songs; a reminder that Saul's first meeting with David was as a "music therapist." David's reputation as a musician led to the erroneous assumption that he produced many of the psalms.

Proper 17: 1 Kings 2:1-4, 10-12. The death of David and the beginning of Solomon's reign as king.

Words ascribed to David at his death conclude our reading of his life story. If you read the entire speech (1 Kings 2:1-11), it sounds like the dying speech of the Godfather! Solomon is to wreak revenge on this and that person who angered David during his lifetime. The final words attributed to David are a vivid reminder that he was remembered for violence and bloodshed as well as for justice and praise of God. The importance of this passage, of course, are the words of hope for the future. God had promised David that his house would reign in power if his sons ". . . walk before me in faithfulness" (1 Kings 2:4). That promise from God was also a threat. "If" is the key word to hear in this passage.

With David's death, Solomon became king. As background for this week's story, read the first chapter of 1 Kings; a vivid description of the court intrigue that led to Solomon being named as king instead of his half brother Adonijah. Then go back and read 2 Samuel, Chapter 19 for the description of David's return to Jerusalem after the death of his son Absalom. This will help to explain the tragic division of the nation into the two kingdoms of Israel and Judah that came after Solomon's death. The tribes of the northern kingdom were offended that they had been not invited to escort David back across the Jordan river in victorious procession. Sharp words ensue between the men of Judah and the men of

Israel. This is an ominous foreshadowing of events that come after Solomon's death.

Propers 18, 19, 20, 21:

As mentioned above, the four week focus on readings from the Wisdom literature will not be treated here since they are not part of the great narrative section of the Old Testament.

Propers 22 through 29:

The Old Testament readings are chosen to be in thematic harmony with the epistle or gospel lections during the last eight weeks of the church year. The lections for five of the eight weeks are already discussed in Chapter Six.

Proper 22: See page 227.

Proper 23: Genesis 3:8-19. "The Fall."

With Proper 22, the Old Testament readings begin to follow the lectionary pattern of the Roman Catholic, Lutheran and Episcopal lectionaries again, and the readings are chosen for their thematic relationship with the gospel rather than for their sequential narration of Old Testament history.

Today's first reading is an exception. The appointed text follows in sequence from last week's Old Testament reading rather than being in harmony with the gospel. Last week we heard the story of the creation of Adam and Eve. In today's reading we hear the story of what Christians call "the Fall." If possible, share all of Chapter 3 in the learning community or liturgy. This story was told by our biblical ancestors in the face of the inevitable questions about the reason for death, struggle and pain.

Though Eve is often blamed for the "Fall," notice that Adam was as much a part of the temptation as Eve was. In the Jerusalem Bible and New American Bible, we read a more accurate rendering of the Hebrew text: "She also gave some to her husband who was with her, and he ate it" (Jerusalem Bible, Gen 3:6).

As you read this story, notice that only the snake and the soil is cursed. It is not God's will that women be subject to men or that men be subject to the struggles of fighting brambles and thistles to bring forth crops out of the soil. Rather it is God's intention that woman and man live as one, and that man and woman will live in harmony with their environment. The struggles that we see in life come as a result of men and women attempting to "become like the gods" by eating of the tree of good and evil and making decisions that are God's alone to make. This ancient story speaks truth.

Proper 24: See page 228.

Proper 25: See page 228.

Proper 26: See page 228.

Proper 27: See page 229.

Proper 28: Daniel 7:9-14.

This reading is appointed for Proper 29 (Feast of Christ the King) in the Roman Catholic, Lutheran, and Episcopal lectionaries. See comments on page 230.

Proper 29: Jeremiah 23:1-6. A future king shall come.

In the Common Lectionary we hear Jeremiah's poem promising that God will shepherd the sheep and "raise up for David a righteous branch, and he shall reign as king and deal wisely" (Jeremiah 23:5). The reading fits the theme of this Sunday.

The Common Lectionary Old Testament Readings Sundays after Pentecost, Year C

In the third year of the Common Lectionary Sundays after Pentecost cycle, we pick up where we left off last year with the reign of Solomon and move through the great stories of the prophets Elijah and Elisha. The narrative section goes on for ten weeks and is followed by a fifteen week focus on the writings of the great prophets. Only the ten weeks of the narrative sequence will be treated here.

Proper 4: 1 Kings 8:22-23, 41-43.

Read all of Chapter 8 as you prepare to share the assigned text. At last the great Temple

that David dreamed of building has been completed by his son Solomon. Now comes the sacred moment of consecration. The sacred Ark carried for a generation through the wilderness has been resting in the city of David ever since David brought it into the city. (See 2 Samuel 6.) The City of David (also referred to as Zion, the ancient name of the city) was the fortified city that David had captured from the Jebusites. The Temple was built further up the hill for the original city. Thus the Ark was carried "up from the city of David, which is Zion" (1 Kings 8:1). The dedication came at a major pilgrimage festival, the Feast of Tabernacles. It was an awesome and wonderful moment. A thick cloud of smoke filled the Temple, the narrator tells us, a sign that God had indeed filled the space with holy presence. The use of incense is a symbol of God's presence in some of our churches today; a symbol that has roots reaching back to the days of the Temple and to Mt. Sinai. "And Mount Sinai was wrapped in smoke because the Lord descended upon it in fire; and the smoke of it went up like the smoke of a kiln, and the whole mountain quaked greatly" (Exodus 19:18).

First, Solomon addressed the people in a joyful statement of fulfillment at being the one to complete the Temple. Then he turned to address God in prayer. Notice that his prayer begins with praise and then shifts to intercession for all people who will come to pray in this great Temple. This pattern of prayer that moves from praise to God for acts accomplished and then turns to intercession and petition is the pattern still followed in the formal prayers of the Church today. The collects of the Book of Common Prayer usually begin by remembering some mighty act of God in creation or history. Eucharistic prayers always begin with praise for what God has done. Part of the text assigned for today's reading is a prayer that even foreigners who come to the Temple will be heard by God. In a moment of vision Solomon saw beyond the nation and embraced the stranger and sojourner.

The Feast of Tabernacles (also known as the Feast of Booths) was a great pilgrimage festival that helped the people remember the days their ancestors spent in the Sinai wilderness

("You shall dwell in booths for seven days; all that are native in Israel shall dwell in booths, that your generations may know that I made the people of Israel dwell in booths when I brought them out of the land of Egypt . . . " Lev. 23:42). As the people remembered their ancestors' nomadic life, they also remembered that God "dwelled" with them in the Tent of the Meeting and that God would always dwell among them wherever they were. (See comments in connection with Exodus 33:12-23, Proper 23, Year A, above.) With the dedication of the Temple on this significant festival, God could be perceived as dwelling in a permanent "tent" or tabernacle. The placing of the Ark within the confines of the Temple was an important symbolic gesture. This was its last resting place. God was at home in Jerusalem.

The idea of containing God within the walls of a Temple is a dangerous one. Perhaps that was one of Nathan's concerns when he told David not to build a Temple. (See 2 Samuel 7:1-7.) On the one hand, the prayer attributed to Solomon recognizes that Temple walls could not contain God. "But will God indeed dwell on the earth? Behold, heaven and the highest heaven cannot contain thee; how much less this house which I have built!" (1 Kings 8:27). And yet these words are also attributed to Solomon. "The Lord has set the sun in the heavens, but has said that he would dwell in thick darkness. I have built thee an exalted house, a place for thee to dwell in for ever" (1 Kings 8:12).

Proper 5: 1 Kings 17:17-24. Elijah restores a widow's son to life.

Since we are going to be living with Elijah and his successor Elisha for the next nine weeks, it is worth taking some time to meet the man and understand his mission. A lot has happened since we left King Solomon dedicating the Temple last week. Read 1 Kings 10:1-29 for a sense of Solomon's power and reputation. Though Solomon is most often remembered for his great wisdom, we need to understand that he was also a ruthless ruler. His power came partly from oppressing his own people. He ruled like any Eastern despot of the time. With his death came the end of Israel's greatest period of national wealth and power.

David and Solomon came from the southern tribe of Judah. Saul had come from the northern tribe of Benjamin. You may recall that it took some time for David to convince the northern tribes that he should reign over a united kingdom. (David's struggle to become king over both the northern and southern tribes is recorded in 2 Samuel, Chapters 1 through 4.) When Solomon's son Rehoboam met with the leaders of the northern tribes and refused to soften his father's harsh policies against the people, the response of the northern tribes was clear. "What portion have we in David? We have no inheritance in the son of Jesse. To your tents, O Israel! Look now to your own house, David" (1 Kings 12:16). From that moment the northern kingdom of Israel broke away from the southern kingdom of Judah resulting in the formation of two weak nations rather than one united kingdom.

The tragedy of the divided kingdom continued with a succession of oppressive kings who had little commitment to the Covenant that demanded justice for the people. Jeroboam, Nadab, Baasha, Elah, Zimri, Omri march through the pages of history as kings of Israel. Each is dismissed by the biblical writers with words of disdain. "Omri did what was evil in the sight of the Lord, and did more evil than all who were before him" (1 Kings 16:25). And so it went until we reach King Ahab who ruled in Israel from 874 to 853 BC. He married Jezebel, a Phoenician princess who brought the worship of her own Baal god with her to Israel. Priests of Baal and the cultic practices associated with Baal worship became a part of court life, a direct affront to Israel's Covenant relationship with Yahweh. Elijah and Elisha were the prophets who stood before Ahab and Jezebel to confront them with the Covenant demands of Israel's God.

As you read the stories of Elijah and Elisha in the coming weeks be aware that some legendary elements form a part of Israel's memory of those prophets. Great figures of history tend to become larger than life as people reflect back on their influence. When Israel later suffered exile and dispersion, Elijah began to be seen not only as a powerful figure in history but as a hoped-for herald of the future. "Behold, I will send you Elijah the prophet before the great and terrible day of the Lord comes. And he will turn the hearts of fathers to their children and the hearts of children to their fathers, lest I come and smite the land with a curse" (Malachi 4:5-6). When Jewish people celebrate the Passover meal together to this day a place is always set for Elijah the prophet, for he represents the hope and expectations of God's final victory and the beginning of God's reign. "Next Year in Jerusalem" is the expression of ultimate peace and harmony with God and with all peoples. Elijah is to be the harbinger of that great day.

People quickly began to see in Jesus the fulfillment of this expectation. At one point Jesus asked his disciples who people were saying he was. The disciples responded, "Some say John the Baptist, others say Elijah and others Jeremiah or one of the prophets" (Matthew 16:13). Some of the stories told about Jesus in the Gospels show the influence of the people's memories and expectations of Elijah.

As background for the first Sunday in the Elijah cycle, read 1 Kings 16:29-17:16. A drought came to the land, and Elijah interpreted the resultant suffering as a judgment on the reign of Ahab. The power of God was evidenced in Elijah as he gave life to a widow and her son first through a miracle of feeding and then through the even greater miracle of raising the son to life.

Proper 6: 1 Kings 19:1-8. Elijah's journey to Horeb.

Though Chapter 18 is not appointed for reading as a part of the lectionary, you will need to share the stories from that chapter in order to appreciate the scene presented in today's text. Elijah ordered a contest between himself and Jezebel's priests of Baal. The priests were to meet Elijah on Mount Carmel. Each was to offer an animal sacrifice to their god. The most powerful god would accept the sacrifice by sending fire to consume the offering. Elijah taunted the priests at the incompetence of their god. He, in turn, made the task of lighting the fire even more difficult for the God of Israel. Water was poured on the sacrifice three times before Elijah called out to

God to accept the offering. The story would have been told with great delight by the followers of Elijah in later years. Needless to say, Elijah won the contest hands down, but in the next scene we find him sulking at the edge of the wilderness. This is where we meet him as the lectionary text is shared on this summer Sunday in June.

Proper 7: 1 Kings 19:9-14. Elijah's encounter with God at Mt. Horeb (Sinai).

(Mount Horeb and Mount Sinai are two names for the same mountain.) We pick up today where we left off last week; Elijah goes up into the mountain following the path taken by Moses. This time he meets God in the "still small voice." Refer to Exodus 33:18-34:35 for a sense of the powerful memory of God's presence Elijah would have carried with him into this moment with God.

Proper 8: 1 Kings 19:15-21. God's instructions to Elijah.

The prophet raised a plaintive cry to God as he stood on the mountain. "I have been very jealous for the Lord, the God of hosts; for the people of Israel have forsaken thy covenant, thrown down thy altars, and slain thy prophets with the sword; and I, even I only, am left; and they seek my life, to take it away" (1 Kings 19:14). Those were the words that concluded last week's reading. This week we begin with God's response to Elijah. God is not very patient with his prophet. There are some 7,000 faithful people left in Israel, God quickly informs the prophet. Take those 7,000 and start a revolution against the house of Ahab. The people of God are called to direct political action. Elijah begins to carry out his instructions from God with the calling of Elisha.

Proper 9: 1 Kings 21:1-3, 17-21. A confrontation between prophet and king over the murder of Naboth.

The storyteller will want to include verses four through sixteen as this episode in Elijah's life is shared in the community this week. The king wants land belonging to Naboth. Greed overrides justice when Jezebel arranges to have Naboth arrested and killed when he refuses to sell the land to the king. This action results in a direct confrontation between prophet and king reminiscent of the meeting between King David and the prophet Nathan (2 Samuel 12) after David had arranged the death of Bathsheba's husband Uriah. Even Ahab is brought to repentance as he faces the judgment of God pronounced through the prophet. As a result of Ahab's acknowledgement of guilt, the doom on the house of Ahab is postponed to the next generation.

Proper 10: 2 Kings 2:1, 6-14. Elijah's death.

Legendary elements in the Elijah/Elisha cycle are heightened with accounts of the latter prophet's activities. Tell the stories of Elisha with the same enthusiasm and sense of wonder as our biblical ancestors did, but help your listeners understand that they do not have to take every detail as literal fact. "It is said that Elisha struck the water and it divided to the right and to the left," is the kind of statement that expresses appreciation for the tradition but signals that we are dealing with the language of the awe-filled storyteller and not the newspaper reporter.

This Sunday we learn of Elijah's death in the presence of Elisha. The mantle of Elijah is passed, and God's power is evidenced in Elisha.

Proper 11: 2 Kings 4:8-17. Elisha's prediction of a son for the woman of Shunem.

For an additional story about Elisha read 2 Kings 4:1-7. In this passage Elisha provides oil for a widow; this scene is reminiscent of Elijah's feeding the widow as recounted in 1 Kings 27:7-16. The storyteller emphasizes that the power of Elijah was now invested in his disciple Elisha.

As a traveler announced the birth of a son to Abraham and Sarah at the Oak of Mamre (Genesis 18:1-15), so Elijah announces the birth of a son to the Shunemite woman in the text assigned for reading this Sunday. A Jew hearing the story of Elisha and the Shunemite woman would make connections with other accounts of birth announcements.

Though only verses 8 through 17 are assigned to be read at the liturgy, you will want to tell the whole story ending with verse 37. The

gift of life is granted a second time when the child is raised up from death and handed back to his mother. Two other stories of Elisha are also found in Chapter 4.

Proper 12: 2 Kings 5:1-15ab. The cure of Naaman.

(The letters "ab" after the verse indicate the first two parts of verse 15). This week we are presented with a delightful story of healing faith that extends beyond the assigned text to the end of the chapter. Naaman was the army commander of an enemy king. Leprosy led a desperate Naaman to seek the healing of the prophet of Israel. After his miraculous healing he wanted to worship the God of Israel, but the only way he could conceive of doing that was to take a piece of Israel back with him to his own land of Aram. "Then Naaman said . . . 'let there be given to your servant two mules' burden of earth for henceforth your servant will not offer burnt offering or sacrifice to any god but the Lord' " (2 Kings 5:17).

Proper 13: 2 Kings 13:14-20a. The death of Elisha.

Though not a part of the lectionary texts, 2 Kings 9 is worth reading on your way to the text assigned for this Sunday. Remember Elijah's commission (1 Kings 19) to anoint Jehu king of Israel? That command from God was finally accomplished by Elisha, you will discover in Chapter 9. Jehu was anointed by the order of Elisha and the whole house of Ahab was finally destroyed. The revolution begun with Elijah's encounter with the "still small voice" at Mt. Horeb (Sinai) is completed.

The last story in this summer's series is the account of Elisha's death. Verse 21 gives us one last legendary picture of the prophet. "And as a man was being buried lo, a marauding band was seen and the man was cast into the grave of Elisha; and as soon as the man touched the bones of Elisha, he revived, and stood on his feet." The overlay of such legendary material helps us to realize the importance of both Elijah and Elisha in the memory of our biblical ancestors. The Elijah-Elisha cycle of stories also remind us that God demands justice for the oppressed and mercy for the suffering. Both prophets were intimately involved in the political struggles of their day. They are remembered for their radical stands against the oppressive Ahab and Jezebel. They proclaimed birth in the face of barrenness, life in the face of death, liberation in the face of oppression. The powerful stories of healing, raising and confrontation are living tributes to their witness before Israel.

Propers 14 through 27:

For the next fourteen weeks in Year C, we will be exposed to the writings of the great prophets of the Old Testament: Jeremiah, Ezekiel, Hosea, Joel, Amos, Micah, Habakkuk, Zephaniah, Haggai, and Zechariah. Their words and actions were influenced by Elijah and Elisha. The readings from the prophets are tied loosely to the gospel reading, but you may want to follow the lead of the earlier Sundays after Pentecost and take the opportunity to tell the stories about the prophets themselves. Talk about the times in which the prophets lived, the struggle they had in attempting to confront the people with the true word of God, and some of the social and religious issues the prophets found themselves addressing.

Proper 28: See Chapter Seven, page 267.

Proper 29: See Chapter Seven, page 268.

Conclusion

We come to the end of the sequential reading of Israel's story. In Year A we heard the stories of our beginnings in the Book of Genesis and we moved with our biblical ancestors across the trackless waste of the wilderness following in the footsteps of Moses. In Year B we joined David, the king, whose memory shapes future dreams of fulfillment for God's people. In Year C we look at the role of the two great prophets of the northern kingdom who confronted the leaders of their own time with the uncompromising Word of God.

Over the three years of the liturgical year, the Common Lectionary exposes us to three key narrative sections of the Bible:

Genesis: stories of our roots.

Exodus: stories of our liberation.

David: stories of God's Word and will revealed through the anointed leader of the nation.

Elijah/Elisha: stories of God's Word revealed as it confronts those who govern and guide the peoples of the world.

Appendix I
Using the Psalms in the Religious Education Setting

In addition to the Old Testament, epistle, and gospel readings appointed for each Sunday and holy day, a psalm is listed as a part of the lectionary. Though I have not mentioned the appointed psalm each week in the lectionary, be sure to look closely at the psalm as you plan your program for the learning community. Many of the psalms offer good possibilities for singing, dancing, or pageantry. All of them add a further dimension and depth to the readings. Some of the psalms and other portions of the Old and New Testament are liturgical in nature. For example, Psalm 24 is a processional hymn. The last four verses, beginning with

Lift up your heads, O gates!
   and be lifted up, O ancient doors!
   that the King of glory may come in,

are a portion of the liturgy at the "ancient doors" of the Temple; the people in procession proclaimed God as the "King of Glory," the "Lord of Hosts." Read these verses; picture the grand procession winding through the Temple gates, with choirs of people chanting the ancient words of praise. You can sense the power of that moment and the power of those words as you see them in their original context. We can still use Psalm 24 in much the same way as it was originally intended! Picture the people

approaching the door of the parish church in a grand procession and chanting "Lift up your heads, O gates. . . ." From inside the church comes the response "Who is this King of glory?" Finally the doors of the church are swung open, and the people enter to a triumphant hymn of praise and majesty. Now the Bible has come alive for us. We will never read the words of that psalm without sensing the wonder of that moment. History will become present for us, too! We are walking in procession up the hill to the Temple in Jerusalem with our ancestors in the faith.

The following guide may be helpful in suggesting various ways to use psalms. This guide is an example of the kind of creative liturgical experience we can enjoy as we share the psalms with a knowledge of how they were used in biblical times.

The Book of Psalms contains some of the most beautiful and meaningful writings of the Bible. They are suitable for adults and children alike, but they can be especially appealing to children. The psalms are poetry, and children can appreciate and enjoy poetry without getting tied up in literalisms. The psalms can be read dramatically; they can be sung, used in slide or picture presentations, read with rhythm-instrument accompaniment, and used in connection with banners and bulletin-board displays.

The following psalms are especially appropriate for religious education. Read the psalm. Let your mind roam freely. Children can enter into the mood and feeling of the psalm in drama, audiovisual presentations, body movement, dance, music, prayer, choral readings. The psalms, many of them at least, were written with this kind of participation in mind. They are meant to be shared in feeling, in mood, and in praise to God.

Psalm 1: The man of God is like a tree planted near water.

Psalm 4: An evening prayer showing the comfort the believer feels.

Psalm 5: A morning prayer asking for guidance.

Psalm 6: Prayer for help by one in spiritual darkness who has lost touch with God. Feeling of despair. Example of a lament in biblical literature.

Psalm 8: Beautiful prayer comparing the greatness of God with the humbleness of man: "What is man that thou art mindful of him?"

Psalm 13: Similar to Psalm 6. It is important to realize that all must struggle in darkness at times.

Psalm 14: Those who do not recognize God live in ignorance.

Psalm 15: Who has the right to enter God's "tent" or inhabit his "mountain"? Excellent for the opening words in a children's liturgy.

Psalm 18: A victory song after a battle. Interesting from a literary point of view. Notice the poetic images of what happened during the battle.

Psalm 19: The glories of the universe declare the greatness of God (verses 1-6). "Let the words of my mouth and the meditation of my heart be acceptable in thy sight. . . ." Great for liturgy, especially with slides or other visuals showing stars, sun, moon.

Psalm 20: Prayer for help. "Some boast of chariots . . . ; we boast of the name of the Lord our God."

Psalm 22: The sufferings that a man of God feels as he sees the suffering of the world and finds himself caught up in it. Compare this with the suffering of Jesus. Jesus uttered the words of verse 1 as he died on the cross. Read the psalm and compare it with the passion narrative. Jesus' suffering was seen in the context of this psalm and of the Suffering Servant described in Isaiah 52:13—53:12.

Psalm 23: The Lord is my shepherd.

Psalm 24: See Psalm 15. Verses 7-10 are an ancient liturgy said as the Ark of the Covenant was brought into the Temple.

Psalm 25: The faithful person's prayer.

Psalm 27: "In God's company there is no fear."

Psalm 29: Seeing God in the power of nature. Fun to act out with children. Great audiovisual possibilities.

Psalm 31: Prayer by one suffering at the hands of personal enemies.

Psalm 32: A beautiful confession of sin. Good for liturgical use.

Psalm 33: Trust in God who watches over his people.

Psalm 38: Lament of one suffering because he feels cut off from God. Link with the Book of Job in feeling.

Psalm 39: The transitory nature of human life.

Psalm 40: A joyful prayer of thanksgiving by one "rescued" from those trying to destroy him.

Psalm 41: Prayer of a sick and lonely person.

Psalms 42, 43: Lament of one in exile who feels cut off from God. Beautiful opening words set the mood.

Psalm 44: A lament at the fall of the nation. Questions God for letting it happen. Interesting historically. Shows the feeling of the people.

Psalm 46: Beautiful song of confidence. "God is our refuge. . . ." Martin Luther's beautiful hymn "A Mighty Fortress Is Our God" was inspired by this psalm.

Psalm 49: The futility of riches. Look to God.

Psalm 50: Perfect example of Old Testament prophecy. People are condemned for honoring God with their lips but not their lives.

Psalm 51: See Psalm 32.

Psalm 57: Faith in time of persecution.

Psalm 65: Beautiful thanksgiving hymn.

Psalm 66: See Psalm 65.

Psalm 67: See Psalm 65.

Psalm 71: Prayer of an old person showing faith.

Psalm 72: The promised king to come. The early Church saw psalms and sayings such as this as foretelling Jesus. Though the psalmist speaks of a king of Judah, Jesus fulfilled for many the hopes expressed.

Psalm 73: A wisdom psalm. Why does evil prosper?

Psalm 78: An outline in symbolic terms of Israel's history and God's role in it.

Psalm 81: The people of God have not kept the Law of the covenant.

Psalm 84: A pilgrim's song sung on the way to Jerusalem. The wonder at being in the Temple (church).

Psalm 90: A wisdom psalm. The human condition.

Psalm 92: "It is good to give thanks to the Lord."

Psalm 94: The justice of God—first questioned, then acknowledged.

Psalm 95: Familiar to many as the "Venite" ("O come, let us sing to the Lord") from the Daily Office.

Psalm 96: Beautiful psalm of thanksgiving; perfect for liturgy.

Psalm 97: Thanksgiving. Note the poetic symbolism.

Psalm 98: Psalm of thanksgiving.

Psalm 99: God in Israel's history.

Psalm 100: Invitation to praise God. Great for liturgy.

Psalm 103: Beautiful psalm expressing "God is love."

Psalm 104: Seeing God in nature. Great with audiovisuals.

Psalm 105: God in Israel's history.

Psalm 106: A continuation of Psalm 105.

Psalm 107: God in Israel's history.

Psalm 115: Glory of the people of God.

Psalm 116: Thanksgiving following close brush with death.

Psalm 117: A summons to praise God. Good for liturgy.

Psalm 118: Liturgy of thanksgiving (notice litany refrain, "His steadfast love endures for ever"). Fun to use in a children's liturgy.

Psalm 121: Help comes from God.

Psalm 122: A pilgrim's song of joy at being at the Temple. Especially good for children's liturgy.

Psalm 128: Blessed are those who "fear" (have respect for) God. The word *fulfilled* may help to define what the psalmist means by *blessed* in this psalm.

Psalm 130: "Out of the depths I cry to thee, O Lord."

Psalm 131: Childlike trust in God.

Psalm 133: How great to live together as brothers and sisters!

Psalm 134: A nighttime prayer. Good for liturgy.

Psalm 135: God in Israel's history.

Psalm 136: A litany of thanksgiving. Note refrain.

Psalm 137: Lament sung by those in exile, cut off from Israel.

Psalm 138: Hymn of thanksgiving.

Psalm 139: God knows our every thought before we think it.

Psalm 145: Praise of God's power.

Psalm 146: Rely on God, not on human power.

Psalm 147: The power of God compared to human power.

Psalm 148: A beautiful psalm of praise. Everything in the universe praises God in its own way. Great for liturgy, especially with audiovisuals.

Psalm 150: Praise God with everything we have: drums, dancing, cymbals. No end of possibilities for using with children and with children's liturgies. Worship is joyful and celebrative as we praise God in thanksgiving. How about a children's band that would respond to each line as it is read in chorus?

Appendix II
The Church's Rites of Passage

The Church marks the turning points of our individual, personal lives by letting us know in outward, visible ways that Christ is with each of us as we move through those transitional and growing times. The sacraments and other rites that both mark those special times and give us strength to face them joyfully and successfully are called rites of passage.

But my personal, individual story is woven into the larger fabric of the story of my people. My people's story is rehearsed continually in the Church's liturgy or worship—in the weekly or even daily celebration of the Holy Eucharist, in the yearly round of festivals, in all the sacraments and numerous other rites that are part of the liturgy.

In this brief appendix, I want to discuss the nature and importance of the Church's rites of passage.

The Episcopal *Prayer Book* makes it clear that the Church is there supporting us at many of our passage points. In the ritual of Thanksgiving for the Birth or Adoption of a Child, the Church welcomes the newborn infant into its midst with a beautiful expression of love and thanksgiving. The rituals of Holy Baptism and Confirmation express the person's growing awareness of the covenant relationship with God as the person is nurtured in the Christian Community called the Church. The Form of Commitment to Christian Service can help to express various stages in the life journey of the individual who is accepting new responsibilities of ministry and witness. Ordination marks those set aside for the vocation of holy orders in the Church. The Celebration and Blessing of a Marriage marks a further step in commitment for many of the faithful. Furthermore, there are liturgies to support those who are sick and those who feel the weight of guilt and want to be restored and healed in an act of penance. And Ministration at the Time of Death and the rites for The Burial of the Dead mark the final rites of passage.

The community gathers to celebrate, affirm, recognize, and support the person at each of these stages of the journey. To the ancient, oft-asked question "Who am I?" comes the response of the Church time and time again:

> You are a child of God. You are created to image his love and power in the world. You are led into covenant . . . into ministry . . . into healing . . . into marriage . . . into penitence . . . into crisis . . . into change . . . into growth and discovery . . . and finally into death and new life. You are not drifting in an endless, meaningless voyage made up of historical accidents. You are on a

pilgrimage leading toward wholeness in God's kingdom that is coming ever more deeply into your life. Moreover, you are an integral member of the pilgrim *people* of God who join with you to mark the passage points of your journey together and to celebrate with you the holiness of each of your days. All of God's people are called to be part of God's liberating action in his world. Together you are the Body of Christ called to suffer, to heal, to point in wonder at the mystery of God in creation. You, as a *people*, have wandered across the face of this earth from the days of Abraham. Your story points to your calling and to your endless quest for liberty and justice. Your life has significance, not insofar as you search alone for power and primacy, but rather insofar as you see yourself as an integral part of God's history-making pilgrim people.

Each step along our pilgrimage calls for a different way of approaching life and responding to covenant. This means that we must undergo radical changes in our world view and in our responses to life. The rites of passage and the preparations for those rites help us to face those radical changes and to grow in doing so.

But there are many other passage points in our society not marked specifically in the *Prayer Book*—important events that we should observe memorably. For example, many high schools and colleges no longer have baccalaureates at graduation, or the baccalaureate observance fails to express in a personal way the significance of that painful, frightening, and exciting passage point in life. Another important passage time that needs to be observed well is when people move from one community to another, for a very real death occurs both for those who move and for those who are left behind. Moreover, the families or individuals who enter a new civic community and a new parish need a rite of passage to help them entwine their life story with the story of their new people of faith. Changing one's vocation, going off to school, or opening a business are other important occasions. Divorce is another kind of death—for the couple, their family, and their friends—, and yet how little support we give to such persons in their crisis! And retirement calls for more than the proverbial gold watch and company dinner.

The Body of Christ needs to join with its individual members in recognizing and celebrating their passage points so as to turn the pain into hope and joy.

The parish family will often need to design these rites of passage themselves. Some of them can be marked with the Form of Commitment for Christian Service (*The Book of Common Prayer,* page 420). In that case the offertory of the Eucharist becomes the time to affirm the person's journey in faith. In other cases the parishioners may meet in the home or parish hall for a celebration they themselves have prepared—one marked with gifts, prayer, ritual, and loving laughter. In the Episcopal church, the *Book of Offices: Services for Certain Occasions Not Provided for in the Book of Common Prayer* (in the process of revision at this writing) would be helpful, since it offers additional liturgies that mark passage points in the lives of the faithful. Similar rites can be found in the service books of other denominations. Other helpful resources are Lawrence Moser, *Home Celebrations*, and John Westerhoff, *Generation to Generation* and *Learning Through Liturgy* (see Bibliography).

As an example of the kind of rite of passage that can be designed in the local parish, here is a tradition from our parish.

When a person or family is about to move from our community, we ask them to come to the altar railing at offertory time. Their friends gather around them and lay hands on them as the community did when Paul and Barnabas were about to leave Antioch. The following brief liturgy is based partly on that scene from Acts 13:1-3.

A Liturgy of "Sending Forth"

"Now in the church at Antioch while they were worshiping the Lord and fasting, the Holy Spirit said, 'Set apart for me Barnabas and Saul for the work to which I have called them.' Then after fasting and praying they laid their hands on them and sent them off" (Acts 13:2-3).

We now lay hands on you, (name) , as sign and symbol that the Holy Spirit calls you forth from us to share the good news and to spread the kingdom of love among new friends in (place) .

We send you forth with our love and our blessing and with deep thanksgiving for the love we have shared together in this place. May the Lord strengthen you with the might of his Spirit. May Christ dwell in your heart by faith, that you may be filled with the presence and power of God. Amen.

We bless you in the name of the Father, and of the Son, and of the Holy Spirit. Go in peace to love and serve the Lord.

Appendix III
Tips for the Storyteller on those Sundays When there is no story appointed in the Lectionary

Telling the stories that come up in the lectionary week after week offers both teacher and preacher an effective way of helping children and adults engage in the study and appreciation of the scriptures. But what do we do for a story on those Sundays where there is no story appointed in the lectionary? We open the Bible to the appointed texts and find a discourse of Jesus as the gospel lection, a reading from the Book of Proverbs for the Old Testament reading, and a difficult section of Paul's epistle to the Romans appointed as the epistle for the day. Teachers find themselves at a loss to link their education time with the liturgy.

First, a few suggestions about those "problem weeks." Behind every biblical text is a story waiting to be told. Look beyond the text to discover the story. Share that story to bring the appointed lection alive for adults as well as children. For example, when Paul's letter to the Philippians is appointed in the lectionary, turn to the sixteenth chapter of the Book of Acts and tell the story of Paul's captivity in the city of Philippi. After telling the story, read or paraphrase the appointed epistle. The text will have new meaning as you put it into the context of the community that first heard it.

Paul did not write his epistles in a vacuum.

He had a reason for writing the churches he had established, and that reason is the story we have to tell to our communities. Tell about Paul's anger at those in the churches of Galatia who insisted that Christians must follow the strict laws of the Torah. Show where the province of Galatia was on a map so that the place takes on character.

Taking another example, the lections for Proper 7, Year A, deal with the theme of suffering for the Word of God, but there is no story in any of the lessons. The Old Testament text is taken from Jeremiah, and the gospel includes words of warning from Jesus to his disciples about the struggles that will come to them as a result of their discipleship. As suggested in the comments about the propers for this week on page 183, the reading of Jeremiah's words is an opportunity to tell Jeremiah's story. The Guide to Stories of the Bible (pages 35-37) lists appropriate stories about Jeremiah. You may have to do a little digging in a commentary, but your efforts will be worth it.

When you begin to look at the appointed lections in this way you will see that there is a story *behind* every reading even when there is not a story *in* every reading! Preachers can include the story of the text as a part of the sermon. People tend to hear and remember stories far more readily than they retain ideas and concepts. Thus a text from the Book of Amos becomes a wonderful opportunity to tell the story of Amos as well as to teach and preach about the words he used to proclaim the impending judgment of God.

What follows is a supplement to both the lectionary and to the commentary in chapters 5, 6, and 7 of this book. For those weeks where there is no story in the lectionary or in the commentary section of this book, an alternative story is suggested here. The alternative story will have some bearing on at least one of the lectionary texts. Look first at the commentary section. If there are no alternatives suggested there, then turn to this section.

Supplemental Bible Stories
Year A

Week	Text	Story (and link to the lectionary)
Advent 1	Gen 32	Golden calf. (Coming judgment)
Advent 3	Gen 16:1-17:7	Manna in the wilderness. (OT rdg)
Epiphany 4	Exodus 19	The giving of the Law at Mt. Sinai. (Jesus the new lawgiver. Sermon on the Mount)
Epiphany 5	Judges 6-8	Story of Gideon defeating Midianites. (OT: God's saving deeds)
Epiphany 6	2 Sam 11	David and Bathsheba. (Gospel: Adultery begins with desire)
Epiphany 7	Exodus 24	Covenant ratified. (People called to life of justice in keeping the Covenant)
Epiphany 8	Ezra 1	Return of exiles from Babylonia. (Isaiah promises return from exile)
Proper 5	Lk 5:1-11	Calling of first disciples. (Jesus calls Matthew as a disciple)
Proper 18	Acts 15	Church council called to settle dispute. (Jesus establishes guidelines for dealing with conflicts in the Church)
Proper 26	1 Kings 22	The prophet Micaiah refuses to predict victory at the behest of kings. (Micah denounces false prophets)
Proper 29	2 Samuel 6&7	David enters Jerusalem with the Ark. David's "throne will be established for ever." (Focus of week: Christ the King)

Supplemental Bible Stories
Year B

Week	Text	Story
Advent 1	Mt 25:1-13	Parable of ten bridesmaids. (Advent theme of being expectant)
Advent 3	Mt 11:1-19 Mt 14:3-12	Two stories about John the Baptist
Epiphany 8	Ex 33:1-34:9	God's mercy expressed in the wilderness. (Hosea dreamed of the day God would take Israel back to the wilderness to reestablish the Covenant relationship)

Proper 15	Exodus 16 1 Kings 19:4-8	Manna and quails in the wilderness. God provides food for Elijah. (Jesus is the bread of life)
Proper 20	Acts 6 and 7	The story of Stephen, the first martyr. (The meaning of true discipleship)
Proper 23	Luke 12:13-21	Parable of the rich fool. (Hard for the rich to enter the kingdom of God)
Proper 24	Acts 7:55-8:3 Acts 9:1-9:30 Acts 21:27-23:35	Paul's persecution of the Church Paul's conversion & his first trials as a Christian Paul's arrest and imprisonment in Rome and Caesarea (Three stories showing Paul's struggle as a follower of Jesus. In today's gospel reading, disciples want glory for themselves.)
Proper 26	Luke 10:25-42	Parable of the Good Samaritan. (Greatest commandment: Love God/Love neighbor)
Proper 28	Daniel, Chapters 1,2,3,5,6	See page 37 for outline of stories about Daniel. (First reading is from the Book of Daniel)
Proper 29		See page 37 for outline of stories about Daniel, or see Proper 29, Year A above. (First reading is from Daniel. Focus of liturgy is Christ the King)

Supplemental Bible Stories
Year C

Advent 1	Mt 24:45-51 Mt 25:14-30	Parable of the steward Parable of the talents (Both parables reflect Advent theme of expectancy and judgment)
Epiphany 6	Luke 12:13-21 Acts 16:11-40 Jer 37:3-39:14	Parable of the rich fool Imprisonment of Silas & Paul Jeremiah's struggles & vindication (Gospel: The beatitudes. Blessed are poor, and persecuted)
Epiphany 8	Joshua 1:1-9 Joshua 24	Joshua's command to Israel. People must be faithful to the Law. Joshua rehearses mighty acts of God and commands people to be faithful to the Covenant. (Jesus warns people to act on his words and not just listen.)
Proper 9	Acts 3:1-10 Acts 5:12-16 Acts 8:26-40	Peter cures a lame man Peter's reputation for healing Philip baptizes a eunuch (Gospel: Jesus sends out the seventy. They are to heal and proclaim the reign of God.)
Proper 15	1 Sam 17:1-18:16	David & Goliath. Note David's struggle with his brothers and later on with King Saul. (Gospel: Jesus warns that following him will bring divisions. The gospel demands decision.)

Appendix IV
Planning the Worship for the Congregation

This book is about planning. The best planning happens when people work together in the planning process. Chapter 4 outlines the step-by-step details for planning programs for education. In this appendix we will look at a process for planning the congregation's worship experience.

All too often the planning for worship is done by the pastor working alone in the study. The secretary enters into the plans as the details of the Sunday bulletin are outlined, and the music director suggests anthems and hymns, but that is the extent of collaborative efforts. Christmas and Easter may prove the exception. Then, at least, we usually find people gathered around a table in the library recalling what they have done in past years and talking together about what they want to do in the current year.

But when planning is restricted to the wisdom of one or two persons, the pattern of congregational worship tends to become stylized. Since there is no one asking the "why" questions, assumptions about what makes for a good worship experience go unchallenged. And so, in the all-too-typical Episcopal congregation we hear statements like, "We're a Rite One parish." or "We always use Prayers of the People, Form IV, because that is what people are accustomed to." As a result, the Book of

Common Prayer tends to fall open at the same place when it is picked up and much of the book goes unexplored and unappreciated.

The introduction to the *Book of Worship, United Church of Christ,* states the planning principle well. "The line between leading the people of God in worship and displacing them in worship is a precariously thin one. It is significant that in the New Testament, as in Judaism, the leadership of worship was a shared responsibility. In the church of the first four centuries, this collegial model of leadership prevailed. It was common for several people to concelebrate word and sacrament in services full of congregational participation.

Then leadership fell into the hands of an officiant acting alone . . . In churches in the East and West alike, liturgical action became remote from the laity, who often paid for rites they did not bother to attend.

. . . History is replete with examples of empty and corrupt worship that afflicted the people of God precisely because a responsibility that belonged to the whole people of God was abandoned into the hands of the few who eagerly assumed it." (*Book of Worship, United Church of Christ,* New York United Church of Christ, Office for Church Life and Leadership, p. 11 & 13.)

A method for planning the worship of the congregation

The planning process begins with a Bible study on the Sunday lections scheduled early in the week. The study group could be composed of the parish musician, a prayer group leader, the church teaching staff, and the lectors and intercessors assigned for the week. Out of their Bible study and dialogue the group begins to make some decisions about the shape of the Sunday Eucharist.

"That's a lot of work," may be the initial response to this suggestion, but taking the time to discuss the text and the texture of the worship experience saves time down the road. Sermon ideas come naturally when we're talking about the scripture passages that are the basis of the sermon. Pastoral concerns about people come up in the dialogue and study. Issues of social justice are raised naturally as a passage from Amos is read in connection with the radical words of Jesus. Decisions are made and responsibilities for offering the worship are accepted. The church's teaching staff find their plans falling into place as a result of their study and dialogue. The congregation begins to feel some "ownership" of what happens on Sunday morning.

The same group of people should not always be engaged in the planning. Different configurations of people need to be involved in the process. The idea is to involve as many people of the congregation as possible over the course of time. For example, a confirmation group preparing to reaffirm their baptismal vows on the first Sunday in June could be given the responsibility of planning for Sunday liturgies for the whole season of Lent. This would require a crash course in liturgics to start with, but the study would have immediate practical results. Next, the group would look at the traditions of Lent; both the recent lenten practices of the congregation and the ancient practices of the early Church. This review of past practices is not made to limit the ideas of the planning group, but rather to enrich their understanding of the possibilities for meaningful worship that is rooted in the traditions of the Church. The planning process would focus first on the entire season and then move to the planning of the five Sundays within the season.

Another group could be called together to plan for the season of Advent and Christmas with a third group planning for the Feast of the Epiphany and the Sundays after the Epiphany. The more people who are involved, the more impact the worship will have on the congregation. Parishioners will begin to hear and understand the familiar words of the liturgy. They will listen to the readings and respond to the hymns as they realize that the music of the worship reflects the theme and focus of each worship service.

Because of the ecumenical nature of the three year lectionary used in many of our churches, another option for worship and education planning is to share at least initial discussion with persons from neighboring congregations. The rich insights of such ecumenical discussion can be an exciting stimulus to the planning process of each individual congregation. Moreover, opportunities to share worship experiences will become more and more evident as time goes on and trust develops.

Liturgical planning is sometimes carried out by a formal worship or liturgical committee. Though an appointed committee offers a taste of collegial planning, it can quickly become ingrown and the people of the congregation will still not feel a part of the planning process. "What did we do last year?" may become the guiding question rather than, "what can we do to bring this Sunday (or season) alive with the full resources of Prayer Book, hymnal, and available people acting under the guidance of the Holy Spirit?"

In the Episcopal church we need to remember that the final authority for parish worship lies with the rector. Someone needs to be responsible for final decisions. That responsibility needs to be clearly stated at the beginning of the planning process.

Planning for Worship

A step-by-step worksheet

This worksheet provides you with a series of steps leading to a completed plan for a worship service. Though the worksheet is keyed to the Episcopal *Book of Common Prayer,* it can be adapted for use by planners from other denominations. (Roman Catholics and Lutherans can adapt this worksheet to the Ordinary and the *Lutheran Book of Worship.* The guidelines for worship offered in the *Book of Worship, United Church of Christ,* are in basic harmony with the outline on the worksheet, as are the worship practices of the other denominations using the three year lectionary). Churches not celebrating the Eucharist (Lord's Supper) each week can use the worksheet up through the section on the Offertory.

A walk through the worksheet:

The Propers for the Liturgy: Space is provided to fill in the readings assigned for the particular Sunday or feast day. In the Episcopal liturgy, the collect of the day establishes an initial focus for the worship, for this is the prayer that draws the people together in community. The collects are beautiful statements of biblical and theological truth reflecting generations of faithful response to the Word. Though the collect often does not reflect the theme of the readings, it needs to be looked at carefully and be included in the study and discussion.

Time restraints will usually require the convener of the planning session to make some initial decisions about the focus of the Bible study. Where the epistle is not in thematic harmony with the Old Testament and gospel lections, there is no point in looking at all three readings with the same intensity. Choose either the Old Testament gospel or the epistle lections as the focus for the liturgy. Thus the group will usually not go through the detailed process of analysis outlined on the worksheet for all three readings.

Dialogue with the texts and theme: Read each of the texts through at least twice with pencil in hand. Listen carefully to the reading and mark images or words that stand out for you. Verna Dozier, a widely respected Bible teacher in the Episcopal church, suggests that a variety of translations be available to a Bible study group. As someone reads one translation of the text out loud, others follow the reading using

different translations. This helps participants see the different shades of meaning that become evident as translations are compared. (Nothing replaces reading the texts in their original language, but having a variety of translations available helps the participants see the range of possible meaning as the text is studied.)

The next step is to encourage participants to share their present knowledge and experience with the texts. For example, a man in the group may start talking about the first time he heard the reading back in his first grade Sunday school class. The text will always carry the association of that memory, and hearing the stories associated with the text is a constant reminder that we read the Bible with several layers of understanding. Someone else may have studied the text some months earlier and will be able to recall some of her discoveries. Sharing associations and memories of the texts can be a valuable group building experience as well. People tend to draw closer as they share their stories and memories. But stories are not the only thing we are looking for here. People come with knowledge that can add to the group's understanding of the texts. Each participant needs to be recognized for their potential as bearers of God's truth.

I am indebted to Verna Dozier for the next series of questions about the meaning and significance of the texts. Her helpful booklet *Equipping the Saints: A Method of Self-directed Bible Study for Lay Groups* (See the Bibliography) offers detailed instructions for Bible study and would be important resource to have on hand for the conveners to review. The questions on the worksheet summarize her Bible study method. Someone in the group needs to do some study ahead of time in order to be able to respond to specific questions about meaning and significance, or the group can spend time together looking at commentaries and other resources to discover the answers to questions raised by group members.

Though some research is necessary when responding to the meaning of words and the significance to the early Church, Verna assures us that everyone is an expert when it comes to responding about the meaning of the texts today. This is the stage where the study moves the group out of the past and into the present moment. Since the Bible's primary emphasis is on people living together in community, social issues need to be addressed first. Move from the concerns of society to the nearer concerns of the congregation and then to the individual issues of the participants. The Bible was written into the political context of its time. As we hear the Word today we must place it in the political context of our own day or we miss the impact of the gospel we are called to proclaim to a society longing for a vision.

Everyone is not going to preach, but it helps to talk about themes and ideas for a sermon as a way of focusing on the planning process that comes next. The preacher need not feel bound by what the group shares, but rather should see the ideas expressed as seeds for sermon preparation. Writing a one sentence statement and title for the sermon is simply a way of defining the discussion.

Planning for the liturgy: Here the group looks at every option available in the eucharistic rite. As noted above, this worksheet is keyed to the Episcopal *Book of Common Prayer,* but it can be adapted to fit the traditions of any denomination. Seeing all of the rubrics and options laid out in one place helps the planning team see the possibilities. For example, the entrance rite can be as elaborate or as simple as the occasion calls for. Sometimes planners will want to include all of the options and offer an extensive entrance rite. This could include a processional hymn followed by the acclamation ("Blessed be God; Father, Son and Holy Spirit . . ."), then the collect for purity followed by the singing of "Glory to God in the highest," or some other hymn of praise. But on other occasions the liturgy could begin more simply with the acclamation and move directly to a hymn of praise and then to the collect of the day. This may seem like a small decision to make, but remember that the entrance rite sets the tone for everything that follows. Is a penitential mood established? Does the group want to emphasize praise with the singing of a hymn and a canticle in close succession? Does the mood and theme of the celebration express a simpler mode of gathering?

The way the group responds to those questions will make a difference in how the liturgy is celebrated on a particular occasion. The discussion leading to the decision can help clarify what the group wants to express as they move from studying the texts to planning the service.

Other points to note about the planning process:

The Lessons: We never hear God's word without offering praise to God in response. This beautiful tradition is one that we have inherited from ancient synagogue worship, and is the rationale behind the singing of hymn, psalm or canticle after each reading in the liturgy. The psalm is the first song of praise. It should be sung, and ideally the whole congregation will join in the singing led by choir or cantor. A hymn of praise should follow the second reading as well. Silence can be a form of praise as participants are given the opportunity to reflect on what they have heard. The lessons need to be well read and rehearsed. If the lector has been a part of the liturgical planning group, the people of the congregation will hear the difference.

The Prayers of the People: The rubric allows creativity on the part of the planners. Episcopalians may develop their own prayer forms or adapt the printed forms so long as they include the "generic" intercessions listed in the rubric. (The Universal Church, all in authority, the welfare of the world, etc). "Adaptations or insertions suited to the occasion may be made in any of these, and there is freedom to devise other forms. A series of collects or occasional prayers may be used (pp. 809-841), or a prayer from some other source, or a prayer composed for the occasion, so long as the directions on page 383 are followed." (Marian J. Hatchett, *Commentary on the American Prayer Book,* New York: Seabury Press, p. 336.) The Book of Worship of the United Church of Christ offers the same kind of guidance for intercessions. Part of the planning process needs to include some discussion about how the assigned lections influence the intercessions. If the gospel deals with healing, for example, then intercessory prayers for healing may play a central role in the Prayers of the People.

The Eucharistic Prayer: The eucharistic prayer is chosen to reflect the theme of the liturgy or season. Each of the four eucharistic prayers is a beautiful expression of the wonderful mystery that is the Eucharist, but no one prayer fully captures the fullness of that mystery. People need to be exposed to all four prayers. Congregational leaders tend to choose the same prayer week after week for fear of confusing people, but the flow of the eucharistic prayers is basically the same even though the words differ. Print the congregational responses in the bulletin to save people having to page through the Prayer Book.

Music for worship: The parish musician can help the planning process by having some suggestions ready for the group. There are a variety of resources available in each denomination that print suggested hymns for each Sunday and feast day in the church year. Singing is a heightened form of prayer and praise and for that reason music is an essential part of the worship experience. Sing as much of the service as you can for as we sing we praise God, ". . . joining our voices with Angels and Archangels and with all the company of heaven . . ." (*The Book of Common Prayer,* p. 362).

Planning for the Parish Liturgy

The Propers for the Liturgy:

Theme of the Collect:

The Appointed Readings:

Old Testament:
Psalm:
Epistle:
Gospel:

Overall theme of the celebration:

Dialogue with the texts and the theme:

Read each text at least twice. Watch for words, and images that strike you in the reading.

What experiences and memories do we bring to these texts?

What else do we need to know in order to understand the texts?*

- •What do the texts **mean?** Questions about words, traditions, etc.*

- •What was the **significance** of the texts to the first century Church?*
- •What do the texts **mean to us today?***
  - •What social issues are raised for us as we look at the texts?
  - •How do the texts address the concerns of the congregation?
  - •How do the texts address our personal situations today?
- •Think about the sermon:
  - •Write a one sentence statement that would provide a focus for a sermon preparation.
- •Write a sermon title for the preacher.

Planning for the liturgy:

Based on our experience with the texts, how will we celebrate the Eucharist on this occasion?

The Entrance rite: Book of Common Prayer, page 355

The first rubric of the rite: *A hymn, psalm, or anthem may be sung*

- •Will we have an entrance hymn, psalm or anthem or will the song of praise after the Opening Acclamation be our first words of sung praise?

The rubric at the collect for purity: *The Celebrant may say [the collect for purity]*

- •The collect for purity adds a penitential note to the entrance rite.

The rubric before the Glory to God: *When appointed, the following hymn or some other song of praise is sung or said, all standing.* (page 356)

The options:

- •"Glory to God in the highest" or "some other song of praise" must be sung in festive seasons; may be sung at other times, may not be sung during Advent and Lent. (See rubric p. 406.)
- •"Lord, have mercy" (may be sung in threefold, sixfold or ninefold form)
- •Trisagion ("Holy God, Holy and Mighty, Holy Immortal One")

The collect of the day: *The Celebrant says to the people* (as appointed—see above)

Alternative entrance rites for penitential times & seasons:

A Penitential Order, p. 351
The Great Litany, p. 48

The Lessons: (page 357)
The rubrics: *The people sit. One or two lessons, as appointed are read . . . A Psalm, hymn, or anthem may follow each reading. Silence may follow. Then, all standing, the Deacon or a Priest reads the Gospel . . .*
The options:
  • How will we offer praise to God following each lesson?

The Sermon: (No option. Sermon focus—see above)
(The sermon flows out of the lessons and into the Creed, prayers and confession.)

The Nicene Creed: (page 358)
The rubric: *On Sundays and other Major Feasts there follows . . .*

The Prayers of the People: (pages 383-393)
The rubric: *Adaptations or insertions suitable to the occasion may be made.*
  • What specific petitions do we want to include that reflect the focus of this celebration along with the immediate concerns of the congregation?
  • Which form (or adaptation) of the Prayers of the People shall we use?
    Form 1 - Litany form; includes confession petition
    Form 2 - Each formal petition ends with invitation for personal prayer
    Form 3 - Shorter form; variety of congregational response to petitions
    Form 4 - Litany form; easy to include people's personal petitions
    Form 5 - Extensive range of petitions with litany response
    Form 6 - Includes confession as option; litany with varied responses

The Confession of Sin: (page 360)
The rubric: *A Confession of Sin is said here if it has not been said earlier. On occasion, the Confession may be omitted.*
  • Is a Confession appropriate for this celebration?
    • As part of the entrance rite, or following the Prayers of the People?
    • Included in Prayers of the People, Form 1 or 6?

The Peace: (page 360)
The rubric: *Then the Ministers and People may greet one another in the name of the Lord. . . . If preferred, the exchange of the Peace may take place at the time of the administration of the Sacrament (before or after the sentence of Invitation).*

The Offertory: (page 361)
The rubric: *The Celebrant may begin the Offertory with one of the sentences on page 376, or with some other sentence of Scripture. During the Offertory, a hymn, psalm, or anthem may be sung. Representatives of the congregation bring the offerings of bread and wine, and money or other gifts, to the deacon or celebrant. The people stand while the offerings are presented and placed on the altar.*
  • Appropriate hymn, psalm, or anthem?
  • Offertory sentence that reflects the focus of the liturgy? (Note that any appropriate sentence from scripture may be used.)

The Eucharistic Prayer: (pages 362, 367, 369, 372)
  Prayer A: Adaptation of Prayer 1 in Rite One. Focus on the cross & Jesus' sacrifice
  Prayer B: Emphasis on Incarnation and age to come
  Prayer C: Litany style—penitential emphasis; creation emphasized
  Prayer D: Ancient eloquent liturgy from Eastern tradition. Ecumenical prayer
  Memorial acclamation: *(Christ is risen . . .)*
    • said?
    • sung?
  Form of the Lord's Prayer (page 364)
    • traditional language
    • contemporary language (obscure words eliminated: "trespasses" changed to "sins"; "temptation" to "trial")
  Fraction anthem: (page 364)
  Rubric: *In place of or in addition to "Christ our Passover" some other suitable anthem may be used.* The hymnal provides following options:
    • Christ our Passover is sacrificed for us (Hymnal S 151-156)
    • Agnus Dei (Lamb of God) (Hymnal S 157-166)
    • The disciples knew the Lord Jesus (Hymnal S 167)

- My flesh is food indeed (Hymnal S 168-169)
- Whoever eats this bread (Hymnal S 170)
- Be known to us (Hymnal S 171)
- Blessed are those who are called (Hymnal S 172)

Ministration of Communion: (page 365)

The rubric: *The ministers receive the Sacrament in both kinds, and then immediately deliver it to the people. . . . During the ministration of Communion, hymns, psalms, or anthems may be sung.*

- How will we distribute the sacrament?
  - Standing? (The preferred form until late middle ages)
  - Kneeling? (penitential emphasis)
  - At the altar rail?
  - At "stations"?
- Is music appropriate at this point in the celebration?

Postcommunion Prayer: (page 365 and 366)

- First prayer—(God has fed us and sends us out to love and serve)

- Second prayer—(We are living members of the Body and heirs of God's eternal kingdom . . . send us out to love and serve as witnesses)

Hymn before or after the Postcommunion Prayer

The rubric: *A hymn may be sung before or after the postcommunion prayer.*

- Liturgical ministers leave in silence?
- Appropriate hymn?

The blessing (optional) (page 366)

- In Rite Two, form of the blessing left entirely up to bishop or priest
- See *The Book of Occasional Services,* for seasonal blessings, pp. 20-27

Words of dismissal—a choice of four options (page 366)

(*Questions are based on the approach developed by Verna Dozier, *Equipping the Saints: A Method of Self-directed Bible Study for Lay Groups,* Alban Institute, 1981)

Bibliography

Alexander, David, and Alexander, Pat, eds. *Eerdmans' Handbook to the Bible.* Wm. B. Eerdmans, 1973. A beautifully illustrated background book for the Bible; explains the complexities of the Bible.

Alter, Robert. *The Art of Biblical Narrative.* New York: Basic Books, 1981. Persons are accustomed to studying biblical stories from a theological background. Alter helps us explore the stories through literary analysis. We discover the tools ancient storytellers used to heighten the dramatic impact of the stories for their audience.

Anderson, Bernhard W. *Understanding the Old Testament.* Englewood Cliffs, N.J.: Prentice-Hall, 1957. A classic college textbook on the Old Testament. For those who want a deeper study of the Bible, this book and its companion, *Understanding the New Testament* (see Howard Clark Kee entry), are excellent. The books are very readable and exciting.

Barclay, William. *The Daily Study Bible Series.* Rev. ed. Philadelphia, Pa.: Westminster Press. Commentaries on all the books of the New Testament; can be read as daily meditations as well as for general study.

Benson, Jeanette, and Hilyard, Jack L. *Becoming Family.* Winona, Minn.: St. Mary's College Press, 1978. A book of guided experiences or exercises designed for use in family religious education programs. The exercises are all built on the Christian message of love and caring. Some of the themes in the liturgy could be explored experientially by using the exercises outlined.

Bettelheim, Bruno. *The Uses of Enchantment: The Meaning and Importance of Fairy Tales.* New York: Alfred A. Knopf, 1976. On the power of the story and the importance of sharing stories.

Borsch, Frederick Houk. *Introducing the Lessons of the Church Year, A Guide for Lay Readers and Congregations.* New York: Seabury Press, 1978. (Reprinted by Harper and Row). Succinct "program notes" explain the background and context of each of the readings appointed for the Sundays and feast days of the year. The notes can be printed in the Sunday bulletin and used as a starting point in planning for education and liturgy.

Brown, Robert McAfee. *Unexpected News, Reading the Bible with Third World Eyes.* Philadelphia: Westminster Press, 1984. We need to hear the Bible stories as if for the first time and be surprised by their radical power to transform our thinking and acting. Our comfortable assumptions about the meaning and message of the familiar Bible stories are confronted in this book.

Browning, Robert L., and Reed, Roy A. *The Sacraments in Religious Education and Liturgy*. Birmingham, AL: Religious Education Press, 1985. The link between liturgy and education is explored in detail.

Charpentier, Etienne. *How to Read the New Testament*. New York: Crossroad, 1985. A good primer in introducing biblical scholarship and understanding to the new Bible student.

Charpentier, Etienne. *How to Read the Old Testament*. New York: Crossroad, 1985. The companion book to Charpentier's treatment of the New Testament.

Children in the Parish Eucharist. New York: Episcopal Church Center, 1987. A major consultation of educators, liturgists, and other concerned church leaders resulted in the production of this important resource. Practical suggestions on how to include children as full participants in the parish Eucharist are offered along with the rationale for their inclusion. The author was a part of the team that designed the consultation.

Cox, Harvey. *The Feast of Fools*. New York: Harper & Row, 1970. The influence of festival and liturgy on the formation of a people's ideas. Excellent. This book has had a very strong influence on my thinking about liturgy.

Craddock, Fred B, et al. *Preaching the New Common Lectionary*. Nashville: Abingdon Press, 1985. (See Chapter Nine for an explanation of the new Common Lectionary) An excellent series of commentaries on the appointed lessons for the Common Lectionary. Three volumes a year for the three year lectionary complete the set. For those using the Common Lectionary, this series gives background on the Old Testament lessons for the Sundays after Pentecost that are missing from most other lectionary commentaries. Except for the Old Testament readings for the Sundays after Pentecost, most of the appointed lections treated in this series are the same as those appointed for the Episcopal, Lutheran and Roman Catholic churches.

Crossan, John Dominic. *In Parables, The Challenge of the Historical Jesus*. New York: Harper and Row, 1973. This book is an important contribution to the study of the parables. Crossan uncovers meaning in the parables that is often lost because of assumptions made that cannot be supported by closer examination.

Crossan, John Dominic. *The Dark Interval, Towards a Theology of Story*. Allen, TX: Argus Communications, 1975. Reading this brief book was a turning point for me in understanding the nature of parable and story.

Dowley, Tim, ed. *Eerdmans' Handbook of the History of Christianity*. Grand Rapids, Mich.: Wm. B. Eerdmans, 1977. An understanding of church history is essential if we are to appreciate the continuing quest of our people to understand their relationship with God. A companion to *Eerdmans' Handbook to the Bible*. Charts, tables, and brief articles make it possible to comprehend the great movement of church history over the centuries.

Dozier, Verna. *Equipping the Saints: A Method of Self-directed Bible Study for Lay Groups*. Washington, D.C.: The Alban Institute, Inc., 1981. The author provides a helpful step-by-step process for Bible study that is suggested as a starting place in the planning of the liturgy as outlined in Appendix IV of this book.

Fuller, Reginald H. *Preaching the New Lectionary: The Word of God for the Church Today*. Collegeville, Minn.: Liturgical Press, 1971. An excellent book designed to help the preacher tie the appointed Bible readings together into the common theme of each week. Helpful to the religious educator and parent for its insights into the lectionary readings.

Goldberg, Michael. *Jews and Christians, Getting our Stories Straight: The Exodus and the Passion-Resurrection*. Nashville: Abingdon Press, 1985. The author is concerned that Jews and Christians understand the two "Master stories" that shape our understanding of God's activity in the world. A key book for the teacher and pastor.

Griggs, Donald L. *Praying and Teaching the Psalms*. Nashville: Abingdon Press, 1984. An example of Griggs' creative work in helping teachers teach the Bible creatively. Look in the Abingdon catalog for a host of other helpful resources by Donald and Patricia Griggs.

Griggs, Donald. *Teaching Teachers to Teach*.

Livermore, Calif.: Griggs Educational Service, 1974.

Groome, Thomas H. *Christian Religious Education, Sharing Our Story and Vision.* New York: Harper and Row, 1980. An important book that treats the theory as well as the practice of Christian education.

Hanchey, Howard. *Creative Christian Education.* Wilton, CT: Morehouse-Barlow, 1986. "Based on a parish year of five liturgical seasons (All Saints, Christmas, Epiphany, Lent and Easter/Pentecost), (the book) offers a wealth of both general and specific suggestions for enlivening the classroom experience and tying it to the larger experience of the whole church. It also offers many insights into the practical realities of managing a consistently lively Christian education program, and is written . . . with infectious enthusiasm, and verve." (Gretchen Wolff Pritchard, "Pastoral Care of Christian Education," *The Living Church,* Vol 296, #1, 1/3/88, p. 18.)

Harrell, John, and Harrell, Mary. *A Storyteller's Treasury.* Berkeley, Calif.: Harrell Press, 1977. Not only provides the reader with a wide variety of stories to tell but also helps the reader appreciate the deep significance of stories in all cultures.

Harrell, John, and Harrell, Mary. *To Tell of Gideon: The Art of Storytelling in the Church.* Berkeley, Calif.: Harrell Press, 1975 (Box 9006, Berkeley, CA 94709). I would suggest that every religious educator be given a copy of this book at the beginning of his or her term in the learning community. Comes with a plastic record so that the reader can hear the art of the storyteller as well as read about it. Brief but thorough. Essential in any religious educator's library.

Hessel, Dieter T., editor. *Social Themes of the Christian Year: A Commentary on the Lectionary.* Philadelphia: The Geneva Press, 1983. The thesis of this book is that the gospel is directed at society and not just the individual. Each season of the church year is examined from that perspective. An important book for the liturgist's and educator's library.

Hovda, Robert. *Dry Bones: Living Worship Guides to Good Liturgy.* Washington, D.C.:

The Liturgical Conference, 1973. An excellent resource for those who plan the liturgical life of the congregation.

Huck, Gabe, and Sloyan, Virginia. *Parishes and Families: A Model for Christian Formation Through Liturgy.* Washington, D.C.: Liturgical Conference, 1973.

Huck, Gabe, and Sloyan, Virginia, eds. *Children's Liturgies.* Washington, D.C.: Liturgical Conference, 1970.

Jeep, Elizabeth McMahon, and Huck, Gabe. *Celebrate Summer: A Guidebook for Families* and *Celebrate Summer: A Guidebook for Congregations.* New York: Paulist Press, 1973. These two books provide a wide variety of ideas for celebrating the summer in liturgy and in shared experiences. Ideas for celebrating the saints' days and festivals of that season.

Kavanagh, Aidan. *Elements of Rite: A Handbook of Liturgical Style.* New York: Pueblo Publishing Company, 1982. This book provides beautifully written guidelines for liturgical planners.

Kee, Howard Clark; Young, Franklyn W.; and Froehlich, Karlfried. *Understanding the New Testament.* Englewood Cliffs, N.J.: Prenctice-Hall, 1957. A companion to Bernhard Anderson's *Understanding the Old Testament.*

Kingsbury, Jack Dean. *Matthew as Story.* Philadelphia, Fortress Press, 1986. Read this book at the beginning of Year A for it will give you an excellent overview of the gospel of Matthew from a storyteller's point of view.

L'Engle, Madeleine. *The Irrational Season.* New York: Seabury Press, Crossroad Books, 1977. In chapter three of *Sharing Our Story,* I suggest that we tell our life story within the framework of the liturgical year. Madeleine L'Engle's book is an example of this kind of approach. The seasons of the church year launch her own reflections about life. Not only is this a worthwhile book for the insights that the author shares but it also helps us understand the depth of the liturgical year.

Lewis, C. S. "The Lion, the Witch, and the Wardrobe." *Chronicles of Narnia.* (New York: Macmillan, 1951; Collier Books). The first of seven books in a series. Written to express the Christian gospel in the imagery of fantasy for children. Helps them experience the gospel by stepping out of the language and imagery of the Bible into a completely different pattern of symbols and metaphors. Highly recommended.

McLendon, James William. *Biography as Theology*. Nashville, Tenn.: Abingdon, 1974. Helps the reader see the influence that our life story has on our understanding of God—how our theological perspective grows out of our story.

Mitchell, Leonel L. *Praying Shapes Believing, A Theological Commentary on the Book of Common Prayer*. Minneapolis: Winston Press, 1985. One of the crucial tasks of the church teacher in the Episcopal church is to open up the Prayer Book with the people of the congregation. Mitchell's book is a valuable resource for the home or parish library.

Neville, Gwen Kennedy, and Westerhoff, John H. III. *Learning Through Liturgy*. New York: Seabury Press, 1987. Insights from anthropology and religious education point out the significance of liturgy and ritual in the learning process.

Porter, Harry Boone, *Keeping the Church Year*. New York: Seabury Press, Crossroad Books, 1977. Easily read; provides an overview of the church year, with many suggestions for deepening our appreciation of the liturgy in the parish family.

Rhoads, David and Michie, Donald. *Mark as Story, An Introduction to the Narrative of a Gospel*. Philadelphia: Fortress Press, 1982. A book for the church teacher and pastor to read at the beginning of Year B, the year of Mark.

Rohrbaugh, Richard L. *Into All the World: A Basic Overview of the New Testament*. Livermore, Calif.: Griggs Educational Service, 1976.

Russell, Joseph P., and Vogelsang, John D. *In Dialogue, An Episcopal Guide for Adult Bible Study*. New York: Episcopal Church Center, 1986. This book was written to respond to the growing interest in Bible study in the Episcopal church today. An Episcopal approach to reading and studying the Bible is offered along with an extensive annotated listing of various Bible study approaches and resources.

Russell, Joseph P. *The Daily Lectionary, A weekly guide for daily bible readings*. Cincinnati: Forward Movement, 1987. An inexpensive four volume set of week-by-week commentaries on the Daily Office lectionary that is shared by Episcopalians, Lutherans and the Anglican Church of Canada. The lectionary guides the reader through the Bible in two years of daily reading. The commentary, designed to be read at the beginning of each week, provides "program notes" for the readings by placing them in their literary, historical and theological contexts. (The Daily Office lectionary is not the same as the Sunday lectionary that is treated in this book.)

Russell, Joseph P. *The ABC's of a Christian's Education*. Cincinnati: Forward Movement. This brief tract outlines the author's feelings about the role of Christian education in the congregation.

Russell, Joseph P. *Daily Prayer and Bible Study with the Book of Common Prayer*. Cincinnati: Forward Movement. A brief tract that explains how to use daily Morning and Evening Prayer as a way of focusing prayer, praise and Bible reading each day of the year.

Sawyer, Ruth. *The Way of the Storyteller*. New York: Viking, Penguin Books, 1970.

Shaughnessy, James D. *The Roots of Ritual*. Grand Rapids, Mich.: Wm. B. Eerdmans, 1973. Background on the meaning and power of ritual.

Shea, John. *Stories of God: An Unauthorized Biography*. Chicago: Thomas More Press, 1978. The stories we tell about God shape our understanding of God.

Shedlock, Marie L. *The Art of the Storyteller*. New York: Dover, 1951. Highly recommended.

Stuhlman, Bryon D. *Prayer Book Rubrics Expanded*. New York: Church Hymnal Corporation, 1987. An excellent and thorough guide to liturgical planning. The author examines the rationale behind the rubrics of the Prayer Book, and in the process helps us see the meaning behind what we are doing together in the liturgy of the Church.

Tilley, Terrence W. *Story Theology*. Wilmington, DE: Michael Glazier, 1985. This book explores the field of "narrative theology;"

the theological perspective that lies behind *Sharing Our Biblical Story.*

Weil, Louis. *Gathered to Pray: Understanding Liturgical Prayer.* Cambridge, MA: Cowley Publications, 1986. A beautifully written book that helps us appreciate the experience of praying the traditional prayers of the Church.

Weil, Louis. *Sacraments and Liturgy, the Outward Signs: A Study in Liturgical Mentality.* New York: Basil Blackwell, 1983. A brief overview of the theology and practice inherent in the Book of Common Prayer.

Westerhoff, John H. *A Pilgrim People: Learning Through the Church Year.* The Seabury Press, 1984. Another one of John Westerhoff's brief works that explores approaches to education and encourages creativity. The argument of this book is that the whole shape of parish life should change with the cycle of the seasons. The author talks about the theology and environment of each season and suggests practical ways to help bring that environment alive in the congregation.

Westerhoff, John H. III. *Will Our Children Have Faith?* New York: Seabury Press, 1976. I recommend this book as required reading for all persons working in the religious education program of the parish. Helps readers appreciate the significance of what they have been called to do in the parish.

Notes